MINNIE FISHER CUNNINGHAM

MINNIE FISHER
CUNNINGHAM

A SUFFRAGIST'S
LIFE IN POLITICS

Judith N. McArthur
and
Harold L. Smith

OXFORD
UNIVERSITY PRESS
2003

OXFORD
UNIVERSITY PRESS

Oxford   New York

Auckland   Bangkok   Buenos Aires   Cape Town   Chennai
Dar es Salaam   Delhi   Hong Kong   Istanbul   Karachi   Kolkata
Kuala Lumpur   Madrid   Melbourne   Mexico City   Mumbai   Nairobi
São Paulo   Shanghai   Taipei   Tokyo   Toronto

Copyright © 2003 by Judith N. McArthur and Harold L. Smith

Published by Oxford University Press, Inc.
198 Madison Avenue, New York, New York 10016

www.oup.com

First issued as an Oxford University Press paperback, 2005

Oxford is a registered trademark of Oxford University Press

Library of Congress Cataloging-in-Publication Data
McArthur, Judith N.
Minnie Fisher Cunningham : A suffragist's life in politics /
Judith N. McArthur and Harold L. Smith
p.   cm.
ISBN-13 978-0-19-512215-2; 978-0-19-530486-2 (pbk.)
ISBN 0-19-512215-1; 0-19-530486-1 (pbk.)
1. Cunningham, Minnie Fisher, 1882–1964.   2. Women politicians—
United States—Biography.   3. Politicians—United States—Biography.   4. Roosevelt,
Eleanor, 1884–1962—Friends and associates.   5. Women in politics—United States—History—
20th Century.   6. Women politicians—Texas—Biography.   7. Women in politics—Texas—
History—20th Century.   8. Women—Suffrage—Texas—History.   9. Texas—
Politics and government—1865–1950.   10. Texas—Politics and
government—1951–   I. Smith, Harold L.   II. Title.
E748.C966M35   2003
976.4'062'092—dc21
[B]   2002193124

3   5   7   9   8   6   4   2

Printed in the United States of America
on acid-free paper

To the memory of Billie Carr

FOREWORD

MINNIE FISHER CUNNINGHAM'S LIFE STILL RALLIES FRONTLINE FEMINISTS like myself. Until now, her story has been written in bits and pieces but not as thoroughly and authentically as Judith McArthur and Harold Smith have done.

I knew and loved Minnie Fish and listened to her whenever possible. As her words ring forth over the years, I realize just how solid her advice was on how to wage grassroots activism. She taught me that the first rule of political activism was "Stamp the letter first, then address the envelope. That way you'll write it and mail it."

I wish I had saved every one of her letters. She wrote them on any size stationery, in the margin, even around the sides of postcards with news or instructions on who to call about what. You could always recognize a Minnie Fish letter before you opened it because she continued to write on the back of the envelope.

One of Minnie Fish's favorite stories concerned the early days of the women's suffrage campaign. When President Wilson was arriving at the Democratic National Convention in Saint Louis, Missouri, the suffragists wished to get his attention. "We all wore long white dresses with yellow sashes across the front proclaiming our cause. We lined both sides of the street to the convention hall so he couldn't miss us." After lobbying the convention delegates to vote for women's suffrage, she told me, the younger women got dressed up and went on to parties, but the oldtimers like herself "just unhitched our corsets, took off our shoes, and talked politics." Worried that women would be reluctant to vote the first time after suffrage was granted, Minnie Fish got her allies to plaster Texas with signs: "Vote, vote as you please, but VOTE."

I loved her looks . . . soft and plump like a grandmother, dressed in comfortable cotton (loyal to the Texas crop) most of the time. Her hair was arranged gently around her face with hairpins and braids. She talked directly but never loudly. Her voice was wise, good humored, and inviting. She had a beautiful even face, with deep brown eyes that could be amused, sympathetic, gentle, or indignant.

The noisy leaders of the 1970s were not her style, but Minnie Fish was not a day behind them on the issues. She had Betty Friedan's foresight, Gloria Steinem's insight, and Bella Abzug's forcefulness. Their goals were the same — the freedom for every woman to be what she can be. Minnie Fish is a basic part of women's story. She knew how necessary it was for women to work together, so she was a moving force in the National League of Women Voters, the Business and Professional Women's Clubs, the Woman's National Democratic Club, and many others. She helped ensure that the Woman's National Democratic Club was "political," not "social," as some of the ladies would have had it. "I just don't like sipping tea and making chit-chat," Minnie Fish often said.

If for no other reason, Minnie Fish will be remembered as a major force for women by Eleanor Roosevelt's comment while speaking in Texas: "It was your own Minnie Fisher Cunningham who aroused my interest in politics." Arousing women's interest in politics was one of the things Minnie Fish did best. By stirring women into political activism during the 1940s and 1950s she helped keep the spirit of the women's suffrage movement alive until the feminist revival in the 1960s.

My own experience with Minnie Fish was certainly part of the inspiration which led me to become a founder of the National Women's Political Caucus in 1971. She would have loved having a chance to be part of its efforts to organize women to secure the passage of the Equal Rights Amendment and to keep *Roe vs. Wade* intact. With the Bush administration's war on women's rights not only here, but around the world, this history of Minnie Fish is especially significant. Perhaps it will reawaken women to the evidence not only of how far we have come, but how far we still must go.

—Liz Carpenter

ACKNOWLEDGMENTS

MANY PEOPLE OFFERED EXPERTISE, RECOLLECTIONS, AND HOSPITALITY as we worked on this book. Mr. and Mrs. R. M. Traylor III, Richard and Cindy Traylor, and Denise Traylor Whetsell graciously shared memories of their great- and great-great Aunt Minnie; Richard and Cindy showed us the Cunningham sites in New Waverly. James Patton of the Walker County Historical Society guided us through the society's Cunningham collection, suggested leads, and acted as host and guide in Huntsville.

We are greatly indebted to Elizabeth Hayes Turner for answering innumerable queries about Galveston women's organizations, and to Nancy Beck Young for sharing her research on left-liberal Texas women of the 1940s and 1950s and drawing our attention to relevant sources in the Western Historical Manuscripts Collection. Jewell Fenzi and the Woman's National Democratic Club gave us unrestricted access to the Club's archives and made us welcome. The national offices of the League of Women Voters and the General Federation of Women's Clubs kindly searched their files and supplied copies of their records on Minnie Fisher Cunningham.

Of the many librarians and archivists whose assistance was invaluable, we especially thank Nancy Snedeker at the Franklin D. Roosevelt Library; Ann Barton and Dawn Letson at Texas Woman's University; Ralph Elder, Patrick Cox, and Don Carleton at the Center for American History, University of Texas at Austin; Sarita Oertling at the University of Texas Medical Branch, Galveston; Ellen Brown at Baylor University; Shirley Rodnitzky at the University of Texas at Arlington; and Bill Page at Texas A&M University, who shared his bibliography of Cunningham citations from the Texas press. At the

University of Houston—Victoria, Karen Locher tracked down sources, and Shirley Parkin and Susan Cobler processed stacks of interlibrary loan requests.

Jo Freeman helped us locate an article by Cunningham at the New York Public Library; Janice Sutton at the University of Texas College of Pharmacy provided us with a history of the College; Debra Reid supplied information on the Agricultural Extension Service; Maurine H. Beasley located Cunningham's film in the National Archives; and Beverly and Bobby Tomek transformed a grainy newspaper photograph of Cunningham and her colleagues at the Woman's National Democratic Club into a glossy print. For sharing their recollections of Cunningham, we thank Orissa Eckhardt Arend, Jean Begeman Bergmark, Liz Carpenter, the late Billie Carr, the late Virginia Durr, Ronnie Dugger, Beulah Grimmet, Creekmore Fath, Nadine Eckhardt, the late Robert Eckhardt, Dell Sackett Goeres, Lawrence Goodwyn, Forest Hill, Dr. Frank Manuel, Pat Mathis, the late Oscar Mauzy, Anne McAfee, Wayne Rasmussen, Dave Richards, Bernard Rapoport, Jean Dugger Sherril, and Kathleen Voigt.

The University of Houston–Victoria Academic Council granted financial support that made research and travel possible. Liz and Al Turner in Houston and Myron Gutmann in Austin extended warm hospitality again and again as we worked our way through the local archives.

We are indebted to Elizabeth York Enstam, George N. Green, Elizabeth Hayes Turner, and Thomas LeBien for reading and critiquing portions of earlier drafts, and to Randy Faulk and Jennifer Chau for computer assistance. We thank Martha Swain for helping move the project forward early on, and for her unflagging interest. Most of all, we are grateful to our editor, Susan Ferber, for her ruthless pencil and infinite patience.

CONTENTS

ABBREVIATIONS

AAA   Agricultural Adjustment Administration
AAUW   American Association of University Women
ADA   Americans for Democratic Action
AFL   American Federation of Labor
AHC-APL   Austin History Center, Austin Public Library
CAH-UT   Center for American History, University of Texas at Austin
CIO   Congress of Industrial Organizations
DAC   Democratic Advisory Council
DNC   Democratic National Committee
DOC   Democratic Organizing Committee
DOT   Democrats of Texas
ER   Eleanor Roosevelt
FDR   Franklin Delano Roosevelt
FERA   Federal Emergency Relief Administration
HMRC   Houston Metropolitan Research Center, Houston Public Library
HRC   Humanities Research Center, University of Texas at Austin
HWS   *History of Woman Suffrage*, Ida Husted Harper, ed., 6 vols.
LBJ-A   LBJ Presidential Library, Austin
LC   Library of Congress
LDT   Loyal Democrats of Texas
LWV   League of Women Voters
MFC   Minnie Fisher Cunningham
NA   National Archives, Washington, D.C.
NA-CP   National Archives, College Park

NDAC	National Defense Advisory Commission
NFU	National Farmers' Union
PLC	People's Legislative Committee
SCL	South Caroliniana Library, University of South Carolina, Columbia
SL	Schlesinger Library, Radcliffe College
TCDWC	Travis County Democratic Women's Committee
TDWC	Texas Democratic Women's State Committee
TFWC	Texas Federation of Women's Clubs
TFU	Texas Farmers' Union
TSL	Texas State Library and Archives, Austin
TSLC	Texas Social and Legislative Conference
TWU	Texas Woman's University
UH	University of Houston
UNC	University of North Carolina
UM-C	University of Missouri–Columbia
UT	University of Texas at Austin
UT-A	University of Texas at Arlington
VCU	Virginia Commonwealth University
WCEF	Women's Committee for Educational Freedom
WCEP	Women's Committee for Economic Policy
WCTU	Woman's Christian Temperance Union
WHMC	Western Historical Manuscript Collection, University of Missouri–Columbia
WNDC	Woman's National Democratic Club
WSHS	Wisconsin State Historical Society Library, Madison

Minnie Fisher Cunningham

INTRODUCTION

OF ALL THE LABELS THAT MINNIE FISHER CUNNINGHAM ACQUIRED DURING a lifetime in politics, the one that captures her best was bestowed posthumously by *Texas Monthly* magazine in a December 1999 retrospective on the most important twentieth-century Texans. It profiled Cunningham under the caption "Agitator of the Century."[1] In the accompanying 1928 photograph she stands with two friends, hatted, gloved, and impeccably ladylike, next to a "Cunningham for U.S. Senate" sign. By then, she had already led the Texas woman suffrage movement, chaired the Congressional Committee of the National American Woman Suffrage Association, been the first executive secretary of the national League of Women Voters (LWV), and served as resident director of the Woman's National Democratic Club and acting head of the Women's Division of the Democratic National Committee (DNC). In the decade that followed, she would become a New Deal activist, director of the "women's division" of the Agricultural Adjustment Administration, and, in the DNC staff's judgment, the South's best female political organizer.

Cunningham was part of a remarkable cohort of American women. Born in the 1870s and 1880s, they were only the second generation of women to attend college, and they went on to invent careers as social workers, labor investigators, public health nurses, and settlement house residents. They were the "municipal housekeepers" of the Progressive Era, who prodded city governments to install sanitary sewers, clean up water supplies, and pass pure food and milk ordinances; Cunningham did her part through the Women's Health Protective Association in Galveston. They took up the languishing woman suffrage crusade by the thousands, transforming it into a mass move-

3

ment. After winning the vote in 1920, they built women's political organizations, ran (usually against heavy odds) for public office, and pressed against male resistance for party positions. In the 1930s they staffed—and sometimes headed—New Deal relief agencies, carrying forward the reform tradition of the Progressive Era as they helped shape the modern welfare state.[2]

It is as a middle-class suffragist and women's advocate that Cunningham is remembered. She entered politics through voluntary associations, and social reform led her into suffrage. After women won the vote she lobbied, as part of the Women's Joint Congressional Committee, for the Sheppard-Towner and Cable Acts. She counted Carrie Chapman Catt, Julia Lathrop, Emily Newell Blair, and Eleanor Roosevelt among her friends and was part of the Washington, D.C., female political network. But Cunningham also had another identity, as a left-liberal grassroots activist, that cast her in the role of an outsider. This one grew out of her upbringing in rural East Texas where, as a child in the 1890s, she listened to Populist Party orators describe how farmers and workers were economically squeezed and politically ignored. Realizing that the oppression of women could not be disentangled from class and racial exploitation, she fought against the power structure that upheld all three.

This blend of feminism and left politics can appropriately be called "left feminism," although Cunningham and her female political allies in the 1940s and 1950s did not refer to themselves as feminists.[3] By then feminism was firmly associated in the public mind with the National Woman's Party (NWP) and its decades-long crusade for an Equal Rights Amendment (ERA). The NWP drew support from middle-class and professional women, and its leadership combined ERA advocacy with a right-wing politics that Cunningham and other left feminists abhorred.[4] Although the NWP's ERA campaign has been portrayed as the link between the suffrage movement and 1960s feminism, the conservatism of NWP leaders fits awkwardly with the left-of-center outlook of the feminists who launched the second women's movement. Feminist historians thus have urged a reevaluation of the role women on the Left played in maintaining the tradition of women's political activism between 1920 and 1960.[5]

Cunningham's life is evidence of this alternative story, an example of how suffrage activism blossomed into left feminism. As the national women's movement declined, she devoted herself to helping build a political Left in Texas, becoming the "very heart and soul of Texas liberalism."[6] She ran for governor in 1944 against the anti–New Deal incumbent, explaining to Eleanor Roosevelt that her candidacy was "one part of the great fight which the little people of this state are making all along the line" for New Deal ideals.[7] The "little people"—farmers, organized labor, women, and minorities—made up the membership of the left-liberal organizations that Cunningham helped found to press for expanded democracy and fundamental social change. The women's groups in which she worked during the 1940s and 1950s were not national organizations like those of the 1910s, but they used the same tactics: grassroots organizing, publicity campaigns to arouse public opinion, legislative lobbying and monitoring.

As a southerner, Minnie Fisher Cunningham belonged to the generation that grew up while racial discrimination and segregation were being written into law during the late nineteenth century and grew old as the civil rights movement peaked in the twentieth. In the Jim Crow South, liberals like Cunningham were reviled as troublemakers by the conservative, white supremacist cliques whose hold on power had to be continually shored up with racial demagoguery. Challenges to racism and sexism exposed the vulnerable seams that held together the political order. Cunningham learned early in her public career that even the mildest expression of racial tolerance gave conservative politicians a weapon with which to beat down reform. In the 1910s the cry was that woman suffrage would bring "Negro domination"; in the 1940s and 1950s it was that civil rights activists were Communist subversives.

The politics of white male supremacy impeded the growth of the southern suffrage movement and kept leaders like Cunningham perpetually on the defensive. As head of the Texas Equal Suffrage Association, she was compelled to sidestep the issue of voting rights for African American women. But she was one of the very few southern presidents to negotiate partial suffrage from a state legislature before 1920, despite white supremacist opposition, and the only one who left documentary evidence of how she succeeded: by taking shrewd advantage of a split in the state Democratic Party. She was also astute enough to keep quiet about the bargain she made with her male allies, allowing them to claim—and historians mistakenly to assume—that suffrage succeeded because the legislators finally recognized the justice of the women's cause. Her extensive papers from the suffrage years are a window on local organizing and its relationship to the national movement, a subject about which historians know relatively little.[8]

Racial politics always constricted the space within which southern liberals could act. Cunningham took her opportunities to oppose inequality and racism where she found them, leaving no manifestos and gently criticizing the idealism of northern friends who advocated more forceful confrontation. "To my mind," she wrote, "the choice lies plainly between doing the work or making the noise."[9] Doing the work meant pragmatic action as an individual. She was a committed and well-liked chair of the LWV's Negro Problems Committee in the 1920s, and during World War II hired Frances Williams of the NAACP to work with her at the National Defense Advisory Commission's Civic Contacts Unit. She welcomed and defended the Supreme Court decisions that outlawed segregated schools and struck down the white primary, regretting only that white supremacist candidates offered black citizens nothing to vote *for*.[10]

Working without noise, she stayed below the radar of the race-baiters, but also largely outside the historical record. Frustratingly incomplete glimpses appear in her correspondence. There is a passing reference to having, with her sister, rescued a black youth from a mob in Galveston, with no hint of the circumstances or at what time during her fourteen-year residence the incident occurred. She mentions having been called names ("only a coward could lose a moment's sleep over that") for having spoken at an unidentified conference, apparently with an interracial theme or audience.[11] The details are unrecoverable, and there is no way of documenting the full extent to which she may have challenged white supremacy.

Minnie Fisher Cunningham's life illuminates, and at the same time complicates, the story that historians are constructing of women in post-suffrage politics. She was among the few leaders of the woman suffrage movement— at least among those prominent enough to merit an entry in *Notable American Women*—who went on to become party activists.[12] But she does not fit easily into the paradigm that separates into divergent groups women who sought influence within the political parties from those who opted to continue the tradition of nonpartisan pressure-group lobbying. Cunningham worked for political change through the Democratic Party, through women's organizations, and through mixed-gender groups (some of which she founded herself), and at every level, from Washington, D.C., to her home county in Texas. She was partisan and nonpartisan, separate and gender-integrated, and always in motion.

Cunningham's forty years of activism after gaining the vote illustrates in bold relief the obstacles women encountered in politics, notably the difficulty of winning office and marginalization within the parties. Equally important, her story helps fill in the still-emerging narrative of women's political activism between the demise of the first women's movement after 1920 and the rebirth of feminism in the 1960s. Much of women's struggle to define political roles for themselves after suffrage remains invisible and unrecorded because it has been played out at the local level, where the barriers to participation are lower. "The study of women and politics," Jo Freeman emphasizes, "is the study of grassroots political activity."[13]

Cunningham, who never missed a precinct meeting, would have agreed wholeheartedly. Just as turning a local lens on the Progressive Era has uncovered the social welfare and municipal housekeeping agendas of female reformers, a closer examination of women in state politics may reveal a new paradigm for the post-suffrage era. The central role of Cunningham's female network in sustaining the liberal wing of the Texas Democratic Party suggests that other stories of women's grassroots political influence wait to be discovered, and historians' understanding of post-suffrage politics will be incomplete without them.

Cunningham's experience as part of the first generation of women who ran for Congress after suffrage likewise invites a closer look at female candidates. Little is known about how they campaigned, the opponents they faced, or how audiences responded. Cunningham's unsuccessful race for the U.S. Senate suggests that women have been shut out of high elective office not only by sexism and lack of campaign funds but also by ambivalence over adopting the aggressive style and ambition-driven values of male political culture. She faced a dilemma with which women candidates still contend: the gendering of politics and the need to be perceived as "tough" in order to be taken seriously.

Politics was Minnie Fisher Cunningham's life. She had no children and her unsuccessful marriage is nearly a blank; there are no letters between husband and wife and no domestic confidences to friends. Not given to introspection or even reminiscence, she left no diaries, scrapbooks, or autobiography to illuminate a private self. But the public activist who emerges from her correspondence is combative, forthright, and funny, with a talent for friendship and a gift for motivating others. Cunningham had remarkably little ego; as long as an organization got the work done, her own role, whether as president or untitled strategist, seemed not to matter. Indifferent to building a personal legacy, she always faced forward, toward the next challenge. It never bothered her that the opposition was more numerous and better funded, or that the odds were against her side. What mattered was airing the issues and being part of the fight—and fight was a word she used frequently. She would have been delighted to be memorialized as an agitator.

A Daughter of the New South

THE THINGS MINNIE SUE FISHER REMEMBERED MOST VIVIDLY ABOUT growing up in East Texas in the 1880s and 1890s were her mother's stories of life before the Civil War and the railroad that was built across the plantation afterward, the romance of the Old South and the reality of the New. To the barefoot Fisher children, hoeing vegetables and picking fruit to be shipped to Houston for scarce cash, it seemed that their hard-working mother had grown up in almost unimaginable luxury. Sallie Fisher described a world of silk dresses and rosewood pianos, personal maids, carriage horses, and full store-houses. Years later Minnie rejected the "moonlight, mockingbirds, and magnolias" mythologizing of the antebellum South and wrote frankly that "the primitive luxuries of a pioneering plantation-owner class contrasted blackly against the lives of their slaves." But as a child she was conscious only of the contrast between storied past abundance and the hardscrabble present.[1]

The Fisher plantation lay in Walker County, in the piney woods region of East Texas. In the nineteenth century East Texas was the western frontier of the cotton kingdom, and Walker County was settled in the two decades preceding the Civil War largely by slaveholders from the lower South seeking fresh cotton lands. Minnie's parents, Horatio White Fisher and Sallie Comer Abercrombie, were part of the wave of migrants from central Alabama who arrived in Walker County in the early 1850s. Sallie was only a child, and her parents, John Comer and Jane Minerva Sims Abercrombie, were early settlers in the new community of Waverly. Their migration followed a pattern common among antebellum planters. John Abercrombie and several other men from Macon County, in Alabama's black belt, made a preliminary journey to

Texas to buy land, and the families later relocated as a group. They named the settlement after Sir Walter Scott's popular Waverly novels.[2]

The extended Fisher family arrived two or three years later from Lowndes County, Alabama. Horatio White Fisher made the journey with his first wife and baby daughter, but the little family was soon broken by Rebecca Fisher's death, and Horatio passed the remainder of the decade as a widower. His brother Lorenzo and their father, William Phillips Fisher, set up separate households. The third brother, Dr. John Fletcher Fisher, migrated later and established his plantation next to John and Minerva Abercrombie. The heavy influx of planters like the Fishers and the Abercrombies, and the slaves they brought with them, more than doubled the population of Walker County between 1850 and 1860. They shaped it economically and socially in the image of the Deep South, and by 1860 the county had a black majority and a fully developed cotton economy.[3]

Cotton and slaves had made the Fishers and the Abercrombies wealthy in Alabama, and they prospered as well in Texas.[4] Most white southerners owned no slaves at all, and only a minority of slaveholders held more than twenty bondspeople, the traditional marker of "planter" status. The Fishers and John Abercrombie belonged to the elite who counted their slaves by tens and their acreages by thousands. Horatio Fisher and his father, with seventy-two and ninety-two slaves respectively, ranked among Walker County's half-dozen largest slaveholders, and John Abercrombie was one of the largest landowners.[5] The value of their real estate, as reported in the 1860 census, put the Fishers in the wealthiest 3 percent of East Texas society, and John Abercrombie in the wealthiest 1 percent. In personal estate—slaves, money, and goods—all three ranked in the wealthiest 1 percent.[6]

Men from this class, the planter elite, also dominated public affairs and politics. Though he had lived in Walker County for only a few years, Horatio White Fisher was elected as its representative to the state legislature in 1857–1858. When the Civil War broke out in 1861, he raised one of the two cavalry companies that Walker County furnished to the Confederate army, and John Abercrombie helped equip it. By then Horatio, thirty-three, was courting sixteen-year-old Sallie Abercrombie and building a new house for the bride-to-be. The following year, while "Rashe" Fisher was home on furlough, he and Sallie were married. The letters they exchanged over the course of the war, carefully bundled in ribbon-tied packets and stored in the tall secretary in the parlor, delighted Minnie and her siblings, who read in them "the history of our land garnished with romance and adventure."[7]

Horatio and Sallie Fisher had eight children; Minnie, born on March 19, 1882, was the seventh, and the youngest daughter. Four girls and two boys survived, and grew up while their parents' generation sought solutions to the political turmoil and economic devastation that followed the Civil War.

Because federal troops never invaded the interior, Texas escaped the military destruction of an occupying army, but the end of slavery disrupted the labor system and the economy. Land values plunged and personal wealth, much of which had consisted of slave property, evaporated. By 1870 the value of Horatio Fisher's real estate had dropped by more than half, and his personal wealth plummeted from $51,750 to $2,000. During the war he had bought additional land, and postwar deflation made paying off the debt difficult. After his father died, he and Sallie let their property go to the mortgage holder and resettled on William Fisher's plantation. Minnie and her brothers and sisters grew up there, a generation that would inherit memories instead of wealth. In the secretary with the Civil War letters, the children found evidence of vanished prosperity: Confederate money, "more than a little of it," and a list of the slaves, "kept carefully because everybody believed that sooner or later the government would pay for them."[8]

By Minnie's childhood, the outlines of a new social and economic order were fully evident. The former planters and the freedmen improvised a new labor system, tenancy and sharecropping, to replace slave labor. Most of the Fisher tenants were black, but a group of Waverly planters also commissioned an agent to recruit a handful of families from Poland; their descendants continued to farm Fisher land even after it had passed to Minnie. In the postwar decades, northern investment capital helped finance a boom in railroad construction and nurtured industrial development across the South. In Walker County the railroad was the Houston and Great Northern, and the industry was lumbering. The railroad, snaking fifty-five miles north from Houston, was diverted from Waverly in 1871 when the village leaders refused to grant it a right of way. Instead, it was built through the Fisher plantation, parallel with the wagon road that ran in front of the house.[9]

Construction of the Houston and Great Northern track became part of Fisher family history. The supervising engineers camped for months in the yard under the giant oaks, near the well, and boarded at Sallie's table. In return, they offered to locate the station on the property and name it—and the village that would inevitably grow up around it—after the family. Had Sallie not flatly vetoed the honor and the "riff-raff" that a railroad town would bring, Minnie's birthplace would have been known as Fisher Station. Instead, the townsite was laid out three miles to the south and called, at first, Waverly Station, and then New Waverly.[10]

Hamlets like New Waverly sprouted throughout the postwar South; in the decade after 1870 the number of villages doubled. Southern entrepreneurs and newspaper editors proclaimed a "New South" to be on the rise in the 1880s, a forward-looking region that cherished its past but embraced urban growth and economic diversification. Yet despite the rhetoric and striving, the New South of Minnie's childhood lagged far behind the North by every economic and social measurement; it was rural, backward, and poor. Southern agriculture was even more firmly wedded to cotton culture than before the Civil War, while demand for the crop was stagnating and the price dropping. The region's industries were largely limited to processing raw materials— coal, iron, timber, tobacco, and cotton—which generated low-wage unskilled and semi-skilled jobs. New Waverly, with a handful of general stores, a grist-mill, two cotton gins, and four sawmills, was the embodiment of the South's underdeveloped economy.[11]

The Fishers, like other cotton-farming families, were cash poor even in good years. In the memoir that Minnie wrote of her childhood, she empha-sized her mother's ceaseless struggle to raise her children according to mini-mal standards of gentility, which included shoes, Sunday clothes, and ex-tended schooling. The youngsters would gladly have forgone shoes well into adolescence, but Sallie was adamant; barefoot summers ended forever when each child reached eleven or twelve. Shoes cost "ridiculous sums of money" and wore out faster than cash to replace them flowed in, a source of perpet-ual distress to Horatio Fisher and embarrassment to the needy child "whose vigorous activity had worn to a frazzle good cowhide and battered out even copper toes."[12]

By the time that they "went into shoes for life," Minnie and her brothers and sisters had completed their primary schooling at home, using textbooks— from geography and spelling to Latin grammar and higher mathematics— passed down for several generations. Their mother, a book lover who could quote long passages from Shakespeare, gave out assignments and checked copybooks. She also improvised lessons out of daily life, using visits from the Greek and Syrian peddlers who traveled the railroad and fascinated the chil-dren, to teach the history and geography of their homelands. Education was a family enterprise. The older children helped the younger ones learn to read, and even the unbookish Horatio was sometimes called upon to give out spelling words while Sallie cooked breakfast.[13]

Minnie early developed a love of reading, although not especially of study-ing. An eclectic collection of books, many of which had belonged to Grand-father Fisher, absorbed her as a child: *State Papers of Washington*, *Pilgrim's Pro-gress*, William Gilmore Sims's *Poems of the Confederacy*, and the novels of Henry Fielding, Tobias Smollett, Victor Hugo, "and other lively tale tellers." At some point, probably around 1890, Minnie was enrolled in the "little county school" several miles away. Supplying her with a "speller" and a geography book used up the family's last 40 cents in cash, and before the week was out, she dis-graced herself by losing both books on the way home. Since there was no money to replace them, she studied at home under Sallie until age twelve.[14]

With adolescence came each daughter's turn for the expensive adventure called "going away to school." Like other southern states, Texas had an inadequate and underfunded educational system and high illiteracy rates; public schools financed with local taxes and organized by districts came late to the region. Antebellum planters had educated their children in private academies, while yeomen, if they got any schooling at all, depended upon church-sponsored common schools. The New South, after rejecting the Yankee-style universal education briefly imposed during Reconstruction, relied on impermanent community schools voluntarily established by local groups of parents and overseen by appointed trustees. Secondary schools, such as they were, existed only in the cities; there was no provision for public high schools in rural areas until well into the twentieth century.[15]

Most rural children thus got only the most basic education at ungraded schools, which were in session for just a few months a year during breaks in the agricultural cycle. Sallie Fisher had been educated in nearby Huntsville, at Andrews Female Academy, but it had not survived the war; her offspring would have to be sent farther afield after primary school. "Going away" for the Fisher girls was a luxury that depended upon Sallie's initiative in finding the extra money. Outfitting the departing student, Minnie recalled, necessitated an "awful burst of spending" for clothes, train fare, and tuition. And every term brought a new demand for "running expenses": board, registration, lab fees, seasonal hats and gloves, and the everlasting problem of shoes.[16]

The money came out of Sallie's private purse. Horatio's reluctance to finance some of the expenditures for what Minnie called her mother's "rigid and unyielding" standard of living resulted in a dual economy for the family, the significance of which Minnie appreciated only in retrospect. Her father oversaw the plantation and dealt with the local merchants who furnished supplies, while Sallie initiated a small market gardening and dairying operation made possible by the nearness of the railroad. Her first customers were the railroad employees themselves, who picked up produce on their regular runs. By the 1880s and 1890s she was dealing with commission merchants in Houston and Galveston, shipping eggs, butter, fruit, and vegetables, and experimenting to find out which fruits sold best and kept freshest. Sallie and her children's labor produced the marketable surpluses; they all helped hoe and harvest acres of strawberries and watermelons, pick peaches and green beans, and churn milk for the buttermaking.[17]

Sallie Fisher consecrated this small supplemental income to educating and polishing her brood, especially her daughters. The two boys, William Phillips and Horatio Jr., could anticipate making a living on the land, but Marion, Comer, Ella, and Minnie were essentially restricted to marriage or school teaching. As an adolescent, Sallie had envied her older brother's departure for the all-male University of Virginia; she had lost her opportunity for a "finishing" course in New York because of the impending the Civil War. A personal sense of deprivation may have heightened her determination that her girls have every opportunity she could possibly afford. The money she and the children earned helped pay for music and art instruction; for refurbishing the parlor when the eldest daughter reached the age for receiving callers; and for the endless expenses of schooling, including college degrees for Marion and Minnie. "The years when we took care of all obligations and were able to afford nice clothes for the absentee we won," Minnie remembered. "The years we were not so successful and had to borrow money to finish the spring term we lost."[18]

When her turn came to "go away" to Houston, however, the experience ended unhappily. Although she did not name the school, it was apparently one of the new graded ones. Minnie found it sharply different from the common school model, under which children studied at their own pace, older learners helped the younger ones, and everyone said their lessons aloud. In graded schools the day was highly structured, and students were grouped by ability and studied silently. Ignorant of this new classroom etiquette, she talked out loud instead of whispering and read other books openly when she had nothing to study. She lasted only a semester and finished the year back home with a woman who ran a small private or "old field" school, such as had been common before the Civil War. Finally, at the age of fifteen, she spent a six-month term at the New Waverly public school. She was the only algebra and Latin student and thus "subject to considerable razzing." That was the extent of her secondary schooling.[19]

In between lessons Minnie preferred to be outdoors, preferably on horseback. She learned to ride early, progressing from a secure perch in the saddle in front of her father to bouncing precariously behind an older sibling on the horse's bare back. As soon as a child was able to "stick on" behind the saddle at all gaits, she or he was deemed competent to handle a horse alone. Minnie proved skillful enough to merit the "amazing grace" of a personal mount. The roan pony complete with sidesaddle and bridle, which her father bought her as a surprise, acknowledged his youngest daughter's aptitude for working cattle and livestock. Had there been more than one older brother in the family, she might not have had the opportunity to discover this talent. But being short on sons and well-endowed with daughters, her father encouraged her ability, "and it was good economy to mount me properly for it."[20]

MINNIE ABSORBED HER RELIGIOUS BELIEFS FROM HER MOTHER, HER passion for politics from her father, and her racial attitudes from both, internalizing ideas that would shape her social and political activism as an adult. Sallie Fisher, a Methodist, had the children read the Bible aloud as part of their daily schooling. Minnie also pored over *The Works of Hannah More*, whose didactic, evangelical poetry and prose had been popular in early nineteenth-century England, and *Foxe's Book of Martyrs*. As a young woman Minnie helped found a Methodist Church at New Waverly and supported it over the years from wherever she happened to be living. Methodism, with its belief in the equality of all souls and creed of social responsibility that urged believers to work for a better world, fired her with moral energy and tenacious optimism. Faith, usually coupled with wry humor, got her through adversity as an adult. Letters to friends urging forbearance in the face of frustration or venting righteous indignation at some piece of political chicanery often included an apt biblical quotation.[21]

Her sympathy for the labor movement, evident as early as the 1910s, and commitment to improving race relations, mirrored the progressive outreach of Methodist laywomen's organizations. In the 1940s and 1950s, as fascism spread in Europe and white southerners at home dug in to bitterly resist black civil rights, she sometimes affirmed her commitment to democracy and liberalism in religious language. Her seven-paragraph credo, "I Believe," sent to the members of the Texas Women's Democratic State Committee as a Christmas greeting, was an eloquent testimony of faith in human perfectibility, social progress, and brotherhood that could have been handed down from a Methodist pulpit.[22]

Minnie also learned a pragmatic and ordinary form of racial tolerance by observing her parents. She grew up before the codification of segregation, interacting daily with freedpeople who had once belonged to Horatio and Sallie Fisher. An elderly ex-slave continued to live in the "yard" behind the main house in return for splitting wood, drawing water, and occasionally minding children. Another former slave was in charge of the fall butchering; still others worked as stable hands and kitchen helpers.

Fisher freedmen dipped their church members at the "baptizing hole" on the plantation and buried their dead in the old slave graveyard (Minnie's favorite place to retreat and read undisturbed). She was entranced by the baptism and funeral processions that passed opposite the house, along the railroad track, and by the hymns and spirituals that echoed from the woods. After a funeral, contemporaries of the deceased always paid a ceremonious visit to Horatio and Sallie, and "in this way we children learned to know most of the ex-slaves even though they did not all continue to live on Fisher Farms." She sketched her father, especially, as a classic paternalist who habitually dug into his nearly empty pockets to help out former slaves and gave his former Civil War body servant (whom the children called "Uncle" George) a small farm adjacent to the family property.[23]

Minnie grew up during the years when the white South began to glorify its Civil War heritage, and newly formed Confederate memorial associations were erecting military monuments on courthouse lawns and in town squares.

But the cult of the Lost Cause, which romanticized plantation life and justi-fied southern resistance to northern "aggression," was not venerated around the Fisher hearth. Other southern children learned, through carefully moni-tored textbooks, to view slavery as a benevolent and paternalistic institution that schooled savage Africans in civilized ways. Sallie Fisher, by contrast, taught Minnie and her siblings that slavery had degraded whites as well as blacks and "brought us up to rejoice that the Negroes were freed." "After I was fully rooted and grounded in this faith I learned with surprise that there ex-isted a less philosophical, idealistic school of thought, members of whom were said to be 'unreconstructed.' I thought and still think that they existed on a lower plane of intellect than that on which my mother lived."[24]

Sallie Fisher's iconoclasm did not spare the Civil War either; Minnie heard from childhood that it had been a mistake brought on by "hot-headed seces-sionists." Sallie had viewed Horatio's cavalry company of small farmers with disdain and his departure with dismay. "The whole thing was fantastic and un-economic, while my mother was a realist even as early as that, and she hated it." Thus despite being the daughter of a Confederate officer and a descendant of the planter elite, Minnie grew up without internalizing an idyllic southern past that could not be questioned or challenged. As an adult, she never hesi-tated to slip a reference to her father's Confederate service into a speech when it served her purpose, but she stayed out of the United Daughters of the Con-federacy, which women of her class joined by the thousands. In crafting pub-lic historical memory, the UDC celebrated images—contented slaves, patri-archal planters, and cavalier blood—that reinforced white supremacy and traditional gender and class privileges. Minnie would devote herself to chal-lenging rather than preserving these inequalities.[25]

From her father, whom she described as "humorous, charming, popular, [and] rather dashing," Minnie acquired her consuming interest in politics. Horatio Fisher probably helped impart her completely traditional view of Reconstruction as a "tragic era" of carpetbagger misrule and "Negro domi-nation," although by the time she was a young adult this was the standard in-terpretation taught in northern universities as well as southern schools. Post-war Republican governance and voting rights for the freedmen, backed by federal military authority, threatened the political dominance of the prewar planter elite. Men of the leadership class, like Horatio Fisher, found them-selves barred from public office for having fought in the Confederate army. In Walker County, where African Americans were nearly 60 percent of the population, white Democratic resistance to black voting and officeholding erupted into violence and temporary occupation by the state militia during Reconstruction.[26] Minnie's memoir implies, without giving examples, that her father had some part in the successful struggle that deposed Republican government in the early 1870s.[27]

Whatever role Horatio Fisher may have played in "redeeming" the state is lost to history, but after the Democrats' return to power, he spent much of his life in public office. He first appears in the record in 1876, running unopposed for justice of the peace in Walker County Precinct Four. Two years later he won a close race to represent Walker and Trinity counties in the state legislature. In 1880 he attempted to move up to the state senate, coming in second in a field of four candidates. This defeat marked his last bid for state office. The following year the justice of the peace of Precinct Four resigned, and Horatio Fisher was appointed to finish the term. Thereafter, the office was apparently his whenever he chose to run. He won in 1882, sat out the next two elections, and beginning in 1888 was elected every two years for the rest of his life. He died in office in 1906.[28]

Minnie wrote little about her father in her family memoir except that his official duties took him frequently away from home. In newspaper interviews, however, she described herself as interested in politics from the time she was in pigtails, riding around the plantation with her father and listening to him talk about candidates and issues. As the youngest daughter, growing up when Horatio was in his sixties, she may have been a favorite companion. She went along to political meetings in Huntsville, the county seat, twelve miles away, and on the long drive home he would discuss the proceedings with her.[29]

Minnie's interest in politics was precocious, but Horatio's was characteristic of his generation. The late nineteenth century was the apogee of "popular" or mass participation politics, an era of intense partisanship, high voter turnout, and hard-fought elections. Parties mobilized supporters through spectacles—rallies and torchlight parades in the North, all-day barbecues in the South—that combined ideology with public theater and gave men (for so-called "universal" suffrage excluded women) a sense that their participation mattered. In an era of few commercial amusements, politics was also entertainment. Minnie vividly remembered the excitement of waiting to see the "grand special train" that carried President Benjamin Harrison and a party of notables past the farm.[30] She was always on the front bench at the county barbecues, listening to the political oratory and shaking her head in dissent when the speakers disagreed with her father's views.

Coming of age at the end of the century, she witnessed a decade of political turbulence caused by prolonged economic deflation. The hard times hit farmers first. Struggling to make a profit, they increased production, which forced prices even lower. The condition of agriculture went from bad in the 1880s to devastated in the 1890s, when a nationwide economic depression struck. Cotton, which had sold for 11 cents a pound in the late 1870s, dropped below the price of production; it hit rock bottom in 1894, at less than 5 cents a pound. "That was when worry really came and abode with us," Minnie remembered. Her mother's market gardening was equally devastated; produce shipped to Houston on consignment did not bring enough to pay the freight costs. "The next year we planted cotton in the orchard, but cotton was cheap too."[31]

To help make ends meet, Sallie and the children raised more poultry and increased their dairy production, selling the eggs, milk, and butter to a sawmill nearby. The transactions brought the family no hard currency; they were paid in the same merchandise "checks" — cardboard discs stamped in varying denominations like coins — redeemable at the company commissary that the millworkers received. Sallie exchanged them for yard lengths of cloth, from which she sewed clothes for the children, but what she really wanted was cash "and that in the nineties was certainly hard for farm folks to come by."[32]

Minnie carried the memory of that depressed decade all her life. Forty years later she still remembered the exact sum — 80 cents — that her mother ended up owing the railroad for a shipment of green beans that brought no profit. Nevertheless, the Fishers were more fortunate than many. They still had their land, while increasing numbers of farmers, trapped in a vicious cycle of falling prices and rising debt, lost their mortgaged acres and became tenant farmers. The distressed condition of agriculture sparked social protest and demands for political reform. Struggling white farmers deserted the Democrats for independent and reform parties, and they joined the Farmers' Alliance. Born in Texas, the Alliance spread rapidly across the South and West in the 1880s, and by 1892 had spawned the People's or Populist Party. Tagging along with her father, Minnie heard Populist candidates expound the most radical political platform of the nineteenth century.

The Populists demanded, in the words of one historian, "a fair shot at making a decent living as it was being defined in the Gilded Age." Most of their grievances were directed against the Northeast, whose financiers and monopolies they held responsible for policies and practices that hurt the South and West: tight credit, an inflexible national banking system, rising rail transportation costs and discriminatory rates that penalized rural areas and small shippers. To overcome the burden of debt and end regional discrimination, the Farmers' Alliance demanded increased coinage of silver and a paper-based currency; reclamation of land and resources from large corporations; and government ownership of the railroad and communications networks. Southern Populists, perpetually in debt to local "furnishing" merchants who demanded crop liens as security, also wanted a subtreasury, a system of government warehouses to be located in agricultural counties. Farmers would be entitled to deposit their crops and receive up to 80 percent of the value in interest-free loans while they waited for the most opportune time to sell.[33]

In sum, the Populists identified farmers and factory workers rather than monopoly capitalists as the backbone of the economy and called for unprecedented government intervention to bring about a more equitable distribution of wealth and power. At a time when the national government was small and did virtually nothing at the local level except operate the post office, Populist proposals for expanding federal power were far-reaching by any standard, but especially so in the South. They clashed head-on with the Democratic Party's devotion to frugal, limited government and local control, at a time when memories of federal power exercised during Reconstruction still rankled.

More radical still was the Populist acknowledgment of shared class interests across the South's racial divide. In the hope of winning black votes, Populist leaders stressed that white and black farmers were caught in the same economic squeeze, and that the old parties were indifferent to their plight. While careful not to advocate "social equality," which was unthinkable in the nineteenth-century South, they defended black political rights. Democrats customarily bought and bullied black voters, bribing them away from the Republican Party with cash or liquor, or intimidating them from going to the polls at all. Populists, attempting to build a biracial coalition, offered them appointments on state executive and county committees.[34]

The unrest of the 1890s split the Democratic Party into three factions: radical agrarians who defected to the Populists; Reform Democrats who embraced railroad regulation and soft (silver) money but rejected the more radical parts of the agrarian platform; and pro-business conservative, or Bourbon, Democrats. Minnie's father was a Reform, or "Hogg," Democrat, a faction led by Governor James Stephen Hogg, who had made his reputation as a railroad-battling attorney general.[35] Even though they supported some Populist proposals, large landowners like Horatio Fisher were attached to the Democratic Party through their tradition of local officeholding and county leadership. Hogg's "middle-of-the-road" stance enabled them to embrace economic reform without leaving the party.[36]

Walker County, however, was a hotbed of Populism, one of a cluster of East Texas counties where radical agrarianism flourished. The Populists won it in 1892, 1894, and 1896, despite Democratic fraud and intimidation. In one heavily black area, election officials saved themselves the trouble of "counting out" votes by changing the precinct lines so that black men found themselves separated from their polling place by a large river. Horatio Fisher's role in the campaigns is unknown, except that he worked fervently for James Hogg's re-election in 1892. Since he, in Minnie's words, "lived, breathed, ate and slept politics," the hotly contested elections of the 1890s must have been the subject of much discussion with his interested young daughter.[37]

By 1896 the Populist insurgency had peaked, but the political aftereffects lasted for generations. Conservative Democrats' determination to suppress dissidence and permanently secure one-party dominance shaped the political culture Minnie would challenge throughout her adult life and constrained

women's political opportunities well into the twentieth century. Most immediately, the backlash against Populism ensured that she and other southern
women would have the hardest struggle in the nation to win voting rights.

Conservative Democrats had "redeemed" their states from biracial Republican government in the 1870s, but they had not been able to eliminate the
Republican Party or undo the Fifteenth Amendment, which guaranteed black
voting rights. In response to the Populists' attempt to elevate class interest
over racial solidarity, Democrats sought to dispense with the tradition of ma-
nipulating elections by violence and fraud and securely enshrine white supremacist politics once and for all. In the second redemption of the 1890s,
however, they had an option not available a generation earlier: a small, newly
organized movement for woman suffrage. Seizing the opportunity offered by
southern Democrats' desire to curb black political power, the National American Woman Suffrage Association (NAWSA) formed a special Southern Committee to help nurture suffrage societies below the Mason-Dixon line. Making
white supremacy the focus of their campaigns, the southern associations argued that enfranchising white women would counterbalance the voting power
of black men. As state legislatures and constitutional conventions debated disfranchisement in the 1890s, suffragists petitioned them to solve their "Negro
problem" by giving white women the ballot.[38]

Conservative Democrats chose instead to maintain racial privilege without
surrendering gender prerogatives, tightly interweaving the two into a nearly
impenetrable breastwork for white male supremacy. They fabricated an epidemic of rape by black men, who they claimed were emboldened by political
power, and used it to justify a wave of terrorism and lynching in the name of
safeguarding white womanhood. White women were invited to political participation not as voters but as symbolic victims, and many played the role willingly. Populist men found not simply their political loyalty but also their status as white men under attack, as conservative Democrats charged them with
betraying white supremacy and endangering their wives and daughters. The
relentless linking of white solidarity with honor and manly independence
helped smash the fragile biracial coalition between black Populists and white
Populists and suppress the nascent woman suffrage movement. In withhold-
ing the ballot from women and stripping it from blacks, the disfranchisers ensured that women would be dependent on male "protection" and that black
men would have none at all.[39]

Coalitions of Democrats, the political configurations of which varied from
state to state, devised new laws to circumvent the Fifteenth Amendment. Secret ballots, literacy tests, multiple-box laws, and poll taxes targeted the illit-
erate and poor, purging a good many lower-class whites from the electorate
along with blacks. By 1904 every former Confederate state had adopted a poll
tax, which had to be paid months before the election and took at least $1.50

(and sometimes more) out of pocket at a time when the average rural southerner handled less than $100 in cash annually. Voter turnout plunged (in Texas
only 29 percent of whites and 2 percent of blacks were voting by 1910). The
adoption of laws restricting party primaries to white voters—on the justification that political parties were private organizations—further eroded black
participation.[40] Constricting the electorate fastened Democratic one-party
rule on the region for more than half a century. In the absence of significant
Republican and third-party opposition, Democratic candidates nominated in
the primary automatically prevailed in the general election.

But the new political order was never as stable and unassailable as the disfranchisers would have liked; it simply "papered over deep fissures in southern life," as one historian has observed.[41] Women challenged it in a new suffrage movement; African Americans by resistance along the color line at great
personal risk; and labor through formal organization and protest. Minnie
would spend most of her adult life in this company. The echo of Populism
was always audible in her quest for economic justice and political inclusive-
ness, but the Populist uprising also taught her pragmatism by negative example. Third-party movements, she learned by observation in the 1890s, could
not prevail. Like her father, she fought conservatism from within the Democratic Party, supporting candidates who sought to move it to the left. The
agrarian insurgency forced southern Democrats to secure their base by adopting populist language to denounce railroads, special interests, and trusts even
as they resisted the Populists' radical vision of full economic and political
democracy. Advancing that vision would motivate Minnie's half-century of
political activism.

ALTHOUGH SHE HAD SPENT LITTLE TIME IN CLASSROOMS, AT AGE SIXTEEN
Minnie passed the state teacher certification exam and was offered a rural
school contract. Teaching was not a career to which she felt particularly drawn,
but few other professions were open to nineteenth-century women, especially
in the South. She put off taking the position and went to Galveston to stay with
her oldest sister, Marion, a graduate of Sam Houston Normal Institute, who
had been teaching elementary school for years. Although the purpose of the
visit was to observe her sister's classroom, Minnie apparently wanted to be
talked out of school teaching altogether. Marion obliged, and the teacher's certificate went unused.[42]

Minnie's real ambition was to study medicine, a profession practiced on
both sides of her family. Her father's brother, Dr. John Fletcher Fisher, was a
farmer-physician in New Waverly, and her mother's late uncle, Dr. J. Marion
Sims, the acknowledged father of modern gynecology.[43] Female physicians,

always a small percentage of the profession, were beginning to confront higher barriers to medical school admission, as male doctors sought enhanced status by exerting greater control over professional training and restricting the number of female students. But like other Victorian daughters, even in the more progressive North, Minnie found her parents' opposition the strongest obstacle. Physicians' training required intimate knowledge of body parts and functions at odds with the prevailing standards of female modesty. Medicine, remembered a Smith College graduate whose decision to enroll in Johns Hopkins University Medical School in the 1890s appalled her family, "was distinctly not a ladylike occupation."[44]

Horatio and Sally Fisher compromised and allowed Minnie to study pharmacy. In 1899 she returned to Galveston to enter the program at the Medical Department of the University of Texas. The School of Pharmacy, established in 1893, was still in its infancy and, unlike the medical school, required no high school diploma. Admittance was open to any student who passed the simple entrance examination: a short essay to reveal grammar and spelling ability and an arithmetic test. But the two-year curriculum, overseen by a faculty of three, was challenging and the attrition rate high. In addition to a lecture-laboratory course on prescription dispensing, Minnie was required to attend two weekly lectures each on pharmacy, chemistry, and *materia medica* (the physical, chemical, and medical properties of drugs). There were weekly lectures on botany and in physics, and labs in pharmacy and chemistry three times a week.[45]

Women students, although a minority, were less scarce than in the medical school (from which only one woman had graduated), and their presence was not disparaged. When Professor Raoul Rene Daniel Cline, a Texas native educated in France and New York, arrived to head the pharmacy school in 1895, he announced himself unequivocally in favor of equal professional opportunities for women. "Since it has been conclusively demonstrated that women reason and imagine as well as men," he declared in an address to the Medical Department faculty, "their education should be of the same kind and degree as that of a man." Minnie became good friends with the sole woman in the class ahead of her, Emma Domingo. The main difficulty they encountered was one that neither sex could avoid: the uncomfortable and inadequate facilities. The pharmacy lab, housed in the basement of the medical classroom building, was poorly lighted and ventilated, and because Galveston Island was only a few feet above sea level, it frequently flooded. Students often had to do their experiments barefoot in standing water, using outdated and improvised equipment, since the university board of regents had not acted on Professor Cline's request to fully equip and expand the laboratory.[46]

Minnie's second year was unexpectedly foreshortened by events beyond anyone's control. On September 8 and 9, 1900, three weeks before fall classes were scheduled to begin, a massive hurricane devastated Galveston. In the deadliest natural disaster in American history, between 6,000 and 8,000 of Galveston's 38,000 citizens perished. The storm surge submerged the entire island. It destroyed or damaged beyond repair more than half of the buildings and blew away the bridge to the mainland. Though the Medical Department campus was left relatively intact, the basement laboratories suffered serious damage. University officials found them waterlogged and wrecked, "one great jumble and tangle of chemical tables, gas and water pipes, bottles, and apparatus."[47]

While funeral pyres for thousands of corpses smoldered on the beach, Clara Barton and the Red Cross undertook a massive relief effort. Marion Fisher volunteered at one of the relief stations, and Minnie made her own contribution from New Waverly. Finding that no one in the community was collecting supplies for the Red Cross, she undertook the job herself. She persuaded Sallie Fisher to give a tea—"we'd never have done anything like that"—and invite the local women to bring used clothing. She rode all over the community distributing notes of invitation, and the guests came laden with donations. Her efforts netted $22.50 in cash, which she sent directly to Barton, and $30 worth of women's and children's clothing, which she expressed to Marion's relief station. She parted with all she could spare from her own slender wardrobe in order to include a private package for Emma Domingo, who lost everything but the clothes she was wearing when the storm struck.[48]

Minnie's class could not begin its second and final year until November 15, when the campus was reopened, and had to work harder to make up for lost time. By eliminating most holidays and squeezing in extra class hours, the eight-month term was compressed into six. Minnie was the sole woman in the fourteen-member class of 1901 (and only the sixth since the program's inception) to earn the Graduate in Pharmacy (Ph.G.) degree.[49] As a "graduate" pharmacist, she was in the minority of the profession, for the state did not then require pharmacists to be degreed. Prospective practitioners had to pass only a district licensing board examination, for which a year of coursework was usually abundant preparation. The majority of students who entered the pharmacy program stayed just long enough to prepare for the exam and did not return for the second year.[50]

Having a degree exempted Minnie from the licensing examination but brought her no advantage in the workplace. Many pharmacies preferred candidates schooled by the traditional apprenticeship with a local druggist, and being a woman was an economic liability in any field. She went to work as a prescription clerk in the Huntsville drug store at $75 a month, half of what her nondegreed male coworkers were paid. "And I was the professional!" she fumed to an interviewer more than fifty years later. At the time, however, she may have simply enjoyed being nineteen, independent, and, in her own words, "flirtatious." A photograph from that period shows a round-faced young woman with brown eyes, a finely etched mouth, and dark auburn hair. There was apparently enough gossip about a romance with a local doctor to annoy both her and the young man, but the suitor who prevailed was a lawyer named Beverly Jean Cunningham.[51]

Nothing is known about their courtship and little about B. J. Cunningham himself. Unlike Minnie, with her large extended family and deep Texas roots, he was alone and a newcomer. The son of English immigrants, he was born in Illinois in 1874, perhaps in White County, bordering Indiana in the southeastern tip of the state. He taught school there in the 1890s and may have then gone to St. Louis. He arrived in Huntsville in time to be counted in the 1900 census, having become a lawyer sometime in the interim.[52] He boarded with a local family, along with two other young bachelors, joined the Masonic Lodge, and undoubtedly passed some of his leisure time socializing at the drugstore.[53] Minnie, apparently smitten, thought him "the best-looking man I ever saw." They were married on November 27, 1902, when she was twenty and he twenty-seven. According to family memory, it was a joint ceremony with her favorite sister Ella, three years older, who married a New Waverly farmer.[54]

In an age that regarded marriage as a full-time occupation for a woman, Minnie thus confronted a very different future from the one she imagined at sixteen, when she aspired to be a doctor. She had spent less time practicing pharmacy than she had invested in qualifying for it and would never again work in the medical sciences. Like many middle-class married women, she would find meaningful activity through clubs and other voluntary associations. Ultimately, she would construct through women's networks the equivalent of a "career" in social reform and political activism.

2

THE RISE OF A PUBLIC WOMAN

THE EARLY YEARS OF MINNIE FISHER CUNNINGHAM'S MARRIAGE ARE THE least documented period of her life. She spent her twenties as convention prescribed, focused on homemaking and her husband's career. She was a helpmate in more than the usual sense when B. J. decided to run for Walker County Attorney in 1904. He concentrated his electioneering in Huntsville, relying on her to campaign in the countryside and win over the farmers, the kind of people with whom she had grown up. "As a city man to a country girl, if you'll hold up your end of the campaign, I'll hold up mine," was the bargain her husband proposed. She did, and B. J. won the race, polling a majority in the rural precincts.[1]

In 1905, however, the Cunninghams left East Texas so that B. J. could begin a new career as an insurance executive. They went first to Houston, where he managed a branch office of the Connecticut-based Travelers Insurance Company. Minnie, the "country girl," felt stifled in a city of 60,000. At her urging, the couple rented a rural retreat midway between Houston and Galveston on Dickinson Bayou. The village of Dickinson, even smaller than New Waverly, was a frequent destination of excursion groups from Galveston attracted by the wooded and pavilioned picnic grounds that had once been part of a private estate. Cattle grazed the coastal prairie on the south side of the tree-lined shallow water, while fruit farmers on the north side grew strawberries for shipment to the Midwest. Minnie drove a fast horse over the unpaved roads to collect visiting family members at the depot and devoted herself to gardening, boating, and fishing. The bayou was full of wildlife, and on one occasion she shot a six-foot alligator.[2]

In 1907 the Cunninghams moved to Galveston, and B. J. took charge of the accident department of a recently established local firm, American National Insurance. The change may have been prompted by the new Robertson Insurance Law, which required out-of-state life insurance companies to invest 75 percent of their Texas reserves in state securities. As a result, nearly two dozen large companies stopped doing business in Texas. Although new and small, American National had the advantage of local roots and a less uncertain future.[3]

Minnie gave up Dickinson Bayou and began a new phase of her life in a city that was still rebuilding from the destruction of the Great Storm of 1900. A protective concrete seawall seventeen feet high had been erected, but an ambitious project to raise the grade of the city took years. Tackling a quarter-mile section of the city at a time, crews jacked up buildings and lifted water, gas, and sewer lines; sand dredged from the harbor channel was then pumped in to raise the elevation. While the work was in progress, residents cautiously navigated their neighborhoods across planks and trestles eight to ten feet in the air.

Galveston was also changing shape politically. Using the storm devastation as justification, the city's business elite successfully petitioned the state legislature to replace the mayor and board of aldermen with the first city commission system of government in the United States. Subsequently copied in many cities during the Progressive Era, the "Galveston Plan" appealed to the reform-minded because it seemed businesslike and efficient, empowering each commissioner with oversight of a designated city department. City commission government also eliminated the representation that black and working-class voters had claimed under the old ward system; they were no longer able to elect their own to city hall.[4]

Inadvertently, elite-dominated government opened new pathways to power for the wives and daughters of the leadership class, and the devastation of the Great Storm impelled them into innovative public work. Six months after the hurricane, sixty-six women active in religious and benevolent societies, clubs, and charitable institutions founded the Women's Health Protective Association (WHPA). The first citywide women's civic organization in Galveston, it was open to any white woman who wished to join, although the elected officers came from the wealthier strata. Its initial priorities were reburying the dead, who had been hastily interred in makeshift graves all over the city, and replanting the denuded island with trees, shrubs, and flowers. The WHPA also constituted a voluntary force of inspectors and enforcers to help the city health department as it struggled with a massive sanitary cleanup. Over the next decade and a half, its membership climbed to 500 women, including Minnie Fisher Cunningham.[5]

Initially, however, Cunningham seems to have entered female public culture through the older tradition of benevolent work. Still childless after six years of marriage, she and B. J. apparently took in two orphaned or semi-orphaned children during their early years in Galveston. There is an oblique reference in a 1914 letter to "Josie and Jimsey" learning to swim, and later in life she made occasional passing references to having reared two adopted children. She never mentioned their names, sex, or ages. Her only direct statement appears in a letter to a friend in the 1920s. She described the pain of being unable to have children and added that "after I lost my two kiddies I quit having anything to do with children at all and have never taken up any of that kind of work again."[6]

While it is impossible to verify what she meant by "that kind of work," Cunningham may have sheltered children from one of Galveston's two orphanages. The Home for Homeless Children, run by the all-female Society for the Help of Homeless Children, had been destroyed by the hurricane, and when Minnie and B. J. settled in Galveston, the Board of Lady Managers was in the midst of a highly visible fundraising and rebuilding campaign. Along with foundlings, the Home for Homeless Children accepted other children, who were classified into two groups: full orphans, whose keep was paid by relatives, and half orphans, usually the offspring of widowed or deserted mothers who were financially unable to keep their families together. Cunningham's "lost" children may have come from one of these two categories and later been reclaimed by their mothers or other relatives.[7]

Minnie and B. J.'s commitment to Galveston deepened after American National Insurance Company underwent a reorganization that led him to establish his own firm, First Texas State Insurance, in 1910. B. J. was president of First Texas State for almost a year and a half, but he lacked the local reputation and access to capital necessary to make the new company a serious contender against American National. In 1911 he relinquished the presidency to Isaac H. Kempner, one of Galveston's wealthiest businessmen, and became vice president and legal counsel. Although it never approached American National in size, the company prospered modestly, subsequently acquiring the Texas Prudential Company of San Antonio and changing its name to First Texas Prudential Insurance. As vice president, B. J. had found the job that he would hold for the rest of his life.[8]

Minnie, like many wives of business and professional men, occupied herself in voluntary associations — clubs, societies, and organizations of every description through which middle-class women structured a separate female public culture. Women's traditional responsibility for religious and charitable work had long been manifested in church societies that supported home and foreign missions, distributed relief to the poor, and built and maintained orphanages and shelters. By the last quarter of the nineteenth century, leisured women seeking to compensate for their lack of formal education had enlarged the voluntary association tradition with a proliferation of study clubs. Self-development through the study of literature, history, and the arts led to cultural enrichment projects; clubwomen raised money to fund traveling art exhibits, establish public libraries, and sponsor musical performances.

After the turn of the century, many clubs devoted portions of their curricula to the problems of urban growth and unrestrained capitalism: dirty, disease-plagued cities; inadequate public services and schools; and factories and sweatshops where children and women worked fourteen-hour days for below-subsistence wages. Vóluntarist women used their clubs and civic associations to lobby town governments for better sanitation, to publicize threats to public health, to restrict child labor, to set up day nurseries and kindergartens, and to establish infant welfare programs. They helped shape the social justice agenda of the Progressive Era and, especially at the local level, supplied vital energy to reform efforts.[9]

Minnie constructed an extra-domestic role for herself through Galveston's female voluntary association culture, moving from fine arts and literature to municipal housekeeping and, ultimately, to woman suffrage. In Houston, she had belonged to a musical club, which provided talented women with opportunities to sing in public. She joined another in Galveston, probably the Ladies' Musical Club, although membership records are lacking to confirm it. Consisting of thirty-five women who met weekly for rehearsals, the Ladies' Musical Club gave three annual performances featuring instrumental and vocal music. Minnie also sang in the Trinity Episcopal Church choir, although she is not listed on the membership rolls and was a lifelong observant Methodist.[10]

In 1912 she was admitted to the exclusive Wednesday Club, a literary study group, and a year later she was elected secretary. Founded in 1891, the club limited membership to twenty-five women; each prospective inductee had to be recommended by two others. Since the Wednesday Club belonged to the Texas Federation of Women's Clubs, which in turn was affiliated with the General Federation of Women's Clubs (GFWC), Cunningham became part of a national network of women united by a common agenda. Following the GFWC's lead, the Wednesday Club had gradually added social issues to its study syllabus, taking up such topics as pure food and drug laws, the need for police matrons and juvenile courts in the criminal justice system, and the benefits of kindergartens in the public schools. Cunningham was admitted just as the Wednesday Club committed itself to discussing "sociological subjects," including two that it had previously rejected: laws affecting women and children and woman suffrage. The 1912–1913 program also gave her the opportunity to hear papers on working conditions for factory women, the social settlement movement, modern educational trends, and socialism.[11]

In 1913–1914, when the Wednesday Club decided to study "the problem of woman," Cunningham read the contemporary feminist theory of Charlotte

Perkins Gilman, Olive Schreiner, and Ellen Key. Schreiner's *Women and Labor* (1911) and Key's *Love and Marriage* (1904) offered sharply contrasting visions of fulfillment for women. Having given up her profession to become a dependent wife, Cunningham must have found special resonance in Schreiner's denunciation of female "parasitism," or economic subordination to men, and her insistence that women were entitled to the satisfaction of self-sufficiency. Swedish writer Ellen Key struck a different nerve with the argument that women would truly fulfill themselves only through nurturing and motherhood—for which they should be entitled to half their husbands' income and assets.[12]

While the Wednesday Club offered Cunningham an opportunity to study and discuss social issues, in the Women's Health Protective Association she became part of a phalanx of women organized for action. By 1911 the WHPA was the largest women's voluntary association in the city, with a multiplicity of departments and an expanded mission: with the city's grade-raising completed, the WHPA turned its attention from replanting the island to a vigorous campaign to improve public health and sanitation. WHPA inspection committees invaded bakeries, butcher shops, groceries, and dairies and reported their unsavory findings at monthly meetings covered by the press. They demanded that the city improve refuse collection; hire food, milk, and building inspectors; force foodsellers to install window screens to keep out flies; and enforce the ordinance against spitting on the sidewalks. Citizens who failed to get satisfaction from city hall took their complaints about garbage collection and food sanitation to the WHPA.[13]

Cunningham joined the WHPA during this second phase of its existence, apparently because Galveston's unsanitary milk supply made one of her adopted children sick. The technology existed to identify the bacterial causes of diseases such as tuberculosis and typhoid fever, and northern cities had been working to curb their spread through contaminated milk for several decades. Galveston, however, had neither pasteurization laws nor a milk commission, and the city's dairies operated with only occasional visits from the understaffed health department. The WHPA stepped into this void, and from 1912 to 1917 it waged a crusade of lobbying, public exposure, legal action, and boycotts that produced results. Under WHPA pressure, the city commissioners finally agreed to a new pure milk ordinance and stringent enforcement.[14]

Although the pure milk campaign was the WHPA's most highly publicized endeavor, the women took every aspect of public health as their province. Cunningham chaired the WHPA's School Hygiene Committee, which in 1913 undertook a complete inspection of the public schools. It found some buildings lacked even such basic amenities as shelves to hold lunch baskets, coats, and hats. The following year she worked with the WHPA's Women's Room Committee, whose goal was to secure public restrooms for women both downtown and on the beach. At the time, such public accommodations were ordinarily found only in saloons and other male domains.[15]

Cunningham and other middle-class women thus took upon themselves civic responsibilities that men had neglected or deliberately ignored. Calling their new work public housekeeping, they challenged the ideology that assigned women responsibility for the private home and gave men control of public space. Cunningham echoed the rationale of Progressive Era female reformers nationwide when she argued in a newspaper article that "modern methods" had rendered such demarcations obsolete. The bakery, dairy, and public school had taken over functions once entirely under the housewife's control, yet she was still held accountable for "the wholesomeness of the food served on her table, the health of her entire family, and the manners and morals of her children."[16]

As they used voluntary associations to force domestic welfare issues onto the political agenda, progressive women expanded the scope of politics and redefined it as an activity to which women had equal claim. The gender consciousness that emerged from female public culture developed slowly, dividing as well as uniting women who shared a reform agenda. The more conservative, fearing that women would be "unsexed" by voting alongside men, clung to the refined female tradition of persuading and petitioning called "indirect influence." Cunningham identified unequivocally with the growing minority who were frustrated by the ineffectiveness of indirect methods and demanded the right to cast a ballot. In February 1912 she became a founding member of the Galveston Equal Suffrage Association (GESA).

The GESA was part of a rebirth of suffragism taking place across the South, where the movement had begun late and accomplished little. Nationally, the struggle for the vote began in 1848 at the famous women's rights convention in Seneca Falls, New York, but the association of feminism with abolitionists hindered it from crossing the Mason-Dixon line before the Civil War. The southern states had no suffrage societies until the 1890s, and most were small, struggling groups that disintegrated or went dormant within a few years.[17] Texas was a typical example. The Texas Equal Rights Association formed with forty-eight charter members in 1893 and apparently never grew much larger. The widespread perception that suffrage was radical and unwomanly made recruiting members difficult, and the association expired in 1896. A subsequent attempt, led by Annette Finnigan of Houston and her sisters Katherine and Elizabeth, produced the Texas Woman Suffrage Association in 1903. Annette Finnigan found women generally "too timid to organize," and local leagues formed in only three cities. When the Finnigans moved to New York City in 1905, the state association ceased functioning.[18]

Beginning in 1912, however, suffrage sentiment blossomed at the local level. San Antonio organized a society at almost the same time as Galveston;

Houston followed before the end of the year; and Dallas started one in early 1913. The same phenomenon was unfolding in other southern states. And unlike their small and fragile nineteenth-century predecessors, the suffrage associations of the 1910s expanded rapidly and stayed viable. The GESA's growth was typical: the initial membership of seventy-four more than doubled within a year and swelled to three hundred by 1915. Cunningham epitomized the women of this second generation of suffragists; like them, she was a "New Woman," imbued with the progressive spirit of the New South. She and the other New Women who led the second suffrage movement shared a common profile: they were urban, likely to be married, middle- and upper-middle-class, and active members of other voluntary associations. Nine of the GESA officers chosen in 1912, including Cunningham, had held or would hold office in the WHPA.[19]

In later years, Cunningham gave two different explanations for becoming a suffragist. To a male interviewer in the 1950s she stressed the wage discrimination she had endured as a prescription clerk in Huntsville. "Equal pay for equal work," she asserted, "made a suffragette [sic] out of me."[20] When traveling on behalf of the LWV in the 1920s, however, she portrayed herself as one of the Progressive Era's legions of municipal housekeepers, telling a female reporter that she "floated into the suffrage movement on a sea of bad milk." When the WHPA pressed charges against the offending dairymen, Cunningham pointed out, "women could bring their knitting to the corporation court and stare at [male] jurors when milkmen were on trial, but they had no voice in the selection of judges nor in the choice of municipal officers who were responsible for conditions."[21]

This emphasis on collective over individual good—what women could do for others with the ballot as opposed to what it could do for them alone—was the hallmark of Progressive Era suffragism and the stimulus for the movement's impressive growth in the 1910s. The early suffrage movement, led by Elizabeth Cady Stanton and Susan B. Anthony, had asserted a radical demand for equality based on natural rights. As a rebellion against woman's "sphere," it had limited appeal in the North and even less in the conservative South. By contrast, Cunningham's generation of suffragists emerged from the dramatic expansion of female voluntary association culture in the late nineteenth and early twentieth centuries and the rise of Progressivism. Through clubs and civic associations, middle-class women developed a political agenda and a maternalist rationale for public activism that accommodated suffrage without contradicting the cultural definition of womanliness. Progressive Era suffragists intertwined "sameness" and "difference" arguments, contending that women should have the vote because they were equal to men yet distinct in perspective.[22]

Although Cunningham and other suffragists of the 1910s did not cease to

speak of woman's rights, they injected new rationales about female responsibilities, drawing their arguments from the writings of Jane Addams and Ellen
Key. Addams, the most admired woman in America, explained in the *Ladies'
Home Journal* that women needed the vote because industrialization and
urban growth had obliterated the old boundaries between the private household and the public domain. Without the ballot, she stressed in "Why Women
Should Vote," wives and mothers dependent on city services and commercial
vendors (like Cunningham's unsanitary dairyman) could not properly care for
home and family. Key elaborated another aspect of women's expanding roles:
"collective motherliness." Women were not, as the Victorians had claimed,
morally superior beings with "finer" natures than men, but they *were* different; innate maternalism made them more intuitive and compassionate. In
Love and Marriage, Key called for votes for women to enhance their work as
"social mothers."[23]

Cunningham used gendered arguments purposefully, tailoring her presentation to the sex of her audience. When she wrote and spoke to male legislators, she focused on the "sameness" argument, women's "inherent right" as
citizens and taxpayers to equal representation. No government that disfranchised half its citizens could rightly be called a democracy, she reminded
newspaper editors and politicians. "We are determined to do our bit to make
it a *real* Democracy, a *real* representative government, a *real* government of,
for, and by the people."[24] To women's groups, she emphasized the "difference" rationale of maternalist feminism. Presenting a program on suffrage to
the Wednesday Club in 1912, she followed Ellen Key's concept of the "bi-
sexuality" of society to argue that women had as much of a stake in society
as men. Having "a point of view and information which is sometimes not pos-
sessed by the men," women needed the ballot "from the standpoint of their
own welfare as well as the welfare of the community as a whole."[25]

Like all suffragists, Cunningham deployed a range of arguments, but she relied on the sexual difference–municipal housekeeping rationale for recruiting
and organizing. It spoke to the same impulse that prompted women to join the
WHPA and appealed to the more conservative women who shied away from
natural rights rhetoric. Although in one sense the sexual difference argument
reinforced gender stereotyping, it at the same time demolished the old ra-
tionalization that men could represent women at the polls. If one *class* could
not legislate for another, Cunningham pointed out, it followed logically that
one *sex* could not either. Women had knowledge and skills that men lacked,
and "the American housewife has delegated her legislative right too long."[26]

From the beginning, Cunningham was part of the nucleus of GESA members willing to undertake the active labor of building a local suffrage movement. She accepted appointment to the executive committee, which was responsible for arranging public lectures, "keep[ing] in touch with the movement

in the state," and lobbying the state legislature for a suffrage bill "when the time is ripe." Cunningham was also in charge of planning and staffing the GESA booth at the city's Cotton Carnival, the annual summer fair that celebrated business and encouraged tourism; the suffragists used the space to hand out literature and solicit new members.[27]

Another major project was the planning and production of an educational "entertainment" that the GESA presented before a capacity crowd at the Grand Opera House in March 1913. The suffrage movement made good use of theatre's drawing power, and the GESA's three-part program offered a characteristic critique of separate spheres ideology while celebrating female accomplishment. It opened with "A Dream of Brave Women," a series of tableaux depicting the lives of nine famous American women, with Cunningham in the role of her favorite, Clara Barton. Two short satires, "An Anti-Suffrage Monologue" by Marie Jenny Howe and "Lady Geraldine's Speech" by England's Beatrice Harraden, tweaked the opposition's arguments and poked fun at gender stereotyping. Both Howe and Harraden were forthright feminists, but the plays softened the message with humor; the Galveston Daily News pronounced it "solid argument sugar-coated with laughter."[28]

That April, delegates from the GESA and suffrage societies in six other Texas cities met in San Antonio to revive the Texas Woman Suffrage Association (TWSA). They elected Eleanor Brackenridge, the state's most prominent clubwoman and philanthropist, president of the organization and listened to a keynote address by the noted English suffragist, Mrs. Philip Snowdon. Cunningham and the other members of the GESA executive committee publicized the reemergence of the state movement by putting together a special suffrage edition of the Galveston Tribune in June. Membership in the TWSA, which in turn was affiliated with the National American Woman Suffrage Association (NAWSA), brought Galveston suffragists into the national network of women agitating for the vote. In 1914 Annette Finnigan, who had returned to Texas, again became president of the TWSA, and Cunningham, who had just turned thirty-two, was elected to the first of two terms as president of the GESA.[29]

Her devotion to the cause notwithstanding, the GESA presidency put Cunningham at the helm of an organization in which she often felt frustrated and constrained. Southern suffragism grew out of the woman's club movement, which was both its strength and, from the point of view of New Women like Cunningham, its weakness. Clubwomen's tradition of genteel activism shaped the GESA's approach to suffragism and manifested itself in events such as the Opera House evening, which raised operating money and brought a controversial subject before the public without giving offense. Cunningham fully appreciated the importance of avoiding stridency, but she was impatient with what she regarded as a timid approach to suffrage advocacy. She pushed the GESA, which in 1914 counted 175 members and was growing steadily, to undertake more energetic organizing.[30]

For advice and assistance, she turned to Annette Finnigan. The privileged daughter of a wealthy Houston businessman, Finnigan was a Wellesley College graduate and a quintessential New Woman. She had done settlement work, learned business management as her father's administrative assistant, and worked for suffrage in New York City through the Women's Political Union, Harriot Stanton Blatch's innovative mix of working-class and wealthy suffragists. She founded the Houston Women's Political Union with the same goal (though not the same success in recruiting working women) and stayed in touch with the New York network. When she took over as TWSA president, Finnigan went to work immediately to raise money, organize the counties, and plan a legislative campaign. She hired Perle Penfield, a former NAWSA organizer studying to become a doctor at the University of Texas Medical Branch, as a summer field organizer and began strengthening ties between the TWSA and the local societies.[31]

Cunningham sought mentoring from Finnigan and developed a warm rapport with Penfield, whose confident public presence and polished speaking style gave her a model to emulate. Eager for responsibility and full of ideas, she assured Finnigan that "you can always count on Galveston for 'team work' & I think the more of such work we can have the better." She responded willingly to Finnigan's suggestion that presidents of local suffrage associations send representatives to speak before business and professional conventions that met in their cities. The problem, she lamented, was having no volunteers: "There is a perfect famine in Suffrage Speakers!" If Finnigan could somehow supply a speaker, Cunningham promised to provide an escort committee. "Please worry about Galveston!" she implored in a subsequent letter. "We should be doing so much more than we are."[32]

NAWSA's call for nationwide suffrage demonstrations on May 2, 1914, gave Cunningham her first opportunity to lead the GESA in the direction she wanted. She made "May Day" the highlight of an entire week of special suffrage activity during which the GESA expounded its message where women could hardly miss it—the department store. In addition to public meetings, the suffragists introduced the "voiceless speech," a text printed on large placards set up on an easel in store windows. Passersby lingered to read as a suffragist slowly turned the cards. On May 2, for the climactic final demonstration, the GESA's principal speaker was Annette Funk, a Chicago attorney and a member of NAWSA's congressional lobbying committee. The crowd that gathered for a downtown street meeting sang "America the Beautiful" and the "Battle Hymn of the Republic," and then adopted a resolution calling on Congress to make America "in truth and reality a democracy" by giving women the ballot.[33]

What Cunningham wanted above all was to move suffrage work out-of-doors—away from tableaux and teas—to storefronts, street corners, and the beach. She followed May's activities by conducting the GESA's regular monthly meetings "open air" during the summer, on a shady lot adjoining a member's house that "decorates up very prettily, with flags & 'Votes for Women.'" The GESA held its business meeting first, with public speaking as the main event. She turned the meeting that fell on July 4th into an Independence Day celebration with short speeches and a special address by Annette Finnigan.[34] The GESA also voted to share with the WHPA the cost of maintaining a restroom for the summer at the Woman's Exchange, which entitled the suffragists to maintain a desk there and distribute literature.[35]

But Cunningham's dream, "the darling hope of my heart," was to establish a headquarters on the beach, where locals and visitors congregated together. Having charge of the GESA's booth at the Cotton Carnival convinced her of the efficacy of taking suffrage where the crowds were, but those few days were "only a 'drop in the bucket' to what we might do," she told Finnigan. "It seems to me we are letting a glorious opportunity to reach all Texas slip right through our fingers." The GESA had money in the bank toward a beach headquarters, but the membership thought the price too high, and the refusal to act left Cunningham simmering with frustration. She suggested to Finnigan that perhaps the TWSA might fill the void and establish summer headquarters of its own at the Galveston seafront if the GESA contributed money and workers. "Come some excursion day when we *have* a crowd," she urged the president, "and see the potential readers of Suffrage literature and listeners to Suffrage speeches wandering up & down the Boulevard with nothing to do!"[36]

When Finnigan seemed disinclined to pursue the suggestion, Cunningham tried another tack. She proposed that the GESA and the TWSA split the cost of a beach headquarters, the details of which she had already mapped out in her head. She envisioned "a nice little pagoda tent of some bright color" from which the suffragists could hand out literature every afternoon and sell sandwiches and cake on excursion days. She would get permission for Perle Penfield to speak from the bandstand on the Seawall Boulevard: "We could choose our time just after the sun leaves it & have a little music to begin with, rent chairs & get a crowd every time I'm sure." Collections taken at these talks and profits from the food booth would cover Penfield's salary, incidentals, and the pagoda tent, the dimensions and price of which she had already discussed with the tentmaker. "Of course it's all in the air," she conceded, "but then most things *are* until somebody pulls them down!"[37]

The beach project revealed all the qualities that would make Cunningham an effective suffrage leader. She was farsighted, enthusiastic in the face of challenge, and resourceful. She sought a way around her own organization's intransigence by urging that Annette Finnigan be the one to propose cooperative headquarters. "Coming from me," she stressed to Perle Penfield, whom she enlisted to help make the case, "the proposition will appear the same as the beach headquarters I have advocated in vain for two years. Coming from Miss Finnigan it will appear to be an entirely new proposition & be judged fairly on its merits." She had an incentive for Finnigan as well: "I don't think the State organization can reach as many up state people with so little expense as it can in this way." Finnigan, however, decided that the TWSA's limited funds could be more effectively spent in organizing work, and Cunningham was never able to pull her cherished beach project down out of the air.[38]

She compensated by planning a week of heightened visibility for suffrage during Cotton Carnival, which annually attracted as many as 60,000 people. The GESA's activities opened with an outdoor assembly at which Perle Penfield and two local women spoke. Since automobiles were still novel enough to attract attention, the suffragists drove along the Seawall Boulevard distributing literature, and Cunningham made her first public speech from the back of a car. She and Penfield turned the cards of the voiceless speech every afternoon on the roof of one of the bath houses, while another crew showed it at night from an automobile on the Boulevard. Penfield spoke daily, tailoring her remarks, at Cunningham's suggestion, to the special recognition days, such as Houston Day, and Army and Navy Day, designated by the carnival organizers. On Children's Day, for example, Cunningham aimed for "something rather special." The GESA intended to decorate store windows and ask merchants to wrap suffrage literature in customers' packages; Penfield's talk would stress "Mothers' need of the ballot to protect children."[39]

Cunningham was also, by Annette Finnigan's appointment, the TWSA's chairwoman for Galveston County and responsible for organizing its smaller towns. She sought out contacts herself but asked initially for help from headquarters in conducting the meetings. "You know I am not experienced at all in organization work and I'm afraid taking them alone I'd not clinch the matter," she wrote worriedly to Finnigan in June 1914. Reassured with the promise that Perle Penfield would speak, she arranged the first meeting in Dickinson, where she still had friends. What she lacked in self-assurance, she made up in enthusiasm. "I'm certainly *crazy* for this meeting to 'go big,'" she bubbled to Penfield. "I suppose when I have worked for suffrage fifty years more or less, and still have it *not*, I will learn to take it easy and not care very much, but I'm so 'new & all' that when I induce an innocent bystander to mother a suffrage meeting, I feel so personally responsible I can't sleep!"[40]

The Dickinson meeting was a success, but a special assignment for the TWSA later that year, to secure the Texas Federation of Women's Clubs' endorsement of suffrage, ended badly. Although a TFWC member herself, Cunningham was profoundly exasperated by clubwomen's preference for extended study and deliberation before committing themselves to action. The

General Federation of Women's Clubs, with which the TFWC was affiliated, had become the country's largest women's organization by avoiding stands on divisive "political" questions such as suffrage, but by the 1914 biennial convention, vocal prosuffrage members outnumbered conservatives. The GFWC officially endorsed votes for women, and Texas suffragists expected the Texas Federation, which met that November in Galveston, to follow suit.

Since the Wednesday Club would officially host the convention and Cunningham was one of Galveston's three delegates, Annette Finnigan assigned her the task of getting suffrage on the program. When the program committee rebuffed her request for time to address the convention, Cunningham countered by setting up temporary GESA headquarters at the hotel, from which the suffragists could distribute literature and talk informally.[41] To their intense frustration, however, the subject was completely suppressed during the convention proceedings. The TFWC president asked the Galveston delegates, "the only strong suffragists present," not to raise the issue, and they felt obliged, as hostesses, to honor the request. Forced to restrain her resentment in public, Cunningham let it boil over in private. "I feel black & blue all over about that business," she fumed to Finnigan, denouncing the TFWC's violation of both reciprocal courtesy and free speech. "I feel so culpable in allowing myself to be bound to silence on such an important subject. . . . And I can't help regretting that I didn't make a *scene!*"[42]

If clubwomen were a frustrating constituency, Cunningham found organized labor to be just the opposite. Labor and suffrage activists supported each other's legislative demands; the Texas State Federation of Labor (TSFL) favored a suffrage amendment, and middle-class women's organizations backed bills to restrict child labor and improve working conditions for wage-earning women. But Cunningham worried that relatively few working women belonged to suffrage societies and that the GESA was not reaching working people generally. She laid her concern before Annette Finnigan, who put her in touch with Eva Goldsmith, a member of both the Houston Women's Political Union and United Garment Workers Local No. 31.[43]

Goldsmith readily traveled to Galveston and other towns to speak on suffrage to working women's groups. She also gave Finnigan frank advice on which middle-class suffragists would be well received by Galveston labor leaders and which were "stiff and cannot reach the laboring people there." Early in 1915 she spent several months in Galveston on a dual mission to promote the TSFL's union label campaign and "to bring about a closer understanding between the Suffrage Association and the labor movement."[44] Goldsmith was the only female member of the TSFL's legislative committee and, like Cunningham, an indefatigable activist. The two easily became friends and co-workers.[45]

Cunningham established cordial ties with the Galveston Labor Council, which invited her to speak to the women's unions. She was wary of forming too close an alliance, which might draw the suffrage movement into labor's problems. But she had been deeply marked by the economic hard times of her childhood, and all her life she would side with labor against capital, small producers against monopolies, and the exploited against the powerful. As a suffragist, she told the Galveston Labor Council, she was not much moved by the argument that taxation without representation is tyranny, "because I consider that the woman who has property to be taxed is in very much better circumstances to stand tyranny and bear injustice than the woman whose only capital is her physical strength, and who, without the protection of the ballot, cannot be sure the state will protect her capital."[46]

Outreach to labor brought Cunningham an opportunity to promote suffrage in the *Labor Dispatch*, the TSFL's weekly paper. Between February and April 1915 she contributed five articles, beginning with an exposition on the progress of labor legislation in the states that had already enfranchised women. The NASWA monitored legislation in these "suffrage laboratory" states, enabling Cunningham to point out the beneficial effects of women's vote: laws that mandated a minimum wage and the eight-hour day for women, prohibited the hiring of children under fourteen, and made schooling compulsory.[47]

A government study reporting that uniform state laws could eliminate 65 percent of child mortality prompted a follow-up piece in which she blamed the women of her own class for failing to ally with laboring women in the name of motherhood. Her repressed frustration with clubwomen spilled out in a denunciation of "women lapped in luxury" who cherished their own children and ignored those less fortunate. Reversing a favorite accusation of the antisuffragists, she charged that they, not the suffragists, appealed to "the selfish side of human nature," by urging women to stay on pedestals and in rocking chairs—where they would not interfere with business-dominated government. Business leaders well knew that if women united across class lines and won the ballot, "what is 'good for business' will stand in its proper relation to what is good for children." If Texas mothers had a voice at the polls, "never again would a much needed child labor law perish on the [legislature's] calendar while precedence was given to a law to protect little shrimp and oysters and fish!"[48]

Cunningham's articles articulated a female view of community and state that suffragists everywhere shared. Maternalist reasoning deftly inverted gender stereotyping without appearing to "unsex" women. It acknowledged the antisuffragists' stubborn insistence that woman's "place" was in the home and then redefined "home" to include the entire community. Suffragists astutely linked this broad new definition of maternal responsibility to the Progressive Era's gospel of efficiency, with which the Victorian concept of guiding men by "indirect influence" was profoundly out of step. "In these days of scientific management," Cunningham briskly informed *Labor Dispatch* readers, "it is an economic blunder to take two hands and two heads to accomplish what one could do as well." Why, she asked, should "a good efficient modern house-keeper" who has discovered that her neighborhood dairy is violating the pure food and sanitation ordinances have to ask some man to take time from his business and finish her job? Indirect influence was a "nonsensical, wasteful" way of managing public affairs.[49]

Outside the South, such arguments were helping suffragists succeed in state legislatures. Eight of the twelve states that permitted women to vote had been won since 1910, all of them in the West and Midwest. The regional contrast was obvious on the "suffrage map" that NAWSA distributed. It depicted the states that had granted full suffrage in white, those that had enacted partial suffrage in gray, and those that still denied women the vote in black. The South, with its deeply embedded culture of states' rights, Negrophobia, and antifeminism, was a conspicuous black mass. When the Texas legislature convened in January 1915, the TWSA was ready with a suffrage bill, hoping to make Texas the first white state below the Mason-Dixon line. From December 1914 through March 1915, Cunningham devoted all her energy to this effort.

Annette Finnigan had begun laying the organizational groundwork months before, implementing NAWSA methods. She announced a plan to organize suffrage work by state senatorial districts and polled the legislators for their views on suffrage. To help convince them that public opinion was on the suffragists' side, she put the TWSA locals to work gathering signatures on two petitions for a suffrage amendment. One was to be signed by women and the other by men, voting constituents whom legislators were more likely to heed. The local societies were to canvass house-to-house and office-to-office, gathering signatures, distributing literature, and recruiting new members. Finnigan urged workers to use the petition drive, wherever possible, to organize new towns. A network of prosuffrage women throughout the state, who could send a steady stream of letters and telegrams to their representatives in Austin, would strengthen the TWSA's lobbying position.[50]

Cunningham, as chairwoman for Galveston County, took up the work wholeheartedly. The tentativeness with which she had approached organizing only a few months earlier had disappeared; she no longer doubted her ability to "clench" a meeting. She planned to devote an entire week in December to canvassing Galveston County. In each town she hoped to get permission to spend a day in a centrally located store, soliciting signatures and distributing literature. Then she would speak to a group of local women and encourage them to form a suffrage society. "It's a little hard on the county to practice on it like that," she joked to Finnigan, "but one must begin somewhere!"[51] Finnigan thought the plan good enough to suggest as a model to other county chairwomen. But a week of cold, heavy rainfall intervened to keep Cunningham from accomplishing as much as she had hoped. Although she gave away large quantities of literature and got some signatures, speaking and holding organizing meetings proved impossible. "But . . . I did a lot of preliminary work," she reported, undaunted, "and I *will* organize this county if I have to do it in a yellow slicker & a pair of rubber boots."[52]

To reinforce local organizing and generate statewide publicity, Annette Finnigan made plans to bring in a professional organizer, Helen Todd, for a speaking tour while the legislature was in session. Todd, then working for Harriot Stanton Blatch and the Women's Political Union in New York, had stumped for California's suffrage victory in 1911 and was considered especially convincing to the men who heard her. Finnigan thought her one of the best speakers in the country, and Blatch concurred: "I always called Helen Todd our 'prima donna,' so clever was she in talking our cause into the hearts of our audience."[53]

Todd's impending tour moved Cunningham from county to statewide organizing. Since the effectiveness of the visit would depend in part on the TWSA's preliminary work to increase the number of local societies that could host (and pay for) Todd's appearance, Finnigan dispatched Cunningham to East Texas. Originally, her departure was scheduled for late January. But Finnigan made a brief post-Christmas organizing tour in North Texas and returned convinced that it was "imperative that we push into new territory at once to precede Miss Todd, and get the people [in] back of the Legislature." She asked Cunningham to delegate the work of organizing Galveston County and start out immediately: "We want to stir up the state *at once*."[54]

Having at last pushed and pulled the GESA into "some sure enough team work," Cunningham accepted the accelerated departure reluctantly. But as she made her way northeast, and then turned west toward Fort Worth, her reports bubbled with the enthusiasm of a woman who had finally found a field big enough for her talents. In addition to persuading suffrage societies to sponsor Helen Todd's lecture, her mission was to organize new associations and to generate constituent pressure in the form of telegrams signed by prominent citizens; NAWSA encouraged organizers to get "names" as well as numbers. Cold downpours, a train wreck, and being stranded in a hotel while she waited for the TWSA treasurer to wire enough money for the bill, did not dampen her spirits. In the East Texas towns of Nacogdoches and Palestine, she held "splendid meetings" and organized a suffrage society of a dozen members in each. When Helen Todd arrived three weeks later, she found that both groups had grown tenfold and were full of praise for Cunningham. They publicized Todd's visit so well that she spoke to capacity crowds in both towns.[55]

In Sulphur Springs the weather prevented an organizing meeting, but

Cunningham found "a very clever woman" who promised to get telegrams signed immediately and take up organizing later. In Mineola her train arrived so early that she had to get the women out of bed, but they were "perfect *trumps*" who got to work promptly on the telegraph campaign. Not until Fort Worth did she meet a refusal. There she found a small group of recently organized suffragists, "but they've been so ridiculed by the Press & so hectored by these miserable antediluvian clubwomen," she wrote Finnigan, that they were wary of hosting Helen Todd. By that time Cunningham was so seasoned that she took on a learner, a GESA colleague who paid her own expenses and traveled along for a while "to see how it is done."[56]

In late January Finnigan called Cunningham to Austin to be part of the TWSA contingent who would attend Helen Todd's special address to the legislature. She stayed on to help lobby for the suffrage bill, and to her great satisfaction the antisuffrage senator whose district included Galveston was obliged "to take me down the aisle of the Senate to register as a lobbyist for a bill he wasn't for.—For his sins!" Expecting to find a dignified, deliberative body, Cunningham was astonished to discover the lawmakers lounging "with their feet up on their desks, looking like nothing I ever saw in a bunch before."[57]

Armed with an arsenal of carefully reasoned arguments, she and other suffrage lobbyists quickly discovered that southern legislators had a bulletproof shield: the alleged threat that woman suffrage posed to the racial order imposed during the 1890s. Refined white ladies would have to pass through "gangs of Negro women" at the polls, one member asserted in a typical racist diatribe, because "the Negro woman will have the same privilege and prerogative that the white woman will have."[58] Southern suffragists dubbed this argument the "Negro bogey" because it was patently untrue—only a handful of African Americans could meet the discriminatory voting requirements.

Cunningham's generation of southern suffragists was caught in an uncomfortable irony. Without disfranchisement, there would have been no suffrage movement below the Mason-Dixon line; white women could not have mobilized until polling places were made "safe" by removing black men. Yet white male supremacy, based on the myth of endangered southern womanhood, trapped white women in a symbolic role that made their campaign for the vote extraordinarily difficult. Southern politicians wanted them voteless, voiceless, and dependent in order to justify and maintain racial repression. Having choked off meaningful party competition, conservative Democrats did not need women's votes, and they did not want female "interference." They responded to women's demand for the ballot by reviving the racist demagoguery they had used to crush Populism.

The TWSA discovered how obdurate a southern legislature could be as debate on the TWSA's bill dragged on. Cunningham spent most of February in

Galveston, on call, and made a side trip to a nearby county to organize constituent pressure, but to no avail; the targeted legislator declared that he would
not vote for suffrage even if everyone in town petitioned him. The GESA's
own meeting for Helen Todd, however, was a triumph. A crowd of a thousand
gathered at the Grand Opera House to hear Todd's rousing speech and to
adopt a resolution calling on Galveston's senator to change his position and
pledge support for the bill. Although the GESA kept up steady pressure, Cunningham judged the senator a hopeless case.[59]

While the legislature deliberated, Cunningham was reelected GESA president. She informed Annette Finnigan of the news without enthusiasm: "It
makes me feel like 'a spell' of sickness to think of another year, but please
don't tell on me!" Finnigan was "rather sorry," too; she wanted Cunningham
for state service. Late in February, ruefully conceding that the suffragists were
"in real politics," she dispatched Cunningham on an emergency trip to get
more constituent telegrams flowing into Austin.[60]

Expecting to be gone only a few days, Cunningham ended up spending two
weeks in North Texas, as Finnigan cabled urgent new requests. The January
trip had been exhilarating; this one was frustrating and depressing. She found
local notables to sign telegrams ("though in each town I was solemnly assured
that nothing would move their particular representative on that subject") but
failed to bring forth any new suffrage societies. In Crockett, the women were
"afraid to organize while we are under fire," and the members of the Shakespeare Club, which claimed to support suffrage, refused to telegraph their legislator despite Cunningham's offer to cover the cost. "As an organizing trip this
has been a flat failure," she pronounced glumly.[61]

In a close vote, the lower house defeated the suffrage bill—with some of
the nays coming from men who had assured Annette Finnigan of their support—and the senate refused even to consider it. Wasting no time on lamen-
tations, Finnigan pushed ahead with plans to organize the state. She arranged
for Dr. Anna Howard Shaw, the eloquent president of NAWSA, to include
Texas on her southern tour, and Cunningham was back in good spirits when
she introduced Shaw at Galveston's Grand Opera House in late March. Paraphrasing Mark Twain, she announced that reports of the death of suffrage in
Texas were greatly exaggerated. The GESA supplied yellow lapel ribbons to
the crowd, and Cunningham vowed that the cause "would not remain quiet
until its purpose was achieved."[62]

Only once, when she and B. J. were overseeing some long-planned home
renovations and it was not possible to "just pick up and run off," did Cunningham decline to make an organizing tour. She so seldom referred to her
personal life that it is impossible to know how she and B. J. structured their
marriage, but he seems to have fully backed her commitment to suffrage.
They had even decided while the amendment was still alive in the legislature

that if it passed, Minnie would devote herself full-time to the voter referendum campaign that would follow. "Mr. Cunningham and I have agreed that the fight is well worth giving up a lot for," she assured Finnigan, "and we will simply close the house and he will board for as long as the state organization needs my services." Although the need did not arise in 1915, their agreement apparently accommodated Minnie's increasingly high profile in the state movement.[63]

Finnigan hoped to find the money to offer Cunningham a permanent position as a state organizer and seems also to have been grooming her for the TWSA presidency. Thanks in part to Galveston's proximity to Houston—an hour by the interurban railway—the two women saw each other frequently. Finnigan's various health problems also required regular visits to a Galveston specialist, and she used those occasions to meet with Cunningham. Although Cunningham always cast herself in the role of a learner, her ability was obvious and her willingness to turn her hand to almost anything drew Finnigan's gratitude. "You are a treasure," she wrote in the midst of the legislative campaign. "How I wish there were more like you, ready to give up anything for suffrage." Finnigan's sister, Elizabeth Fain of New York City, who had passed the winter in Houston helping out, unequivocally wanted Cunningham to head the TWSA. While Finnigan spent the spring at a West Texas health resort, Fain took charge of planning the May 1915 convention and was "*firm* in the idea that I am to be '*it*' next," Cunningham reported to the absent president.[64]

And all indications pointed that way. Finnigan had appointed her chair of the committee to revise the TWSA's constitution, and Cunningham also volunteered herself as Elizabeth Fain's assistant. The two of them made all the convention arrangements and put together the program. The convention was held in Galveston, Cunningham's own venue, and as GESA president she formally welcomed the delegates. Annette Finnigan, after announcing that she would not stand for reelection, reported a year of encouraging growth and the inauguration of "businesslike" methods. The number of local suffrage societies had increased from eight to twenty-one, representing 2,500 members, and committees of interested women had formed in eighteen additional counties. For the first time, records of all correspondence, press, and legislative work were being preserved, and a card file system had been set up to keep data on each state legislator for future lobbying purposes.[65]

The convention gave Cunningham the opportunity to shine before a state audience. In addition to her visibility as chair of an important committee, she was one of the program speakers; her topic was "How to Organize." She also proposed a money-raising strategy, "self-sacrifice week," which was received with enthusiasm. Each member would forgo some item of personal luxury—a new hat, for example—and cut back on her household expenses, and then donate that money to the TWSA. The individual sums would not be large; for Cunningham, the real value of a week of self-denial was the underlying principle that each woman should make suffrage a personal commitment. The delegates approved self-sacrifice week without a dissenting vote. On the final day of the convention, they elected Cunningham president of the TWSA.[66]

Like Carrie Chapman Catt, who became president of NAWSA that same year, Minnie Fisher Cunningham rose to leadership through her marked talent as an organizer. Effective fieldwork required not simply the eloquence to win hearts but also the ability to recruit bodies, to "clinch" a meeting, as Cunningham phrased it, by forming a new group of working suffragists at each destination. The same demonstrated effectiveness that brought Catt to the attention of NAWSA leaders earned Cunningham the admiration of the Finnigan sisters and would soon attract Catt's notice as well.

Like Catt, Cunningham was convinced that the movement should concentrate its focus on practical organizing and canvassing, a view resisted by some of the older generation, who were steeped in the tradition of agitation. She saw no value in the old-fashioned crusading of the Woman's Christian Temperance Union, which had been advocating votes for women for decades without building a political organization. One WCTU suffragist, who aspired to be a TWSA speaker, complained of being shut out by Cunningham. But Annette Finnigan supported her successor wholeheartedly: "The women prominent in suffrage work in Galveston all backed Mrs. Cunningham, and my personal experience with her this past year made me feel that she was the best one for the Presidency."[67] Over the next four years, Cunningham would validate Finnigan's judgment and prove herself one of the most able leaders of the southern suffrage movement.

SUFFRAGE FIRST

MINNIE FISHER CUNNINGHAM WAS ELECTED PRESIDENT OF THE TEXAS Woman Suffrage Association with no expectation that she would be its longest-serving (1915–1919) and last president. She held the office for four terms because the membership would not elect anyone else and the executive board refused to accept her resignation. In the succinct evaluation of one TWSA officer, Cunningham was "the spinal column of the suffrage body in Texas."[1] The TWSA, which changed its name to Texas Equal Suffrage Association (TESA) in 1916, grew and succeeded in large part because Cunningham refused to concede to the financial, geographic, and political obstacles against the organization.

Of all the women who joined the suffrage crusade, those in the South waged the least fruitful struggle. But within the region there were notable variations in suffrage activity and organizational strength. Some states, like North Carolina and Florida, had barely visible suffrage associations, while others, such as Virginia, had large memberships and leaders of national reputation. And while most southern suffragists lobbied their legislatures to no effect, there were pockets of success: women in Arkansas, Texas, and Tennessee won partial voting rights before 1920. In her four-term presidency, Cunningham built one of the few suffrage associations in the former Confederacy that could claim both organizational strength—about 10,000 members—and political effectiveness.

Cunningham does not quite fit the image of southern suffrage leaders as privileged women motivated by noblesse oblige.[2] She could claim descent from wealthy slaveholders and a father who had served the Confederacy, but not the pedigree or social position of women such as Laura Clay and Madeline McDowell Breckinridge of Kentucky or Virginia's Lila Meade Valentine. Her family's fortunes had never recovered after the Civil War, and while the Fisher name was respected in Walker County, it opened no doors in Austin. She had not attended an exclusive girls' school, or been "finished" in the East, or traveled in Europe. Her husband had neither an old name nor political connections, and he lacked the money to subsidize the extensive traveling and organizing that her more privileged comrades could afford.

Instead of the conventional advantages, Cunningham had youth, optimism, and a sound grasp of practical politics. Only thirty-three when she assumed the TESA presidency, she was a generation younger than the majority of southern suffrage leaders, many of whom had been born during the Civil War. She was both a good platform speaker and an effective administrator, talents not granted in equal measure to every suffrage leader. She brought to the TESA presidency the same energy and initiative that she had displayed in Galveston, always urging the organization to think bigger and do more. Cunningham was ever confident (and sometimes overconfident) that if everyone worked hard and gave until it hurt, the money to implement ambitious plans could somehow be raised. In political strategy, by contrast, she was a realist who understood the necessity of tactical compromise, alliances of convenience, and the art of shaping information, now called "spin." Both sides of her personality were essential to her success as a suffrage leader. Idealism and tenacity built a sturdy organization, and political pragmatism wrested victory from a conservative legislature.

WHEN SHE TOOK OVER AS STATE PRESIDENT IN 1915, CUNNINGHAM'S immediate concerns were finding enough money to meet operating expenses and building an organization strong enough to lobby effectively in Austin. The never-ending struggle to finance the work—which Carrie Chapman Catt at NAWSA described as "eternal begging"—would always be Cunningham's biggest frustration. The TESA's only guaranteed income was the 25-cent-a-year membership dues that each local association was supposed to remit annually, and when Cunningham was elected at the May 1915 convention, there was $162.18 in the treasury. The delegates pledged to raise more than $2,500, with the four largest locals—San Antonio, Houston, Dallas, and Galveston—promising $500 each.[3]

By fall, however, finances were still severely pinched, and the only field-worker, First Vice President Kate Hunter, had been withdrawn because there was no money to cover her expenses. The beginning of 1916 saw no improvement. Just a tenth of the convention pledges had been redeemed, and many local associations withheld part of their state dues to finance local activity. "They seem to think that this work is to be supported by the ravens!" Cunningham lamented, comparing her situation to that of the biblical prophet Elijah, to whom the birds brought food in the wilderness. Her home served as the TESA's "office," and since hiring a secretary was out of the question, she answered correspondence herself, spending six to ten hours a day at the typewriter. If she left Galveston to do field organizing, the office work went undone.[4]

The empty treasury, as much as lack of time, confined her to Galveston. As a substitute for money, she drew on her past experience as a field-worker, and a lifetime of "cutting my garment according to my cloth," she ruefully admitted to a local suffrage officer. She assured women who wrote asking for an organizer from headquarters that they could do the work themselves and explained in detail how to proceed. As added inspiration, Cunningham frequently recounted her favorite anecdote about a woman who was for years the only declared suffragist in the village of Dickinson. "She used to go and sit in her buggy near the post office when the mail was being distributed (about once a week) and give away Suffrage Flyers to all who would accept, and gradually, she won that whole town. When I went up to help her circulate a petition last spring, only two men refused us and every body that could read knew what 'Votes for Women' meant. It doesn't take numbers to start with, but it does take real interest and *consecration*."[5]

For those with a fledgling organization already underway, she had another strategy, also based on NAWSA leaflets and personal work. The president of the San Marcos ESA, for example, received a batch of "The Revolution in Woman's Work Makes Votes for Women a Practical Necessity," which Cunningham considered "one of the clearest expositions of the housekeeper's right to an interest in government that I have ever read." She then outlined a simple procedure. The president should assemble a half-dozen committed members and with them "select from the telephone book the names of twenty of your most influential women who are not Suffrage workers, parcel them out among yourselves and write them personal notes calling attention to the enclosed leaflet, giving your personal reason for being a Suffragist, and closing with a cordial invitation to join the Association. This is one of the most effective ways of rousing interest and increasing the membership. It is best if you have paper and pens ready and get the letters written on the spot."[6]

This same faith in "personal work" underlay her efforts to organize Texas by state senatorial districts, following the NAWSA model that Catt had initiated; election district organizing down to the precinct level was the suffragists' best hope of defeating the political machines and "rings" that opposed them. Cunningham appointed chairwomen for the thirty-one districts, each of whom was then responsible for appointing a chairwoman for every county within the district. In a fully organized district the county chairwomen, in turn, would appoint chairwomen for the towns, who would select those for the wards, who would then choose chairwomen for each block. The goal was to get suffrage information to every individual and gradually erode opposition as relentlessly as water wearing down rock; Cunningham called this the "constant dripping theory." Such labor cost relatively little, much less than the time of a professional organizer, "and by this plan we have personal work so simplified that any and all of us can do it."[7]

She recognized, however, that the TESA had little chance of persuading the next legislature to pass a suffrage bill without more trained workers, publicity, and resources. While she encouraged the local suffrage societies in self-reliance, Cunningham pleaded with Catt to send an experienced organizer to train the local women and good speakers to tour the state and bring out crowds. She wanted not only a headliner for the large cities but a secondary speaker to spend a month in the smaller towns "to follow up and clinch" the organizer's work. "You will, perhaps, think I am asking an awful lot of help, but *please*, dear Mrs. Catt, see your way clear to giving it to us. Our need is so urgent, and help given to Texas now will repay itself many fold in the end in getting that big black blot off the map in 1917!"[8]

While she waited for Catt's reply, Cunningham plunged ahead. With the executive board's authorization, she engaged a freelance organizer, Elizabeth Freeman of New York, for a tour beginning in January of 1916. The TESA had only about $200 in the bank, and Freeman's four months in Texas would cost several times that; Cunningham counted on the promised convention pledges to meet the deficit. But the local associations failed to pay, and by March there was not even enough money in the treasury for stamps. Cunningham paid the office expenses out of her own pocket and cut short Elizabeth Freeman's tour by a month. Nor could Texas meet its share of the expenses for the NAWSA organizer, Lavinia Engle of Maryland, who followed; Cunningham personally borrowed $60 to finish Engle's tour.[9]

The emphasis on fieldwork produced dramatic growth for the TESA. The number of local associations grew from twenty-one to eighty during Cunningham's first presidential term. By her second, in 1916, there was enough revenue—barely—to rent a headquarters office in a downtown building and hire an indefatigable secretary, Edith Hinkle League. Cunningham even persuaded Lavinia Engle, who had worked for NAWSA in several southern states, to give up her position and return to Texas as the TESA's field secretary. The money problem, however, remained intractable, despite Cunningham's determination to set an example by raising $1,000 personally. Pledges made at the 1916 convention were as tardy as those of the year before, and the TESA continued to limp from one financial emergency to the next.[10]

Cunningham also had to cope with the potentially destabilizing influence of the national suffrage movement's emerging left and right wings. In 1913 Alice Paul, who had gotten her suffrage training from British militants, had formed the Congressional Union (CU) to vigorously prosecute the campaign for a federal amendment. The dedicated and uncompromising Congressional Unionists, who employed attention-getting tactics such as parades and open-air rallies, were soon at odds with the staid NAWSA leadership. Breaking with NAWSA in 1914, Paul and the CU adopted the British strategy of holding the party in power responsible for the failure to pass a suffrage amendment. In the congressional elections that fall, CU organizers campaigned in the full-suffrage states of the West against Democratic candidates. In 1915 Paul's organization began building state affiliates and the following year changed its name to the National Woman's Party (NWP).

A smaller insurrection took shape in the South from the opposite view-point, as conservatives led by Kate Gordon of Louisiana organized the Southern States Woman Suffrage Conference (SSWSC) to oppose a federal amendment and preach states' rights. Gordon, an outspoken Negrophobe, embraced the argument put forth by many southern politicians that suffrage by any route except state referenda would endanger white supremacy. A congressional amendment, she claimed, would empower the federal government to scrutinize the South's racially restrictive voting laws, give the ballot to black women, and sound the death knell of state sovereignty.[11]

Gordon therefore proposed to blackmail her fellow racists in the state legislatures into giving southern women the ballot. Southern suffragists could use race as "a club over the heads of Democratic leaders," she insisted, forcing them to pass state amendments in return for women's silence on the illegality of racial voting restrictions. She made her case to Texas suffragists when she was a guest speaker at the 1915 state convention in Galveston, and her call for the Texas association to affiliate with the SSWSC provoked vigorous debate. Outgoing president Annette Finnigan firmly opposed affiliation, maintaining that "we don't want to bring the Negro question to Texas." Cunningham, then GESA president, said the same thing off the convention floor. The convention voted to affiliate with Gordon's organization, but it also elevated Cunningham to the presidency. She dealt with the SSWSC affiliation by ignoring it; the action was never again mentioned, and Gordon did not get another opportunity to speak in Texas.[12]

Cunningham was equally unwilling to endorse the NWP, whose southern organizer, Mrs. E. St. Clair Thompson, arrived in Texas in the fall of 1915. She considered the NWP's exclusive focus on a federal amendment and rejection of state work "short-sighted," although admittedly appealing. "If there is any short cut, I want to take it too," she conceded, "but Educate and Organize is the only thing I see that will win in the end." A federal amendment would still have to be ratified by three-fourths of the states, "and how is it to be gotten

past those Legislatures unless we educate our voters to elect [male] Suffragists and to insist on the enfranchisement of women?" The logic of punishing
the party in power at the polls struck her as both unfair to its blameless prosuffrage members and unworkable, especially in the one-party South. "What,
in the name of all things practical, could we in Texas put up to defeat [the
Democratic Party] with? And what would it do to our chance for a hearing
from our own men, who are largely Democrats?"[13]

A handful of TESA members also joined the NWP, and although Cunningham discouraged dual affiliations, she chose to emphasize peaceably that
"there is room for all in our great Cause." Privately, she thought that belonging to both groups made no more sense than joining both the Episcopal and
Baptist churches, but she issued no ultimatums to those who did. With some
TESA members leaning toward the NWP and others to the SSWSC, "I feel
sure that the middle of the road is the place for us," she told a dual-affiliated
officer, "and you will have to forgive me while I steer for it, because if we steer
to one side or the other we will inevitably split."[14] This did happen in other
states. South Carolina's NWP followers seceded from the state organization,
and Tennessee's Sue Shelton White defected to the NWP after Catt told her
to choose between NAWSA and Alice Paul's organization. In a vast state like
Texas where the suffrage movement might easily have fractured, Cunningham's "big tent" philosophy prevented similar schisms.

AS A PROGRESSIVE DEMOCRAT, CUNNINGHAM SPENT A GOOD PART OF 1916,
an election year, at war with her party. Texas Democrats were bitterly divided
into conservative "wet" and progressive "dry" camps over the issue of prohibition, and the wets were in power. They were led by Governor James E. Ferguson, one of the populist demagogues who flourished in nearly every southern state in the wake of disfranchisement and one-party rule. Ferguson was
one of the milder incarnations of the breed, not given to the racist diatribes
that were the stock in trade of Mississippi's James K. Vardaman and South
Carolina's Cole Blease, but flamboyant enough to stir up crowds and play on
class resentments. Ferguson, a banker and lawyer who reinvented himself as
folksy "Farmer Jim," the poor man's advocate, made the farm tenancy problem the centerpiece of his noisy 1914 campaign. He had coupled a pledge to
seek legislation that would set a legal limit on the amount of rent landowners
could collect with a vow to veto any liquor legislation that crossed his desk.
The former won him a large following among struggling farmers, and the
latter eventually brought around powerful conservatives initially apprehensive about Ferguson's populist rhetoric.

By 1916 his allies included former U.S. Senator Joseph Weldon Bailey and the "border bosses" of the Rio Grande Valley. Bailey, tainted by an old conflict-of-interest scandal, was a spotlight seeker whose reactionary speeches championed states' rights and white supremacy. The border bosses were equally devoted to localism and limited government, but they worked more quietly. Their county machines controlled the votes of thousands of Mexican American laborers, who by inclination and instruction voted against prohibition.[15]

Politically, opposition to prohibition and to woman suffrage went hand in hand; it was widely assumed that enfranchised women would vote with the prohibitionists. Enmity between antiprohibitionists and suffragists dated back to the nineteenth century, when the Woman's Christian Temperance Union began its crusade to close saloons and endorsed the ballot for women as a means to that end. In the 1910s progressives like Cunningham viewed alcohol restriction less as a moral issue than a political one; they deplored the "liquor trust," whose money bought elections and financed political campaigns.

With antiprohibitionists dominating the Democratic Party councils, suffragists were certain to be luckless petitioners. Cunningham put the TESA to work to get more prosuffrage legislators elected, and in 1916 the organization passed a resolution asking the state Democratic Party to include a woman suffrage plank in its platform. But at the party's spring convention in San Antonio, Bailey's impassioned denunciation of woman suffrage as an open invitation to the federal government to force black voting rights on the South foretold the outcome: the wets flattened the disunited drys. Bailey and Governor Ferguson wrote the platform, which took a states' rights stand on both suffrage and prohibition, and declared the delegates' "unalterable opposition" to imposing either by federal amendment.[16]

That June, Cunningham led a large contingent of TESA women to the Democratic National Convention in St. Louis to take part in NAWSA's demonstration for a plank endorsing equal suffrage. She was one of 6,000 suffragists wearing white dresses accented with yellow parasols and yellow "Votes for Women" shoulder sashes—NAWSA's colors—who formed a line on both sides of the street between the delegates' hotel and the convention building. NAWSA leaders feared that a suffrage parade, like the one they were planning for the Republican convention, would only alienate conservative southern Democrats; a "ladylike" demonstration of women with hands outstretched in mute appeal seemed a safer alternative. On opening day, the Democratic delegates had to pass through this "golden lane," of which the TESA women and their state banner formed half a block. It was Cunningham's first convention, and years later she recalled that "some of the girls went to parties around the hotel, but several of us just wanted to unhitch our corsets, take off our shoes, and talk politics."[17]

The Democrats nominated Woodrow Wilson for a second term and rejected NAWSA's proposed equal-suffrage plank; the platform committee in-

stead brought in a weak endorsement that upheld the rights of states to decide the issue themselves. Even that was too much for James Ferguson, who
presented the dissenting minority report in a speech studded with injunctions
about woman's nature and "the purpose for which God Almighty intended
her," which drew hisses from suffragists in the balcony. The Texas delegation,
which loudly encouraged Ferguson, led the jeering against Senator Key
Pittman, the member of the Resolutions Committee who rose to defend the
plank. While both sides shouted at each other, the women in the gallery rose
as a body to cheer Senator Pittman, waving flags, twirling parasols, and fling-
ing reams of "golden lane" bunting down onto the convention floor.[18]

Furious and humiliated, Cunningham led the Texas suffragists in an additional protest against Ferguson: they paraded in front of the convention hotel
carrying a Lone Star flag draped with mourning, which she had improvised
by cutting up a black crepe dress. She went home fired with a "message" and
worked off more frustration by embarking on an auto tour of South Texas, a
wet stronghold, with Lavinia Engle. In the blazing summer heat, they covered
thirty-five towns, organizing for the TESA and urging voters to defeat Ferguson in the July primary. By the end of the tour, Cunningham was sunburned
and hoarse from speaking in the open air as many as four times a day, but she
felt "blissidly [sic] sure that we pried quite a few votes loose from Governor
James E. Ferguson." He won the customary nomination for a second term despite their efforts, but a nonbinding referendum calling on the legislature to
submit a state prohibition amendment to the voters passed narrowly.[19]

At the postprimary state Democratic convention in Houston that August,
Cunningham managed to secure a hearing before the platform committee.
She expected to be "walloped" by Ferguson and Bailey but looked forward to
the fracas: "If we can find a hero who will head a minority report, we aren't
licked yet." She was perfectly aware that the suffragists were granted an audience because the men expected to get some amusement from it. The insult
beyond bearing, however, was the appearance of state senator Claude Hudspeth of El Paso, "the biggest Anti in the state barring J. F.," to escort her little
group into the hearing room. Pale with anger, Cunningham abandoned both
politeness and prepared remarks and extemporized "the *hottest* and best
speech that I have ever made." The committee listened with "cold hostility,"
she reported to Lavinia Engle and Catt, "but the more I abused their methods
and stated our claims, the more they seemed to like it. And in the end gave us
quite an ovation and many of the men followed us out to shake hands."[20]

The outcome, nevertheless, was a foregone conclusion. All proposed resolutions were referred to a subcommittee chaired by a state senator who was
an attorney for the Texas Wholesale Liquor Dealers Association and consisting of "nine of the brewers' most faithful henchmen." The convention ignored both the national party plank on suffrage and the state primary vote

calling for the submission of a prohibition amendment. It "openly, shame-lessly and insolently steam rollered completely out of the platform what was the will of the people," she wrote indignantly to Catt. To Lavinia Engle, with whom she shared a warm bond and a wicked sense of humor, she added that if she had not been brought up to believe in the Methodist Hell, the "Con-demned Democratic Convention" would have converted her. "I don't see what else *is* to become of these outrageous men who have so far forgotten all decency and honesty, as J. Ferguson et al."[21]

She was nearly as disgusted with President Wilson, a fellow southern Dem-ocrat, who was resisting suffragist pressure to endorse a federal amendment by "gluing himself" to the St. Louis platform. The party's states' rights stance, she said flatly, was a hypocritical policy, invoked only to avoid giving women the vote. Texas Democrats, in refusing to endorse even state-granted suffrage, had shown how little the St. Louis plank was worth, and she considered Kate Gordon's SSWSC politically naive for embracing it. While Gordon was lobby-ing in St. Louis, Cunningham wrote in exasperation, "her own state legislature was busily turning down their Suffrage Amendment, and yet, she rejoiced over that plank! Doesn't she *want* Suffrage?"[22]

Wilson's assurance that he would do all he could to influence the states to support suffrage did not mollify Cunningham. It was an empty promise, since there was nothing he *could* do, and an inconsistent one ("if it *is* a state affair, what business has he as President of the U.S. using National influence in state affairs?"). So angry was Cunningham with her party that she was almost will-ing "to say Suffrage First with all of my heart" and campaign for Wilson's Re-publican opponent, Charles Evans Hughes, who endorsed the federal amend-ment in his speeches, even though the Republican Party was only weakly supporting suffrage. Not that working for Hughes would make any differ-ence, she told Catt with resignation, for "of course 'the solid South' will make the mistake of *being* solid."[23]

In light of both parties' failure to endorse NAWSA's demand, Catt, too, was reassessing strategy. Advancing the date of the organization's annual gather-ing by three months, she summoned the membership to an emergency con-vention in September in Atlantic City. Cunningham was one of seven south-ern women scheduled to speak at the "Dixie Evening" program. As a state president, she was also a member of NAWSA's executive council, which Catt called together in a closed preliminary meeting before the Emergency Con-vention formally opened.

Crowded into a stuffy room in the hotel basement, Cunningham and the other council members listened as Catt pointed to a huge wall map of the United States and outlined her new strategy—the Winning Plan—a coordi-nated drive for securing the vote by 1920. It gave primacy to the federal amendment and assigned contributing roles to the states. The eleven states that had passed full suffrage amendments were to get resolutions from their legislatures asking Congress to pass the federal amendment. A second group, states in which political conditions indicated a good chance of securing full suffrage, was authorized to pursue state referenda. The third category, intractable states in which referenda were unlikely ever to succeed, were to ask for partial measures that could be granted by legislative act alone: presidential suffrage (the right to vote for presidential electors), or primary suffrage (the right to vote in primary elections). Catt asked the state presidents to sign a compact pledging adherence to the plan, the details of which they were not to reveal except to their own membership.[24]

The Winning Plan gave the difficult southern states only a small supporting role. It completely wrote off the lower South, where Catt had concluded success was impossible and money wasted, and restricted the border and rim states, including Texas, to campaigns for partial suffrage only. Nevertheless, Cunningham signed the compact willingly. She was weary of being "whip sawed" with states' rights, and Catt's strategy merely confirmed her own conclusion that neither Kate Gordon's SSWSC nor the NWP's anti-Democratic campaigning would yield results in the South. A federal amendment seemed the only realistic hope for most women below the Mason-Dixon line, and by targeting money and labor on the most promising states, NAWSA could win the thirty-six votes necessary to ratify it. Like Catt, Cunningham was a political pragmatist, and the Winning Plan confirmed her own conviction that federal and state work had to advance together.[25]

When the Texas legislature convened in January 1917, Cunningham had her first opportunity to deliver the state for NAWSA, and she moved suffrage headquarters to Austin for the two-month session. She pinned her hopes on a bill for primary suffrage, which was tantamount to full enfranchisement in the one-party South, where the Democratic primary was the only election that mattered. Primary suffrage had the additional advantage of sidestepping the vexed "Negro question," since African Americans were barred from primary elections. The suffragists were thus, as Cunningham said, "'calling the bluff' of those who resent the Negro vote."[26]

Despite the TESA's persistent lobbying, the primary bill failed. But the legislative defeat was balanced by an unexpected gift from fortune, the growing possibility that Governor Ferguson might be removed from office. That summer Ferguson escalated the vendetta he had been conducting for months against the University of Texas. He vetoed the university's appropriation and attempted to fire the president while his handpicked board of regents dismissed six professors whose views the governor disliked. An angry constituency of middle-class reformers, alumni, and students rallied to defend the university and urged the speaker of the House to call the legislature into special session to consider impeachment charges. "This is the chance of a life time to get rid of Ferguson and break the power of the liquor ring and straighten out some of the awful things that have been going on in our state," Cunningham exulted to a fellow TESA officer.[27]

Her opportunity for a direct role came in mid-July through Professor Mary Gearing, who chaired the university's home economics department. Ferguson's regents had criticized the program as a useless expense and implied that both it and Gearing might be eliminated. Gearing, an officer in the Austin ESA, immediately sought advice and assistance from ex-regent George Brackenridge, the brother of the TESA's honorary president, Eleanor Brackenridge. He provided $2,000 to fund a "women's uprising" against Ferguson, which Gearing asked Cunningham to come to Austin and coordinate.[28]

While she and Mary Gearing formulated a long-range strategy, Cunningham started the TESA on a behind-the-scenes campaign to intensify public pressure for impeachment. Since nothing could happen unless the speaker of the House called the legislature into special session, she instructed suffragists to deluge him with letters requesting one. Ordinarily, Cunningham's "Dear Suffragist" directives emphasized the importance of getting press coverage for even the smallest activity, but this, to avoid giving Ferguson a target, was to be a stealth campaign: *"Give no publicity to this action."*[29]

Cunningham, Gearing, and a small group of Austin ESA members and other volunteers worked sixteen-hour days in the summer of 1917 to launch the public face of their impeachment drive, the Woman's Campaign for Good Government (WCGG). An umbrella organization, the WGCC consisted of a dozen women's voluntary associations whose presidents responded to telegrams from Cunningham's headquarters group. Their names, with Cunningham's and the TESA unobtrusively positioned far down the list, graced an appeal sent to a thousand women asking for volunteers "to put before the people of Texas the full facts" of Ferguson's unconstitutional attack on the university. The WCGG worked in conjunction with the Ex-Students Association, guided by businessman-philanthropist Will Hogg (son of the late Governor James Hogg), to arouse public indignation that the legislators could not ignore.[30]

Conversations with leaders of the party's progressive wing convinced Cunningham that Ferguson had survived a previous investigation for misuse of public funds because the legislators "received practically no support [and] encouragement from the moral forces of the state. This we must not, and shall not, let happen again. They must have letters every day, each one of them, constantly expressing our faith in them and our desire for a better government in Texas." The 2,000 individuals who responded to the WCGG's appeal for volunteers received a three-page dossier of Ferguson's misdeeds, to which Cunningham attached a detailed list of instructions for conducting public awareness campaigns. The tactics replicated those of the suffrage movement:

a stream of letters, telegrams, and resolutions to legislators; appearances before all the social, educational, religious, and fraternal organizations of a town or county; and well-publicized mass meetings.[31]

After the House speaker yielded and called a special legislative session, the WCGG produced a one-page "dodger" to hand out in the streets. Intended to produce a flood of constituent mail, it listed the charges against the governor that the speaker had enumerated in his call and concluded with Cunningham's summons to action: "What do YOU as a tax payer think of all this? Write your representative in the Legislature and tell HIM." The WCGG used its vast network of women's clubs and suffrage leagues to distribute 100,000 of these fliers to constituents and at public meetings in the districts of doubtful legislators. Cunningham divided her time between the WCGG's office and the capitol building, where she put at the disposal of the proimpeachment forces the TESA's extensive files on the background and voting records of each member of the legislature.[32]

The House brought twenty-one articles of impeachment, and Ferguson resigned the governorship the day before the Senate voted to convict on ten of them. "Our people are awake and informed as to the corrupt political ring and its activities as never before," Cunningham wrote jubilantly to Catt, "and I hope the result may be a reform wave that will sweep the state of these shameless men." She was certain that the impeachment battle had enhanced the suffragists' chances of success in the next legislative session. "It has been a full six weeks since I have found any man with the temerity to look us in the eye and say he opposed women's voting in the face of the outrageous condition that has been proven to prevail in our state government."[33]

FOLLOWING NAWSA'S DIRECTIVE, CUNNINGHAM MERGED CONTINUING agitation for the vote with a full agenda of war service work. Some southern suffrage associations suspended their annual conventions during World War I and let suffrage activity slide, but the TESA adopted its most ambitious budget ever in 1917. With characteristic enthusiasm, Cunningham committed both the organization and herself to extra responsibilities. The day after the United States declared war on Germany, she issued the first war service letter to Texas suffragists, urging them to help increase the food supply by planting gardens and eliminating waste. Other directives followed regularly, for war work was both patriotic and strategic. When she declared, to applause, at the 1917 TESA convention that suffragists would do war work selflessly, even if Congress continued to withhold the vote, it was not without an awareness of the benefits to the cause. Suffragists could justly point out that women's disfranchisement contradicted the democratic principles for which America was fighting abroad, and home-front service presented a unique opportunity to attract positive publicity. Cunningham took on the high-profile task of chairing the third and fourth Women's Liberty Loan campaigns in Texas, an endless effort that required appointing and coordinating the work of 253 county chairwomen as well as extensive travel and speechmaking.[34]

She also headed a TESA-backed effort for what she and other reformers called "clean moral conditions" for young recruits at the state's army training camps. The Selective Service Act prohibited the sale of alcohol to soldiers in uniform and permitted Secretary of War Newton Baker to ban prostitution within five miles of a military establishment. Military and civilian officials commonly flouted both regulations. In Texas and across the nation, red-light, or "vice" districts, were a fixture of the urban landscape. Some were legally sanctioned, others tolerated for the fees and fines that prostitution generated for city councils and law enforcement officials. The four Texas cities in which the army set up training camps—San Antonio, Fort Worth, Houston, and Waco—all had flourishing red-light districts heavily patronized by off-duty soldiers.

Suppressing the sex trade was a long-standing goal of Progressive-Era reformers, who merged the Victorian moral imperative to rescue and reform prostitutes with the new physician-led social hygiene movement. Warning that venereal disease had reached epidemic proportions, social hygienists targeted prostitution as the cause. They portrayed the prostitute as a menace to public health and a threat to the middle-class family: young men who contracted venereal disease in brothels infected their unsuspecting brides, and babies born of such unions risked birth defects and blindness. (There was no cure for syphilis until the invention of penicillin in the 1940s.) Secretary Baker's desire to maintain an army "fit to fight" added legitimacy to the social hygienists' crusade to close vice districts and encouraged middle-class women to demand that the army safeguard their sons in camp. For Cunningham, the issue was intensely personal: her younger brother, Horatio, was in the army.[35]

The idea for a women's anti-vice crusade in Texas grew out of reports on alarmingly high rates of syphilis and gonorrhea in the training camps presented at the 1917 TESA convention. The delegates decided to ask the War Department to take action and voted "that our whole machinery of organization be at once thrown into the fight." Cunningham chaired the committee formed to do the work and commissioned Elizabeth Speer of the Austin ESA as its investigator. The next phase of the antiprostitution campaign grew from the public awareness campaign that Cunningham launched. Through the presidents of women's voluntary associations, she issued a call for a mass meeting in San Antonio, notorious as one of the few remaining American cities still licensing and inspecting prostitutes. Its Fort Sam Houston had the highest rate of venereal infection in the nation.[36]

More than 300 women assembled on June 5, 1917, registration day for the new military draft, responding to Cunningham's call to "stand together" and demand that young recruits be protected from "temptation, downfall, shame, misery, and in some cases death from wholly unnecessary causes." The heads of fifteen voluntary associations joined her to form the Texas Women's Anti-Vice Committee. After electing Cunningham president, the committee drafted resolutions to the War Department asking that prostitution be suppressed both as a matter of keeping soldiers fit for duty—the army's rationale—and of protecting the health of their future wives and unborn children. Cunningham immediately telegraphed Secretary Baker, whom she had been keeping abreast of her plans, that Southern Department Headquarters in San Antonio was not carrying out his orders and demanded that soldiers be prohibited from visiting prostitution districts.[37]

With sixteen women's organizations united behind her, Cunningham optimistically planned "the biggest single piece of work that has ever been attempted in the state." First, the Texas Women's Anti-Vice Committee aimed to mobilize local women into "camp mothers" committees that would offer soldiers wholesome alternatives to visiting bars and prostitutes. Second, it would monitor conditions around the camps and arouse public sentiment for stronger law enforcement.[38] Cunningham arranged mass organizing meetings in Houston, Waco, Dallas, and Fort Worth to get the work under way and drew up guidelines for grassroots activity. She advised local women to form themselves into an investigative group, survey local vice conditions, and then, armed with the names of property owners, besiege city hall and insist that the mayor enforce the laws against using property for immoral purposes.[39]

Ever mindful that the real coercive power lay in Washington, D.C., Cunningham, from the beginning, sought cooperation and counsel from the War Department's Commission on Training Camp Activities (CTCA). Created to enforce the prohibition of liquor and prostitution near the army camps and to provide alternative recreation for the soldiers, the CTCA was directed by Raymond Fosdick. He welcomed civilian assistance, and Cunningham sent regular reports from the Texas Women's Anti-Vice Committee. In Fort Worth she and Elizabeth Speer discovered that the percentage of soldiers hospitalized for venereal infection was rising rather than declining, and city officials "plainly prefer to cover up rather than clean up." In Waco, Speer and another woman, disguised as maids, infiltrated brothels to gather information that Cunningham telegraphed to Fosdick. Civilian and military officials proved so uncooperative in suppressing the sex trade there that Cunningham asked Fosdick to send in a CTCA undercover detective.[40]

Although pressure from the War Department ultimately forced the prostitution districts to close, the vice situation proved intractable. The evicted prostitutes simply moved into lodging houses and cheap hotels, and Cunningham was soon lamenting that "until we devise *some* way of taking care of these women our problem will not stay solved." She passed on to the CTCA the Anti-Vice Committee's resolution deploring the traditional punitive solutions and suggesting that the federal government take a hand in helping the women find new employment and "a decent place in society." A nonplussed Fosdick, admitting that the CTCA had "no specific policy to recommend," put Cunningham in touch with Maud Miner of the New York Probation and Protective Association, which worked at "rescuing" working-class girls from promiscuity and casual prostitution. Miner, the well-known author of *The Slavery of Prostitution*, offered Cunningham empathy and encouragement, but she clearly had no idea how to help thousands of displaced professional sex workers.[41]

The problem was far too big for the Anti-Vice Committee, and stricter law enforcement merely forced the purveyors of illicit pleasures and their khaki customers to become more resourceful. Cunningham's fellow members of the Texas Women's Anti-Vice Committee disappointed her equally; none contributed the effort or money pledged at the June 5 meeting. Cunningham financed the anti-vice work out of the TESA's treasury, miscellaneous sums raised at mass meetings, and her own pocket; by the end of the summer, the outstanding debt was more than $1,500. Voluntary associations found their resources stretched thin by competing demands from other war service organizations, such as the Red Cross, Liberty Loan, and Woman's Committee of the Council of National Defense. As the CTCA assumed a higher profile, some women thought the difficult and controversial anti-vice work could be safely left to the government and gave priority to collateral projects, such as setting up recreational canteens for soldiers.[42]

In October 1917 the presidents of the organizations that made up the Texas Women's Anti-Vice Committee voted unanimously to disband and join the newly founded Texas Social Hygiene Association. The committee's demise was a failure that Cunningham felt keenly, the more so because she still had to find a way to pay off the outstanding debt. Frustration permeated her postmortem report, in which she reminded the members of their enthusiasm at the San Antonio meeting and rebuked them for their failure to follow through. Those who failed to assist the Texas Social Hygiene Association in its attempt to suppress commercialized vice, she charged, would have to bear "the guilt of many hundreds of ruined lives of our boys and girls of today and the yet unborn children of the future."[43]

For the remainder of the war, Cunningham pursued her commitment to the anti-vice crusade through mixed-gender associations. She was elected one of the five vice presidents of the Texas Social Hygiene Association, and in the spring of 1918 the governor appointed her to the Texas Military Welfare Commission. Formed to coordinate work and avoid duplication of effort among agencies concerned with soldiers' welfare, the twenty-one member commission included a number of prominent women. Cunningham's appointments to the executive committee and the subcommittee on law enforcement indicated that the work of the Woman's Anti-Vice Committee had not gone unnoticed, despite its failure to fulfill its mandate.[44]

BY THE END OF 1917 CUNNINGHAM WAS WORN DOWN PHYSICALLY AND emotionally from the stress of leading the TESA for two and a half years, plus the added burden of war work. Speaking and organizing kept her frequently on the road, and during legislative sessions she spent entire weeks in Austin. She had not wanted to be elected to a third presidential term the previous spring, insisting before the convention that "nothing on earth" would induce her to accept: "I just must have a whole year's rest from that money-raising strain!" Giving way reluctantly, she had told the assembled women that yielding to "conscription" entitled her to ask others to make equal sacrifice.[45]

And having been forced to borrow money to cover the TESA's expenses, she meant "sacrifice" literally. She was frustrated that so many women structured their suffrage work on the study-club model: talking more than doing and adjourning for the summer months. Rhetorical support for suffrage was not enough. Cunningham wanted a deep personal commitment of time and money from every suffragist that included a willingness to give up cool summer sojourns in the North and to practice financial self-denial to help fund the work. Too few gave themselves fully; "this Cause," she admonished, "is not a one woman affair."[46]

She also struggled to reconcile the demands of leading the movement with the responsibility of managing a home, although she said little about it. Uncommonly for a middle-class southern woman, she had no African American household help, and despite B. J.'s position as an insurance executive, money always seemed to be tight. A revealing letter to her closest friend, Jane Yelvington McCallum of the Austin ESA, implies that Minnie did without domestic servants and personal luxuries in order to give more money to suffrage. "Of course if Husband knew about all of the work I *do* he'd *beat* me, and get a cook and things," she confided to Jane. "But this thing has already cost us so much more than we can afford that I have not the heart, nor the right, to let him know. When he leaves home in the morning I'm there and when he gets back I'm there and so is a hot dinner ready to serve (that is to say when he or I are in town)."[47]

In December 1917 Cunningham submitted a request to the TESA executive board for a salary of $200 a month. With a small regular income, she explained to Jane, "I could have a cook and have some sewing and mending and things done, and pressing, and such little nagging personal services so when I *go* home I could rest . . . and have some massage treatments and my hair and teeth put back (they are coming out because I've let myself get so run down) and generally rejuvenate, besides having some clothes so that when I'm called upon to represent the organization on 'state occasions' . . . I needn't pretend to be sick or pawn the 'family jewels' either!"[48]

The issue of compensation had come up before, at the spring convention. In their eagerness to retain Cunningham as president, the delegates had been ready to authorize an income; she had prevented the vote because the TESA was so short of money. The executive board's approval was thus almost a foregone conclusion, but the vote was not unanimous; two dissenters thought a paid president would hurt the public's perception of the suffrage movement. Stung by the implied criticism, and feeling overburdened and underappreciated, Cunningham sent the board her resignation, noting tartly that in practically every town she visited the women assumed that she *did* draw a salary.[49] The crisis was resolved with a formal profession of appreciation and loyalty from her coworkers. At its January 1918 meeting, the board refused *"vehemently"* to accept Cunningham's resignation or to rescind the salary.[50]

Thus mollified, Cunningham resumed work with renewed energy, donating the salary back to the treasury every month lest it provoke any suggestion of egotism. Barely six weeks after insisting that "I cannot go this pace very much further," she issued a letter of vigorous presidential instructions for the coming months. For the war effort, each suffragist was directed to plant a victory garden, buy a thrift stamp weekly, and volunteer for service with the Women's Liberty Loan Committee in her county. For suffrage, there would be an unexpected opportunity to lobby again for a primary elections bill when the legislature convened in a special session at the end of February. "See to it that *your* representative has *daily* advice from home, from men and women, to pass this amendment," Cunningham admonished.[51]

The legislative session presented her with an extra challenge, since by law a special session was restricted to issues enumerated in the governor's call. And the acting governor, William P. Hobby, who had assumed office after James Ferguson's impeachment, continued to resist putting suffrage on the agenda, despite Cunningham's repeated requests. In the months since his promotion from lieutenant governor, Hobby had been undergoing a political metamorphosis, which was not yet complete. Initiated into politics by conservative mentors and elected as an antiprohibitionist, he had moved gradually closer to the progressive-prohibitionist wing of the Democratic Party. Dry leaders courted him assiduously, stressing that he could justify endorsing prohibition as a war exigency to conserve grain and protect servicemen. Secretary of War Baker added to the pressure by suggesting pointedly that the training camp at San Antonio would be moved if conditions there did not improve.[52]

Suffragists worked just as hard to present their own cause as a wartime necessity. Following Catt's suggestion and example, Cunningham proclaimed the need to arm the mothers, wives, and sisters of absent soldiers with the ballot in order to offset "Kaiserism" at home. Like seven other states, Texas allowed "first paper" aliens who had filed a preliminary citizenship application to vote. Since many were German and the United States was in the throes of violent anti-German nationalism, suffragists made full propaganda use of the fact that the "alien enemy" could vote, while loyal American women were disfranchised. Cunningham hit the theme hard, offering Hobby, who had never made any public declaration on either side of the suffrage question, a rationale for endorsing the woman's ballot. But he remained unmoved, even after the TESA executive board formally offered the suffragists' "influence and organization" in returning him to office in exchange for a primary suffrage bill.[53]

Cunningham and other southern suffragists shared a common problem: NAWSA's pressure-group politics was designed for a two-party system, not the one-party South. Without competition between parties—or intense factionalism within a dominant party—suffragists lacked leverage: potential allies who could reap political benefits from helping them win the vote. Unexpectedly, the reemergence of James Ferguson, Cunningham's worst enemy, gave her bargaining advantage. Despite having been banned from holding public office after his impeachment, Ferguson defiantly declared himself a candidate for governor in 1918. An anathema to the progressive-prohibitionists, "Farmer Jim" was still popular with rural voters. His chances were further enhanced because several progressive dry candidates had announced in opposition to Hobby, who, if no longer actually wet, was still damp from his previous affiliation. Young and inexperienced as a campaigner, with only a few months in the executive office behind him, Hobby lacked the usual advantages of incumbency. Sizing up the field, Cunningham saw what was likely to happen: competing prohibitionist candidates would split the dry vote, and Ferguson would regain the governor's office.

At that point, she proved herself as shrewd a political negotiator as any of her male opponents. Bypassing the obdurate Hobby, she made a deal—the vote for women in return for women's votes—with key dry legislators. She asked Representative Charles Metcalfe, a suffrage ally who was also a Hobby supporter, to use his influence in persuading the governor to ask for primary suffrage, hinting broadly that "a large number of new and grateful voters would be his salvation, I should think!" Metcalfe asked for a guarantee that she could turn out the female vote for Hobby, and she provided an "unofficial" letter for him to circulate among progressive-prohibitionist legislators. "Vote in hand we will quite naturally concentrate on the man who enfranchised us," she stressed. With the drys divided and Ferguson certain to win the wet and machine-controlled vote, "whomever the women of Texas concentrate on in the July primaries, that man is just as good as elected. But without us, it is Ferguson with a plurality. . . ."[54]

Metcalfe, a blunt-spoken West Texas rancher, frankly told Cunningham to keep her organization out of the limelight and let him handle the negotiating; *"masterful* women" irritated him and would only antagonize the men who needed persuading. She passed along TESA's breakdown of the legislators according to their views on suffrage—supportive, opposed, or undecided—and Metcalfe lined up the votes. Hobby, fearful that endorsing suffrage would cost him more support than he would gain, remained an impediment to the end. He did not mention suffrage in his call to the legislature and told Cunningham that he would ask for a bill only if presented with a petition signed by a majority of both houses. As soon as the suffragists had gathered the signatures, Charles Metcalfe and a half-dozen cosponsors introduced a primary suffrage bill, taking care to waive the 1917 poll tax so that women would be able to vote that summer. In a matter of days, the same legislature that had defeated primary suffrage the previous year passed it in 1918, by large majorities in both houses, and Governor Hobby signed the bill on March 26.[55] The suffrage victory in Texas was a bargain of political expediency made possible by a factionalized Democratic Party and Cunningham's shrewdness in exploiting this rift.

At the jubilant TESA convention two months later, Cunningham listened to testimonials praising her leadership and insisted—although less vehemently than the previous year—that she would not stand for reelection. She was nominated anyway, along with two other candidates; one withdrew and the other, arguing that "horses should not be changed in the middle of the stream," urged the delegates to vote for Cunningham. The convention reelected her by acclamation and authorized a massive campaign to register women voters during the seventeen-day period mandated by the new legislation. Cunningham appointed a chairwoman for each county, charging them with compiling statistics, designating precinct chairwomen, and forming a broad-based citizen advisory committee to stimulate community interest.[56]

In the middle of the registration campaign, an African American women's club applied for membership in the TESA, a potentially damaging quandary. Cunningham laid the problem before Catt, who suggested telling the black club's president "that you will be able to get the vote for women more easily if they do not embarrass you by asking for membership." On her own, Cunningham added that since the application was without precedent, it would require a vote at the next convention, by which time she hoped all women would have full suffrage by federal amendment.[57] The action was evasive, but no southern suffrage association could have survived if it had failed to uphold the color line. The white male supremacists controlled the debate, forcing suffragists, like the Populists before them, perpetually on the defensive. Any suffragist who voiced even mild support for black voting rights risked retaliatory race-baiting, which the antis coupled with a studied pretense that the disfranchisement laws did not exist.[58]

By 1918 Cunningham had learned the futility of defending black voting rights. Two years earlier she had written an open letter to the *Galveston Daily News* disputing its assertion that woman suffrage would guarantee the Republican Party an additional 160,000 black votes. After pointing out the fallacy of assuming that all black women would vote for the GOP, since the same was not true of black men, she asked: "Is there really a Democrat in the state of Texas who is so little an American that he would willingly see anyone disfranchised purely because that person might vote the Republican ticket?" It was a rhetorical question, intended to shame, and an astonishingly frank assertion of two ideas considered radical in her time: that African Americans were entitled to vote—and for whomever they chose—and that the Democratic Party should win elections by fairly contesting them rather than by disfranchising the opposition.[59]

Bruising rounds of legislative lobbying taught her to keep such convictions to herself; white supremacist legislators could not be shamed into expanding democracy. Evaluating Cunningham's statements on voting and race requires keeping the different political reality of the 1910s, and suffragists' struggle to rebut lies with facts, always in primary focus. Like other mainstream southern suffragists, Cunningham saw no solution to racist intransigence except to assure suspicious legislators that suffragists were "not for any radical revision of the voting qualifications in any State." She even tried to move white supremacists by linking their own logic to reliable statistics. Since more girls than boys graduated from high school, she pointed out, enfranchising women would inevitably increase the literate white vote.[60]

Such statements are easily misinterpreted. They reflect not Cunningham's own views but her attempts to find a way around or through the racial bigotry of the opposition, and they appear only in private lobbying letters to legislators. Never in any public forum or printed medium did Cunningham raise the race issue. Exasperated by the deliberate distortions of the *Houston Post*—for example, that woman suffrage meant "placing the ballot in the hands of 300,000 Negro women and prostitutes"—she placed a carefully factual rejoinder in the suffrage-friendly *Chronicle*. The rebuttal reminded readers of the restraining effect of the poll tax and white primary, but Cunningham had it printed without a signature, lest she or the TESA appear to be endorsing such laws.[61]

During the TESA's registration campaign, the *Post* inadvertently proved that the suffragists had been right about the "Negro bogey"; the paper did not even bother to keep an accurate count of the African American women who came forward to register, knowing that they would be turned away from the polls on election day. But all of the metropolitan papers gave front-page coverage to white women's registration, which the suffragists counted a grand success. In all, some 386,000 women signed up, "enough to make Ferguson sick," Cunningham noted happily. Walking out of the Galveston County tax collector's office with her own registration receipt, she compared her exultation to that of a mockingbird bursting into full song "when he perches on the topmost swinging bough. . . . But for a hundred and sixty pounds of excess baggage and the trifling matter of lack of voice, I could have done it myself!"[62]

To turn out the women's vote for Hobby, Cunningham combined grassroots political organizing with an appeal to gender interest. Knowing that many women might hesitate to join their local male-dominated Hobby organizations, suffragists took the lead in forming a parallel network of Women's Hobby Clubs. Cunningham, who was unanimously elected a member of the Hobby Campaign Committee in Galveston, organized Galveston's women's club herself, guiding the women through the process of electing officers and explaining the need for precinct and block chairwomen to coordinate house-to-house canvassing. Women's Hobby Clubs instructed women in marking ballots, handed out campaign literature on street corners, and distributed yellow badges for women to pin on their lapels, signifying their intention to vote. Galveston's club had a speakers' committee that visited factories, laundries, and other employers of female labor during the noon hour.[63]

To give women an even stronger motive to vote, Cunningham made certain that there was a woman on the ticket. Six weeks before the election, Annie Webb Blanton, a suffragist and professor of English at North Texas State Normal College, agreed to run for state superintendent of public instruction. Cunningham managed this subtly, first persuading Blanton, and then arranging for the TESA convention to pass a resolution calling on her to enter the race. Since public education was considered a female domain and several other states had elected woman superintendents, the office was an apt choice, and Blanton an ideal candidate. She had just completed a term as the first woman president of the Texas State Teachers' Association and was thoroughly connected to the web of women's voluntary associations through memberships in the TESA, the TFWC, and several patriotic-hereditary associations.[64]

In addition to directing suffragists to work actively on Blanton's behalf, Cunningham helped refine her platform and draft campaign literature.[65] Cunningham, in turn, sought guidance from Dr. Alexander Caswell Ellis, the TESA's unofficial counselor. A professor of education at the University of Texas, Caswell Ellis had spent the previous five years building the University's extension division. In the process, he acquired a network of political contacts and skills as a publicist that the suffragists tapped into. Married to Mary Heard Ellis, a mainstay of the Austin ESA, he was the author of a NAWSA pamphlet, "Why Men Need Equal Suffrage for Women." Carrie Chapman Catt (whom he teased for making "an indecent exposure of her brains" when she lobbied Congress) prized him as the rarest kind of ally, a genuine southern liberal, and Cunningham considered him a fountainhead of political wisdom.[66]

Cunningham and Blanton planned an "educational" campaign in the style of female voluntarist politics, laying out Blanton's qualifications against those of her opponent so that voters could make an informed choice. But when Caswell Ellis read the draft of a proposed campaign circular, he immediately predicted failure because "it hasn't any punch or shock in it." In a series of long, frank letters, he gave Cunningham a crash course in the realities of winning elections. The incumbent superintendent, Walter F. Doughty, was no less qualified than Blanton; he was a career educator with a master's degree from the University of Chicago, an unassailable record in office, and the endorsement of the *Texas School Journal*. Blanton could not expect victory unless she was "willing to sail in with the gloves off," Ellis warned.[67]

The election offered a foretaste of the dilemma that suffragists everywhere would confront after enfranchisement: should they persist in issue-oriented "female" politics or adopt the values of male political culture? Men had one set of expectations and women another. Suffrage locals targeted antisuffrage, antiprohibitionist candidates for defeat, to the great irritation of Charles Metcalfe, who also gave Cunningham a lecture on playing the political game. Former opponents who had pledged future support for women's causes should be accepted as friends, he admonished, and he asked her, as a personal favor, to call off the women campaigning against El Paso's Claude Hudspeth. When Cunningham declined, citing TESA and NASWA policy that candidate records be given out impartially, Metcalfe rebuked her testily for pursuing a "vindictive" policy and "failing to defer to the judgment of your [male] friends."[68]

But she did follow Caswell Ellis's counsel to play politics in the Doughty-Blanton contest, not daring to risk failure after having promised to deliver the women's vote. Following the lead of the Hobby campaign, which accused Ferguson of disloyalty because of his ties to the state's German-American brewing industry, Ellis drafted a Blanton campaign flyer that charged Doughty with being a tool of the brewery interests. The evidence was flimsy and Doughty vigorously protested that he was being unjustly attacked, but Cunningham moved aggressively. She distributed the circular to the press with a letter contending that Doughty was "unfit" for office. TESA members received it along with a presidential appeal to organize telephone committees for Blanton.[69]

Working in cooperation with Hobby's campaign manager and speakers' bureau, Cunningham stumped the eastern part of the state, giving Hobby-

Blanton speeches. At her suggestion, Lavinia Engle went on the Hobby campaign payroll for several weeks and made a speaking tour. Confronted with an outpouring of support for Hobby, Ferguson, in top "Farmer Jim" form, tried to divide women along rural-urban lines. He urged farm women not to be influenced by the "pink tea" women of the cities, who would rather nurse a poodle dog than a baby, a taunt that the childless Cunningham thought deliberately directed at her. The suffragists countered with a cross-class portrait of Hobby as the "woman's candidate," emphasizing the unprecedented reform legislation—suffrage, statewide prohibition, and enlarged anti-vice zones around military training camps—passed during his administration.[70]

When the ballots were counted, Cunningham had more than delivered on her bargain with Representative Metcalfe. Both Hobby and Annie Webb Blanton won by a large margins. Hobby's total was more than twice as large as Ferguson's, while Blanton carried every county but one. Since women's ballots were not counted separately, it is impossible to know how many voted, but the press reported heavy turnouts. The newspapers exaggerated in crediting women with the victory, but the female vote clearly gave Hobby his landslide. Even Ferguson conceded that women had apparently voted ten to one against him. Cunningham was so elated that she did not mind being defeated as a delegate to the September state Democratic convention. She had wanted to be a delegate in order "'to rub it in,' but who cares—it rubs itself in, that majority."[71]

Although the State Democratic Executive Committee selected her to be the convention's temporary chair, the suffragists discovered that male and female political self-interest still diverged. The TESA's male allies of convenience would not give more ground willingly—every foot would have to be contested. Cunningham wanted the state Democratic convention to go on record for the federal amendment, but Hobby declined to introduce the necessary resolution. And the "honor" of chairing the convention was disingenuous, a maneuver by Ferguson men on the state committee to prevent her from speaking for the federal amendment from the floor. Forewarned by the mother-in-law of one of the plotters, Cunningham declined to preside, feigning a sudden conviction that since women were attending for the first time, the convention offices should go to "more experienced persons."[72]

Thus free, and "still feeling a little pert" from women's impressive showing during the election, she warned Hobby that the women would spend the entire night preparing for a floor fight on the suffrage resolution. Reproached by a Hobby-backer for possibly jeopardizing the governor's "fine political future," she retorted, "if he doesn't support this amendment, he doesn't *have* any future." Two years earlier, with James Ferguson in power, Cunningham had been an unsuccessful supplicant before the resolutions committee. But now she was a political player who had proved that she could mobilize women voters. The committee brought out the desired resolution, and the convention approved it. "We really did organize a fine floor fight," Cunningham recalled. "It's a pity we didn't have to use it. We would have shown them something in termagants they had never seen."[73]

She did not reveal this confrontation until forty years later, her choice of words reflecting frustration carefully suppressed at the time. Termagance was no part of her suffrage persona. Women followed Cunningham—and men listened to her—because she maintained the requisite image of southern ladyhood in a region profoundly suspicious of feminism. As one suffrage neophyte noted with relief after hearing her speak, Cunningham was "a true womanly woman." Without that persona, she would have had no access to men like Charles Metcalfe, who was nearly apoplectic in his denunciations of the National Woman's Party suffragists picketing the White House. She walked a careful line between assertiveness and deference, mindful of legislators' distrust for "the naggers and militant fanatics."[74]

Part of Cunningham's success as a suffrage leader stemmed from this ability to conceal herself as a politician. Primary suffrage and the state Democratic convention's endorsement of the federal amendment were triumphs of quietly executed and publicly invisible "personal work on the ground," as she termed it, about which she was purposely "discreet," even in reports to Catt.[75] She never divulged the backstairs bargain that produced the primary suffrage bill, and for good reason. Political horse trading contradicted the self-image that suffragists cultivated as a "front-door lobby" for a just cause. Their official explanation credited fair-minded men with rewarding women for selfless war service.

Deliberately obscuring her own role as a tactician and distributing praise to half-hearted male allies, Cunningham helped shape the image of Texas suffragists as earnest petitioners who succeeded through perseverance. But by the time of the twentieth anniversary commemoration of woman suffrage, after two decades of hearing women disparaged as a "failure" in politics, Cunningham was finally ready to acknowledge in print the politician inside the southern lady. "The time has come to dispense with this starry-eyed babes-in-the-wood twaddle about suffragists. We went up against and helped to break the most ruthless and powerful machine that had ever fastened its tentacles on Texas and the United States and we knew what we were about." In a private letter to Jane McCallum, she expressed it better still: "At the moment we were the smartest group of politicians in the state."[76]

WASHINGTON LOBBYIST AND NATIONAL LEADER

BY 1918 MINNIE FISHER CUNNINGHAM HAD BECOME ONE OF THE BRIGHT stars in NAWSA's dim southern firmament. She had been initiated into national service in 1916, working for a month in West Virginia's suffrage referendum campaign and making up to three speeches a day. The TESA, as usual, was struggling financially and unable to make the contribution NAWSA requested for the 1916 "campaign states," so Cunningham volunteered her labor instead.[1] The role she was assigned in the drive to pass the federal amendment reflected her growing stature in the national movement. She was the last secretary of NAWSA's Congressional Committee in Washington, D.C., and in 1919, after the Nineteenth Amendment finally passed, she was sent out to help organize support for ratification.

A combination of talent and geography propelled Cunningham's rise. In terms of what Carrie Chapman Catt expected from state presidents, her performance had been flawless. Cunningham could see the importance of national strategy and of her assigned role within it, which made for a smooth working relationship with NAWSA. There was never any foot-dragging from Texas, and no outbursts of ego; Cunningham admired Catt and relished collaboration and teamwork. Whatever the directive from headquarters, she could be counted on to get it done.

Most important, Cunningham was one of the very few southern presidents who had gotten results from a state legislature, which made her especially desirable for national work. Southerners dominated President Woodrow Wilson's administration and were disproportionately represented in the leadership of Congress. Bostonian Maud Wood Park, who arrived in Washington in 1916 as a NAWSA lobbyist, recalled that for months she had trouble following the debates because so many members and floor leaders spoke with heavy Dixie drawls.[2] With southern Democrats constituting the largest block of congressional opposition to the federal amendment, articulate and effective southern women, like Cunningham, were valued spokeswomen for NAWSA in Washington.

As a state president, Cunningham was one of the gears in the national suffrage "machine" that Catt built after taking over the NAWSA presidency late in 1915. Catt transformed the organization into a single-issue pressure group, shifting focus away from a campaign of public education and toward the "practical politics" of getting suffrage amendments through state legislatures and Congress. Pressure-group politics required suffragists to work both inside and outside the political system: inside, through NAWSA's Congressional Committee, and outside, by applying the pressure of public opinion from the states. Cunningham served in both capacities: mobilizing outsider pressure from Texas and working as an insider lobbyist in Washington. Catt considered her especially gifted at "political work," and Cunningham slipped easily into assignments at the national level.[3]

CUNNINGHAM DID HER FIRST WASHINGTON LOBBYING STINT IN DECEMBER 1917, as head of the TESA's delegation to NAWSA's annual convention. With a vote on the federal amendment pending in the Sixty-fifth Congress, Catt planned the convention's opening day to include a ceremonial descent on the Capitol by delegates from the nonsuffrage states. A majority of Texas congressmen and one senator were adamant antis. Martin Dies, for example, contended that anyone could "look at the barnyard, at the cockrel who protects his hen" to see that suffrage was against nature. Sam Rayburn, the future House Speaker, insisted that women were adequately represented by their husbands and other male relatives. With absurd gallantry, he offered to represent personally a widowed NAWSA lobbyist who called at his office, despite the fact that she lived in Kentucky. Pursuant to NAWSA instructions, Cunningham arranged with Texas's prosuffrage senator, Morris Sheppard, to invite the state's entire congressional delegation to his office to meet the Texas suffragists and hear their arguments for the federal amendment.[4]

The NAWSA considered these meetings—thirty in all—a success, but Cunningham's efforts for the federal amendment were abruptly interrupted by a case of German measles so severe that she was hospitalized in Washington for the rest of December. Representative Marvin Jones had told her that no one in his district cared about the ballot, and from her hospital bed, she issued instructions to have constituent signatures gathered on a petition that would convince him otherwise. Since so many southern congressmen shared Jones's belief, Maud Wood Park, director of the Congressional Committee, instructed the southern suffrage associations to inundate their representatives with telegrams as the date for the vote drew near. Cunningham was back in Texas, coordinating a barrage of "home pressure," when the amendment passed the House of Representatives, in a tense vote, by exactly the required two-thirds majority on January 10, 1918. The "heavy artillery down in Texas," as Catt dubbed Cunningham and the TESA, persuaded six of the state's eighteen congressmen—including the heavily pressured Marvin Jones—to vote yes.[5]

By the suffragists' count, they were several votes short in the Senate, where the amendment would be stalled for months. The TESA went after Texas's Charles Culberson, an aging and infirm states' rights Democrat, "by laying down the strong arm." Cunningham and Caswell Ellis undertook to persuade every Texas newspaper to come out for suffrage so that the women could overwhelm Culberson with editorials. By February she was forwarding between five and fifty editorials a day. She instructed TESA members to intensify the pressure by making sure that he received a "ceaseless number" of telegrams and letters from prominent citizens until the very day of the vote.[6]

While the Senate delayed, Cunningham proved her lobbying skills by winning primary suffrage at home. Within weeks she was called to Washington to assist NAWSA's Congressional Committee, whose sole function was to persuade Congress to pass the federal amendment. As described by chairwoman Maud Wood Park, the committee's responsibility was "to keep our friends in the Congress active for the Amendment, to direct pressure of every sort upon doubtful or opposed men, to make an accurate poll . . . to study the floor situation and be ready to take advantage of favorable opportunities and to avert a threatening action." The committee was always poised "to bring in delegations of our women from the states when we needed help," and Cunningham was summoned several times.[7]

She and the other Congressional Committee lobbyists worked in pairs, for propriety's sake and because having two listeners made it more difficult for a congressman to go back on his word. The goal was to secure the politician's pledge of support or, failing that, at least to make a positive impression. Maud Wood Park laid down firm procedural guidelines:

> Don't nag
> Don't boast
> Don't threaten
> Don't lose your temper
> Don't stay too long
> Don't talk about your work in corridors, elevators, or streetcars
> Don't tell everything you know

Don't tell anything you don't know (i.e., don't repeat rumors)
Don't do anything to close the door to the next advocate of
    suffrage

Every interview required thorough preparation and follow-up: before calling on a member, the lobbying pair read the Congressional Committee's dossier on him and afterward wrote a full report for the file.[8]

Cunningham spent part of the spring of 1918 in Washington, and Maud Wood Park found her congenial and effective. When the House Woman Suffrage Committee held hearings on Hawaii's petition for woman suffrage, Cunningham was chosen, along with Park and Anna Howard Shaw, to testify on its behalf. The Hawaiian bill passed, but two attempts to bring the federal amendment up for a vote in the Senate failed before Congress adjourned for the summer recess.[9]

NAWSA called Cunningham back to Washington in September for two special assignments. Maud Wood Park wanted her to take charge of persuading New Mexico's Andrieus A. Jones, chair of the Senate Woman Suffrage Committee, to bring up the amendment. Jones doubted that the suffragists could find the two votes still lacking for passage, and Park found him "very rasped" by the Congressional Committee's past pressure. She believed, however, that Jones had some Texas connections that "may give [Cunningham] a new hold on him." And because the Texas primary suffrage victory and the Hobby campaign had made Cunningham NAWSA's best southern headliner in 1918, Catt designated her to lead a delegation to President Wilson, a fellow southern Democrat, despite his years of residence in New Jersey.[10]

The White House delegation was NAWSA's response to the National Woman's Party's well-publicized demonstrations against the Wilson administration, part of Alice Paul's strategy of holding the party in power responsible for the failure to pass the federal amendment. Catt and the nonpartisan NAWSA, certain that such confrontational tactics only aroused hostility, appealed instead to the Democrats' self-interest. Cunningham's mission was to get the President's help in bringing about an immediate Senate vote; his party, the NAWSA suffragists stressed, could reap the benefit in the November elections.

Women from the West, where the Democrats worried about losing seats, and from the South predominated in the delegation. The southern members emphasized that sentiment below the Mason-Dixon line was beginning to shift, and Cunningham had the most impressive story to tell. Suppressing the backstairs politics of winning primary suffrage, she attributed the Texas victory to "the sweeping change in sentiment" wrought by the suffragists' unselfish war work. "We feel we have answered for all time the charge that southern women are not interested in voting," Cunningham declared, recounting that "nearly four hundred thousand" Texas women had registered.

"Now that we are confident that the Federal Amendment will pass, we Democratic women naturally are anxious that it shall pass as a Democratic measure—that is why I am here."[11]

The deputation met with Wilson on September 16, two hours before an NWP demonstration announced for Lafayette Park, across the street from the White House. Inadvertently, the NAWSA women changed the shape of the NWP protest. Immediately after the interview, Cunningham released Wilson's brief statement of sympathy with the cause and his promise to use his influence with Congress. She praised the President as a "wonderful listener": "That is real democracy—to be able to go to the head of the nation with the problems of the people." To the NWP, however, Wilson's assurance that he would "urge the passage of the amendment by early vote" fell short of an actual promise to act. Therefore, with banners flying and police clearing the way, several dozen NWP members marched to the park and burned a copy of the President's statement at the foot of the Lafayette monument, protesting that "today women receive more words."[12]

Both the NWP and the NAWSA moderates claimed credit when Senator Jones announced that the amendment would be taken up. The President fulfilled his promise by making an unprecedented personal appeal on the Senate floor. The NWP demonstration may have stiffened Wilson's resolve, and it certainly gave him an opportunity to reward NAWSA's "polite" approach. But the outcome—the amendment lost by two votes—revealed the flaw in Alice Paul's policy of holding the governing party accountable, a tactic borrowed from the British militants. Despite the NWP's scorn for Wilson's mere "words," they were all he could offer; unlike a British Prime Minister, an American President could not compel fellow party members to follow his lead. This was always the core of Cunningham's opposition to the NWP. She never complained that the demonstrations were offensive or the militants "unladylike," only that their strategy was futile against southern Democrats, who held the most secure seats in Congress. She considered threats useless, and persuasion the only realistic hope.

The NWP's street theater was vital in making suffrage a live political issue and forcing Congress to resume hearings (the last had been in 1887). But it was Catt's pragmatic and low-key Winning Plan that steadily built the necessary clout in Congress, with each state victory adding more prosuffrage votes in Washington. The NAWSA responded to the narrow Senate loss by holding both parties responsible. It targeted four antisuffrage senators for defeat in the November midterm elections and succeeded in retiring two of them; barring death or broken promises, success could be expected when the new Congress met in 1919. And Minnie Fisher Cunningham, back in Texas once more, was tapped to be the next secretary of the Congressional Committee. Again, she was chosen because she was a successful southern president, and the fifteen-member committee had no southern representation. (Mrs. William Jennings Bryan of Florida did not count, by anyone's definition, as a daughter of Dixie.)

Maud Wood Park and Carrie Chapman Catt wanted Cunningham to return to Washington immediately, but she claimed pressing responsibilities; she was absorbed in wrapping up the Fourth Liberty Loan campaign and in planning a conference of the TESA's district chairwomen in preparation for the opening of the Texas legislature in January.[13] There is a significant silence in her list of reasons for delay: she did not mention any need to discuss the offer with her husband or arrange to have her household looked after. By this time, she and B. J. had probably separated, or decided to, although the split would not be known in suffrage circles until the following year.[14] There is no indication that suffrage broke up the marriage. The few references to B. J. in her correspondence show him to have been extremely supportive of her work. (Catt and Park had similarly structured marriages—childless, with much time away from home—and theirs were successful.) Nor is there any hint of marital discord in Minnie's letters to her closest associates, and if she confided the reason for the separation to anyone, before or afterward, the correspondence has not survived.

A plea from Park that "we need you desperately," finally prompted Cunningham's departure in late November. Her new home was Suffrage House, on Rhode Island Avenue, where she had stayed during previous lobbying trips. Formerly a European embassy, it served as both office and living quarters for the Congressional Committee and was open to the public for suffrage teas and receptions. Suffrage House was huge, ornate, and impossible to keep warm in winter. The state dining room, complete with music gallery, was so enormous—and so cold—that the women ate instead in an adjoining alcove. They turned the small drawing room into a memorial to Susan B. Anthony; it housed her portrait as well as furniture and mementos lent by the family. The large formal drawing room was the suffragists' evening gathering place, where, after a day spent cornering congressmen and writing up interview results, they exchanged reports and political gossip. On the third floor were sixteen bedrooms, including one to which Catt had first claim when she visited from NAWSA's New York headquarters.[15]

There were usually at least a dozen women in permanent residence at Suffrage House, plus any number of temporary visitors from the state associations. Before a crucial vote, the third floor resembled an overcrowded college dormitory, with extra cots tucked into the residents' rooms, lights ablaze, and chatter echoing in the halls. The atmosphere suited Cunningham perfectly, and the secretaryship was an ideal job for her. In Washington she was part of a contingent of "consecrated" suffragists, a focused, hardworking team of women whose drive and dedication matched her own. Although she and chairwoman Maud Wood Park, a New Englander and Radcliffe College graduate, could hardly have been more different in background, the two admired each other's talents and developed a warm friendship. Cunningham nicknamed Park "the Chief" (Catt was "the Great Chief") and looked up to her as a mentor.

In the lame duck session of the Sixty-fifth Congress that met from December 1918 to March 1919, the Congressional Committee made one more try in the Senate. A prosuffragist had been elected to fill the unexpired balance of the late "Pitchfork" Ben Tillman's term in South Carolina. If the suffragists could find just one more vote, the amendment would pass. The Republicans would hold both houses of Congress in the new Sixty-sixth Congress and would be able to claim the amendment as a GOP measure if it succeeded then, as the suffragists anticipated. The Democrats, as Cunningham pointed out, "ought to want us to have it now, if they have a grain of sense." While the state associations geared up for another letter-writing campaign, the Congressional Committee targeted likely converts, especially Edward Gay of Louisiana. Cunningham wrote confidentially to Caswell Ellis in Texas wondering if the publisher of the *Dallas Morning News* "could help you get newspaper stuff going in New Orleans and other strategic spots" without being let in on the reason.[16]

In January 1919, however, Gay declared his intention to vote "No," and the Congressional Committee was glum; "in our judgment," Cunningham reported to Catt, "the Democratic bacon is not going to be saved." Maud Wood Park was justifiably despondent, and even her own natural optimism was somewhat wilted: "We have traced down every clue and followed every gleam of hope and they have brought us nothing definite." The two remaining possibilities were Senators Park Trammel of Florida and George Moses of New Hampshire, who might change their position if their state legislatures passed resolutions endorsing the amendment. Cunningham suggested that Catt might personally take a hand in New Hampshire; she herself was "working a little line on Trammel through an Oklahoma congressman who lives at the same [boarding] house." Having learned thereby that Mrs. Trammel, who disagreed with her husband on suffrage, was en route to Florida, Cunningham arranged to generate publicity for her arrival.[17]

Within days, Cunningham, too, was on a train to Florida. Catt had initially opposed sending workers on such an expensive and uncertain lobbying mission, but the situation was critical. On the advice of Louisiana's Joseph Ransdell, one of the Democratic friends on the Woman Suffrage Committee, Catt changed her mind and dispatched Cunningham and the Congressional Committee's talented press secretary, Marjorie Shuler. They spent nearly two weeks getting favorable newspaper comment, citizen endorsements, and convention resolutions. The effort paid off, and the Florida legislature passed a resolution asking that the amendment be passed and submitted to the states. In the end, however, Trammel proved unmovable and New Hampshire's Moses insincere. When the amendment was finally brought up again in the Senate on February 10, it lost by one vote.[18]

Cunningham was not in Washington to witness the defeat. She had been called back to Texas to deal with a suffrage crisis that came to a head in January 1919. Against the wishes of the TESA leaders, the Texas legislature passed a constitutional amendment authorizing full suffrage for women, subject to approval by voter referendum. Catt had wanted no more state amendment campaigns in the unpromising South, and she especially did not want one now, with the federal amendment on the verge of passing. A failed referendum in Texas—and every southern referendum *had* failed—would be an embarrassment that might cost NAWSA essential votes in Congress. That was certainly the hope of the antisuffragists in the Texas legislature, all of whom voted for submission. As Cunningham's lieutenant in Texas succinctly summarized the situation, the Texas suffragists "were forced into this referendum by some friends backed by some enemies and had to make the best of it."[19]

Before she left Texas, Cunningham had spent months trying to head off this situation. The 1918 primary election returns had hardly been counted before the progressive-prohibitionists began offering to introduce a full suffrage amendment in the 1919 legislative session—for entirely self-serving reasons, as she explained to Catt. "They need us and they know that they would never have gotten this far without us." The constitutionality of the primary suffrage law was being challenged, and "it is nearly giving these men, who didn't hardly lift a finger to help us get it, nervous prostration that we are not more diligent as to the courts and as to getting full Suffrage."[20] At the September 1918 state Democratic convention in Waco, Cunningham and the other women delegates derailed—or so they thought—a resolution calling for a state amendment. At their request, the platform plank had been amended to "recommend" (which they thought nonbinding) rather than "demand" one.

But the proamendment sentiment did not dissipate, and the suffragists were caught in a politically delicate situation. Refusing this generously proffered reward would make them appear ungrateful; accepting would violate NAWSA's directive to work only for the federal amendment. Nor, since Catt's Winning Plan had to be kept within the inner circle of suffragists, could Cunningham explain to prosuffrage legislators the rationale against a state constitutional amendment. Forced to dissemble, she used the war as an excuse, stressing that war work was completely absorbing the available womanpower that would be needed for a state campaign. And raising the enormous amount of money to finance it would be impossible while people were being asked constantly to give money for the war effort.[21]

The situation worsened after Cunningham left for Washington. Prohibitionist women's groups refused to support the TESA's position and announced that they would lobby in Austin for a full suffrage amendment. More seriously, there was dissension within the TESA itself. Cunningham had taken care to secure a convention resolution against undertaking a state amendment campaign, in effect a ratification by the TESA membership of the compact with NAWSA to work only for the federal amendment. But the effusive praise for women voters that followed the Hobby campaign convinced some suffragists that the majority of men were on their side and that a state amendment would pass easily. Cunningham thought this politically naive, a judgment that Catt heartily seconded.[22]

At the same time, a semantic debate arose over the wording of the suffrage plank adopted at Waco. In Cunningham's absence, Martin M. Crane, a leading progressive who had been the convention's temporary chairman, asserted that she was misconstruing the platform and that every plank was binding, regardless of whether it was "recommended" or "demanded."[23] Brushing aside suffragist concerns over the difficulty and expense of a state campaign, he said bluntly that the decision belonged to the Democratic Party, to which women were obligated for the "favor" of suffrage. Cunningham, who still vividly recalled the humiliation of 1916, when the Ferguson-controlled state convention had rejected suffrage and neither Crane nor any other progressive dry delegate had been willing to introduce the TESA's resolution, was furious. Other suffragists could "stick by that miserable old creature" if they chose, she fumed, "but . . . I am 'off'n' him. . . . The things which I would like to do to him are not civilized!"[24]

Realizing that it would be impossible to keep a state amendment from being brought up, Cunningham crafted a counterstrategy. She arranged for a friendly legislator in each house to introduce a suffrage bill that set the referendum date for the 1920 general election. By that time the federal amendment would undoubtedly have been passed, rendering a state amendment unnecessary. The sponsors, both highly influential progressives, further agreed to keep the suffrage legislation from coming up for consideration until after the U.S. Senate had voted on the federal amendment. Covered from both directions, she thought the plan a sure thing: "We ARE fixed and General Crane can go hanged!"[25]

Cunningham also had complete confidence in Jane McCallum, the officer she had left in charge of the legislative work. McCallum chaired the Ratification Committee that NAWSA had instructed all state affiliates to form for the last phase of the federal amendment push. The committees were to persuade their legislatures to pass resolutions asking the Senate to approve the federal amendment and then lobby in advance for ratification. McCallum was a former president of the Austin ESA and Cunningham's right-hand lobbyist; she was also the TESA's unofficial historian and a publicist who contributed columns on suffrage and women's issues to both Austin newspapers. The friendship that she and Cunningham forged in the 1910s lasted a lifetime and united them in political crusades for three more decades. To assist McCallum, Cunningham designated a younger protégée, Jessie Daniel Ames, who was the TESA's treasurer.

The correspondence that passed between Texas and Washington as Mc-Callum and Ames tried unsuccessfully to hold back the state amendment revealed Cunningham's conception of leadership. In long letters of guidance written late at night from Suffrage House and on her knee while she waited to talk to Senators, she boiled it down to tactics and tenacity. She advised McCallum to "make rather an intensive study of your Legislative list [the legislators and their personal histories] and your Ratification Committee list [which included all of the TESA's senatorial district and county chairwomen] & make them yours, so that when you want pressure on a man you can call on the woman from his Dist. to come down." She suggested lunching every day at the hotel where the legislators and the press gathered; in that relaxed setting, Cunningham had found that the men "are sometimes moved to hand out information they'd *never* hunt you up to give."

A bit of guile and good people skills were essential too: "1st I ask few direct questions & give out little information. 2nd I *listen* with a very interested and deferential air. Not at all as tho I was just waiting until it's my turn to talk!" These tactics she forbade divulging, to "*any* one," on threat of murder, because "they sound so crude put into words."[26]

Cunningham believed firmly in a democracy of leadership and in mentoring other women, just as Annette Finnigan had encouraged and guided her. She wanted to bring others forward not only to share the burden but also to benefit the movement. McCallum and Ames were mothers and therefore immune to the taunt that suffragists would rather raise trouble than a family. Both were capable women—a decade later McCallum would be appointed Texas secretary of state and Ames would found the Association of Southern Women for the Prevention of Lynching—and Cunningham was certain that they would quickly "find their feet." But she underestimated the significance of being "the Chief" herself to Texas suffragists, who were apprehensive about facing a legislative crisis without her. Cunningham's special gift was the ability to inspire confidence, a resourceful determination that others admired and responded to. Ames alternately demanded and pleaded that Cunningham come home, complaining that McCallum was "panicky" and "not a leader in any sense." The emergency took priority over personal desires and even NAWSA's needs. "WE must have our leader back and you will have to come."[27]

For Cunningham, the crisis was personal as well as political. Having separated from B. J., she could no longer afford to donate her labor in Texas, an embarrassment that she did not care to have revealed. She needed the salary

she was earning as Congressional Secretary and any other potential employment that might arise with NAWSA. Catt was equally reluctant to relinquish
her. A state amendment campaign in Texas would be "a great calamity," but
the work of the Washington lobby was even more critical. "Mrs. Park has
great confidence in you and you were the one she chose of all the South," she
reminded Cunningham. "To desert her now may mean the loss of the passage
of the amendment." If she were still badly needed in Texas after the federal
amendment passed, NAWSA would release her, but Catt would want her back
afterward to work for ratification in the southern states. If, in the worst case
scenario, the federal amendment remained hung up in Congress for another
year, NAWSA would also yield to the TESA's claim. But in the meantime, "we
simply cannot let you go to prevent a referendum."[28]

In the end, Governor Hobby asked for a state amendment with an early
submission date, the worst possible scenario, and the suffragists' defenses
were quickly overwhelmed. The senator who had written and introduced
the TESA's bill specifying a 1920 referendum promptly capitulated to pressure to call it for 1919 instead. Even house speaker Robert Ewing Thomason,
a longtime ally to whom Cunningham had appealed for assistance, counseled that there was "so much enthusiasm over the matter and so much confidence on the part of many sincere friends of woman suffrage" as to make
resistance futile.[29]

If Cunningham had been in Austin, she might well have kept her strategy
alive, but from Washington there was little she could do. Even some TESA officers thought it better "to fall into line and boost rather than oppose the inevitable." Reluctantly, she wired McCallum not to keep resisting if all of
TESA's "real friends" supported an early referendum, adding the consolation
that Jane had "done the very best that anybody could have done." The amendment passed both houses unanimously, the prosuffrage forces misreading the
"Aye" votes of the antis as evidence of a change of heart. The legislators also
passed a state prohibition amendment, which progressives of both sexes had
long sought, and fixed May 24 as the referendum date for both.[30]

Catt received the news with predictable unhappiness, lamenting that "there
is no time to do the work, much less raise the money." In addition, a loss
might prompt Senator Culberson, whom the TESA had worked so hard to
turn, to swing back to the antis. NAWSA could not afford to lose *any* votes and
defeat in Texas possibly "would throw us out of suffrage for some years to
come." Pulling Cunningham out of Washington was a "tragedy unspeakable,"
Catt concluded, but in terms of NAWSA's overall strategy, it was more important that she take charge of the Texas referendum.[31] Cunningham was
back in Texas by February, putting on an appropriate public face. At the formal signing of the hated suffrage amendment, she posed, smiling, with Hobby
(whose political future she was determined to torpedo if he ran again for of-

fice) and a group of legislators and suffragists. In press statements she feigned appropriate gratitude for the men's supposedly generous "gift."[32]

Having no illusions that the prosuffrage men would exert themselves to carry the election, she consulted closely with the NAWSA leadership in planning a campaign strategy. Carrie Chapman Catt and Corresponding Secretary Nettie Rogers Shuler mobilized the resources of the suffrage "machine" behind her, offering literature, money, and trained organizers. Catt and Shuler considered it an enormous advantage that the Texas amendment also contained a provision disfranchising aliens. A state amendment structured in the same fashion had passed the previous year in South Dakota, which, like Texas, had allowed the ballot to "first paper" aliens who had filed a declaration of intent to seek citizenship. Six prior referenda in South Dakota had failed due to mobilization of the foreign-born vote, but after the disfranchising clause was added in 1918, wartime nativism carried the South Dakota suffragists to victory. "You see, no one could vote against suffrage without at the same time voting to give the vote to unnaturalized Germans," Catt explained to Cunningham, adding that she thought the same strategy would work in Texas.[33]

Catt voiced her antipathy toward immigrant voting freely and frequently. Like many progressives, she favored removing "ignorant" voters from the electorate, either by tying an educational qualification to the ballot or by outright disfranchisement. Cunningham shared some of this sentiment, which was interwoven with her disgust for machine politicians, like the South Texas "border bosses." To suffragists, the consequences of manipulated immigrant voting—poll taxes paid by county machines, votes exchanged for cash or liquor, and commonplace election fraud—seemed a travesty of democracy, cynically perpetrated by anti-reform political hacks. But even though the TESA had always supported progressive-prohibitionist attempts to withdraw the ballot from aliens, Cunningham was conflicted about voting restrictions. She had opposed a provision in the primary suffrage bill requiring a woman to fill out the registration form in her own hand. It was a de facto literacy test aimed at Hispanic women in the machine-controlled counties, and she had reluctantly acquiesced, she told Catt at the time, because electoral corruption there was undeniable.[34]

Cunningham certainly resented having to plead for her own voting rights with men who were not even full citizens, but until World War I unleashed a national epidemic of anti-German prejudice, she had always kept these sentiments out of her suffrage rhetoric. And she had tactical reservations about emphasizing the amendment's alien disfranchisement provision. The foreign-born, she worried, would vote against it just as surely as prosuffrage men would support it.[35] But she had always cooperated closely with NAWSA and regarded Catt's political acumen, which had brought the movement within striking distance of victory, as superior to her own. Following NAWSA's lead, she made nativism the focal point of the campaign, stressing that aliens constituted as great a menace during reconstruction as they had during war. Making Texas an "All American Democracy" was the theme of press releases, instructions to suffrage workers, and mailings to interest groups.[36]

The 1919 referendum was a textbook NAWSA campaign in tactics as well. Cunningham based her overall organizing strategy on NAWSA's secret campaign plan, used in the successful Michigan referendum the previous year. It followed the election-district model Catt had pioneered, organizing down to the precinct and block level. Separate committees handled various aspects of the campaign: Finance; Press and Publicity (under Jane McCallum); Speakers' Bureau; and Advisory (chaired by U.S. Senator Morris Sheppard). The "big general piece of work" consisted of three parts: collecting petitions from women asking men to vote for the amendment; canvassing county by county to reach every man eligible to cast a ballot; and publishing a free weekly suffrage paper for Saturday afternoon street distribution. Cunningham sent a copy of the plan to each senatorial district chairwoman, with instructions to read every word and discuss it with the workers but to make certain that it did not get into the newspapers.[37]

Catt considered the petition to the voters "the one thing that is tried and tested and brings results," and a key factor in the success of referenda in New York, Michigan, South Dakota, and Oklahoma over the previous two years. "Whatever else you do, you must have that petition," she emphasized, and Cunningham's directives to campaign workers underscored the necessity. The purpose of the petition was to demonstrate to male voters that women *did* want the vote, and the work of gathering signatures was combined with the second task, the voter canvass. Cunningham instructed county chairwomen to get a copy of the list of men who had paid poll taxes (eligible voters) and divide it among the precinct workers, who would carry it with them in house-to-house visitation. As the precinct workers asked each woman to sign the petition, they could also ask how her menfolk intended to vote and record the information against the names on the poll tax list.[38]

By the time they finished the canvass, local workers would thus know how many women favored suffrage in their precinct, county, and district, and how many favorable votes they could count on for the amendment. "You can then plan intelligently to place your speakers and literature to advantage to win the rest," Cunningham stressed. She encouraged workers to get as much publicity as possible: newspaper stories at the beginning and end of the drive and "Petition Day" rallies the Saturday before the election to display the signatures and gather an audience for speakers. To train workers, she put together, with advice and literature from NAWSA, a three-day "suffrage school" in Austin, with sessions that covered precinct work, public speaking, publicity, and fundraising.[39]

Cunningham planned the campaign with thoroughness and imagination; Nettie Rogers Shuler, at NAWSA headquarters, judged her proposed budget "about right" and her plan of work "exceedingly good." The success of the latter depended heavily on raising funds, and the TESA, as always, was struggling just to meet operating expenses; in February 1919 there was $252.60 in the treasury. Catt had warned that a campaign in so vast a state as Texas (253 counties) would require forty-five trained organizers and a minimum of $100,000—and everyone knew there was not the remotest chance of getting either.[40] Cunningham, out of necessity, planned to rely on volunteers and calculated a bare-bones budget of roughly $76,000. It took weeks, however, to find someone willing to chair the Finance Committee, and Cunningham had no time to devote to fundraising. She and Treasurer Jessie Daniel Ames revised their ideal downward to $50,000, and then $30,000. In the end, the suffragists collected only a little more than $13,000, including $5,000 from NAWSA, which also sent in four organizers.[41]

Lack of funds forced Cunningham to curtail some projects. Catt had recommended holding three suffrage schools, but the TESA could barely scrape up enough money for one and could not afford to bring in the district and county chairwomen. Plans for the free weekly paper, budgeted at $15,000, had to be dropped entirely. As the campaign peaked in May, Caswell Ellis, the strategist of the women's Hobby campaign, and Jane McCallum put together a one-time edition, the *Texas Democrat*, and 200,000 were distributed on the streets. Weekly papers were offered a four-page suffrage fold-in, with Cunningham's assurance that local suffragists would gladly do the folding. Streetcars in fourteen cities displayed "car cards," advertising suffrage and urging a vote for the amendment. County chairwomen received semiweekly bulletins to use in supplying news for their local papers, and Cunningham urged these women to seek publicity creatively.[42]

The opposition, with James Ferguson playing a leading role, mobilized just as effectively, disseminating reams of antisuffrage literature. Legislators received mailings postmarked from Selma, Alabama, accusing suffragists of advocating racial intermarriage and social equality between blacks and whites. Ferguson began with well-honed populist diatribes against rich, idle city women (his caricature of Cunningham) colluding with prohibitionist preachers against country folk. In the final weeks he took his cue from the race-baiters and changed tactics, proclaiming for the first time in his career that "equal suffrage means equal nigger."[43] The real issue, Cunningham advised Catt, was whether Ferguson could swing as many votes against suffrage as he had won for himself in 1918. "If he can we are beaten, because Hobby would never have been elected without the women and the women cannot vote for themselves."[44]

Despite following a campaign strategy that NAWSA had used successfully in other states and a statewide speaking tour given by Anna Howard Shaw, the Texas suffragists were defeated. The suffrage amendment lost by some 25,000 votes while the prohibition amendment succeeded, even though the two might have been expected to appeal to the same constituency. Catt and Shuler had miscalculated the effectiveness of the alien disfranchisement theme: the circumstances in South Dakota and Texas were quite different. While South Dakota suffragists had been able to prove that the manipulated German-Russian vote had repeatedly denied them victory, in Texas, where the amendment was up for the first time, there was no comparable level of public resentment for the TESA to tap. The Texas referendum failed, Cunningham thought, because the suffragists had been crucially short of time, money, and workers, and their male allies complacent and unhelpful. "I honestly think that the German vote was not more effective against us than was the overconfidence of our friends," she told Catt. "From the time that they forced submission to the hour when we began to lose ground it was not possible to make them believe that it was not a walk over."[45]

There may also have been election fraud. NAWSA always expected it, since the suffragists confronted political machines and special interests with deep pockets, especially the brewing and distilling industries. Cunningham's final letter to campaign workers had instructed each precinct chairwoman to secure "in writing, a statement from the Election Judge as to the result of the election in her precinct BEFORE SHE SLEEPS" and turn it in to the county chairwoman.[46] But substantial evidence of underhandedness surfaced. The official ballot provided by the secretary of state's office listed the suffrage amendment in second place, and suffrage workers had frequently referred to it as Amendment Two. On election day, as women outside the polls politely reminded voters to vote for the second amendment, it was discovered that twenty-eight counties in East Texas—a Ferguson stronghold—had been furnished a ballot with the amendments in a different order. Worse yet, the tally sheets did list the amendment in second place, resulting in inaccurate counts. In the ensuing days, suffrage headquarters received reports of ballot boxes left unguarded and polls that never opened.[47]

On June 4, less than two weeks after the referendum failed, the Senate of the new Sixty-sixth Congress—at last—narrowly passed the federal amendment. The antisuffrage forces in Texas, with Congressman Robert Lee Henry in the lead, promptly called a planning meeting to prevent the state from ratifying. The strategy of the suffrage opponents in the legislature, who had voted to submit the state amendment, then became clear: the antis could claim that the amendment's defeat in the May referendum was a popular mandate against suffrage. The legislature was therefore obligated, they argued, to follow the will of the people and vote against ratification—and to repeal primary suffrage as well.[48]

Cunningham dropped the pursuit of election fraud, which would have been almost impossible to prove, and concentrated on damage control and preserving Texas's chance of ratifying, for NAWSA badly needed the state.[49] Fewer than one-third of southern Congressmen and Senators had voted for the Nineteenth Amendment. Although Cunningham and other southern suffragists had done impressive work to build that base—only 2 percent of southern House members had voted yes in 1915—the amendment had, in essence, passed over the opposition of most of the South. The NAWSA needed to win thirty-six of the forty-eight states in order for the Nineteenth Amendment to become law. If the thirteen in the South stood together and voted no, as the governor of Louisiana urged, they could defeat ratification. The Texas legislature was scheduled to meet in special session in late June, and preventing rejection in a state where women had won partial suffrage was essential.[50]

Here, even more than in the women's Hobby campaign, Cunningham showed herself to be the antithesis of the popular conception of women as highly principled amateurs. The embodiment of this image was Jane Addams of Hull House, dressed in white, seconding Theodore Roosevelt's nomination for President at the Progressive Party convention in 1912. One side of Cunningham's public persona did indeed match this representation. She was an ardent progressive, a reformer, and a champion of "good government," with boundless contempt for machine politics. But when winning really mattered, she could be as hard-boiled as any ward politician. To get primary suffrage in 1918, she had stumped for a candidate whose only attraction was not being James Ferguson and portrayed him as an advocate of political equality for women. Salvaging some credibility from the state referendum defeat likewise followed a script that was mostly spin. With help from Caswell Ellis, who compared voting statistics with county census data, she blamed the referendum defeat on the "German vote."

It was the best way to rebut the antisuffragists' claim that "the people" had rejected suffrage, although her correspondence clearly shows that she knew reality to be more complex. "Disloyal" voters and the alien disfranchisement clause thus became the TESA's explanation for the amendment's failure. The election, Cunningham emphasized, was not a fair expression of popular sentiment. The suffrage amendment was "handicapped" by the alien clause and the election held while 200,000 "good American men" were away in the army and unable to vote.[51] At the same time, she reminded members of the legislature that the referendum had no political force: the Democratic platform adopted at Waco bound them to support ratification and only another convention could release them from that obligation. Knowing better than to rely on politicians' honor, she put the TESA "machine" to work in the election districts, repledging each legislator.[52]

In contrast to the grinding months of the referendum campaign, the ratification battle was six days of intense drama. Cunningham was fairly sure of majorities in both houses, but she anticipated a tactical fight and worried that the antis might "out general us and split our forces on some technicality or side issue." The lower house, where she had counted votes to spare and the speaker was a staunch supporter, passed the resolution quickly by a large margin. In the senate, she had secured just enough pledges to prevail, but the support was shaky. The antis had drafted a bill requiring a voter referendum on ratification, which several nominally prosuffrage senators intended to support if it came up first. Waiting anxiously in New York for the verdict, Catt conceded that Cunningham had "the most ticklish job and the most crucial problem of any of the states at this moment."[53]

The antis' referendum resolution was where Cunningham most feared being "out generaled." When it was ruled out of order on a technicality, the antis then tried to break the quorum by attempting to get ten senators to resign and run again on the issue. The suffragists, breathing easier, began to enjoy themselves. "We openly rejoiced at the idea," Cunningham reported to Catt, "and urged them to do it, pledging them that there would be ten new faces in their places at the end of the necessary twenty days and we would still have time to ratify this session." An attempt to spirit enough members out of town to break the quorum also failed, because TESA women and Caswell Ellis were on guard at the train station. On June 28 the senate passed the resolution by a bare majority, making Texas the ninth state in the nation to ratify, and the first in the South. Caswell and Mary Ellis hosted a ratification party at which Cunningham and the other lobbyists, giddy with triumph and apricot brandy, staged a grand march around the dining room table, singing and cheering.[54]

Pulling off such a victory only a month after being defeated in a state referendum was a remarkable feat. This time, Cunningham judged, it was the antisuffragists who had been overconfident. The TESA had the advantage, she told Catt, "because we went to work the day after we knew we had lost our referendum, whereas the Antis were too busy counting up a great big majority against us so we wouldn't contest the election and expose their cheating." Years later, she emphasized that lining up legislators and making allies of key men had been crucial.[55] With Texas finally safe, Cunningham was again called to national service, this time to organize support for ratification in the West and South.

Although most of the South held little promise, suffragists there had asked for assistance, and NAWSA agreed to help fund suffrage schools and send in professional organizers. The situation in the West was an ironic reversal. Women there had been voting for so long that the ballot was taken for granted; most of the suffrage societies had disbanded, and western governors showed no disposition to call special legislative sessions. Initially, Cunningham was to be dispatched to Alabama and Virginia; she declined because the Texas antis, fighting to the bitter end, were attempting to repeal primary suffrage. By the time the danger had passed, Catt had a different assignment. The NAWSA board voted in mid-July to send four envoys to find out why western governors had not called special sessions and to urge them to act. Two Republicans were assigned to the Northwest, where the GOP predominated, and two Democrats to the Southwest. Cunningham and Jessie Jack Hooper of Wisconsin were the southwestern delegation, responsible for Nevada, Utah, Arizona, and New Mexico.[56]

Cunningham reported to NAWSA headquarters in New York a few days after the board meeting for instructions and expense money ($1,500), which she carried in a cloth purse pinned inside her dress. From there she went to Washington, D.C., to ask key Senators to use their influence with the Democratic governors and then on to connect with Jessie Jack Hooper in Chicago. In a facetious letter to Jane McCallum describing the "nerviness" of descending upon the unsuspecting governors as a "Commission," she revealed her apprehension about Hooper, a NAWSA director whom she had never met. "I don't want her—I'm afraid she's a high up person of some kind who will intimidate me something *awful*. . . . If I have to do all this hard job in Washington, why do I have to have her at all to scare me to death?"[57]

Although Hooper was considerably older than Cunningham, the two women turned out to be well-matched and compatible. Both were resilient, unflappable, and quick to see the humor in unexpected situations. The tone for the journey was set in Chicago, when the conductor examined their tickets and loudly announced that their destination was Reno; heads swiveled and the other passengers' faces plainly registered the suspicion that Cunningham and Hooper were going to Nevada to get divorces. Upon arrival they were met by a member of the legislature, a lean ranching woman whose one-seated buggy could barely accommodate her rather plump guests. Squeezed between them, the Nevada woman had to brace her knees against the dashboard to keep from sliding off the seat as she drove down the main street. While Cunningham wrote their report that night, Hooper drew a cartoon of the comic trio in the old buggy, which brought work at NAWSA headquarters to a hilarious halt when the letter was opened.[58]

The governor of Nevada received Cunningham and Hooper cordially, but they had to pursue Arizona's governor, who was on a speaking trip, from Phoenix to Flagstaff. He was astonished—not pleasantly—to see them. A storm that washed out the railroad bridges delayed their departure for Santa Fe, and when they reached New Mexico at last, Hooper and Cunningham discovered that the governor was in California. Their attempts to interrogate the state Democratic Party chairman met a wall of silence until Hooper remembered an item from the local paper. Not daring to look at Cunningham for fear that they would both lose their composure, she inquired with seemingly sincere interest about the epidemic of black leg among calves, which put the politician in a talkative mood and eventually produced the information they needed. They finally found the New Mexico governor in Salt Lake City, at the National Governors' Conference, where they spent their last week and helped present NAWSA's formal appeal for quick ratification. All of the governors they visited pledged to call special sessions, although only Utah acted as early as hoped.[59]

In the fall Cunningham worked as an organizer for ratification in the South, where the local women were not taking hold of the work as NAWSA desired. She spent time in Florida and Oklahoma before going to Mississippi in December to help its ratification committee prepare for the 1920 legislative session.[60] Catt and Nettie Rogers Shuler considered her the state's only chance, and Cunningham went dutifully but without much eagerness. The situation was as difficult as she anticipated. The ratification committee had organized only in November, and its chairwoman was distracted by her mother's serious illness. "The State President is not a leader but an *incubus* that has to be placated," Cunningham reported, and the committee had "no headquarters & no data except such as I establish & collect & so it moves around with me."[61]

Despite "really doing the best piece of work I ever did in my life," Cunningham assessed the odds bluntly: "It's going to take a miracle to ratify 'Ole Miss.'" She was tired and fervently hoping someone else could take her place in January, but after spending the Christmas holidays in New York, she went reluctantly back for the opening of the legislative session. Both the incoming and outgoing governors favored ratification, and the chairman of the Democratic National Committee (DNC) urged it, but the prosuffrage *Jackson Daily News* polled the legislators and found not even a "ghost of a show for ratification." Mississippians, a discouraged worker wrote Cunningham from the field, "are all balled up on the negroe's [*sic*] vote and the States Rights Idea. If it isn't one its the other—and sometimes both." After endless speechmaking on the threat to white supremacy and state sovereignty, both houses of the legislature overwhelmingly voted against ratification.[62] (Mississippi, the very last state to ratify, finally approved the Nineteenth Amendment in 1984.)

By the time Cunningham departed for NAWSA's Victory Convention, which opened on February 12, 1920, thirty states had ratified the Nineteenth Amendment. The governors of Arizona and New Mexico had fulfilled their promises to Cunningham and Jessie Jack Hooper and called special sessions; both states ratified while the convention was in progress. With women on the brink of being able to cast ballots everywhere in the country, the suffragists assembled in Chicago formally transformed NAWSA into the League of

Women Voters. Through it, they hoped to preserve NAWSA's organizational momentum for the new challenge of training women to become voters and the continuing one of removing the remaining legal discriminations against women.

The LWV had been created as an auxiliary organization at the previous year's convention and had been operating in the enfranchised states under the governance of a council of state presidents. The Victory Convention voted to transform the LWV into a permanent organization with a new structure and headquarters in Washington, D.C. Maud Wood Park was elected president and Carrie Chapman Catt honorary president. Full legislative agendas, with a total of sixty-nine planks, were authorized for eight standing committees that would continue to pursue the social reform goals women's voluntary associations had been seeking throughout the Progressive Era. From this legislative program, the LWV chose thirteen planks to present to the Republican and Democratic National Conventions, a "woman's platform," for which it hoped to secure party endorsements.[63]

Although the Nineteenth Amendment was not yet law, women could vote in 29 states, and they were delegates to both conventions. In Texas, Cunningham was one of four women, all prominent members of the TESA, elected delegates at large to the Democratic National Convention in San Francisco; she won nearly as many votes as Governor Hobby. When the Texas Special train stopped in Amarillo on its way west, she joined the male party leaders in addressing the crowd gathered at the station platform. She and Jessie Daniel Ames, also a delegate at large, recalled for a reporter that four years earlier women had stood outside the convention headquarters in St. Louis as petitioners. "We wore badges pleading for votes, and now we have them. It's absolutely delicious to think of the transformation." All together, women made up 7 percent of the Democratic delegates to San Francisco and 24 percent of the alternates.[64]

Cunningham and Ames went before the Resolutions Committee to urge acceptance of the planks that Maud Wood Park and an LWV delegation had formally presented. Of thirteen demands, the Democratic Party accepted all but the one calling for the creation of a federal department of education. It incorporated the LWV's request for federal support for infant and maternal health care; the prohibition of child labor; increased funding for the Children's Bureau; programs to combat illiteracy and teach citizenship to immigrants; independent citizenship for married women; and an end to sex discrimination in the civil service. Cunningham led the women in the Texas delegation in praising the "splendid, progressive, outspoken platform upon which all people who . . . do not desire to evade issues or compromise fundamental principles can take their stand."[65] Her only disappointment was the failure of former Treasury Secretary William Gibbs McAdoo, a dry progressive and Woodrow Wilson's son-in-law, to win the presidential nomination. She and the other Texans supported him through forty-four votes until Ohio Governor James Cox finally prevailed.[66]

Both the Democrats and the Republicans fêted women at their national conventions and passed resolutions encouraging the state legislatures controlled by their respective parties to ratify the Nineteenth Amendment. But Minnie Fisher Cunningham's experience in Texas was a foretaste of the difficulty women would encounter after 1920 in the continuing struggle for political equality with men. In the language of her day, Cunningham was the kind of woman who "got on" with men; she understood political negotiation and compromise and made no one uncomfortable by her presence. She had mobilized a constituency that helped elect a governor and had been effusively praised, but she had not been accorded the status within the party that would have been a man's due for an equivalent accomplishment. At every critical turn after primary suffrage, she found herself in conflict with party leaders who wanted women's votes but not their input. Having the vote did not guarantee having a voice, and the hard work of fulfilling the promise of the ballot had barely begun.

5

IN LEAGUE WITH WOMEN VOTERS

IN CHOOSING TO COMBINE LEADERSHIP IN THE LEAGUE OF WOMEN Voters with Democratic Party activism, Cunningham embraced the strategy of dual political identity that Carrie Chapman Catt believed would bring newly enfranchised women the greatest influence. The passage of the Nineteenth Amendment presented the former suffragists with a political dilemma. To abandon the tradition of female separatism risked diluting the potential power of women's votes. The two major parties had begun creating separate women's divisions even before 1920, aiming to capture female voters without actually sharing political power. If women channeled all their work through the parties, they would surely be taken for granted and ignored. Yet to stay aloof from the parties would be pointless: if women were to continue as petitioners, then of what use had been the fight for the ballot?

Catt proposed separation *and* integration. Through the nonpartisan LWV, women would continue to work collectively, as a pressure group, for a female reform agenda. Women's "distinctive experience," argued President Maud Wood Park, inclined them to focus on human development issues, and this "social welfare" perspective was as necessary to government as the male "business interest" viewpoint. But to get their concerns on the political agenda and enacted into legislation, women would have to work within the party system. Therefore Catt urged women, as individuals, to join political parties and seek power within them, warning that they would not be welcome in the inner sanctum, "the real thing at the center, with the door locked tight."[1]

Catt anticipated that some women would reject dualism. Those to whom party loyalty was "a superstition and a fetish" would be "partisans only," while others, "who fail to see the good in parties because they know much they cannot admire," would be "Leaguers only." But her confidence that a majority would embrace her vision proved misplaced, not the least because the LWV was immediately attacked from all directions. President Warren Harding reproached it for attempting to unite women as a "class." Republican and Democratic leaders alike, suspicious of the LWV's nonpartisan stance, accused it of aspiring to be a third party and trying to divide the electorate along "sex lines." Many women with strong partisan loyalties also denied the need for continued organization as a gender group and urged women to work exclusively through the parties.[2]

Minnie Fisher Cunningham had expressed a similar view in 1918. At the beginning of the campaign to elect Governor Hobby, she declined a fellow suffragist's invitation to serve on the Hobby Executive Committee for Women, explaining that she had already joined her local gender-integrated Hobby Club. She was not sure of the wisdom of a separate women's organization: "Mostly I believe that men and women do their best work together." By the same token, she opposed gender segregation within the parties. She wanted women integrated directly into the party organizations, with a "reasonable" proportion of offices and power—or better still, according to the "Colorado Plan," which gave women equal representation on party committees. "Only so," she warned, "can we be advised as to the machinations within the party, and only so, can we hope to defeat them."[3]

Watching the parties deliberately marginalize women undoubtedly helped convince Cunningham of the need for a countervailing women's organization. When the Democrats decided in 1918 to appoint a national chairwoman from each state, the Texas Equal Suffrage Association's Washington lobbyist, Elizabeth Herndon Potter, warned that the men were known to prefer a political wife, "or a fool who would be wax in the hands of the politicians." Potter wanted to see "a fine & true hard working *Suffragist*" in the position, and she wrote the chairman of the Democratic National Committee proposing three names, including Cunningham's. No one was surprised when the Texas appointment went instead to the state's best-known clubwoman, whom the suffragists heartily disliked because she had endorsed the cause reluctantly and late.[4]

Frustration that party women were not allowed to choose their own leaders made the LWV seem essential to former suffragists like Cunningham. She considered Elizabeth Bass, head of the Women's Bureau of the Democratic Party, undistinguished and ineffective, and was incensed when Indiana party boss Tom Taggert dispatched his own candidate for the post to speak to the LWV convention in 1921. "I could talk a book full on the general stupidity of trying to get enough of the women's vote to elect anybody to anything by offering the women the old type of politician for leader—*pants* or petticoats," she fumed to a Democratic correspondent. "We *won't* follow 'em and there's that."[5]

Cunningham was also drawn to the LWV because she shared Catt's hope that enfranchised women, by demonstrating how citizenship ought to be practiced, could advance the nation's progress toward a "reformed democracy." She articulated the views of many voluntarist women when she humorously described being "much shocked" the first time she attended a political convention. Men who had been "saying perfectly terrible things about the candidates they were not supporting" while glorifying their own would undergo an abrupt change of allegiance after the opposing candidate won nomination. A man might see no contradiction in "standing in a chair and waving his hat and cheering his head off" for a nominee he had vehemently denounced a few hours earlier, but "that is not the League of Women Voters' method with candidates." The "League method" taught women to choose a party on the basis of platform and ideology, to study the issues, and to examine candidates' records. LWV leaders aimed to "improve" partisan politics by infusing it with the values of female voluntary association culture.[6]

Cunningham's search for a political role in the 1920s was grounded in this optimistic vision. Catt's dislike of parties proved so strong that she was never able to follow her own advice and join one, but Cunningham successfully practiced what Catt preached, operating from both inside and outside the party system. She plunged into Democratic Party politics in Texas, at the same time helping to launch the state chapter of the LWV. Although she began the decade intending to focus on local politics and family duties, in 1921 she was called to Washington, D.C., to serve as the first executive secretary of the national LWV. From 1921 to 1923 she helped push the LWV's legislative agenda through Congress and wrestled with two controversies that immediately confronted the organization: how in practice to interpret and apply the nonpartisanship policy and whether to defend the voting rights of African American women. Her experience illuminates the promise and problems the former suffragists faced as they worked to renegotiate the gendered boundaries of politics.

THE TEXAS EQUAL SUFFRAGE ASSOCIATION FORMALLY TRANSFORMED itself into the Texas League of Women Voters (TLWV) at a jubilant convention in San Antonio in October 1919. Cunningham exhibited a large map showing the states that had already ratified the Nineteenth Amendment and told reporters that it had "caused a number of men to jump violently." Politicians everywhere were wondering—and worrying about—how women would vote. The national LWV's study program on social, economic, and political conditions, which Cunningham explained to the convention in intimidating detail, would prepare them to act. She stressed that nothing constructive would come of blaming men for the state of society; the sexes must cooperate and women must share responsibility "to the last detail." Woman's sphere, she announced, belonged to history.[7]

Although the TLWV was ready to elect her president, and Jessie Daniel Ames was willing to raise a salary for her as an inducement, Cunningham stuck to her resolve that it was time for other women to lead. The top office went to Ames, and Cunningham accepted only the chairmanship of the Committee on Improvement of Election Laws and Methods and the presidency of the local Galveston league.[8] But she worked closely with Ames during the TLWV's first year, functioning as something of a silent co-president. In the spring of 1920 while Ames underwent and recovered from surgery, Cunningham, not the vice president, took over; she even stayed in Georgetown and looked after Ames's children.[9]

In order to focus on Texas politics, Cunningham also initially chose only a small role in the national LWV. She declined to be a candidate for director of the southern (Third) region, accepting only a contract for six weeks' work as a paid organizer.[10] Her priority in 1920 was settling an old score with former U.S. Senator Joseph W. Bailey, a vocal critic of Woodrow Wilson's administration, who had declared his candidacy for governor. Bailey, who had testified against the Nineteenth Amendment before the House Committee on Woman Suffrage, stood beside James Ferguson at the top of Texas suffragists' list of most detested opponents. Cunningham and Ames had helped hand him one setback a few months earlier, when Bailey sought to win enough support in the county and precinct conventions to control the selection of delegates to the Democratic National Convention. The leaders of the party's progressive wing had countered with a mass meeting at which Cunningham and Ames were elected to the resolutions committee. They helped write a lengthy document defending Wilsonian progressivism; Bailey, in turn, ridiculed the committee members as "six sissies and two sisters." Although his forces lost decisively at the precinct conventions, Bailey's gubernatorial bid was unaffected.[11]

The 1920 elections forced the TLWV and other state leagues to grapple with the practical application of the organization's policy of nonpartisanship, which was still evolving and flexible. Like NAWSA before it, the national LWV had voted not to endorse or oppose any political party, but NAWSA had frequently targeted antisuffrage politicians for defeat, and some state LWVs were eager to retaliate against men who had fought women's enfranchisement. The New York LWV launched a highly publicized campaign to unseat Senator James Wadsworth, who had been one of NAWSA's bitter enemies, while Cunningham and the Texas LWV mounted an equally determined but historically overlooked effort to defeat Joe Bailey. The TLWV executive board passed a formal resolution declaring 's Bailey's candidacy inimical to the state's welfare, and that spring and summer the organization publicized his reactionary record. Ames and Cunningham deferred all other projects, such as holding citizenship schools, and channeled the TLWV's energy and resources into the Bailey fight.[12]

At the same time, Cunningham worked to mobilize women behind the most liberal of Bailey's opponents, Robert Ewing Thomason, speaker of the Texas House of Representatives. Thomason was a longtime ally of women reformers and their causes, including suffrage, the Ferguson impeachment, and the World War I anti-vice crusade. Cunningham regarded his candidacy as "one of the first fruits of women's participation in affairs of government"; he was the "higher type of man, intellectually, morally, and spiritually" that she hoped women's votes would put into office. Jane McCallum affirmed the same: Thomason was "honest, clean, and has right ideals. . . . such an improvement over anything we've had in ages."[13]

The other leading contender, Pat Neff, was also honest, clean to the point of boasting that he had never touched tobacco or liquor, and a skillful campaigner. He was a moderate, who had done nothing for suffrage, nor had he been, like Thomason, "in the frontline trenches fighting for decent government." Cunningham found him more show than substance, a politician without a vision running on a platform of "glittering generalities." When Neff's opening campaign speech appeared in the newspapers, she went through it paragraph by paragraph, scribbling indignant comments in the margins: "bombast," "rhetoric," "old stuff!"[14]

Throughout the spring of 1920, Cunningham worked at organizing a Woman's Committee for Thomason. His inexperienced campaign manager, struggling on a limited budget, let her structure her own role, grateful for her advice not only on reaching women but on designing literature and planning strategy. The campaign could not afford a separate women's organization, so Cunningham urged women to join the local Thomason clubs, stressing that he was the only candidate "who can lay claim to having furthered the cause of women in the state." While she frankly used the Texas LWV to oppose Bailey, Cunningham was more circumspect about the Thomason effort. The TLWV did not endorse any candidates, but the line between what Cunningham and Jessie Daniel Ames did as individuals and as LWV members was somewhat blurred. The Thomason campaign paid for the Woman's Committee organizational mailings that Cunningham got out, but she apparently did the work at the TLWV office in Georgetown. When Thomason spoke there, Ames issued an invitation to women on TLWV letterhead in which she praised the candidate's "splendid record of having worked and voted for constructive measures."[15]

It soon became clear, however, that no female voting bloc would emerge.

Neff had his own contingent of female supporters who, because of his strong prohibitionist image, were willing to overlook his past indifference to suffrage. After one of them, a prominent Dallas clubwoman, released a pro-Neff statement incorporating misleading information about Thomason, Cunningham drafted the rebuttal that the Thomason campaign ran in the *Dallas Morning News*. It was a perfect example of LWV-style voter education; in parallel columns, she compared the two men's records on prohibition and suffrage, to Neff's disadvantage, all the way back to 1912. At the end, she appended her own strong endorsement of Thomason.[16]

To the former suffragists' frustration, Thomason was eliminated in the primary; neither Bailey nor Neff polled a majority and were forced into a runoff. Resigning themselves to supporting the "second best candidate," Cunningham and Jessie Daniel Ames intensified the TLWV's campaign against Bailey. One of the leaders of the progressive wing of the party supplied Ames with material from Bailey's political record, which she compiled, printed at TLWV expense, and distributed through the local leagues. He was finally vanquished at the second primary, but the "great grand *awful* campaign" into which she and Cunningham had poured all of the TLWV's resources for six months left the membership exhausted and the organization itself nearly $1,000 in debt.[17]

Despite its success, the TLWV's campaign against Bailey, like the New York LWV's against James Wadsworth (which reduced his majority but failed to unseat him), caused dissension and debate over the proper boundaries of nonpartisanship. A complaint by the local league in Waco (Neff's hometown) that the TLWV's candidate profiles contained editorial comments reflected the sentiments of a growing number within the national organization, who interpreted nonpartisanship to mean strict neutrality. Cunningham was among those who resisted this turn. Reporting for Texas at the 1921 national LWV convention, she proudly recounted how the TLWV had adapted to its own purpose the voter education schools prescribed by the national organization: "What we did was to teach the women how to vote against Mr. Joseph Weldon Bailey."[18]

At the following year's national convention, during a debate on the subject of endorsing or opposing candidates, panelist Jessie Daniel Ames likewise argued for flexibility. Endorsing candidates was generally inadvisable, she conceded, especially in a one-party state like Texas, where the choice was usually "between the kettle and the pot." But a formal policy forbidding endorsements would also prohibit leagues from opposing unacceptable candidates, as had been "necessary" in the Bailey case. The discussion was inconclusive, but the national board continued to reaffirm its abstention policy. State and local leagues were not required to follow suit, but women like Cunningham, who had envisioned the LWV as a fighting organization as well as an educational one, found themselves increasingly defending a minority viewpoint.[19]

WHILE TEXAS SUFFRAGISTS SOUGHT RETRIBUTION AGAINST JOE BAILEY, NAWSA continued to pursue the thirty-sixth and final state necessary to ratify the Nineteenth Amendment. Cunningham took time out to join the "Suffrage Emergency Corps," which Catt dispatched to Connecticut, the most promising possibility. The forty-eight women, chosen for their "oratorical and leadership qualities," represented every state in the union. Divided into small groups, they toured Connecticut staging rallies to generate public pressure for ratification. Cunningham was quoted cheerfully asserting that "if we could make all of Texas white for suffrage, and record its ratification of the Federal Suffrage Amendment within the first few weeks after it was passed in Congress, we ought not to stop at a little thing like whitening Connecticut." The tour concluded with a mass meeting on the capitol grounds in Hartford and an audience with the governor, who remained unmoved.[20] The Bailey-Neff runoff prevented her from going to Tennessee, which provided the crucial thirty-sixth vote in August 1920.

With the happiness of being "ratified and released," Cunningham confronted a difficult period of adjustment. The failure of her marriage forced her to look for some means of financial support, even as it left her the daughter most "free" to help care for her widowed mother, Sallie, who was seventy-six and in poor health. Both of Cunningham's brothers had died, and the Fisher family now consisted of four daughters. Comer and Ella were raising families in New Waverly; Marion, the unmarried eldest, was superintendent of the primary department of the Galveston public school system. Sallie Fisher spent intervals in Galveston with Marion but lived most of the year with Ella and her husband, Richard M. Traylor, who managed Fisher Farms. In 1920 Cunningham joined the Traylor household, designating herself Sallie's primary caretaker and chief worrier over Ella, who she thought was "playing fast & loose with a nervous breakdown." The time that she had intended to devote to political writing that fall she instead spent in the kitchen, because there were no cooks to be had during cotton-picking season.[21]

For much of the 1920s, the last decade of her mother's life, she alternated stints of public work with periods of nursing both her mother and sometimes Ella, her favorite sister. Balancing the pull of family against her desire for work and independence frustrated and sometimes defeated Cunningham. She referred to her intermittent bouts of isolation in New Waverly as "building character," reminding friends who lamented the burial of her talents that one's first duty was always to one's family in need. "But you'll never know what this particular duty costs in the doing," she admitted to Jane McCallum. Job opportunities and political volunteerism had to be weighed against the current state of family health and needs in New Waverly.[22]

She was temporarily drawn back to Washington by her friendship with LWV President Maud Wood Park and by the national organization's legislative agenda. The ballot having given women the clout to back up their traditional pressure-group politics, Park and the LWV moved quickly to mobilize a female legislative lobby. At the LWV's invitation, ten national organizations created the Women's Joint Congressional Committee (WJCC) late in 1920 and elected Maud Wood Park president. Charter members included the General Federation of Women's Clubs, the Woman's Christian Temperance Union, the National Consumers' League, and the National Federation of Business and Professional Women. As an umbrella organization, the WJCC worked through subcommittees; whenever a designated number of member groups (initially three, later five) agreed on a legislative goal, a subcommittee was formed to lobby for the measure in Congress. The WJCC's first objective, endorsed by all ten groups, was the legislation that became the Sheppard-Towner Maternity and Infancy Act, the country's first federal social welfare program and the first "women's bill" passed in the aftermath of suffrage.[23]

Research by the federal Children's Bureau had revealed that the United States had one of the highest maternal and infant mortality rates in the industrialized world and that as many as half the deaths might be prevented by improving prenatal and infant care. Director Julia Lathrop wanted especially to extend public health programs to rural areas, where maternal mortality was higher than in the cities and infant mortality nearly so. Backed by middle-class women's organizations, she proposed federal grants-in-aid to the states to set up prenatal and infant care education programs. The funds would pay for instruction in nutrition and hygiene, baby and child clinics, midwife training, and visiting public health nurses for pregnant women and new mothers. Each state would be required to appropriate a matching amount and create an agency to administer the funds and oversee the program.[24] Senator Morris Sheppard of Texas and Representative Horace Towner of Iowa, reliable allies of voluntarist women, introduced the legislation in 1919. When the WJCC formed its Sheppard-Towner subcommittee in 1920, chairwoman Florence Kelley of the National Consumers' League launched a massive lobbying effort that took Cunningham back to Capitol Hill.

From December 1920 until April 1921 she served as legislative secretary for Maud Wood Park, assisting Park and Florence Kelley on the Sheppard-Towner legislation. She worked closely with Dorothy Kirchwey Brown of Boston, chair of the LWV's Child Welfare Committee and sister of *The Nation*'s Frieda Kirchwey, and formed a lasting friendship. The Sheppard-Towner bill passed the Senate that December but died in the House when Congress adjourned, and the women's lobby spent the beginning of 1921 preparing for resubmission while the White House changed from Democratic to Republican hands.[25]

Standing in the crowd that watched Warren G. Harding's inaugural procession, Cunningham pondered the end of Wilsonian progressivism and tried not to feel like "a citizen in a conquered land" at the prospect of four years of Republican conservatism. The frail and sickly Woodrow Wilson, seated in the open car with Harding, seemed to her almost a prisoner of the glittering cavalry troop that followed behind. Eyes fixed on the pageantry in the street, her mind reviewed the GOP's anti-reform record in the last Congress: victories for the meat packing and railroad lobbies; salary cuts in the Women's Bureau; the elimination of the Social Hygiene Board; the languishing Sheppard-Towner bill.[26]

Nevertheless, Sheppard-Towner *was* going to pass, she wrote Jane Mc-Callum, because women would not give up while the lives of 250,000 babies and 20,000 mothers were needlessly lost every year. "They might just as well let us have these things, because the more they *won't*, the more we *will*." And at the LWV convention in Cleveland, she put the same passion into a speech that made an indelible impression on New York delegate Eleanor Roosevelt, who would later become a friend. Cunningham, Eleanor wrote to Franklin, was "emotional & idealistic, but she made nearly everyone cry!" Almost twenty years later, Roosevelt credited her own sense of civic responsibility to Cunningham, "who first made me feel that you had no right to be a slacker as a citizen, you had no right not to take an active part in what was happening to your country as a whole."[27]

Cunningham was hardly resettled in Texas, preoccupied with spring planting and Ella's plans to build a new house, when Maud Wood Park wrote on behalf of the LWV board asking her to become the organization's first executive secretary and take charge of its Washington headquarters. She said yes immediately, reluctant to be a "slacker" in the Sheppard-Towner effort and fearful of being drafted as the next Texas LWV president. The 1920 TLWV convention in El Paso the previous fall had been disappointingly small—Jessie Daniel Ames went so far as to call it a "a complete failure"—and the organization counted only 280 members.[28] Cunningham foresaw herself trapped again in a perpetual presidency and financially embarrassed, as she had been in the TESA. "They said they'd raise the money to pay me a salary," she confided to Dorothy Kirchwey Brown, "and bless their hearts they'd mean to— but if they fell down I couldn't raise any of the money because I *cannot* raise the money to pay myself a salary. I just couldn't *do* it. So I must run for it."[29]

She arrived in Washington to take up the executive secretaryship in July 1921, as both houses of Congress debated the Sheppard-Towner bill. A chorus of medical associations and right-wing organizations attacked it as creeping socialism and federal intrusion in state affairs, charges Cunningham immediately refuted in a press release for the WJCC. She was on Capitol Hill daily for the Senate hearings and on August 1 was elected acting chair of the WJCC's Sheppard-Towner subcommittee, to take charge while Florence Kelley went abroad. Having passed the Senate, the bill was stalled in the House, where the hostile committee chairman had adjourned the proceedings for three weeks. The hearings had not been printed, and until they were, there could be no committee report and no House vote.[30]

It was a deliberate delaying tactic, and Cunningham responded by reactivating the old suffrage "home pressure" strategy, requesting that all state LWV presidents deluge the committee members with constituent mail. To this she added a tactic that made ingenious use of women's new status as voting constituents with congressional access prerogatives. She encouraged LWV presidents to have women write their congressmen and request copies of the printed hearings. "This will insure a constant stream of secretaries to the Committee rooms asking for these hearings and may impress upon the Committee Secretary that the matter is not slipping." At some point, she even had a private conference with President Warren Harding.[31]

Thanks to relentless lobbying—by fall the WJCC was seeing fifty congressmen daily—the Sheppard-Towner Maternity and Infancy Act finally passed the House on November 19, 1921. Critics persistently denounced it as Bolshevism, and the large margins by which it cleared both houses of Congress were deceptive. One member admitted that if the vote could have been taken secretly, the measure would have been emphatically killed. The politicians' fear of alienating the newly enfranchised female voters gave the women's lobby its first and most significant legislative success.[32]

Nevertheless, partisan loyalties and organizational rivalries that the suffrage movement had temporarily obscured were already beginning to reemerge among organized women. Responding in irritation to an attack on the LWV by the Woman's National Republican Club, Catt justified the need for the LWV by asserting that it had done more than any other group to put through Sheppard-Towner. Partisan and voluntarist women took offense in equal measure, which Cunningham summarized with detached humor. Republican women, who had helped secure President Harding's backing, were "*furious!*"; the WJCC coalition "*furiouser!!*" Maud Wood Park attempted to make peace with a letter to the *Woman Citizen* lavishing credit all around and "sent it to Mrs. Catt, who was evidently *furiousest!!!* Said if Chief [Park] had drawn up a brief to show that the LWV was ineffective and not worth supporting she couldn't have done better."[33]

Following the triumph of passing the Sheppard-Towner Act came the hard work of persuading the states to accept it and authorize matching appropriations. Cunningham dispatched nearly 10,000 leaflets from LWV headquarters for the state presidents' use in petitioning their legislatures and governors. Maud Wood Park was "shocked to the center of her being" at such lavishness, Cunningham admitted to Dorothy Brown, "and I don't blame her, but they *were* needed." Especially worried about states' rights sentiment in the South,

Cunningham made sure that each southern LWV president received one hundred copies of Morris Sheppard's Senate speech, hoping that the sentiments of a Texas Democrat would carry more weight with southern legislators. By mid-1922, forty-two of forty-eight states, including all those below the Mason-Dixon line except Louisiana, had accepted Sheppard-Towner.[34]

The executive secretaryship was a demanding job that Cunningham found both enjoyable and trying. The Washington office was the LWV's nerve center. Its congressional service handled lobbying on behalf of the standing committees and monitored appropriations for successful legislation. The publicity department supplied news releases to 750 newspapers and, beginning in September of 1922, a four-page insert called "The Woman Voter" to the *Woman Citizen*. A bureau of information filled requests from individuals and state leagues. Individual secretaries were responsible for the work of the divisions, while Cunningham coordinated the overall operation and oversaw all functions of the main office. She ruefully compared the latter to being the mother of a family who "picks up after, sews and mends for, and feeds and generally supplements the activities of her brilliant husband and children."[35]

Whether hiring an efficiency expert to help reorganize the office or lobbying Democratic senators for LWV bills, Cunningham embodied versatility. She sat on the executive committee and attended meetings of the board of directors; approved the weekly copy for "The Woman Voter"; and managed the finances of the Washington office, authorizing expenditures and worrying over budget shortfalls.[36] Most significant, she was Maud Wood Park's first lieutenant and right hand. The two reprised the teamwork of their days with NAWSA's congressional lobby to guide the LWV at a time when the fledgling organization "seemed to have before it all the unresolved questions of the universe," as one officer later recalled. The struggle to build membership imposed a heavy traveling and speaking schedule on Park; Cunningham helped arrange it, substituted when she was ill, handled her correspondence, and kept her abreast of Washington affairs.[37]

Wherever Park could not be, Cunningham went. In three especially busy days in January 1922, for example, she was scheduled to speak in Philadelphia in the morning, at the Virginia LWV convention the same evening, in Alexandria, Virginia, the following night, and in Maryland the evening after ("unless I can brow beat M[aud]. P[ark]. into doing it.") That year she addressed five state LWV conventions and spoke to the University of Maryland summer school and miscellaneous gatherings in nearby states. She stood in for Park at the Permanent Conference for the Abolition of Child Labor, which convened to hammer out a proposed constitutional amendment; spoke to the annual conference of the Consumers' League on the LWV's behalf; and represented the LWV in a lawsuit in Toronto. As the only southern officer at headquarters, she was frequently dispatched to bring greetings and inspiration from the national organization to state LWV conventions in the South. In South Carolina in 1923 she spoke not only to the LWV but, by invitation, to the state legislature on bills that the women were promoting.[38]

Cunningham and Park also played essential parts in putting over the WJCC's second successful initiative, the Married Women's Independent Citizenship Act, better known as the Cable Act of 1922. Prior to that date, a wife's citizenship followed her husband's: a native-born woman who married an alien lost her American citizenship, even if she remained a resident of the United States, while an immigrant woman who wed an American automatically gained it. A number of prominent women who married foreigners found themselves summarily deprived of their birthright, including Ruth Bryan Owen, the daughter of William Jennings Bryan, and suffragists Harriot Stanton Blatch and Inez Millholland. During World War I, American women married to unnaturalized German and Austrian immigrants had been designated as enemy aliens in their own country.[39]

With suffrage finally achieved, the federal nationality law stood as one of the most conspicuous remaining barriers to women's autonomous political identity. The LWV made independent citizenship for married women one of its first legislative goals and secured pledges of support from both the Republican and Democratic conventions of 1920. When the WJCC took up the cause, Maud Wood Park oversaw the independent citizenship subcommittee. She helped shape the bill that Representative John L. Cable of Ohio introduced in the spring of 1922 and testified at the hearings. While the WJCC lobbied to get the bill out of committee and brought up for a vote, Cunningham, expecting the usual protracted delay, took a month's vacation in Texas. Returning to Washington on June 20, she was barely off the train and still shampooing the dust of the two-day journey out of her hair when a telephone call summoned her to Capitol Hill. Hurriedly binding up her wet hair, she reached the House just in time to see the Cable bill go through. It deserved, she reported to the LWV, "the blue ribbon for speed in passage over any piece of women's legislation I have ever known anything about."[40]

Equally quick action was promised in the Senate, but it was not forthcoming. Park departed for her own vacation in Maine while the Cable bill languished in the Committee on Immigration. Cunningham's attempts to move it along were stymied by the Senate's preoccupation with tariff legislation and the Bonus Bill for veterans. She reluctantly summoned Park back to Washington, and together they interviewed senators, repeating the familiar routine of their Congressional Lobby days. Told that it would be impossible to assemble a quorum of the committee during the late summer lethargy, Park assigned female lieutenants to persuade each of the necessary six senators. Cunningham's was "a gentleman who was so busy that no one dared to ask anything of him," but she had no choice. "Mrs. Park sat on a bench outside of the door and checked them off as they came in," she recalled, "and if your man did not come in, woe unto you." The bill was voted out of committee on September 8 and passed the Senate the next day.

Before the Cable bill reached President Harding for signature, however, it had to be passed through the Departments of Labor and State, which were affected by its provisions. Cunningham spent two tense weeks working to get the bill sent forward before Congress adjourned, while Congressman Cable, who was eager to have the bill signed before he went home to campaign for reelection, besieged her with anxious telephone calls. Finally, in the last days of the session, an unidentified "great and mighty friend" intervened and moved the bill to the White House. For organized women's efforts on behalf of the Cable Act, Maud Wood Park collected two ceremonial pens: the one President Harding used to sign the bill, which was then sent to LWV headquarters, and the one that a relieved Cable handed Cunningham after writing Park a letter of thanks for the WJCC's work. Cunningham presented it to her at the LWV executive committee meeting in Boston, where all of the officers posed for a publicity photo.

Although Cunningham judged the Cable Act "a dramatic and wonderful piece of legislation," it did not grant women citizenship on identical terms with men. American women who married foreigners and sought to reenter the country became naturalized citizens, subject to the same restrictions as a foreign-born naturalized citizen. And reflecting the racism embedded in American immigration policy, the act stripped citizenship from women who married Chinese immigrants, who were ineligible for naturalization. Foreign-born women no longer became citizens automatically when their husbands were naturalized, a prospect that had appealed to congressmen concerned about the immigrant vote. Married women's citizenship did not become fully independent until the Cable Act was revised in 1930 and 1931, with the WJCC again acting as the driving force.[41]

WHILE THE LWV WORKED WITHIN THE WJCC FOR A SHARED LEGISLATIVE agenda, it also labored to build its own strength and visibility. The meeting that it staged in Baltimore in 1922 was its most ambitious and imaginative, combining the annual convention with a Pan-American Conference of Women. Women from twenty-one Latin American countries and Canada assembled with the convention delegates to discuss the status of women and social reform. The LWV hoped to promote "international friendliness" and to encourage Latin American women, none of whom were fully enfranchised, to seek political equality. The director of the Pan-American Union lent his support, and Secretary of State Charles Evans Hughes permitted the foreign delegates'

invitations to be issued through diplomatic channels. Britain's Lady Astor, the first woman to sit in Parliament, gave a keynote address, and there were receptions at the White House and the Maryland governor's mansion. Cunningham, by appointment of the LWV executive board, chaired the planning committee.[42]

The Pan-American Conference of Women was the brainchild of Lavinia Engle of the Maryland LWV, who had worked in Texas as a NAWSA organizer during Cunningham's presidency. Engle saw the possibilities of generating publicity for the LWV and getting financial assistance from the Baltimore Board of Trade, which would benefit from promoting the city as a shipping center. The Maryland LWV offered to raise $10,000 if the national organization would contribute an equal amount, a prospect that Maud Wood Park faced reluctantly. Cunningham, however, was enthusiastic, and her "venturesome courage" helped persuade Park to recommend undertaking the conference to the LWV executive committee. Cunningham and Engle spent months working on the details of the Pan-American Convention: arranging publicity, drafting the program, and securing everything from flags and translators to accommodations for Lady Astor's secretary.[43]

Secretary of Commerce Herbert Hoover, by discreetly enlisting the aid of commercial attachés in Latin America, helped Cunningham and the planning committee make sure that the delegates were women of achievement rather than the wives of diplomats posted to Washington.[44] The Pan-American Conference addressed "the common problems of women everywhere," and the roundtable speakers were prominent in their fields: Grace Abbott of the Children's Bureau on child welfare; her sister Julia on education; Mary Anderson of the Women's Bureau on women in industry; Dr. Valeria Parker on the suppression of prostitution; Assistant Attorney General Mabel Walker Willebrandt on the civil status of women; and Carrie Chapman Catt on the women's political status. Cunningham and the planning committee expected about 600 attendees, and when more than 1,000 arrived, the Baltimore hostesses had to scramble to find a larger hall. Most satisfying of all for the LWV's investment of effort and prestige, the conference concluded by forming a Pan-American Association for the Advancement of Women, to keep the spirit and goals of the assembly alive, and elected Catt president.[45]

LWV women found international outreach easier than forming ties of sisterhood at home with African American women. While some state LWVs in the North included black members, and a handful of black chapters existed, the national LWV made no attempt to organize among African American women. And southern black women, who were frequently denied their voting rights under the Nineteenth Amendment, found little sympathy among their white counterparts. The LWV first confronted the racial dilemma at its 1921 convention, when Addie Hunton, a prominent African American clubwoman and field secretary for the NAACP, led a delegation to ask the LWV's assistance in protesting voting discrimination. The black women were granted time to speak, but some southern delegates protested, and the incident pointed up the difficulty of mending the continuing racial split that had divided the suffrage movement.[46]

The board of directors' meeting at the close of the convention then grappled with the "Negro question." Several prominent northern women offered a resolution to form an Interracial Committee to study ways of promoting racial harmony; it was turned down in favor of one drafted by southern women to create a Special Committee on the Study of Negro Problems. Presented by Eulalie Salley of South Carolina, director of the Third Region, the resolution called for the Special Committee to be composed of representatives from states with an African American population of 15 percent or greater. The board, at Salley's request, created the committee by its own authority, without bringing the controversial issue before the convention. It offered the chairmanship to Julia Lathrop of the Illinois LWV, who had backed the rejected Interracial Committee proposal. Addie Hunton was notified of the action by letter.[47]

Cunningham viewed the race issue from the perspective of a southern moderate who had learned through hard experience that race-baiters always held the upper hand and that progress would be made gradually, or not at all. She was convinced that, as a matter of strategy, a noisy, soul-satisfying confrontation did less damage to an enemy than steady indirect pressure. The LWV, she argued, could accomplish more for black rights "by going at it from one end on Education and from the other on Clean Elections and simple, understandable election laws. But of course going at it that way we do not occupy the heroic position of attacking, bravely and from the front, a great evil, and we will not, when the work is done, get the credit."[48]

Southern LWVs courted trouble by doing even that much, and Cunningham thought it prudent to leave black disfranchisement measures out of their election law study programs. "Quiet work," she advised the LWV's national director of political education, might help change such laws, but "any publicity at all" would bring out the white supremacists in full cry. Maud Wood Park's preference for a more direct assault prompted Cunningham to a rare criticism: "I know how the Chief feels about the Negro question; strongly as she feels, I don't think she can feel any more strongly on it than I do—and with all due deference I think I know more about it than she does."[49]

Although the "problems" the Negro Problems Committee were to consider were not elaborated, its mandate included social as well as political issues, with the objective of "creating better feeling between the two races." The first year of the committee's existence, however, produced nothing but an unresolved debate over membership criteria: the advisability of including cities as well as states and of lowering the cutoff to include states with a 10 percent African American population, thereby bringing in some from the

North. By the spring of 1922, only seven states had named representatives to the committee, and only three of those had responded to Julia Lathrop's queries. Admitting regretfully that overcommitments had limited her own effectiveness, she resigned as chair.[50]

After Lathrop's resignation, the responsibility for filling out the Negro Problems Committee devolved to Cunningham. Getting the southern LWVs to appoint their members required persistent prodding. "Unfortunately many of our women do not see the responsibility or feel the obligation to work at this," the Alabama LWV president admitted, in a typical response. Cunningham also tried, at the Executive Committee's request, to persuade Lathrop to reconsider. An appeal to another noted social investigator, Sophonisba Breckinridge of the University of Chicago, likewise failed to produce a chair. Following Lathrop's suggestion, Cunningham then spent several months soliciting nominations from the committee members themselves. The effort produced two serious possibilities but no acceptances. Although she was not officially designated acting chairman of the Negro Problems Committee during 1922–1923, all the labor of trying to keep it alive fell to her.[51]

By the time of the LWV's 1923 convention in Des Moines, Cunningham had persuaded all of the southern states to appoint a representative to the committee, and Blanche Rogers of Mississippi telegraphed her willingness to take the chairmanship. Equally important, the Des Moines convention produced an unprecedented dialogue between white and black members. In attendance were seven African American delegates from the Midwest, most of whom were also clubwomen active in the National Association of Colored Women. The black women met with Park, Cunningham, Lathrop, first vice president Belle Sherwin, and several other white members in a quiet, unpublicized conference to discuss racial concerns.[52]

The African American delegates, led by Irene Goins of the Illinois board, Beatrice Grady of the Missouri board, Sue M. Brown of Iowa, and Alice Webb of Chicago, suggested a plan of cooperation that avoided the touchy subject of black disfranchisement. Concentrating on the LWV's mission of voter education and citizenship training, they asked for outreach to the black community and cooperation with such groups as the NACW and the Commission on Interracial Cooperation. After the Executive Committee voted to accept the proposals, Cunningham passed them on to Blanche Rogers, who continued to seek her guidance in working out a program for the committee.[53]

MINNIE FISHER CUNNINGHAM CEASED TO BE THE LWV'S EXECUTIVE secretary at the end of September 1923. She had tried to resign a year and a half earlier, apparently because of wounded southern sensibilities. Southern women were a minority in the LWV, as they had been in NAWSA, and barely represented in the leadership. Throughout the 1920s only Cunningham, Pattie Ruffner Jacobs of Alabama, and Adele Clark of Virginia held national office. The women who led the LWV tended to be from the Northeast and Midwest, and many were graduates of elite colleges. In their private politics they were often Republican; the GOP, born as an antislavery reform party, had traditionally been more hospitable to activist women. Cunningham always felt something of an outsider in this company, aware of being country-bred and lacking the polish of a liberal arts education, a daughter of the provincial Democratic South.

Although the particulars are not recorded, some Executive Committee members apparently criticized Texas and other southern states for slowness in getting LWV work organized and financially stable, and praised Cunningham as an exception to southern backwardness. Whatever the specific slight, she brooded deeply over it, confiding to Dorothy Kirchwey Brown in February 1922 that she didn't "care a continental for any approval personally which lists me as different or exceptional from my own people . . . *I think* lumping people by states or sections is silly any how . . . How *can* they feel that way?"[54]

She concealed her hurt from Maud Wood Park, determined not to be perceived as "a supersensitive professional Southerner," and made a general excuse for wanting to leave. (Some thirty years later she had a more spirited recollection of "my rebellious attitude toward 'Chiefie Park' for *her* snooty attitude toward Texas.") Park received the news with such dismay that Cunningham agreed to stay on. Devotion to "the Chief," whom she considered "the greatest woman of this generation," as well as her own real satisfaction in the work, kept Cunningham in the executive secretaryship until Park decided not to stand for reelection in 1924.[55]

In returning to Texas to again help care for her mother, Cunningham regretfully closed the door on an opportunity to do significant work in the 1924 presidential election. With Park's consent, she had begun acting "*very* quietly in an advisory capacity" to the campaign of William Gibbs McAdoo, the Democratic front-runner, in the summer of 1923. McAdoo's principal adviser, Daniel C. Roper, approached her confidentially, and Cunningham found him likeable and noncondescending, a man who "talks to you like he actually thought you had sense as a person!" Roper wanted her to organize women for McAdoo, a job she would have welcomed had not family considerations stood in the way. She did, however, stay a week in Washington after her departure from LWV headquarters, to train a group of Democratic women as political organizers for the 1924 campaign. The Democratic Party, not wishing to give the Republicans inspiration, refrained from publicizing the event.[56]

Helen Gardener, an old NAWSA comrade and the first woman appointed to the Civil Service Commission, used the occasion of Cunningham's departure to celebrate women's postsuffrage gains in public life. Gardener hosted a bipartisan testimonial dinner for Cunningham at the Woman's City Club, announcing that she intended to invite "all of the women who are holding high official positions in Washington." In addition to the LWV leaders, she assembled a group that represented women's achievements in political preferment, including two judges and the heads of the U.S. Employees Compensation Commission, the District of Columbia Commission, and the D.C. Rent Commission. Among the best known attendees were Grace Abbott, Mary Anderson, Mabel Walker Willebrandt, Emily Newell Blair, vice-chair of the Democratic National Committee, and Harriet Taylor Upton, vice-chair of the Executive Committee of the Republican National Committee.[57]

It was expected that Cunningham, only forty-one, and with years of experience in both voluntarist and partisan politics, would soon be back in Washington. "The only question disputed about," the *Woman Citizen* mused, "is whether she will sit in the Senate or the House." Cunningham made sure her return to Texas was noted by the state press, including a front-page story in the *Galveston Daily News.* Sailing from New York City to Galveston, she was accompanied by two close friends, Dr. Anna Rude of the Maternal and Infant Hygiene Department of the Children's Bureau and with whom she had shared an apartment near Dupont Circle, and Mabel Costigan, chair of the LWV's Committee on Living Costs. Rude had retired and was on her way home to California; Costigan was beginning a speaking tour. The three women used the notice their arrival attracted to discuss the implementation of the Sheppard-Towner Act, the LWV's advocacy for a federal child labor amendment, U.S. membership in the World Court, and Cunningham's future. The *Dallas Morning News* noted that while Cunningham had not announced any plans to run for office, "league women feel she will not be able to escape a destiny so obvious."[58]

Despite Cunningham's resolve to devote herself to her mother and family in New Waverly, Washington continued to beckon. In December she forced herself to turn down another appeal to organize women's work for McAdoo, this time from the campaign manager, David Ladd Rockwell. She left open the possibility of a few weeks' work in Washington later that winter, when her mother would be staying with the eldest sister, Marion, in Galveston. Rockwell welcomed the prospect, and he planned to discuss it with Daniel Roper and Texas National Committeeman Thomas B. Love when he met with them in Washington.[59] Instead, Cunningham found herself back at the LWV in a new role. When the LWV held its convention in the spring of 1924 in Buffalo, she was nominated for second vice president.

Although Cunningham had steadfastly refused to consider new service, either as a vice president or a regional director, Pattie Ruffner Jacobs's decision not to stand for reelection left the board of directors without a southern member. The Virginia LWV nominated Cunningham and begged her not to decline: "Everybody wants you." The only southerner on the ballot, she was elected overwhelmingly. "Honestly, I *couldn't* not, it was such a desperate sort of a situation," she only half-joked to Dorothy Brown. "Now *I* am 'the Democrat' and Pattie Jacobs is kicking up her feet in a disgustingly frisky fashion. Only of course you know, in spite of this railing & weeping & wringing of hands I'm horribly flattered that they wanted me."[60]

Becoming a vice president brought Cunningham back in touch with the Special Committee on Negro Problems, which had made little progress under Blanche Rogers. At the Buffalo convention, Cunningham and several other officers again met with a group of African American delegates, led by Irene Goins, president of Chicago's Douglass LWV, and Carrie Horton of the Chicago Federation of Colored Women's Clubs. The black women, astutely stressing the need to prevent "exploitation by unscrupulous politicians," asked that the LWV cooperate with African American women's clubs and black colleges in citizenship education work. Equally important, the Board of Directors appointed Cunningham chair of the Negro Problems Committee. As the only LWV member who had been continuously involved with the committee and a prominent southerner, she was the obvious choice.[61]

Although the Negro Problems Committee had no budget and the LWV insisted that its activities not be publicized, Cunningham took the chair with enthusiasm. As a Methodist, she belonged to a denomination whose women's home missionary societies had begun reaching across the color line in the 1910s, establishing settlement houses in black neighborhoods with biracial staffs and governing boards. Cunningham had also been deeply impressed by the report of the Chicago Commission on Race Relations, created in the aftermath of that city's 1919 race riot. *Literary Digest* published a summary of the commission's conclusions, based on three years of study, that Cunningham called "probably the most important publication on the subject that has been printed." White prejudice, not black inferiority, had created the "Negro problem," the biracial commission declared. Every group in society helped perpetuate it, and "every citizen, regardless of color or racial origin is in honor and conscience bound to seek and forward its solution."[62]

Cunningham certainly saw the LWV committee as part of that solution and a way to implement the Chicago Commission's recommendation that "the nation must make sure that the Negro is educated for citizenship." She immediately scheduled a conference with Blanche Rogers in Mississippi and sought lists of individuals, organizations, and educational institutions to contact from Irene Goins, who expressed pleasure at Cunningham's appointment. She went to Chicago for a follow-up meeting with Goins and the other African American delegates, and as a result of that discussion had six recommendations ready to present when the Executive Committee met in July.[63]

Two of Cunningham's resolutions were especially notable. She suggested, for the first time in the committee's existence, that black women be encour-

aged and assisted to vote. She saw nothing to be gained in the LWV's batter-
ing itself hopelessly against the brick wall of southern prejudice. But in states
where the black vote was "a material and accepted fact," that is, in the North,
state presidents were requested to arrange ballot marking classes for African
American women, just as they did for whites. Cunningham also proposed that
the committee itself be reorganized to include representatives from three additional regions and, more significantly, that black women be appointed as
members (a suggestion that the white southerners could be expected to resist).[64] Relieved to see progress at last, the Executive Committee adopted the
entire report "with profound appreciation."[65] Without any fanfare, she had
advanced the committee's agenda further in six months than her predecessors
had in the previous three years.

CUNNINGHAM FOUND THE LWV BOTH FULFILLING AND FRUSTRATING. AS A
social welfare lobby, cooperating with other women's organizations in the
WJCC, it helped push the well-established tradition of female voluntarist politics briefly to new levels of legislative success. Lobbying was familiar territory to organized women, and achievements such as the Sheppard-Towner
and Cable Acts were the culmination of long-practiced skills backed by the
new potential of the ballot. The LWV offered Cunningham a means to work
for what she and other activist women called "improved conditions": cleaner
politics and laws to protect health and welfare. And despite the antisouthern
snobbishness that sometimes wounded her, the organization offered Cunningham an opportunity to pursue the kind of interracial outreach that she
had never felt able to risk at home in Texas.

Countervailing frustrations emerged as the LWV explored the unfamiliar
terrain of women's new political citizenship. In this, the presuffrage voluntarist experience provided little guidance. Gaining influence for women in the
parties and working to change the tenor of politics brought Cunningham and
the other leaders sharply up against entrenched male interests, voter indifference, and the unwillingness of women themselves to join and support the
LWV in significant numbers. These difficulties would be the focus of Cunningham's labors during her term as second vice president.

Minnie, ca. 1900. This may have been taken at her graduation from college or before her wedding, a year and a half later. COURTESY OF THE CENTER FOR AMERICAN HISTORY, UNIVERSITY OF TEXAS AT AUSTIN, CN 00414 A, B.

~ Minnie, seated right, watches Governor William Hobby sign the bill authorizing a woman suffrage amendment to the Texas constitution, 1919. COURTESY OF AUSTIN HISTORY CENTER, AUSTIN PUBLIC LIBRARY, FP E.4 B.7 29.

Women members of the Texas delegation to the Democratic National Convention in San Francisco, 1920. *From right*: Margie Neal, Minnie, Jessie Daniel Ames, Jane Spell, Florence Sterling (holding flag), Birdie Robertson Johnson (holding hat). FROM THE COLLECTIONS OF THE DALLAS HISTORICAL SOCIETY, JESSIE DANIEL AMES COLLECTION.

Minnie, ca. 1921, probably about the time she became executive secretary of the League of Women Voters. COURTESY OF THE AUSTIN HISTORY CENTER, AUSTIN PUBLIC LIBRARY, FP E.4, B. 7 (3).

 At a meeting of the League of Women Voters Executive Committee, Minnie presents Maud Wood Park with a pen used to sign the Cable Act, 1922. *First row, from left*: Minnie, Belle Sherwin, Park. *Second row*: Katherine Ludington, Elizabeth Hauser, Mrs. Robert DeNormandie, Louise Griffith, Pattie Ruffner Jacobs.

Minnie, ca. 1926. Taken in Washington, D.C., while she was resident director of the Woman's National Democratic Club. COURTESY OF THE LIBRARY OF CONGRESS.

Members of the Woman's National Democratic Club at the opening of the club's headquarters at 1526 New Hampshire Ave., NW, Washington, D.C., May 1927. Minnie, second from left, stands between the president, Mrs. Andreius Jones, whose husband chaired the Senate Woman Suffrage Committee, and former First Lady Edith Bolling Wilson. Behind Minnie (in tall hat and pearls) is Marion Bannister, and looking over her shoulder is her daughter Margaret. Mrs. Edward Meigs is at the far right, last row. COURTESY OF THE SPECIAL COLLECTIONS, UNIVERSITY OF HOUSTON- UNIVERSITY PARK. COMPUTER ENLARGEMENT BY IMAGES BY BOBBY, SHINER, TEXAS.

The candidate with her campaign sign at the entrance to Fisher Farms, New Waverly, Texas, 1928. COURTESY OF AUSTIN HISTORY CENTER, AUSTIN PUBLIC LIBRARY, #F E.4 (28).

Minnie, right, and two unidentified friends, in front of her campaign Ford, 1928. COURTESY OF AUSTIN HISTORY CENTER, AUSTIN PUBLIC LIBRARY, #PICA 16817.

Minnie speaking at a campaign rally for Texas gubernatorial candidate Ross Sterling, 1930. COURTESY OF THE CENTER FOR AMERICAN HISTORY, UNIVERSITY OF TEXAS AT AUSTIN, R.S. STERLING PAPERS, CN02460.

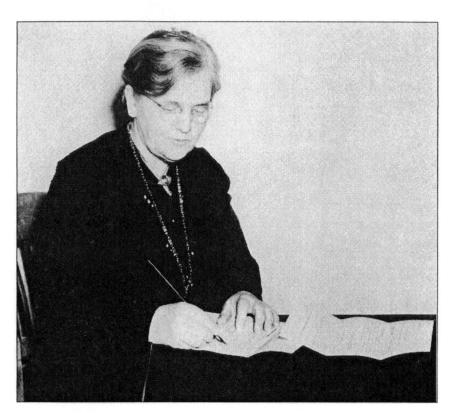

Signing the federal oath of office upon being appointed Senior Specialist in the Information Division of the Agricultural Adjustment Administration in Washington, D.C., 1939.

Members of the Civic Contacts Unit of the Consumer Division, National Defense Advisory Commission, Washington, D.C., 1940. *Clockwise, from center*: Frances Williams, Gladys Baker, Caroline Ware, Loda Mae Davis, Frank E. Manuel, Dr. Leland J. Gordon (consultant), Minnie (presiding), Dickson Reck, Virgil Parr, Frances Montgomery. COURTESY OF THE NATIONAL ARCHIVES AT COLLEGE PARK.

Candidate for governor of Texas, 1944. COURTESY OF THE HOUSTON METROPOLITAN RESEARCH CENTER, HOUSTON PUBLIC LIBRARY.

Texas State Democratic Executive Committee banquet, 1946. *From left*: Jim Wright, Minnie, Marion Storm, Lillian Collier. FROM THE *FORT WORTH STAR-TELEGRAM* PHOTOGRAPH COLLECTION, THE UNIVERSITY OF TEXAS AT ARLINGTON LIBRARIES, ARLINGTON, TEXAS.

Minnie, ca. late 1950s. Probably taken around the time she was honored as "Mrs. Democrat" of Texas. COURTESY OF THE HOUSTON METROPOLITAN RESEARCH CENTER, HOUSTON PUBLIC LIBRARY.

6

WOMAN CITIZEN AND DEMOCRATIC PARTISAN

BY THE MID-1920S IT WAS CLEAR THAT WOMEN'S QUEST FOR POLITICAL empowerment would be no less arduous than the struggle for the vote itself. At the same time that women sought influence in the parties, they retained distinctive "female" political values from their presuffrage voluntary association culture. The LWV, with its citizenship schools and emphasis on informed voting, was one manifestation of female political culture. Another was the disinclination to embrace the male standard of party loyalty; women were more likely to support candidates who shared their position on the issues, even if it meant crossing party lines. In making political choices, Cunningham thus balanced the values of citizenship, female or "independent" partisanship, and Democratic Party membership. In 1924 she embraced all three identities at once: serving as a national officer of the LWV, sitting on the Women's Advisory Committee at the Democratic National Convention, and defiantly voting for the Republican gubernatorial candidate in Texas.

As the decade advanced, Cunningham moved gradually and without comment away from the national LWV and into Democratic organizing. She remained convinced that the LWV performed an essential political function, which she described in a speech called "The Dividing Line Between the Work of the League and Political Parties." Despite politicians' claims to the contrary, there *was* no dividing line between the LWV and the parties, she told the 1924 LWV convention; like water and sand together in a goblet, they occupied the same space separately. The parties got out only their own registered voters; the LWV urged all citizens to go to the polls. The parties touted only their own candidates; the LWV assembled full and impartial dossiers on all. The

109

parties instructed in partisan ballot marking; the LWV taught how to cast an intelligent vote.[1]

Cunningham admired such LWV leaders as Belle Sherwin and Julia Lathrop, elected president and first vice president, respectively, in 1924. But they were social reformers rather than NAWSA veterans like her revered mentor, Maud Wood Park, and she despaired of their political naiveté: "They are so *good* and as *innocent!*"[2] She had more in common with Emily Newell Blair, head of the Women's Division of the Democratic Party, who like herself was a seasoned suffragist and party activist. Recruited by Blair into the inner circle of Democratic women, Cunningham focused her energy on partisan politics after 1925. As the first resident director (1925–1928) of the Woman's National Democratic Club (WNDC), she became a party spokesperson and helped build a semiautonomous base of authority for Democratic women.

CUNNINGHAM MOVED BACK TO WASHINGTON, D.C., IN THE SPRING OF 1924, torn between her desire to be at the center of activity and guilt over leaving her mother in her sisters' care. "I'm confessing to having lost my head," she admitted to Jane McCallum, describing the pressure brought on her to take the LWV vice presidency. The board of directors unhesitatingly accepted the conditions she attached to her willingness to serve. She was to be free to go home whenever her mother needed her and, being without private financial resources, to have a "decent" expense account.[3] As second vice president her responsibility would be to oversee the LWV's organizational work in the states and to head its national campaign to increase voter turnout in the fall elections.

Both jobs were enormous challenges and constricted by circumstances outside Cunningham's control. The LWV attracted only about 5 percent of the estimated 2 million women who had affiliated with NAWSA, and it never overcame the Democratic and Republican parties' head start in mobilizing women. In 1916, with women eligible to vote in a dozen states, both Democrats and Republicans created Women's Bureaus as subcommittees of their national party committees. The Democrats in 1917 and the Republicans in 1918 then set up women's versions of the national party committees and planned full-scale partisan organizing, adding women to the state and local party committees. While NAWSA was engrossed in the Nineteenth Amendment ratification campaign, both parties enlarged their executive committees to make half the membership female, and the women's divisions worked to enroll the new female voters.[4]

The LWV could not begin to match the parties' success, but it was Cunningham's responsibility to build strength and numbers. As second vice president and director of the Department of Organization, she worked atop layers of LWV bureaucracy. Below her were the directors and secretaries for each of the seven geographic regions, the presidents of all the state organizations, and finally the individual local leagues. In theory, each was to be a smoothly revolving cog within an efficient national machine, fully engaged in lobbying, educating voters, and raising funds to sustain itself. In reality, many of the cogs were barely synchronized. Finding money and members was a continuing struggle for the state organizations, which might profess loyal support for the national program while doing little or nothing to promote it.

The Texas LWV, for example, was organized in only ten of the state's eighteen congressional districts, yet in 1923 the Sixth Region's secretary considered it one of the *better* organized states. President Jessie Daniel Ames (1920–1923) had nursed it through indebtedness and low membership, but her successor, former TESA vice president Helen Moore, was less well prepared for the continuing challenge. Moore admitted that the Texas LWV "has been going backward instead of forward" and doubted that it could have survived if the regional secretary had not undertaken organizing work in the state early in 1924.[5]

The Department of Organization's mission was to strengthen the state leagues, pressing them to maintain functioning boards, implement the national program, attract new members, and induce local leagues to active participation. It was a difficult and delicate undertaking, for the national LWV had no coercive authority nor did Cunningham wish it to. Only the year before, as executive secretary, she had defended local autonomy in a speech to the Florida LWV stressing that "every state is a power unto itself" and that the national LWV's function was to serve the state leagues rather than dictate to them.[6]

The burden of this service fell to the regional secretaries, the national organization's field-workers. Cunningham concentrated on filling vacant secretaryships and improving efficiency. She drafted general standards of excellence for which regional secretaries should strive, and wrote a detailed set of procedures explaining how to guide state presidents in setting up headquarters and in adopting a fund-raising plan. Cunningham insisted on receiving a monthly regional report, a biweekly report of visits made, and advance travel schedules with stated objectives; at her request, the national board made these reports compulsory. She urged the regional secretaries to be tactful and realistic, making each visit helpful for the "brave but often untrained leaders" in the states. "Simplify things—get them down to their bare naked bones and show the framework of organization and finance which always does exist under a good permanent piece of work."[7]

While she managed the Department of Organization with one hand, with the other Cunningham directed the LWV's 1924 Get Out the Vote Campaign, an ambitious effort to reduce the drop-off in voter participation, which had fallen to 49 percent in the 1920 presidential election. Scholars now recognize the nationwide downturn in voting that began in the early twentieth century as part of a fundamental, long-term change in American politics. Party competition declined because of growing Democratic hegemony in the South and Republican dominance in the North, while the good government "reforms" of the Progressive Era reduced the size of the electorate and made voting more burdensome.[8] But in the 1920s these complexities were not yet evident; it seemed that the fault for low turnout lay with an indifferent electorate.

Emphasizing the danger of "minority rule," the LWV called for "a crusade to restore democracy." It began planning in 1923 an attempt to increase voter turnout to 75 percent. The 1924 convention authorized the new president, Belle Sherwin, to appoint a committee to assist Cunningham, who was "simply crazy" to undertake the challenge. Because the Get Out the Vote campaign was the brainchild of Maud Wood Park, Cunningham was certain that it would be "the greatest adventure in politics that this country has ever seen." "I shall come home laden with great glory and much political prestige because of it," she predicted, "but it all belongs to *her*."[9]

The Get Out the Vote Campaign was elaborately planned on paper to spread the message everywhere, from movie theaters to church pulpits. National LWV headquarters generated publicity and oversaw the production of leaflets, fliers, and posters for distribution at nominal prices to the state leagues. They in turn were to carry out the fundamental labor by forming general state committees with subdivisions for various facets of the work: publicity, voter information service, candidates' meetings, house-to-house canvassing, and the like. Cunningham's first initiative was to edit a forty-page "campaign handbook" of suggestions, statistics, and sample publicity, which state leagues could use for guidance and inspiration.[10]

Cunningham also quietly oversaw the preparation of planks for the LWV to present at the upcoming presidential nominating conventions. She had doubted whether, as head of the voter turnout campaign, she ought to be so publicly associated with the parties; the board authorized her to do both jobs but cautioned her against publicizing the liaison work.[11] As it had in 1920, the LWV was drafting planks to present to both party platform committees. In 1924 it trimmed its demands to three general issues: public welfare, efficiency in government, and international cooperation to prevent war. The international cooperation plank called for the United States to join the World Court. Efficiency in government (a favorite LWV phrase) urged the merit system of appointments and promotions rather than patronage. Under the category of public welfare, the LWV asked for ratification of the federal child labor amendment; adequate appropriations for the Women's Bureau and the Children's Bureau; continued support for the Sheppard-Towner Act; and the creation of a federal department of education.[12]

Cunningham and President Belle Sherwin edited and amended the planks into final form. When they were presented at the Republican National Convention that nominated Calvin Coolidge, Sherwin considered the reception a success. She was satisfied to have the child labor act mentioned even without a call for enabling legislation; Cunningham, on the other hand, bluntly judged such evasion "a total loss" and was disturbed that the LWV's press secretary credited the GOP with incorporating all of the planks. If the organization was going to settle for half measures and be thankful, she warned Sherwin privately, it would not take the politicians very long to realize that they could ignore the LWV with impunity.[13]

As the ranking Democrat at headquarters, Cunningham took responsibility for pulling together the LWV's representation for the Democratic National Convention. Pattie Ruffner Jacobs, a former member of the Democratic National Committee, headed the delegation, with Cunningham as chief aide. (Jacobs had asked that the roles be reversed, but the board of directors eventually decided that Cunningham was carrying too many other duties.) Since Jacobs lived in Alabama, it was Cunningham who secured the speakers to present each plank, arranged for the LWV's convention headquarters, and circularized the delegates.[14]

At the same time, she accepted Eleanor Roosevelt's invitation to become a member of a special Democratic women's advisory committee, the first time the party had acknowledged the agenda of women's organizations. Emily Newell Blair, vice-chair of the Democratic National Committee, was behind this initiative. Knowing that the LWV and other women's groups wanted to present planks, and feeling that such proposals should come from Democratic women rather than those who held themselves aloof from parties, Blair convinced DNC Chairman Cordell Hull to authorize the committee.

The members, all prominent in party politics and social reform, included Dorothy Kirchwey Brown, Elinor Morgenthau, Charl Williams, Pattie Ruffner Jacobs, and Gertrude Ely. Under Roosevelt's chairmanship, the Democratic Women's Advisory Committee held hearings in New York in June to solicit input on social welfare needs from women's organizations and formulate "a woman's platform of legislation." Groups as old as the Woman's Christian Temperance Union and as new as the League of Nations Non-Partisan Association presented dozens of requests for inclusion. Cunningham both served on the committee and led the LWV delegation that appeared before it.[15]

Working in small groups, the Women's Democratic Advisory Committee evaluated the proposed planks and reduced them to a manageable number. Cunningham reported for the subcommittee on prison reform, which recommended instituting vocational training, abolishing convict labor, and creating a federal system of parole and probation. As chair of the subcommittee on law enforcement, whose primary concern was the widely flouted prohibition laws, she brought out a report indicting the Harding-Coolidge administration for laxity.[16] In addition to the numerous subcommittee proposals, the full committee endorsed the LWV planks, the League of Nations, and measures to improve the welfare of employed women: equal pay, a shorter work week, and safe, healthful working conditions.

When the Democratic National Convention opened in Madison Square Garden, there were more female participants than ever before. Women made up 14 percent of the delegates and 29 percent of the alternates, and there were "hundreds" of female visitors. A woman chaired the credentials committee and women made seconding speeches for the candidates. But as the *Woman Citizen* pointed out, "positions of honor and decoration" did not constitute shared power. There were no women on the platform committee, which refused a hearing to the Democratic Women's Advisory Committee. Eleanor Roosevelt, Cunningham, and the other members sat outside the locked door all night while the men voted three times against a reconsideration. Roosevelt always remembered the frustration of discovering "where the women stood when it came to a national convention. . . . They stood outside the door of all important meetings and waited."[17]

In her capacity as a member of the LWV's delegation (led by Pattie Ruffner Jacobs), Cunningham eventually did get inside the dark, uncomfortable room in the Waldorf-Astoria Hotel where the platform committee met. Straining to be heard above the noise from the street and from the electric fans whirring futilely against the 100 degree heat, Cunningham and Jacobs, along with Susan F. Hibbard, Dorothy Kirchwey Brown, and Gertrude Ely, presented the LWV's planks. The subcommittee that met at the conclusion of the hearings reported favorably on the LWV proposals, and its report was adopted.

But the women's satisfaction was short-lived. During the next several days, as the full committee wrangled over the fine points of the platform, Cunningham concluded that most of the members "gradually lost a sense of values in their effort to win or defeat certain cherished or despised propositions." She and the other LWV women discovered how easy it was for their measures to be sabotaged in the confusion of subcommittees and cliques through which the platform committee operated. The LWV planks were reconsidered and voted out twice; the second time, Cunningham talked to five important men who were unaware that it had happened again. The last attempt to have them reinstated failed by a vote of 18 to 22, the same count that had defeated Eleanor Roosevelt's committee.

Cunningham's report to the LWV board of directors criticized her party unsparingly. Next to each of the LWV's planks, she counterposed the platform committee's language: "The feeble, stumbling, sometimes two faced words which were most frequently given us in exchange." She advised beginning the preparations to present planks much earlier the next time and adopting a new strategy: the LWV should contact all of the women delegates well in advance and invite them to a preconvention conference that would help women increase their political leverage.[18] Although the term had not yet been invented, she was advocating a women's caucus.

The outcome of the convention itself proved no more satisfying. The Democratic Party was bitterly divided over prohibition and the second Ku Klux Klan, which after being reborn in the South in 1915 had spread like a virus into the North in the 1920s. Nourished by anxieties over social and cultural change, the KKK entered politics on the side of prohibition and traditional morality while preaching intolerance toward African Americans, Catholics, and Jews. The presence of Klan members as convention delegates—they made up about half of the Texas delegation, for example—precipitated a wrangle over whether or not to denounce the KKK by name in the platform. Cunningham, who had watched the hooded order's rise with dismay, had already lodged her own protest through the Democratic Women's Advisory Committee. Her report for its subcommittee on law enforcement pointedly condemned "all groups, open or secret, which attempt to take the law into their own hands" and denounced "the attempts of organizations or individuals to create prejudice against groups of citizens because of race or color or religion."[19]

Ideological fissures produced a deadlocked convention. Northeastern urbanites, backing New York's wet, Catholic governor, Alfred E. Smith, vied for control with rural southerners and westerners, who supported former Treasury Secretary William Gibbs McAdoo. The Klan favored McAdoo, who was southern-born and an unequivocal prohibitionist. He was Cunningham's choice because he attacked Wall Street interests, held enlightened views on women, and appeared to embody the moderate progressivism of his father-in-law, Woodrow Wilson. Her hopes for a McAdoo victory were dashed as he and Smith battled hopelessly in Madison Square Garden for the required two-thirds majority. After seventeen sweltering days, John W. Davis, a conservative corporate lawyer, was chosen as a compromise candidate on the 103rd ballot.

Cunningham, who by then was at Belle Sherwin's home in Cleveland for an LWV board meeting, heard "the dreadful thing" happening over the radio. "It was almost the death of me," she lamented to fellow Democrat Dorothy Kirchwey Brown. "And all my nice little Republican friends were so pleased . . . They said what a nice candidate I now had instead of that awful person McAdoo. They talked about it at all meals and if Miss Prudence Sherwin's sweet cups and glasses and beautiful silver ware have not hunks bitten off'n by me while I listened, it's a tribute to my self control which no one but me knows about! I came away with a very bad name as a Partizan [sic] Democrat."[20]

The demands of the Get Out the Vote Campaign, however, left her no time to brood over the disappointing convention. Being "a Pied Piper to the Slacker Voter," she realized belatedly, was "the biggest and most impossible job women have ever tackled."[21] By letter, she secured the endorsement of nineteen women's, professional, and civic groups, and in late July and early August she toured Arkansas, Missouri, Nebraska and Iowa, speaking and organizing. To drum up more interest, the national LWV promised a trophy to the state that showed the greatest increase in turnout and sponsored a national newspaper cartoon contest. By September only nine state LWVs were not participating in the campaign. Cunningham's handbook had gone into a second printing, and a voter information pamphlet, *The A B C of Voting*, was in production. Fifty thousand copies were printed for distribution through the Haskin newspaper syndicate. A smiling Cunningham was photographed next to an enormous poster that urged the public to "VOTE as You Please, but VOTE" and given to another syndicate that reached 600 newspapers.[22]

The campaign was moving into the final stages when Cunningham was abruptly called home in September to deal with a crisis in her mother's health. She was forced to cancel the trip she had planned through the southern states and to abandon the day-to-day management of the last six weeks of the campaign. Her office staff took over, consulting with Cunningham by mail and managing the speakers' bureau. Optimism remained high. At LWV headquarters, plans were laid for an election-night gala and open house; a special telegraph line was installed to receive election returns, and a police detail secured to handle the anticipated crowds. The LWV's press secretary promised Cunningham a telegram of congratulations as soon as the figures were in.[23]

As it turned out, there was small cause for celebration. Although some states showed higher gains, the nationwide turnout rose only to 50.9 percent, far short of the 75 percent goal. The LWV put the best possible face on the disappointing returns, stressing that the country had at least returned to majority rule. The National Civic Federation, however, pronounced the Get Out the Vote campaign a failure, prompting Cunningham to demand indignantly that the LWV issue a rebuttal. The LWV's own postmortem judged that only eighteen state leagues had made an effort that could be described as good or fair; twenty-four others were classed as having done poor work or none at all.[24]

Even if every state LWV had gone all out, their efforts would have made little difference. The era of mass participation politics was over, and middle-class reformers like the LWV women had helped hasten its demise. Reformers' relentless advocacy of nonpartisanship, "efficient" government, and "responsible" voting had curbed the power of parties to turn out and reward supporters; transferred patronage jobs to the civil service; replaced party voting tickets with the secret ballot; and restricted voter eligibility with registration and residency requirements. However much the educated elite deplored "blind partisanship," it had produced the spectacular campaigns and high turnouts of the nineteenth century, when party organizations were part of the fabric of local communities and casting a ballot was a social act. Earnest women like Cunningham and her LWV colleagues failed to grasp that they could not have it both ways: sanitized, cerebral politics was less interesting to voters than boisterous partisanship.

The LWV's small membership and weak state organizations reflected the limited appeal of its civics textbook approach to politics. Good government and "responsible citizenship" were not causes that stirred the blood as suffrage had, and women with a passion for politics tended to desert the LWV in favor of party organizations. This was partly the fault of its increasingly rigid non-partisanship policy, which by the mid-1920s made it difficult for women to hold LWV rank and do party work. State leaders reported that indifference and partisanship ate away potential support; in the summer of 1924, twenty-eight of forty-five state boards were operating only partially or not at all. Women "think [the LWV] is a fifth wheel and so why bother," the regional secretary for New England lamented to Cunningham.[25] Although Cunningham remained involved in the Texas LWV for another decade, she too seems to have concluded that party work offered greater promise. She never again held office in the national LWV, and when she returned to Washington late in 1925, it would be under Democratic Party auspices.

IF WOMEN DID NOT TRANSFORM POLITICS IN THE 1920S, THEY nevertheless challenged its traditions. Male political culture stressed party loyalty and supporting one's friends, while women's, shaped in the presuffrage era by voluntary associations and reform agendas, had been essentially nonpartisan. After enfranchisement, these middle-class women tended to embrace "independent partisanship" that valued issues and the quality of candidates over unconditional allegiance to a party, which Carrie Chapman Catt deplored as "the kind of thing that blinds the sight and paralyzes the judgment." The LWV encouraged this attitude with its candidate profiles, information disseminated to help voters choose the best of both parties. Former NAWSA officer Mary Garrett Hay, who had held both national and state office in the Republican Party, claimed that she never voted a straight ticket: "All the angels are not in the Republican Party and are not in the Democratic Party." Women regarded this as "intelligent" voting; in male eyes it made them unreliable allies who did not deserve positions of authority.[26]

Cunningham had even semiseriously suggested in 1922 that Democratic women would be justified in refusing to work for the party, or deserting to the GOP, if Democratic politicians continued to appoint mediocre women to leadership. "It doesn't do a mite of good to say nobly we ought to stand by the party no matter who is in charge of the work," she wrote indignantly to Dorothy Brown, "the practical fact is we will not do it." The appointment of former suffragist Emily Newell Blair to oversee the women's side of the Democratic Party had stayed those rebellious thoughts, but in the 1924 election Cunningham did choose independent partisanship. She was a "partizan Democrat" for McAdoo in June, and in November deserted the Texas Democratic Party to vote for the better-qualified Republican gubernatorial candidate.[27]

The Texas governor's race pitted organized women's old enemy, James Ferguson, against the Ku Klux Klan, a choice many of the former suffragists found insupportable. The Klan backed Judge Felix Robertson for governor, and they dominated that spring's precinct, county, and state Democratic conventions. Ferguson wanted to regain the office from which he had been ousted in 1917, but the articles of impeachment barred him from running again. He circumvented the legal obstacle by entering his wife, Miriam, in the crowded Democratic primary in his stead and running her campaign. Her husband's supporters gave Miriam Ferguson, a home-focused woman who had not been a suffragist or club activist, enough votes to force a runoff primary between her and Robertson. The Fergusons made opposition to the "invisible empire" the essence of their platform, and the Klan became the central issue of the gubernatorial campaign.[28]

Considering "Fergusonism" distinctly the lesser of the two evils, prominent women, including Jessie Daniel Ames and state LWV President Helen Moore, announced their support for Miriam Ferguson. Cunningham, detesting the Klan, had done the same, "in a very small way," by writing letters from Washington. With the support of most of the progressive Democrats who had worked to impeach her husband, Miriam Ferguson decisively defeated Robertson for the Democratic nomination and showed that the KKK was not politically invincible. After Cunningham returned to Texas in September, she assured a curious Belle Sherwin that Miriam Ferguson would probably be "a fairly good executive, quite as good as any man we have had in Texas for a number of years." Despite her husband's backing from the liquor interests, she had imposed strict prohibition in the governor's mansion and "has a reputation of her own as being rather clear-headed and having a firm personality." "I for one," she added in a tantalizingly vague reference to her own marriage, "could not consistently hold a woman responsible for the iniquities of her husband."[29]

Seven weeks later Cunningham changed her mind. Bolting the Texas Democratic Party, she announced that she would vote in the general election for the Republican candidate, George C. Butte, dean of the University of Texas School of Law. Under ordinary circumstances, the winner of the Democratic primary hardly bothered to campaign against the token Republican opposition, but the choice between the Fergusons and the Klan had split the party. Anti-Ferguson Democrats, calling themselves the Good Government Democratic League of Texas, announced that they would campaign and vote for

Butte. The unexpected momentum for Butte prompted James Ferguson to launch a campaign of demagoguery on his wife's behalf, undermining Cunningham's faith that Miriam Ferguson could keep her promise to be governor in her own right.

In addition to ridiculing the esteemed Dr. Butte in classic "Farmer Jim" style, Ferguson disingenuously accused Republicans and disaffected Democrats of being Ku Kluxers. ("Think of *me!*" Cunningham moaned to Dorothy Brown.) By the end of October the campaign had become for Cunningham a question of whether party loyalty should matter more than moral and ethical standards. In a public statement addressed to women voters, she asserted that voting for "candidates who will not recognize public office as a public trust" betrayed democratic government. "Where the lines are clearly drawn between right and wrong, every courageous citizen is under a moral obligation to stand up and be counted on the side of right."[30]

Cunningham's "frantic-last-minute-pulled-in-by-the-hair efforts to elect a Republican governor in Texas" fell short of success, but Butte polled four times the vote that the GOP candidate had mustered in 1922. Jane McCallum implied that women's ballots contributed significantly to the total, although many men found that "the party collar was too firmly fixed around their own necks for them to join with their independent spouses."[31] Cunningham wore the Republican collar loosely; she was irritated with the GOP for not making a more vigorous effort to defend itself against Democratic calumny and concluded that the minority party was more interested in handling national patronage than winning elections. The Texas Democratic Party had temporarily forfeited her support, but the Republicans had not won it; she voted for a principle instead of a party.

CUNNINGHAM'S INVOLUNTARY RETURN TO TEXAS DID NOT IMMEDIATELY terminate her link to the national LWV. The board was not willing to let her resign as second vice president before her term expired; at its request, she remained in office in an advisory capacity. From New Waverly, she wrote two pamphlets, "Shall We Have a Membership Drive?" and "Writing a Constitution," for the organization department and outlined a program for a regional directors' conference at the end of the year. Her final recommendation called for breaking the regional administrative structure into smaller units, increasing the number of districts from seven to eight.[32]

At the same time, she tried to revitalize the declining and dispirited Texas LWV. At the November 1924 state convention, Helen Moore reluctantly agreed to another term as president because no one else was willing to take the office. Had she declined, Moore wrote Belle Sherwin, "the burden would have fallen on Mrs. Cunningham . . . and I could not with a clear conscience unload the work of the League in Texas on her." It was Cunningham, however, who prepared a month-by-month schedule of work for 1924–1925 adopted in convention, hoping that it would be a "blood transfusion."[33]

To lift her own spirits, weighed down by family worries, she emulated the "modern" young women who pursued female emancipation through social freedoms rather than political rights. Following the new fashion (and perhaps her nieces' example) she bobbed her auburn hair daringly short. More adventurously still for a forty-two-year-old woman, she learned to drive. Women drivers were no longer the curiosity they had been before World War I, but they were still a decided minority, especially outside urban areas. Cunningham must have been one of the few women in New Waverly mastering this new skill, and she enjoyed it. Having only put the car into a ditch once, run into two other vehicles, and stalled it twice in the sand, she was "getting on very well," she joked to Dorothy Brown. "You've no idea what a cheerful and exciting interest it is in my life. I recommend it highly to all the forlorn and broken hearted of the earth!"[34]

Her return to Texas enabled Cunningham to take up an interrupted interest in prison reform, a longstanding concern of women's voluntary associations. In 1918, after winning the fight for primary suffrage, she had tried unsuccessfully to get a woman appointed to the Penitentiary Commission and had targeted prison reform as the "next 'big job' in Texas." She wanted to see a "general overhauling . . . according to the most modern ideas available." Like most southern states, Texas incarcerated the largest part of its prison population on plantation-style "farms," where the main concern was not rehabilitation but saving the taxpayers money. Convicts were forced to raise cotton and other marketable crops in order that the state might recoup as much as possible of the cost of feeding and housing them. Living conditions were usually primitive and unhealthy and punishments brutal.[35]

Advocates of "progressive penology" viewed such systems as both inhumane and ineffective in preparing inmates to return to society. In 1920 the Texas LWV, under Cunningham and Jessie Daniel Ames, had pressed Governor Hobby to invite the National Committee on Prisons and Prison Labor to undertake a scientific survey of the state's penal system. Early in 1923, while Cunningham was in Washington, a Texas Committee on Prisons and Prison Labor (CPPL) finally formed. Elizabeth Speer, who had worked closely with her on the 1918 women's anti-vice crusade, was named executive secretary. Under CPPL pressure, the Texas legislature authorized the prison survey but refused to fund it. While the organization scrambled to raise private financing, Cunningham had assisted from afar, helping to draw in former attorney general Thomas Watt Gregory, who was returning to Houston.[36]

After her own return to Texas in 1924, Cunningham served concurrently as chair of the TLWV's Committee on Prison Reform and as a member of the CPPL executive committee. Old colleagues from the pre-war voluntary association network also held prominent CPPL positions, including Jessie Daniel Ames, who was the recording secretary, and Jane McCallum. When the prison survey was completed, Elizabeth Speer named Cunningham to choose and chair a committee to present the findings to the legislature in 1925 and to lobby for remedial legislation. Cunningham had no illusions about the undertaking. Prison reform was "a frightfully big piece of work . . . and it can easily absorb all that all of us are and have and still be unfulfilled unless the Lord Himself will perform a miracle."[37]

The CPPL report called for numerous changes, including a professional administrator to replace the politically appointed prison commission, vocational training for prisoners, and the abolition of physical punishment. But the dominant issue was replacing the abusive commercial farms with a single prison facility to be built near Austin. Governor Miriam Ferguson immediately fulfilled organized women's misgivings about her by vetoing a relocation bill, claiming the state could not afford the expense. The CPPL managed to secure some administrative changes, but its continuing pressure on the conservative and tight-fisted legislature failed to bring about significant reform. Cunningham was too much of a political realist to be surprised: "With the Fergusons back in power, *we* are just a lot of po' miserable sinners again."[38]

Personal and professional frustrations also depressed her. She carried most of the burden of nursing her mother, whose condition did not improve. Sallie Fisher was probably slipping into dementia, but Cunningham believed that her mother would benefit if she could be treated by a nerve specialist and live in quieter surroundings. She herself was physically and financially drained. Summer would bring her sister Marion from Galveston to relieve her briefly, and Cunningham longed to make a trip to Austin, but she could afford neither the train ticket nor the clothes. She needed and wanted a job that would take her away from New Waverly and enable her to hire the care she desired for Sallie.[39]

A promising opportunity opened up in the summer of 1925. Helen Hamilton Gardener, whom Woodrow Wilson had appointed the first woman member of the Civil Service Commission in 1920, was planning to retire because of failing health and hoped to see Cunningham installed in her place. A NAWSA vice president, the venerable Gardener had been vice-chair of the Congressional Committee and one of its most valuable members. Now she reminded Cunningham that "I have always said that when I went out of this job either you or Maud Wood Park were the only two people that I knew that I would be happy to leave in it." The civil service had been created to fill offices through merit rather than party patronage, and for women reformers, the commissionership was nearly a sacred trust. Gardener wanted it occupied by "a woman who won't be stampeded by men, one whom men wouldn't dare ask to do a dishonest thing, and yet whose tact, finesse and agreeable qualities wouldn't let the men know that she was brow-beating them."[40]

Park and Carrie Chapman Catt also wrote to ask if Cunningham would be willing to be a candidate, a prospect that she received with mixed emotions. Extremely flattered that three distinguished colleagues valued her abilities so highly, she nevertheless doubted that she had a realistic chance of winning the appointment. "Common sense *is* common sense, isn't it?" she told Park, pointing out that she was not the kind of Democrat likely to find favor with the Republican White House. Since the other two commissioners were Republicans, President Coolidge was required to appoint a Democrat, but he was likely to prefer an easterner "with a bit of tariff protected industry in her background." But, unwilling to say no to Gardener and honored by the support of "you three wonderful women," she pronounced herself game for the attempt.[41]

Gardener, who had decided that she would formally ask the President to consider appointing Cunningham when she sent in her resignation, began mapping strategy from her hospital bed. But she died suddenly, without having tendered her resignation or her recommendation to President Coolidge. Her plans for "just the right kind of campaign" devolved on her secretary, Rena B. Smith, and Maud Wood Park, both of whom were determined to carry out her wishes. Park wrote immediately to the President, informing him of Gardener's unfulfilled intentions and Cunningham's qualifications and followed up with a visit to the Summer White House in Massachusetts. She and Catt also sent letters to Senator Charles Curtis, the Republican whip.[42]

Cunningham, given the assignment of generating GOP support from Texas for her appointment, secured the endorsement of the state's lone Republican Congressman. Influential friends approached the Republican National Committeeman and contacted George Butte, who had been rewarded for his gubernatorial race with an appointment as attorney general of Puerto Rico. In Washington, Elizabeth Hauser, secretary of the LWV, and Rena Smith planned strategy in consultation with the two incumbent civil service commissioners, who also backed Cunningham.[43]

The position paid $6,500 annually and was one of the highest to which a woman had been appointed in government. Coolidge had announced that he would definitely choose another woman, and the number of names quickly multiplied. Cunningham soon found herself one of a half-dozen candidates, including Lida Hafford, director of the General Federation of Women's Clubs (which had endorsed Cunningham), Ethel Smith of the Women's Trade Union League, and Jessie Dell, a founding member of the National Woman's Party (NWP) and chair of its Government Workers' Council.[44]

Rena Smith dismissed Dell, a Georgia Democrat who had worked for twenty-five years in the War Department, as "an $1800 clerk" who lacked the appropriate professional standing. The NWP, however, backed her candidacy much more skillfully than the LWV advocated Cunningham's.[45] While Rena Smith and Maud Wood Park concentrated on the Democratic leadership in Congress, the NWP lobbied the GOP, with which it had close ties, mindful that Coolidge would be most receptive to a Democrat recommended by his fellow Republicans. Securing the powerful Republican senator Reed Smoot to sponsor Dell's candidacy gave the NWP an invaluable advantage. The organization itself worked as a political machine, gathering letters of endorsement for Dell from Republican women in its state branches.[46] The decentralized and nonpartisan LWV could do nothing similar for Cunningham.

Although she tried to keep her expectations realistically low, Cunningham could not quite repress her hopes. "I want it very hard but . . . I want it for very low reasons!" she admitted. Her family had finally agreed that she could take her mother and go seek her fortune. The civil service commissionership would be "a nice quiet fortune," a job that she could do in Washington with a salary large enough to cover proper care for her mother. When Coolidge announced at the end of the summer that he would appoint Dell, Cunningham was not surprised, but in spite of herself she was disappointed. "I *think* I'll get over it — long about the time I'm seventy odd," she wrote glumly to Jane McCallum.[47]

THE FRUSTRATION AND LACK OF DIRECTION THAT DOGGED Cunningham's personal life in the mid-1920s likewise affected the women's movement. Observing that women voted in smaller numbers than men and that politics appeared unchanged, journalists and political analysts pronounced suffrage a failure. No female voting bloc had materialized, although NAWSA had always contended that suffragists did not expect — or desire — one. The *Woman's Journal* had tried to debunk the idea in 1912 by polling state suffrage presidents on their preferences in the presidential election; it found 17 for Wilson, 13 for Roosevelt, 3 for Taft, and 1 each supporting the Socialist and Prohibitionist candidates. By 1924 politicians had grasped that women, like men, divided along class and ethnic lines and posed no special electoral threat. Party leaders ceased to respond to women's demands for more committee representation, and lawmakers rejected their attempts to influence policy. The LWV's string of legislative successes ended: over its protests, Congress reduced funding for the Women's and Children's Bureaus, and renewal of the Sheppard-Towner appropriation had to overcome a Senate filibuster. (In 1927 it was funded for the last time and marked for expiration in 1929.)[48]

As a Democrat, Cunningham also endured the doldrums of a decade of Republican ascendancy. Out of power since 1920, the Democrats were divided, demoralized, and financially distressed. The party's women's division, always a low priority, suffered most. In the retrenchment following the 1920 defeat, the Democratic National Committee allowed the Women's Bureau to lapse, curtailing office space and destroying files; when Emily Newell Blair was appointed to take charge of women's work in 1922, she had to start from scratch. The Republican landslide of 1924 repeated the scenario. The party again compressed the Women's Bureau and destroyed Blair's files to save the cost of storage space.[49]

By that time, however, Blair had enlisted a group of Washington-based Democratic women in founding another organization to promote the party. Early in May 1922 she had dinner with Cunningham and Caroline Reilley, another LWV staffer, and talked over her plans for organizing Democratic women. Blair's vision included opening a house in Washington to serve as "a Democratic gathering place to tie together the Hill and the National Committee." Cunningham pronounced it "a splendid idea," but because she was an LWV officer she refrained from taking part in the preliminary planning that summer at Florence Jaffray Harriman's townhouse.[50] The Woman's National Democratic Club was officially organized in November, and by the end of 1923 fifty women, including Cunningham, had paid the $100 fee that entitled them to the status of founding members. The club opened formally in January 1924 in a run-down rented row house on Connecticut Avenue with Harriman as president. Blair, by then the DNC's first vice-chair, was secretary, and former First Lady Edith Bolling Wilson headed the board of governors.[51]

Members included both the wives of prominent Democratic politicians, who contributed their own furniture and china to equip the house, and serious party activists. The clubwomen aimed to do educational work for the party, host social gatherings, and maintain a headquarters for the Democratic women's organizations that Emily Newell Blair was nurturing in the states. Like the Democratic Party itself, however, the WNDC suffered from lack of leadership and money. Although Blair continued to have charge of women's work, she was called home to Missouri by domestic responsibilities after the 1924 election and was in Washington only intermittently thereafter.[52] The WNDC was not attracting enough new members to meet operating expenses, and the work of organizing Democratic women languished.

Blair, however, was not willing to give up. In the spring of 1925, she approached Minnie Fisher Cunningham about taking charge of the WNDC. Cunningham expressed tentative interest, provided that the club was planning "a real piece of work," but nothing happened for several months. Although DNC Chairman Clem Shaver agreed in principle to hiring an executive officer, he would not allow Blair to raise the salary as a separate fund. While the two negotiated, the WNDC ran out of money and the clubhouse doors closed; Florence Harriman's personal loan of $2,000 paid the outstanding bills and overdue rent. In late October the board of governors authorized Blair to appeal to the DNC to underwrite the club's expenses and pay the salary of a resident executive officer, specifying that the position be offered to Cunningham.[53]

Blair went personally to Texas to plead the WNDC's case with Jesse Jones, the Houston multimillionaire who served as the DNC's finance director. She came away with the promise of $1,000 a month for ten months—and in retrospect thought Jones probably conceded because he was glad to get rid of her so easily. Half of the money was to be paid to Cunningham in salary and half to support the club directly. Jones and Shaver donated part of the sum themselves and raised the rest.[54] When Cunningham arrived in Washington at the beginning of December 1925, she presented to the board of governors a three-part plan of work that laid out a program, a financial policy and tentative operating budget, and suggestions for expansion. She was eager to begin, but the women seemed in no hurry to reopen the clubhouse. After living for thirteen days at the Mayflower Hotel, she astonished the board by moving into the chilly house alone and catching cold as she scrubbed and mopped to make it habitable.[55]

As executive officer, Cunningham was the club's manager and spokeswoman. Her first task was to put the WNDC's business affairs on a sound footing and oversee an expansion of its activities; she, not Blair, spent and accounted for the DNC money. Second, she was to act as Blair's representative in Washington, in effect, to take de facto charge of women's work for the Democratic Party. In Blair's words, Cunningham was brought in "to save the Club." Cunningham assessed the situation with characteristic humor and pragmatism: the Democratic women were depressed and lethargic, and her job was to "poke them up."[56] For the next two years, she and Blair did the work of the party's dismantled Women's Bureau indirectly, through the WNDC.

To attract publicity and build membership, Cunningham worked closely with the program committee to structure a series of weekly program luncheons and forum dinners. Held on Wednesday afternoons and Saturday evenings, they were occasions for guest speakers to discuss current events, Democratic policies, and world affairs.[57] She quickly revived the defunct newsletter that Blair had established for the women's division; the DNC had stopped funding it after the 1924 election debacle. Renamed *The Bulletin*, it debuted in February 1926, reporting on Democratic policies, the status of legislation on Capitol Hill, and the WNDC's activities and ambitions. Former editor Marion Banister wrote glowingly in the first issue that since Cunningham, "one of the best known organizers in the country," had come to take charge of the club, the rebirth of the *Bulletin* was one of the "miracles" she had performed. Over the next decade the WNDC polished and expanded the publication until, as the *Democratic Digest*, it again became the DNC's official newsletter.[58]

The *Bulletin* was one of a cluster of new WNDC outreach initiatives to women's Democratic clubs in the states. The first issue announced that the Club had set up a speakers' register, an information service, and a bureau that would assist local clubs in program or special event planning. By March, Cunningham was proposing a trial campaign service to be offered for six months during election years. For a fee of $10, every officer in each participating club would receive copies of *The Bulletin*, which would carry special news from the Democratic congressional and senatorial campaign committees. Clubs would also be entitled to request advisory service, by mail, on campaign organization problems and on setting up an autumn–winter program. Cunningham's objective was to gauge potential demand for such services; if clubs proved indifferent or the WNDC found the election service burdensome, it could disappear after October 31 without explanation or "any loss of dignity" to the WNDC.[59]

Cunningham literally worked herself to exhaustion and had to spend several weeks in a Washington sanitarium in the spring of 1926.[60] The pressure of an election year left no time for a lingering recovery. Acting in Emily Newell Blair's absence, as director of women's work for the DNC, she set up the WNDC's first summer training school for political organizers. Each member club was entitled to send a representative to the week-long short courses offered between July 6 and August 28 — one hundred women attended in all. The topics were permanent club organization, campaign machinery, political parties, and the federal government in action (which included observation visits to government departments). Cunningham taught the sections on permanent organization and campaign machinery, and served as the seminar's public relations spokeswoman. She reported happily to Blair in late August that the school had concluded in "rather a blaze of glory," with newspaper people at the clubhouse nearly every afternoon: "I've talked with them until I am *dead!*"[61]

A paradoxical situation thus developed. Although women were losing ground within the party structures, the WNDC became de facto headquarters for the Democratic National Committee. Too financially strapped to maintain its own offices, the DNC stored its archives and desks in the clubhouse.[62] Under the guidance of Blair and Cunningham, the WNDC served as the party's educational arm and organizational hub. While the Democrats were out of power, the volunteers at the WNDC articulated the party's message and reached out to an expanding network of state Democratic women's clubs. Equally significant, the WNDC chose its own leaders and planned its own agenda rather than having both dictated by male party heads. Clem Shaver had approved Cunningham's appointment, but she was Blair's choice, and the WNDC elected its own president and board of directors. Assiduously nurturing good relations with Shaver, Cunningham used DNC money to support a women's organization run by the women themselves at time when the party-controlled women's division had been shut down.

During the 1926 election campaign Cunningham substituted for Emily Newell Blair as the official voice of Democratic women. She took Blair's place when the *Woman Citizen* offered Blair and Sallie Hert, her counterpart on the Republican National Committee, space to present the issues. "Red Herrings," which appeared with Blair's authorization, charged that "Republican prosperity" and the "Coolidge economy" were boastful diversions to draw voter attention away from the GOP's high tariff and taxation policies.[63] At the same time, Clem Shaver chose her to lead off for the Democrats at the first of a series of radio addresses. Cunningham gave a passionate Jeffersonian defense of the Democrats as the party of the people, while reminding listeners that the GOP propounded "a centralized form of government administered by a chosen, privileged class." Paired against Republican Congressman Frederick Zihlman of Maryland, she spoke as a Democrat for the party, and not as a woman to the female faithful. She admitted to Jane McCallum that the prospect unnerved her, but she could hardly refuse because "Mr. S[haver] had just done a lot of things I wanted *him* to do."[64]

For Cunningham, working with the socialites and congressional wives— the "great ladies," she privately called them—who made up the WNDC's board of governors was much like her experience with the clubwomen suffragists in Texas a decade earlier. Once again, she was the energetic visionary prodding the others to think bigger and do more. She and the DNC money would "expire" on October 1, 1926, and planning in advance, she had set up a sinking fund from entrance fees and donations that could be used to meet emergencies, pay the club out of debt, and purchase a permanent home. She was confident that, if necessary, the newly solvent WNDC could "proceed 'as is'" without the subsidy—and equally convinced that it should aim instead for continued expansion. She had worked out a proposed budget for 1927, estimating operating expenses at $13,000, and laid it before the board of governors in April 1926, urging "that we ought to go to the men *with a plan*" and ask for further financial support. "There sat Mr. Shaver and Mr. Jones having already manifested ten thousand dollars worth of interest in our work— and manifesting a genuine approval of the Club in general," she recalled. "It seemed frightful to me to let it slip."[65]

Nevertheless, the board adjourned for the summer without acting or even sending formal thanks to the DNC for the past year's funding. Only Cunningham appeared to grasp that the funding would not be renewed automatically and that the DNC's cooperation had to be cultivated. With the board members scattered to cool northern resorts, it was left to Blair and Cunningham to rescue the situation. Clem Shaver promised Cunningham that the DNC would cover whatever expenses the club could not meet in 1927, and Blair persuaded him to continue underwriting Cunningham's salary.[66] When the board reconvened in the fall, it elected her to a seat and moved a special vote of thanks for her "untiring devotion."[67]

Cunningham was likewise the moving force behind the WNDC's move into larger quarters. The club was outgrowing the rented house on Connecticut Avenue, which was both expensive and shabby—pieces of tin were nailed over the mouse holes in the kitchen floor. Cunningham and Blair believed that a bigger house with more room rents and a larger membership would help the club become self-supporting. An investigating committee had been appointed in June 1926, with Cunningham as the member responsible for house hunting. By January 1927 the Connecticut Avenue house was proving too small to accommodate the work, but the owner of a property at 16th Street and Massachusetts Avenue, to whom the club had made an offer, had changed his mind about selling. "Three-fourths of my time I spend looking at houses and talking to people about houses and the other fourth I spend reporting to Committee on the status of the situation," she informed Blair gloomily, "because by now everyone is so eager to move that we can hardly bear to live in this place another month."[68]

In early spring the housing problem committee recommended a spacious three-story, turreted brick dwelling at 1526 New Hampshire Avenue, a block from Dupont Circle. It was assessed at $110,000, and the club was far short of the required down payment. Despite the housing committee's enthusiasm, some of the executive committee and board of governors were apprehensive; the WNDC had only just managed to become solvent, and no one knew what its future income would be. Cunningham, who was by then the assistant treasurer as well as resident director, argued tenaciously that the house was ideal and the purchase price reasonable.[69]

Margaret Meigs resolved the dilemma by volunteering to lend the club $20,000, and as Cunningham described the meeting, "the 'pressure of public opinion,' which was me, and the 'money power,' which was Mrs. Meigs, won out." When the WNDC moved in May to the late-Victorian mansion, which it still occupies, Cunningham oversaw every detail, even revamping the committee responsible for meals and servants. "Now then, take your pen in hand and nominate for the 'ignoble prize' everything that ought to be revised," she wrote happily to Blair. "We *gotter* be stylish in this house. O Emily, it is *grand*!!!"[70]

Acting as the WNDC's attorney in wrapping up the final details of the purchase, Cunningham also chaired the Ways and Means Committee, charged with drafting a plan to pay off the debt. Her particular enthusiasm was inviting wealthier women to purchase lifetime memberships. By mid-May she had secured four and was intently seeking a fifth in order to take up the first $5,000 note immediately and save the interest payments.[71] Her financial reports for the fall of 1927 showed that the WNDC, which two years earlier had been temporarily closed and nearly bankrupt, was generating enough income to cover operating expenses and had accrued $5,000 toward repaying Margaret Meigs's loan. Clem Shaver and Jesse Jones signified their approval a few months later with a contribution of $13,000 toward the mortgage.[72]

As her second year at the WNDC drew to a close in 1927, Cunningham had already decided that it would be her last: she was going back to Texas to run for the U.S. Senate. In a special report to the board that November, she summed up the WNDC's accomplishments and addressed its future needs. The club had "far exceeded" the ambitious goals it had set for 1926–1927, holding a full schedule of educational meetings with programs and publicity that had produced "substantial evidence of approval from our brother man." Financially, the year had been a resounding success. The club had adopted a budget of $13,000, even though its resources at the time had consisted of only $4,000 anticipated from 1927 dues; with two months left in the year, revenues had already exceeded the budget by $11,000.

The WNDC's newfound fiscal stability cushioned the news that the DNC was unable to offer more than limited financial support in 1928. Cunningham had already dissuaded the executive committee from dropping publication of The Bulletin, which the DNC money had been subsidizing, arguing that it was an indispensable link to the membership. Now she contended that the WNDC was strong enough to assume all operating expenses except the bookkeeper's salary and her own position—which she believed could be dispensed with temporarily and the slack taken up by the board and the young women who had been her assistants. She had already made up a list of the individuals who could assume her work on the half-dozen committees on which she served.[73]

The WNDC parted with her reluctantly. The board asked Clem Shaver whether the DNC would underwrite Cunningham's "services" again if she became available. The executive committee repeated the request early in 1928, hopeful that Cunningham might be lured back after the Texas primary to help with the fall election campaign.[74] In January 1928 she presided over an all-day meeting of some fifty Democratic women from across the country, who gathered at the clubhouse to discuss organizing women for the upcoming election. Her final public event was the District of Columbia LWV's annual political forum dinner, at which she explained her political platform to an audience that included women prominent in politics and public administration. She left the WNDC in February, expecting to return to Washington in 1929 as the junior senator from Texas.[75]

For Cunningham and other Progressive-Era reformers, the transition from voluntarist to party politics was a sustained tug-of-war between contrasting political styles and values. Politicians pulled them into the existing party structures, granting token representation but not real power and demanding fealty to the party line. Women pushed back, introducing candidate questionnaires and voter education guides into election campaigns and emphasizing issues over rigid party loyalty. In moving from the LWV to the WNDC, Cunningham did not so much cross a political divide as narrow her focus from voter education for everyone to voter education for Democrats. She made the transition easily and was successful at the WNDC because the club, despite its partisan nature, operated in the familiar voluntary association mode. All of its functions served the common goal of educating on the issues, specifically the Democratic position on the issues. Though a spokeswoman for the party, Cunningham operated from a comfortable female space that her male counterparts found both useful and nonthreatening. Running for office was a transition of a different magnitude, one that would necessitate competing with men for power on their own terrain.

"Too Gallant a Walk"?
Running for the Senate, 1928

MINNIE FISHER CUNNINGHAM WAS THE FIRST TEXAS WOMAN TO RUN FOR
the U.S. Senate, and she knew that victory was unlikely. Organized women's
success in lobbying their legislative agenda through Congress after suffrage
was not replicated in their electoral politics. Few women had won seats in the
House, and none in the Senate. As early as 1922, when six women lost Senate
races and all but one of 21 House candidates was defeated, the *Woman Citizen*
concluded that "the barriers in the way of women being elected to any political office are almost insurmountable. The dominant parties do not nominate
women for political office if there is a real chance of winning."[1]

Cunningham, then LWV executive secretary, was less discouraged. "Women
must expect to go slowly in overcoming the prejudices of the conservative element against women in obtaining high offices," she told a reporter, "and in
the meantime they can better train themselves to fit into those high offices
when the time comes."[2] If she had followed this counsel herself, she might
have run for the Texas Legislature from Walker County, where victory would
have been nearly certain. But Cunningham was already accustomed to the national stage and committed to a broader agenda. She watched in frustration
as fellow suffragists Anna Dickie Olesen of Minnesota, Jessie Jack Hooper of
Wisconsin, and Izetta Jewell Davis of West Virginia lost Senate races, while
politicians' widows and women who had been opposed or indifferent to suffrage won House seats.[3] The most galling counterfeminist victory of all was
Miriam Ferguson's election to the Texas governorship in 1924 as a stand-in for
her disgraced husband, Jim. She allowed him to run state affairs, with corruption and scandal as the result.

To friends who warned of the futility of running for the Senate, Cunningham cited Mrs. Ferguson as "probably *the* deciding factor" in her decision. "Fancy letting Ma Ferguson stand to the world as the type of woman who seeks and gets office in Texas," she complained to Jane McCallum from Washington, D.C. "I may not get it—almost certainly won't I guess—but by the great horn spoon I'm well enough known in the Americas and England (through the Pan-American Conference) to take the sting out of some of the ridicule we've gotten—and I simply do not know any other answer to make but to toss my hat in the ring." As an acknowledged leader of women, she felt compelled "to decide things on a higher ground than 'safety.' That Senatorial race is my one and only chance to pull up the standing of women candidates in Texas."[4]

Cunningham entered the race with significant assets. She was a practiced and effective public speaker, an experienced political strategist, and a national leader in the women's division of the Democratic Party. Nevertheless, being "the woman candidate" carried a multiplicity of negative consequences. The gender handicap deprived her of the kind of political and financial support that a male candidate could expect; she had to run a shoestring campaign, which relied on female volunteers instead of male sponsors. Her difficulties were unexpectedly compounded by the Democratic Party's contentious nomination of Al Smith for President. Smith's candidacy prompted an acrimonious debate over prohibition and pushed many dry Democrats—especially women—temporarily into the Republican fold.

Cunningham, however, made choices that influenced the campaign's outcome as decisively as gender prejudice and party disharmony. In the same way that many suffragists hoped that women's votes would "improve" politics, she believed that female candidates could raise the standard of political campaigning. She purposely structured her race as a challenge to the male-defined campaign paradigm, substituting an issue-oriented "female" political style for the male gladiator-style politics of personal attack. Hers would be the kind of educational, high-road campaign that she and other former suffragists believed voters really wanted instead of rhetorical combat and mudslinging. She intended to set a standard that public approval would compel other candidates to meet.

When Cunningham announced her candidacy, the *Dallas Morning News* observed that "friends are said to believe she will amass a huge feminine vote and that she is by far the most powerful woman politician in Texas." The *Houston Post-Dispatch* reacted more thoughtfully, noting that women voters had not shown any preference for female candidates. "But Mrs. Cunningham has one great distinction," the editor commented. "She is not proposing to ride into office on the coattails of any male relative, dead or repudiated. Her political capital will be her own record, and her ability to appeal to the voters for her own individual ability." Therefore "it will be interesting to see how a woman, admittedly of large capability in public leadership, fares at the hands of an electorate when she runs strictly on her own merits and without the 'pull' of a family relationship with some male politician."[5]

Whatever doubts she may have had about her electability, Cunningham was entirely confident that she was better qualified for the Senate than the incumbent, Earle B. Mayfield, for whom she had a long-standing distaste. Mayfield had been Texas Railroad Commissioner in 1919, when Congress passed the Nineteenth Amendment. He promptly requested a meeting with Cunningham and Jane McCallum at TESA headquarters and, without embarrassment, offered Cunningham a well-paid patronage job—as an oil pipeline engineer. The two women knew what was up: Mayfield was contemplating a run for governor and wanted Cunningham to influence the female vote. "Had some quiet fun over it," McCallum confided to her diary, praising Cunningham's incorruptibility. Their amused disdain deepened into real contempt when Mayfield won the U.S. Senate seat in 1922 with heavy backing from the Ku Klux Klan. Cunningham had followed the race from LWV headquarters in Washington, feeling guilty for "not stepping out on faith and running for the Senate myself."[6] In the ensuing six years, Mayfield had made a lackluster showing in the Senate and was politically vulnerable. He was likely to fall short of a majority in the primary and be forced into a runoff, where a strong challenger might finish him off.

Cunningham began planning her campaign well before she knew who else besides Mayfield would be running. Ultimately, there would be four other contenders: Congressman Tom Connally, Congressman Tom Blanton, former Congressman-at-large Jeff McLemore, and Colonel Alvin Owsley, a former American Legion commander. An experienced politician would have waited and sized up the field before making a decision, but Cunningham released a press announcement from the WNDC in July 1927, a full year before the primary. The following month she departed for a working vacation in Texas, where she made her first speech as a candidate. She also solicited advice and support from the men with whom she had collaborated during the progressive-prohibitionist crusades of the 1910s. None offered encouragement; the collective verdict was that a woman had no chance of being elected.[7]

Undaunted, she worked up a detailed campaign plan. The schedule called for sending out a letter requesting support to all her former associates—the old network of suffragists, reformers, and clubwomen—by the beginning of October. At the same time, she would issue an appeal to voters to pay their poll taxes. (The tax books would be open only between the end of October and the beginning of February, and those who failed to pay then would be barred, months later, from voting). A press release would go out before the end of November, along with another poll tax reminder. In January 1928, as she prepared to leave Washington, she mailed the press and her old voluntary association colleagues a full package of information: a summary of her platform; a reprint of the *Woman Citizen*'s announcement of her candidacy, which included a photo and short biography; and an invitation to her opening rally in March.[8]

Everything about the way Cunningham began her quest for the Senate indicated that she intended to run a campaign based on the values of the separate political tradition that women had developed while excluded from the ballot. Although observers in the 1920s did not speak of "gendered" political styles, they identified marked differences in the way men and women approached politics. Emily Newell Blair compared male political style to war: men relished proving their worthiness on the battleground and were perplexed and suspicious at women's preference for issue analysis over verbal combat. Eleanor Roosevelt, then a leader in the Women's Division of the New York State Democratic Committee, used a sports metaphor: men saw politics as a game to be played hard a few weeks a year, while women regarded it as a continuous pursuit of serious objectives.[9]

Blair dubbed male style the fight-game method and emphasized that men structured politics like combat because they enjoyed the contest of strength. It was not that women were incapable of being fighters. Ruth Hanna McCormick, who had learned political gamesmanship from her famous father, Senator Mark Hanna, was a notable example. But few women, Blair emphasized, liked a fight for its own sake. Most women came to politics from clubs and other voluntary associations and, consequently, brought a different perspective. They were accustomed to working cooperatively to advance a program, an approach that tended to value issues over partisanship. A political cartoon from the 1920s likened women's view of elections to choosing apples at a fruit stand. A woman labeled "intelligent voter" selected the best from both the Republican and Democratic baskets offered by the dismayed vendor, Mr. Partisan Politics.[10]

The corollary to intelligent voting was intelligent campaigning, which Cunningham intended to demonstrate. Deliberately rejecting the male fight-game approach, she chose the "program," or issues-oriented, philosophy of female voluntary association politics. If the male standard of political competition was to choose the strongest candidate, the female counterpoint was to select the smartest. Cunningham structured her campaign to give voters detailed information about her positions, thereby demonstrating that she was the most knowledgeable of the senatorial candidates—the best apple in the basket. She was the only one who wrote out a platform. Ten typewritten pages long and worthy of a party convention committee, it covered issues on which she would be expected to vote in the Senate. There was no doubt that she knew as much about policy as any of the men—and probably more.

She defended prohibition and denounced the Ku Klux Klan, the decade's most polarizing issues, but devoted much more of her platform to criticizing Republican pro-business policies that hurt working people. Taking the traditional Democratic stand against high tariffs, she charged that the GOP, under the guise of protecting "infant industries," was subsidizing special interests and raising consumer prices. Tariff reform was also central to her farm relief plank. Forced to pay more for manufactured goods in a protected market, the farmer had to sell in an unprotected one abroad, "and the economic stage is all set for his ruin."[11]

With populist fervor, she argued the need for publicly owned flood control and hydroelectric power dams, such as those at Muscle Shoals, Alabama, for which the federal government was seeking permanent operating authority. Republican administrations opposed such competition with private enterprise; Cunningham called for hydroelectric power that would "belong to the people—to you and me who own the government and all its works" rather than to profit-seeking utilities. She took another poke at the power of special interests in a plank called "secrecy in government," the Senate's practice of going into closed session to vote on presidential appointments. Railroad, trust, and tariff lobbyists were nominated to the federal commissions charged with regulating them and confirmed in closed sessions. As a consequence, "the country has no way of knowing which Senators cooperated to corrupt these government agencies." She promised to demand open, roll call votes.

Cunningham's platform dwelt at greatest length on foreign affairs, the Senate's special area of responsibility. She announced that she was "sorry and ashamed" that the United States did not belong to the League of Nations and praised the League's achievements toward preserving world peace. American foreign policy needed to be entirely rethought, she maintained, especially the tradition of heavy-handed intervention in Latin American affairs. With the interests of American investors in mind, President Coolidge had unilaterally dispatched thousands of Marines to combat an uprising against large landowners in Nicaragua, and Wall Street bankers were helping finance munitions for the antirevolutionaries. "Whose war *is* this?" she demanded, calling for withdrawal. "When did Congress vote to invade that sovereign state?"

To run her campaign, Cunningham chose three colleagues from the women's club and suffrage movements. Mrs. Sam J. Smith of Austin, campaign chair, was a district president of the Texas Federation of Women's Clubs and a former senatorial district chairwoman of the Texas Equal Suffrage Association. (Jane McCallum, more experienced and a closer friend, would probably have filled this position had she not been serving as secretary of state.) Ruby Neale Long, the former secretary of the Texas Committee on Prisons and Prison Labor, was the assistant director and handled Cunningham's itinerary.

Florence Floore, a TFWC past president and vice-chair of the GFWC board of trustees, served as treasurer.[12]

For campaign contributions, Cunningham relied on the network of LWV and Democratic women with whom she had worked in Washington. The locus of fundraising was not Texas but Boston, the home of Dorothy Kirchwey Brown, who was active in the Massachusetts Democratic Party as well as the national LWV. Brown began soliciting contributions from eastern women early in 1927 and continued until the end of the campaign, a task that turned out to be harder and less lucrative than she and Cunningham had anticipated. Donors included such noted former suffragists as Gertrude Foster Brown, Harriet Burton Laidlaw, Jessie Jack Hooper, and Mabel Willard, who had managed NAWSA's Suffrage House in Washington, D.C. Maud Wood Park and Belle Sherwin, ever mindful of the LWV's nonpartisan image, gave anonymously. Among the well-known Democratic names were Eleanor Roosevelt, Alice Brandeis, Elinor Morgenthau, and Woodrow Wilson's daughter, Jessie Sayre.[13]

In every sense, then, Cunningham's was a "female" campaign, funded and run by women and conducted in the educational, issues-focused style characteristic of women's voluntary associations. The only male Democrat who offered money and advice was Caswell Ellis, who had moved to Ohio and Case Western Reserve University. He and Mary sent $100, and Ellis, eager to reprise his old role as political adviser, began ruminating on "some possible lines of attack"—the fight-game style.[14]

For the first time in their friendship, Cunningham declined Ellis's advice. She had been his enthusiastic acolyte in 1918, when he designed a strategy of personal attack against the incumbent state superintendent of public instruction. "Didn't we hand poor old man Doughty one glorious *wallop?*" she exulted. "It's lots of fun to fight with you because you always win!"[15] In 1919 she had collaborated with him in a blame campaign against German-American voters, to explain away the defeat of the state suffrage amendment. During those years Cunningham and the TESA had been locked in a struggle for survival with powerful, well-funded, and often unscrupulous enemies. Bareknuckle tactics seemed justifiable: the fate of primary suffrage and the federal amendment was at stake. But suffragists had not sought the ballot in order to practice politics like the men they disdained. With the cause victorious, Cunningham felt free to abandon battlefield tactics. If voluntarist women were to remake electioneering in the image they wanted—serious, substantive, and civil—female candidates would have to show the way.

The correspondence between Cunningham and Ellis during the Senate race was a dialogue between male and female political styles. Ellis found nothing in her platform that he recognized as political strategy and pressed her to identify which constituencies she sought to win and her "bait" for each. "Are you pursuing a quiet still hunt, so as not to let the opposition think you are dangerous, or do you want to make a noise and attract more attention to you? Are you trying to get in on a conservative platform that will scare no one, or are you proposing a positive measure to get yourself differentiated clearly from the rest?" Arguing that she was offering nothing to stir voters' passions, he challenged her to defend her emphasis on such sober subjects as tariffs, trusts, and utilities. Cunningham refused to budge. The economic planks were her "pet children," she countered, "and I'll stand by them till the last vote is counted!"[16]

Unasked, Ellis drafted a campaign brochure in the "advertising" style by which candidates "sold" their personalities and virtues to the public.[17] Featuring a long and quite good biographical sketch of Cunningham, it compared her to Thomas Jefferson, Woodrow Wilson, and Texas's own Jim Hogg; like them, she was a breed apart from the politicians who filled public life with "hypocrisy, hot air, bunk and incompetence." Cunningham thanked him tactfully for "the excellent flattery" but never used it. Instead she designed a brochure that was the obverse of Ellis's sample, an LWV-style educational pamphlet, which devoted more space to her platform than to her biography.[18]

Still trying to be helpful and to put "pep and aggressiveness" into the campaign, Ellis suggested that Cunningham take advantage of the widespread desire to avoid another war and define herself as a peace innovator. She could promise to introduce a bill in the Senate to create a new cabinet post, Secretary of Peace, and move that at least one dollar be allocated to the Department of Peace for every hundred dollars authorized for war. Ellis even wrote out a sample campaign speech on the Peace Cabinet theme and suggested she use it verbatim.[19] Cunningham, perhaps not trusting herself, said nothing at all about this proposal.

On March 2, she opened her campaign in Huntsville, at the Walker County courthouse, with the chairman of the county Democratic Party presiding. State Senator W. L. Dean of Huntsville, an old friend and legislative ally during the suffrage fight, introduced her to the overflow crowd with a speech that recounted their former collaboration. The state press reported on her dress ("black crepe trimmed in lacy white and a black hat") as well as her speech and noted the rabbit's foot on a gold neck chain that her Washington friends had given her for luck. Only the unsophisticated reporter for the local weekly raised the gender stereotype, in the form of a lame compliment: "She appeared younger than one might expect a woman candidate for the Senate to be and less mannish and political looking."[20]

The hometown crowd gave Cunningham a standing ovation when she rose to speak, and she responded with a full explication of her platform. The *Huntsville Item* noted that she pledged to run a constructive rather than destructive campaign and "made no pronounced attacks on anyone, not even referring to Earle B. Mayfield, whose reelection she is opposing." The *Austin Statesman* reported the platform in full and asked, "Is this a warning to rival contenders for the senatorial prize that live issues must be discussed in the campaign from now on?" The opening was "a *gorgeous* success," the candidate bubbled to Caswell Ellis and Dorothy Brown. "Now that I've this thing launched, I find that I've a surprisingly good chance to win out."[21]

But before the campaign could gain momentum, Cunningham received word that her estranged husband, who had been ill for months with cirrhosis of the liver, was near death in Galveston. Although she and B. J. had been separated for ten years, nothing indicates that they ever considered divorce, and they seem to have been sporadically in touch. She was photographed at his company's summer watermelon party in 1925, and he never altered the will he had made early in their marriage making her his executrix and sole heir.[22] Apparently he had no other relatives, and she was still legally his wife. Being called to the deathbed of an estranged spouse was an ironic twist on the "family claim," a summons that a man in the midst of a political campaign might not have heeded, but Minnie suspended her schedule and went to Galveston.

Despite their long separation, B. J.'s death on March 20 filled her with an unexpected sense of loss, and the memory of his last painful days woke her at night for weeks. "I *miss* him so," she confided to Dorothy Brown. "Isn't that awful? And unexpected too." She mourned alone and went through the motions of resuming her campaign, longing "to go somewhere and find a hole and crawl into it."[23] Thirty years later, in the only public statement she ever made about B. J., she told an interviewer: "You know I can't talk very much about him. He was the best-hearted man, he was always helping people. He encouraged me in all my naughtiness and financed me in much of it."[24] Whatever their story, she kept it private to the last.

Just as she was beginning to recover her stride, the presidential nominating conventions intervened. The Democrats had been signaling for months that their party was polarized into wet and dry factions and that no candidate was likely to satisfy both. Cunningham's first choice, William Gibbs McAdoo, had been unable to build the momentum for another run. Her second, Senator Thomas Walsh of Montana (who reciprocated her esteem and told the *Boston Globe* that Cunningham was "easily the peer" of any of the men running in Texas), had done poorly in the primaries. New York Governor Alfred E. Smith emerged as the front-runner. Wet, Catholic, and nurtured by the Tammany Hall machine, Smith was an anathema in the rural, Protestant, dry South. While other dry Democrats were voicing doubts about supporting a potential Smith ticket, Cunningham had not yet made up her mind. She left open the door to desertion by telling a reporter that national welfare should come before party.[25]

Two prohibitionist women's organizations, however, were vigorously calling for principle over party loyalty. The National Woman's Democratic Law Enforcement League (NWDLEL) released a list of acceptable — dry — Democratic candidates, and the nonpartisan Woman's Christian Temperance Union (WCTU) issued lists for both parties.[26] The GOP chose Herbert Hoover, who was on the WCTU's list, at its Kansas City convention in mid-June and reaffirmed its commitment to prohibition. When the Democratic National Convention convened in Houston two weeks later, the NWDLEL and the Texas branch of the WCTU were a visible and vocal presence outside the hall; both organizations threatened to campaign for Hoover if Smith prevailed.[27] With no viable opposition, Smith won the nomination on the first ballot and then telegraphed his support for modifying the prohibition laws. The "bone-dry" southern element that had opposed him, with Texas Democrats in the lead, promptly bolted the party.[28]

Smith's candidacy posed a personal and political dilemma for Cunningham. Her eastern friends, women such as Eleanor Roosevelt, chair of the party's Women's Advisory Committee, and Dorothy Brown, backed Smith. But the dry, Quaker Hoover became the "woman's candidate," and the GOP actively courted the female vote. Cunningham's old mentors, Carrie Chapman Catt and Maud Wood Park, served on his advisory committee, and officers of numerous national women's organizations lent their signatures to Hoover campaign ads. Mrs. Clem Shaver of the NWDLEL (and wife of the DNC chairman) announced that anyone who backed Smith was a "booze-o-crat." The president of the Texas Women's Democratic Association, Mrs. Larry Mills, seconded the sentiment and urged the women of her organization not to support the platform and candidate of "Tammany's delegates."[29]

Although she felt no enthusiasm for Smith, Cunningham finally announced her support. Her campaign platform unsparingly indicted Republican policies; she could not, with any credibility, take refuge in the GOP. She was convinced, moreover, that the defecting "Hoovercrats" were deluding themselves. Keeping the Eighteenth Amendment from being repealed, she pointed out, "depends on the people you send to Congress because both great political parties are headed by men who do not care a snap about prohibition." The Republicans' poor enforcement record during their eight years in power testified "either to inefficiency or dishonesty" at the Justice and Treasury departments.[30]

Her decision to support the Smith ticket put Cunningham at odds with women whose support she needed. State WCTU president Lala Fay Watts, proclaiming that "organized motherhood is for Hoover," made good her vow to lead her followers out of the party. She called on WCTU women to organize Democratic Hoover clubs in every county and announced that field secretaries would canvass the state for the Republican nominee. Watts, Mills, and Gertrude McWhirter Bloodworth, the state's outgoing Democratic National

Committeewoman, helped organize the convention of bone-dry defectors, who met in Dallas on July 17, to come up with a plan for carrying the state against Smith.[31]

Cunningham was ensnared in an uncomfortable irony. The bolters followed the same principle that she had embraced during the 1924 gubernatorial election, when she had encouraged other women to put principle above party and had refused to support Miriam Ferguson.[32] Women who took seriously the concept of "independent partisanship" could hardly do otherwise when their party nominated a candidate whose views offended them. Some planned to sit out the Democratic primary in order to vote for Hoover in the fall. Others admired the Ku Klux Klan's vigilantism against bootleggers and backed Mayfield, the Klan-approved candidate. It was clear that Cunningham had lost an important segment of the female vote when Gertrude Bloodworth, a WCTU district president who had been prominent in the Klan, assessed the gubernatorial candidates in a press statement. Cunningham, she said noncommittally, was "a Christian woman," before praising Earle Mayfield as "a good senator" who "stands for our principles."[33]

By the time she confronted the Smith dilemma, Cunningham was losing momentum as a candidate. Her bereavement had taken her out of the public eye for part of the spring, and she had suspended campaigning again during the Democratic National Convention in order to assist Emily Newell Blair in Houston.[34] The campaign badly needed workers, publicity, and especially money. Dorothy Brown continued to solicit funds from prominent Democratic women in the East, but most of the contributions were small. Elinor Morgenthau and Eleanor Roosevelt, for example, wrote apologetically that women's work for Al Smith in New York State had first claim on their funds.[35]

Adele Clark, a Virginia suffragist who had succeeded Cunningham as second vice president of the LWV, and Dorothy Brown took the initiative in revitalizing the campaign. Brown and Clark attended the Democratic National Convention to help present the LWV's platform proposals, and before leaving Houston they met with Cunningham and her friends and mapped out a new strategy.[36] They suggested assembling a committee of sponsors, fifty to a hundred prominent citizens (a number that proved impossible to get) who would allow their names to be used on campaign publicity and serve as "disseminating points" for information. Nell Doom, an old friend from the Austin Equal Suffrage Association, and Jane McCallum sent out the telegrams of invitation and follow-up letters. Assistant Campaign Manager Ruby Neale Long, who had de facto charge of operations, scrapped the unfulfilled county organizing plan and drafted a simplified one, which relied on informal committees rather than formal campaign clubs.[37]

In the reassessment, neither the candidate nor her female advisors ever considered changing the issues-based, educational style of the campaign.

Cunningham had vowed "to deal honestly and squarely with the people," and she believed that intelligence and civility would win votes. Her LWV colleagues concurred completely. Dorothy Brown forwarded the advice of the Massachusetts LWV's publicity director, who suggested that campaign workers emphasize two things: that Cunningham was campaigning on issues rather than personalities and that the "distinctive contribution" of newly enfranchised women was the return of statesmanship to politics. Adele Clark clipped and underlined a notice that credited Cunningham with "placing the race for the senatorship on a higher plane and politics in general in a more refined light by her candidacy."[38]

The Texas press, while invariably headlining Cunningham as "the woman candidate," responded favorably to her educational approach, reporting her speeches in detail and noting that she seldom mentioned her rivals by name. She concluded every address with an open forum, answering questions about her platform and public policy, an innovation that made the pages of the *Christian Science Monitor*. She was elated when the *Fort Worth Star-Telegram* and the *Dallas Morning News* assigned special female correspondents to cover the rejuvenated campaign. One of them was "almost *dead* of it," the candidate wrote cheerfully to Dorothy Brown, "but her stuff has rec'd the same recognition and placing as the paper's star political writer so she will die *happy*! You see she's a 'first' as well as *me*."[39]

In the days before air conditioning and interstate highways, campaigning for a midsummer primary meant enduring weeks of ninety-degree temperatures and miles of dusty roads. Traveling up to 150 miles a day in a small Ford bought especially for the campaign, Cunningham demonstrated, for any who doubted, that she had as much stamina as the male contenders. She even turned the car's inevitable tire punctures into opportunities to shake hands with other motorists stopped in city traffic and to attach her stickers to their vehicles. In contrast to Miriam Ferguson, who had let her husband do most of her campaign speaking, Cunningham made as many as four speeches a day to good crowds. "After every meeting, men have told me that if I am physically able to make the campaign all over the state in the hot weather, I will certainly be in the second primary because of the platform upon which I am running," she reported to a friend.[40]

The Senate race was in reality two parallel campaigns, structured by contrasting female and male political styles. Cunningham talked only issues and legislation: the Fordney-McCumber Tariff, the McNary-Haugen farm bill, the Esch-Cummins Act, the proposed Box bill to limit immigration from Mexico (which she opposed). To make her case for government-owned hydroelectric power generators, she cited statistics from Canada, where farm families lighted their homes and barns, milked cows, churned cream, and washed clothes and dishes for just over $3 a month. A campaign poster designed by women at the

Austin headquarters proclaimed her "the brainiest speaker of them all." The male candidates, by contrast, traded accusations and insults in a classic demonstration of the male fight-game style. They charged each other variously with belonging to the Ku Klux Klan, doing nothing in Congress, misusing the franking privilege, and evading military service in World War I. Colonel Alvin Owsley, the only man not serving in Congress, denounced the others as "nothing more than pussyfooting politicians."[41]

Congressman Tom Connally, the front-runner among the pack of challengers, left an unselfconscious account of the fight-game strategy in his autobiography. Devoting less than three lines to his positions on the issues, he described at length the struggle for dominance that ambitious men relished and middle-class women deplored. Connally wrote triumphantly of "outmaneuvering" Owsley, a former national commander of the American Legion, by turning on "full patriotic oratory" to get the veterans' vote. He reveled in Congressman Tom Blanton's "immense error in judgment" in abandoning the slashing rhetoric for which he was known, and temporarily becoming "mild as a bluebonnet," alienating both old and new supporters before reverting to character.[42]

Connally's strategy was simple and devastatingly effective. He ignored the other challengers as much as possible and concentrated on demolishing the incumbent, Mayfield, whom he denounced as the "bedsheet-and-mask candidate." The political power of the Klan had long since waned, but its presence lingered; Cunningham saw the first flaming cross of her life while campaigning in the Rio Grande Valley. Connally early discovered that attacking Mayfield's Klan support never failed as a crowd pleaser and made that his campaign theme. After Mayfield offered a new suit to anyone who could name a single thing that Connally had accomplished in Washington, Connally exhorted crowds to insist on a good new one that could be worn in the daylight, not Mayfield's old sheet and pillowcase from 1922. Audiences accustomed to stump speeches in which candidates lacerated their opponents shouted back approvingly "Pour it on Tom!"[43]

Men whom Cunningham had expected to support her issues-focused campaign, the leaders of the old progressive coalition, turned out to be unapologetic advocates of the fight-game philosophy. Nearly all whom Nell Doom and Jane McCallum asked to lend their names to a Cunningham sponsorship committee declined. Martin McNulty Crane, long since forgiven for pressing the 1919 state suffrage referendum against the TESA's wishes, rebuffed Cunningham's personal appeal with stark pragmatism. He acknowledged their long friendship and agreed that she was entirely qualified to be a senator. But the only relevant criterion, Crane said frankly, was the ability to pound Mayfield in the runoff primary. He planned to endorse the strongest challenger, and therefore was leaning toward Connally, but if Blanton surged, he would "cheerfully" back him instead. Former TESA legislative ally Dudley K. Woodward concurred that the only real issue was Earle Mayfield, and Connally was hitting him hardest.[44]

None of the male candidates acknowledged Cunningham until late in the race. Emily Newell Blair had observed that men regarded women as pacifists on the political battlefield; from that point of view, Cunningham's renunciation of personal attacks rendered her a harmless noncombatant. In the last weeks of the campaign, Colonel Owsley, who appeared to be the weakest of the male candidates, finally made gender an open issue. Cunningham, he remarked patronizingly, was a nice little girl (she was forty-six), and he was too much of a chivalrous southern gentleman to say anything against her, but she should not be elected because being a senator was a man's job.[45]

At first, Cunningham responded with humor, recounting a story about a man who was diagnosed with hydrophobia (rabies) and immediately began scribbling on a sheet of paper. Assured by the doctor that he could be cured and that there was no need to write a will, the man replied that he wasn't making a will, he was making a list of people to bite. "Most candidates are like that," she asserted. "Instead of discussing the issues, they proceed to bite all who oppose them." She drew more laughter and applause by waving one of the souvenir thimbles that Owsley distributed to the women in his audiences, deriding such gimmickry as a pathetic demonstration of so-called chivalry. Real chivalry, she added dramatically, was what Texas men had shown when they enfranchised women as their equals. In fighting back, Cunningham showed audiences what they expected from a candidate, and one male listener called out the ultimate compliment: "Lady, if you wanted to you could pour it on them, couldn't you?"[46]

Until that point in the campaign, Cunningham had dealt with the gender issue by ignoring it as much as possible. Now, in addition to Owsley's claim that a woman should not serve, she began to hear open talk that a woman could not win. Ruby Neale Long suspected Tom Connally's people of spreading it to draw off Cunningham's supporters; Connally also began duplicating her speaking schedule, turning up just ahead of her and securing the best venues.[47] As she was forced on the defensive, Cunningham found it difficult to maintain her ideals. For the first time, she asked audiences "not to erect my womanhood as a barrier between men and your vote" and to accord her an "even break." Belatedly, she confronted the reality that audiences relished male "pour it on" style. In the final days she partially succumbed, adding to her speeches a description of her opponents' political shortcomings.[48]

Without her knowledge, the volunteers at the Austin headquarters decided that an open appeal to gender was the campaign's best hope. Having found it impossible to recruit anyone but women to the proposed committee of sponsors, Nell Doom and Jane McCallum abandoned the original concept and appended the names to an eleventh-hour pitch for the female vote. "To the Women Voters of Texas," signed by seventeen well-known clubwomen and former suffragists, reminded women that they owed the ballot to Cunningham. Stressing that Texas deserved the "honor" of electing the first woman to the U.S. Senate, the appeal pointed out the importance of putting women in Congress to vote on issues of child and family welfare. "Since the men candidates are so soundly berating each other, thousands of their supporters are flocking to Mrs. Cunningham's standard," the appeal concluded optimistically. The signers urged women to "divide the poll tax list or the telephone book among a committee and cover your town or community."[49]

In mid-July Adele Clark returned to Texas as a campaign speaker and organizer. From Boston, Dorothy Brown forwarded the latest batch of small checks to help cover Clark's expenses and urged her to make the local workers "blow in every last cent on publicity." Maud Wood Park, who was quietly assisting Brown with fundraising, sent encouragement. In Beaumont Clark met up with Cunningham, whom she found "tired and hoarse but happy"; after conferring with Cunningham and the East Texas volunteers, she went on to Houston. With only a week remaining until the primary, Clark set up headquarters and joined forces with the little group of clubwomen striving to organize Harris County.[50]

Cunningham, buoyed by crowds and applause, remained optimistic, despite the signs that her chances were slim. "I'm *dead*—but very popular & almost elected!" she exulted to Dorothy Brown. The *Fort Worth Star-Telegram* made a sharply different assessment. It predicted a runoff between Mayfield and Connally with Blanton and Owsley dividing the Ferguson supporters; Cunningham did not get even passing mention. When the ballots were counted Mayfield and Connally, with 200,246 and 178,091 votes respectively, qualified for the runoff. Owsley placed third with 131,755 and Blanton fourth with 126,758. Cunningham finished a poor fifth with 28,944 votes. Since the sixth-place finisher, Jeff McLemore, had not bothered to campaign, she essentially came in last. In only two counties, Harris (Houston) and Tarrant (Fort Worth) did she poll more than one thousand votes, and she carried only her own county, Walker.[51]

Given Connally's obvious strength—he went on to defeat Mayfield in the runoff—Cunningham could hardly have expected to finish near the top, but she did not anticipate the humiliating bottom. Ten thousand hot, dusty miles and 200 speeches had brought her an abysmal 4 percent of the vote. The most painful shock was voter inconsistency. She was incredulous at "the unanimity with which people commended me and my campaign and then strolled off to vote for my opponents. . . . And apparently it never occurred to any of them that what I wanted was *votes* not compliments." To Jane McCallum she observed ironically, "If as many people had voted for me as wrote and thanked me for running in order to raise the standard of campaigns I'd be in the runoff!"[52]

Losing the women's vote was an especially severe disappointment. She laid a generous share of the blame on the prohibitionist defectors. "Why *do* the good have to be so *dumb*—Dottie—why *do* they?" she wailed to Dorothy Brown, castigating "the pious W.C.T.U. ladies who bolted the primary and left me to my fate" in order to vote for Hoover in November. Postmortems from friends and supporters revealed a more complex picture. Rural women, by far the largest contingent of the so-called "female vote," knew little about Cunningham. Her support came from the smaller pool of city and town women who belonged to clubs and other voluntary organizations. But even among this group, personal and political pressures siphoned off votes. A volunteer reported that "lots of my friends voted for Tom Connally. Their husbands did and wanted them to."[53]

Conjoined with the certainty that a woman could not win was an underlying conviction that a woman should not run—at least not at the level Cunningham had chosen. Many former suffragists believed that women should not scramble for office. As beginners, they should have modest aspirations and, lest they resemble self-serving male politicians, seek only offices for which they had undeniable credentials or special expertise. A former TESA vice president who greatly admired Cunningham concluded that she "stepped up a little too much when she wanted to go be a Senator. She had not the political experience, legal ability, grasping of foreign conditions, etc. I didn't support her. I would gladly have done so if she had run for Congress."[54]

Privately, Cunningham lamented "the long long row women have to hoe before they even respect themselves and their own intelligence enough . . . to be willing for one of them to be elected to anything." But she refused to let friends chastise women for not standing by her: "How we vote is nobodies' *business!*" In her published postmortem, she likewise absolved women voters and blamed the men who had relentlessly "dinned into their ears" that a woman could not win. She titled the piece with a quote by an elderly former slave at Fisher Farms, who had opposed her suffrage work with the argument that going to the polls was "too gallant a walk for a lady to take." Although certain that women would eventually find their way to the Senate, she concluded ruefully that in 1928 the road was still too gallant a walk for women.[55]

The gender handicap notwithstanding, the campaign also suffered from inadequate organizing, an ironic failing since Cunningham had done such work for the Democratic Party. She knew very well what was needed, but plans for a speakers' bureau, publicity people, and a campaign committee never came to life. The network of Cunningham For Senator clubs, envisioned to work at the precinct level in each county, likewise failed to materialize. Even after Ruby Neale Long simplified the structure, county-level organizing remained a hit or miss affair that relied on local initiative—which was sorely lacking. "Making the women work politically is a real job," Adele

Clark reported. Ruby Long found that many county workers, although personally enthusiastic, lacked leadership ability and did not know how to organize other women.[56]

Male candidates, by contrast, had the advantage of well-established political networks and machines that mobilized votes. Tom Connally "earned" the support of one machine-dominated county with a single appearance, after which the boss promised to back him and told Connally he could save himself the trouble of further campaigning in the county.[57] There were no women politicians to render such assistance to Cunningham and no existing base of female power to tap into. The suffrage associations that had functioned at the city, county, and precinct level had been deactivated, and the small, nonpartisan, LWV forbade endorsements and electioneering.

The only former suffragist elected to Congress in the 1920s, Ruth Hanna McCormick (R-IL), won with the help of a partisan women's organization built well in advance. Her Republican Women's Club of Illinois reached into every county and counted nearly 200,000 members. McCormick had been initiated into politics through the male rituals of popular partisanship rather than the female voluntary association tradition. She refused to join the LWV and was one of the few women of the era willing to call herself a politician. Cunningham, by contrast, regarded herself as a political educator; she recruited women to the Democratic Party by explaining its ideology and stance on the issues. In that sense, she still upheld the LWV's civics-textbook approach to politics, despite her Democratic partisanship. She salved her loss with pride that her campaign had been "so tremendously successful educationally" and that she had "stooped to no temptation to play politics."[58]

That fall Cunningham returned temporarily to the Woman's National Democratic Club in Washington to help with the presidential campaign. Emily Newell Blair asked her to run a two-week organizing school for women at the clubhouse, and Cunningham also "worked out," speaking for Al Smith in Tennessee, North Carolina, and Wisconsin. The bone-dry prohibitionists in the Democratic Party remained unreconciled and contributed their ballots to a landslide victory for Herbert Hoover. The "solid South" cracked; six southern states, including Texas, went Republican. Too disgusted with the Texas "Hoovercrats" to trust herself on a podium after she got home, she declined postelection speaking engagements with the excuse that she was resting.[59]

ALTHOUGH CUNNINGHAM NEVER MADE ANOTHER ATTEMPT TO REACH Congress, she insisted that she did not regret her failed Senate race. She would do it over, even knowing the outcome, she maintained, because there was no better forum for engaging people in a discussion of the issues.[60] Her public optimism notwithstanding, she was deeply disillusioned by her defeat. She had run to discredit noisy combats fought around stump-speech "side issues" and to demonstrate how elections should be contested. "If I can help it, no future campaign will be fought on Klan or anti-Klan or wet and dry while the people are sold out to the special interests," she had vowed as she launched her bid.[61] Yet despite her efforts, the Senate race had been precisely that. Her model campaign had been doubly rejected: by the other candidates, who persisted in fight-game tactics, and by the electorate, which failed to validate her effort with a respectable total at the polls.

In "Too Gallant a Walk," Cunningham gave the same explanation for her defeat that other unsuccessful female candidates offered and that historians have continued to emphasize: the unyielding prejudice against women in politics. But her campaign suggests that male resistance to female officeholding was interwoven with women's own reluctance to adopt the values of male political culture—to be aggressive, tough, and openly ambitious. Eleanor Roosevelt, who had learned electioneering from the men in her family, argued that women had to "play the game" male style and "elect, accept, and back women political bosses." She conceded that the prospect would horrify many women, and it did. The president of the California LWV pronounced the election of Ruth Hanna McCormick (a boss's daughter) "no victory at all for women, for Mrs. McCormick campaigned and fought like a man."[62]

Cunningham would probably have disagreed with the first part of the statement—she welcomed the success of any qualified woman—but campaigning like a man was a divide she and many other women, shaped by voluntary association politics, refused to cross. If seeking office was about owning power rather than debating policy, and if bellicosity rather than "braininess" was always going to be the standard for victory, there was scarcely any point in running. It would take several generations and another feminist movement for women to enter the game in more than token numbers.

As the tenth anniversary of woman suffrage approached and feminists assessed the disappointments of the decade, Cunningham tempered her frustration with faith in enfranchised women's still unrevealed possibilities. "Women's influence in politics is great—*tremendous*—not only potentially but actually," she mused to Jane McCallum. "*But* not our very best friend could say that we are doing much independent thinking, or studying or leading as yet in the political world." The great questions for Cunningham were "Where are we going to *begin*? The stage is set—the foot lights and spot lights are burning—where are the actors? What is the play to be? Where are the stars?"[63]

Bewailing what women had so far failed to accomplish was pointless, she counseled McCallum, who was planning a severe speech to a women's organization. "Don't belittle what they *have* done, it's good mostly as far as it goes. But show them the greater things going undone." This would be her own preoccupation for the next three decades while the women's movement waned and lost visibility, and the gendering of politics and power persisted.

A Woman's New Deal

CUNNINGHAM'S DEFEAT IN THE SENATE RACE WAS A TURNING POINT IN her career. Although she maintained ties to the network of voluntary associations that had led her into public activism, the limitations of middle-class women's voluntarist politics were evident. Women continued to be excluded from high office, and their organizations experienced repeated setbacks: Congress terminated the Sheppard-Towner Act, a promising Texas child welfare program collapsed, and both the Texas and the national LWV were struggling to survive.

Although the women's movement, by itself, lacked the strength to bring about significant social change, Franklin Roosevelt's election as president in 1932 opened up a new possibility: a women's movement within the Democratic Party allied with the political Left. The result, for Cunningham, was a form of left feminism. Although she was not a socialist, she combined an understanding of the systematic oppression of women with an appreciation of the economic power structures underlying society and an awareness that the emancipation of all women—working-class and non-Caucasian as well as white middle-class women—required fundamental changes in class and race as well as in gender relations.[1] Southern women who sought reform in all three areas encountered an even more hostile political climate than their counterparts in the more liberal northern states. But the New Deal encouraged southern left feminists, such as Cunningham, Lucy Randolph Mason, and Virginia Durr, to believe that their vision of a transformed South was a possibility.[2]

Cunningham admired Roosevelt for giving new life to reform movements, which had become almost moribund during the Hoover administration, and, like other female progressives, considered his New Deal to be a continuation of their reform efforts.[3] But his election was especially important to her because it placed Eleanor Roosevelt, a powerful women's advocate, in the White House. Cunningham became a member of her women's network early in the new administration; by 1939 she was back in Washington, D.C., with access to the White House through her ties to Eleanor.

During the 1930s the Democratic Party began to change from a white, male, middle-class party as women, blacks, and organized labor gained influence.[4] Prodded by Eleanor and by Molly Dewson, the director of the Women's Division of the Democratic National Committee, President Roosevelt supported efforts to make his party, rather than the GOP, the "women's party." More women were given positions of authority in the federal government, and at the 1936 Democratic Convention women were Platform Committee participants for the first time. The Women's Division's increasing importance within the party was in part due to the grassroots organization it created to "sell" the New Deal to other women, which in 1936 helped eliminate the electoral gender gap that had benefited the Republican Party in the 1920s.[5] After Cunningham returned to Washington, she contributed to the party feminization that Dewson had begun; by 1944 DNC staff members regarded her as the South's most politically astute woman.[6]

ALTHOUGH SHE LIVED IN TEXAS FROM 1928 TO 1939, CUNNINGHAM continued to be part of the national women's network. Emily Newell Blair and Eleanor Roosevelt were among those who wrote to her regarding possible employment opportunities after her Senate defeat.[7] Belle Sherwin, national LWV president, kept her informed about Washington political developments affecting women's interests and recommended that Cunningham be included when Molly Dewson planned to appoint an Advisory Council to the Women's Division in 1934.[8] But Dorothy Kirchwey Brown—whose sister, Freda Kirchwey, edited *The Nation* during the 1930s and 1940s—remained her closest confidant outside of Texas.

Cunningham was eager to help when a group of female activists—some of them from the national LWV—initiated a campaign to get President Hoover to appoint Grace Abbott, the Children's Bureau's director, to a cabinet position. She urged Texas Senator Morris Sheppard to complain in the Senate that women were making no progress in public life, even though they were being credited with Hoover's victory.[9] She also reminded AFL President William Green that he owed her a favor, which he could repay by supporting Abbott.[10] But Hoover declined to appoint her, and the failure to get a woman in the cabinet was compounded by the termination of women's most important legislative achievement—the Sheppard-Towner Act—in 1929. Cunningham wrote anxiously to Belle Sherwin about the Act's prospects during the debate, lamenting that Texas newspapers were full of reports on "cruisers and cabinets" but ignored matters relating to mothers and babies. She had intended to focus on the Act in a speech on laws of special relevance to women, but Congress ended the program before her address.[11]

Like other suffragists, Cunningham had expected the vote would give women the power to reshape society to reflect women's values. But by the end of the decade, business interests opposed to the expansion of government authority had blocked much of the legislation that she had fought for while working for the LWV. Since many leaders of women's groups, including the national LWV, were Republicans whose husbands were businessmen, some were reluctant to acknowledge the conflict between the women's movement and the business community. But Cunningham considered this crucial to understanding why women had been able to bring about so little change since they gained the vote. If women didn't ensure that government was concerned with human welfare, she warned, then it would be controlled by a "privileged class" for its own interests.[12]

She channeled her disappointment over the demise of Sheppard-Towner into helping her longtime friend Mary Gearing, a home economist and former suffragist, launch a new child welfare initiative.[13] In 1930 Cunningham became one of the founding members of the committee Gearing founded that sought to establish a Foundation for Child Development and Parent Education at the University of Texas. Modeled after similar foundations at Yale and other northern universities, it appeared to have a promising future when the UT Board of Regents granted approval in 1930.[14] Cunningham was the committee's publicity officer, and after the Foundation was established, she continued to speak on its behalf at women's gatherings, such as the 1930 Texas Congress of Mothers and Parent-Teacher Associations' annual convention.[15] But despite this promising beginning, the Great Depression dried up funding, and the Foundation remained inactive for the next quarter of a century.[16]

The Depression also severely weakened the LWV; the national and many state leagues experienced sharp declines in income and membership. In an attempt to revive morale, the national LWV celebrated the tenth anniversary of women's suffrage in 1930 by establishing a Suffrage Honor Roll. Each state was encouraged to nominate its outstanding suffragists and was asked to pledge $1,000 to the Anniversary Memorial Fund for each name proposed. Despite the deepening financial crisis, the LWV raised nearly $250,000 for a huge bronze memorial tablet that was inscribed with the names of the suffrage leaders and displayed at the LWV's Washington, D.C., headquarters.[17] Cunningham was the only Texan among the eighty-seven women honored.

As part of the nationwide commemoration of the suffrage victory, the

Texas LWV sponsored a luncheon at which Cunningham gave the keynote address. She seized the opportunity to remind her audience that their work was not done and that the vote was a weapon to bring about gender reform, not an end in itself. Acknowledging that suffrage had been a great thing, she drew attention to how little enfranchised women had been able to change society to reflect their values. Were women going to hang up the battle axe and memorialize their leader, she asked, or were they going to take it "and fight for the principles as we once did."[18] But financial instability and declining membership left the Texas LWV almost moribund even before the Depression, and speeches could not invigorate it.[19] Although she insisted that "a piece of my heart will always be in the League," after serving on the Texas LWV's board of directors from 1929 to 1935, Cunningham focused her energies elsewhere.[20]

WHILE SHE WANTED TO BECOME A FULL-TIME POLITICAL ACTIVIST, Cunningham needed paid employment following her Senate defeat. On July 16, 1930, she was appointed associate editor at the Texas Extension Service and relocated to the small East Texas town of College Station. Her ties with agriculture were reinforced when she acquired Fisher Farms (the 1,187-acre family estate near New Waverly) following her mother's death in 1930.[21]

Cunningham's new job placed her in a strikingly different gender environment. After having spent most of the 1920s working in women's organizations, she was now required to work not only with men but also under male supervisors. The Extension Service was headquartered at the Agricultural and Mechanical College of Texas (now Texas A&M University), where all the faculty were men and the Board of Directors was attempting to maintain a male-only student body.[22] Despite the masculine culture, Cunningham assured her female friends that she genuinely enjoyed her work.[23] But while she formed close friendships with some of her male political allies, privately she admitted to a female confidant that "I hate it when the World Series or the Cornell football game has to be listened to."[24]

Cunningham was promoted to acting editor on July 1, 1934, when Wayne Darrow went on leave, and replaced him as editor when he resigned a year later. In her annual report for 1935, she acknowledged that the "pleasure in success did not entirely serve to abate the weariness of overwork."[25] In addition to editing the monthly *Texas Extension Service Farm News*, she prepared a weekly "Press Letter," provided "hot news" press releases to daily papers, wrote feature articles for farm magazines, edited bulletins, circulars, and leaflets, and was secretary of the Extension Service committee that prepared three weekly radio broadcasts. With her output increasing each year, by mid-

1937 Cunningham admitted that "luncheons, teas, etc. are all now relegated to the past and PRINT IT NOW has become the watchword of my existence."[26]

The philosophical differences between Cunningham and the Extension Service increased her job stress. She disagreed with its "feed sack" approach to rural poverty, which taught poor farm women to "make do" with such scrimping strategies as making clothing from the cotton sacks in which animal feed was sold. In addition to encouraging people to believe poverty was inevitable, Cunningham considered it bad policy at a time when the federal government had millions of surplus cotton bales in storage. She proposed a mattress-making scheme as an alternative.[27] Low-income people were provided free cotton by the federal government and were taught how to sew the ticking into which the cotton was stuffed to make mattresses.[28]

Through her Extension Service position, Cunningham became involved in New Deal antipoverty programs. Southern employers, fearful that federal relief programs would undermine employees' willingness to work for low wages, welcomed publicity that portrayed relief recipients obtaining a "handout" for make-work. It was important, therefore, that new programs require productive labor, and even more vital that they be seen doing so. Cunningham supported the expansion of federal relief programs and helped defend a local work center by writing a documentary film script about it, which was used by the Federal Emergency Relief Administration and the Extension Service.[29] She sent the film to Eleanor Roosevelt, who showed it at the White House one night when Henry Wallace, Secretary of Agriculture, and Harry Hopkins, the FERA administrator, were dinner guests.[30]

Agricultural work also brought Cunningham back into reform politics. By the 1930s the radical Texas farm organizations of her youth had been replaced by the anti–New Deal Texas Farm Bureau Federation. After helping dissident farmers withdraw from it and form the pro–New Deal Texas Agricultural Association (TAA), Cunningham devoted considerable time and money to the TAA.[31] She usually attended its annual conference, was one of the speakers at its 1937 annual meeting, and in 1938 served as an advisor to the TAA Board of Directors on ways to improve its journal, the *Farmers' Banner*.[32] Thus, when Texas Extension Service leaders persuaded the TAA to become a Texas Farm Bureau branch in 1941, Cunningham protested that Texas farmers had been "betrayed," but to no avail.[33]

CUNNINGHAM HAD RESERVATIONS ABOUT ACCEPTING THE EXTENSION Service position because it would take her out of politics. Her yearning to resume political work became acute when Franklin Roosevelt sought the presidential nomination.[34] Although she thought the Roosevelts to be "splendid people," she did not join the Texas Roosevelt-for-President Club because she considered its female vice president, Mrs. J. E. King, a "camp follower": "No woman in Texas who is 'in the know' will follow her."[35] But during the 1932 election campaign, she could barely restrain herself from working for Roosevelt. She admitted that if she had enough money to live on, she would resign her position and be on the stump the following day: "I *will* be free. I *will* get myself an economic independence from which I can do as I please as a citizen."[36] She welcomed Roosevelt's victory as "the best thing that has happened in the world since Armistice Day"[37] and admired him even more after he used his presidential powers to force "the capitalists of *this* country [to] publicly beg him for a dole for the unemployed."[38]

She was equally delighted to have Eleanor Roosevelt in the White House. Cunningham became part of the women's network that kept the First Lady informed of how New Deal programs were working and how they affected women. She drew ER's attention, for example, to the mismanagement of the FERA program in Texas.[39] Eleanor forwarded her letter to the appropriate FERA official in Washington with a note that she had "great confidence" in Cunningham and requested that he look into it.[40]

During the 1930s Cunningham's left feminism was strengthened by her friendship with Robert H. Montgomery, an ardent New Dealer and a charismatic University of Texas economics professor. Montgomery was primarily responsible for UT's reputation as having the most radical economics department in the country.[41] Although he was not a socialist, corporate interests tried repeatedly to get him fired because of his criticism of monopolies, especially the Texas sulfur industry.[42] Montgomery introduced Cunningham into his circle of Progressive Democrats, which included several men who became leaders of the post–World War II Texas Democratic Party's left wing: Robert C. Eckhardt (labor lawyer and Congressman), Creekmore Fath (New Deal lawyer and White House advisor), and Otto Mullinax (labor lawyer). Mullinax later recalled how surprised he was that Cunningham was as "dominant" in the group's discussions as any of the men, something quite unusual for Texas political gatherings in that period.[43]

When the Tenth District's Congressman died in 1937, Cunningham was eager to play "kingmaker" by helping Montgomery win the seat. President Roosevelt also wanted him elected; Roosevelt's assistant, Tommy Corcoran, helped Cunningham raise a campaign fund of over $20,000 to encourage him to run.[44] But when Montgomery hesitated, Lyndon Johnson announced his candidacy and Montgomery decided not to compete. Johnson created his own women's organization, stymieing Cunningham's aspirations to elect men who would grant independent women a more significant role in the state Democratic Party. Her experience as the acting head of the DNC Women's Division was actually a liability: male party leaders preferred female leaders who were dependent on them. When the Texas Democratic Party created a Women's Division in 1936, Senator Tom Connally made sure it was chaired by one of his supporters, Mrs. Frances Haskell Edmonson, rather than Cunningham, who had run against him.[45]

CUNNINGHAM WANTED THE WOMEN ACTIVISTS TO CONTINUE THEIR reform efforts during the 1930s, rather than live on their memories of the suffrage victory. The problem was to find an issue that would revive the crusading "women's consciousness" that had sustained them during the suffrage campaign. Although she supported citizenship reforms, such as women's right to jury service, that the Texas LWV was seeking, these lacked the emotional appeal to arouse a new women's movement. What stimulated her sense of moral outrage was poverty and its consequences for family health, an issue which had the potential to draw women back into political activism: "Should we go on shadow boxing for reform we don't really care about . . . while the health department records people dying of starvation—and of food deficiency diseases (just polite names for starvation so as not to stir up our sympathies . . .)!"[46]

Cunningham's concern with the "slavery of poverty" and the "slavery of ignorance" that usually accompanied it grew during the decade.[47] Some of the worst poverty existed among the rural people she encountered in her job. When she began working for the Extension Service, 60 percent of Texas farm operators were tenant farmers, and Texas's per capita income was only 68 percent of the national average.[48] Poverty combined with ignorance of good nutrition often resulted in a diet that contributed to poor family health.

President Roosevelt's 1937 declaration that one-third of the nation was ill-fed was a call to arms for Cunningham. The southern states had the highest incidence of vitamin deficiency diseases, such as pellagra; Texas ranked second in the nation with 544 reported pellagra deaths in 1938.[49] The 1937 discovery that pellagra was caused by nicotinic acid (niacin) deficiency led to a nationwide effort to inform people of the foods to eat to prevent it.[50]

Since nutrition highlighted the mother's importance to family health, Cunningham realized it could become the basis for a revived women's movement. Working closely with home economists, who provided the information needed to plan low-cost healthy diets, she became one of the leaders of the 1938 Texas educational "foods campaign." It developed a model diet, and she served as Associate Editor of the *Texas Food Standard*, an Extension Service pamphlet that explained basic nutrition.[51]

After Cunningham went to Washington, D.C., in 1939 to work for the Agricultural Adjustment Administration (AAA), M. L. Wilson, Federal Extension

Service Director, appointed her to a working committee set up to advise the National Defense Advisory Commission's Nutrition Policy and Planning Committee, which prepared a national nutrition policy and program.[52] She was also a delegate to President Roosevelt's 1941 National Nutrition Conference that endorsed the committee's recommendations as a defense measure.[53]

As the nation prepared for the Second World War, Cunningham was among those who considered good nutrition essential to national defense. About 45 percent of the first Texans drafted in 1941 were rejected, due primarily to years of inadequate diets. Reflecting the extent of rural poverty, the percentage of rejections was higher among farm boys than city dwellers.[54] Convinced that large numbers of young people had grown up in poor health because of malnutrition, Cunningham urged that every child, no matter how poor, should be provided a hot school lunch. This was a controversial position for a AAA employee to take publicly, because powerful agricultural interests had been preventing the Department of Agriculture from distributing surplus food to schools for this purpose.[55]

Because the milling process commonly used at the time removed most of the vitamins from flour, the Texas Federation of Women's Clubs (TFWC) and other women's groups advocated enriching flour with niacin, thiamin, and (when it became available) riboflavin. This brought them into conflict with food manufacturers, who were unwilling to change voluntarily. From Washington, Cunningham organized a group of about twenty women who lobbied the Texas legislature to make enrichment mandatory. Wearing sunbonnets and long dresses, they sat in the gallery of the Texas House of Representatives in 1943, with a loaf of bread under one arm and a placard under the other, until legislation was passed requiring that white flour be enriched with vitamins.[56]

CUNNINGHAM WAS A NEW DEAL ENTHUSIAST IN PART BECAUSE IT embodied the women's movement's preference for an activist government defending the underprivileged. Since the latter conflicted with Texans' antipathy toward taxes, she used her frequent public speaking engagements to explain why government intervention was advantageous. She considered it crucial that women understand that they benefited from government services more than men did and that progressive taxes (which linked the tax burden to income level) were necessary to achieve women's vision of social improvement in such areas as education and social security. "You get more back from a tax dollar than from a dollar spent in any other way," she argued.[57]

While Cunningham drew some of her economic policies from her LWV background, she went beyond its program in identifying chronic poverty as the South's fundamental economic problem. She shared Robert Montgomery's

view that the southern states were economic colonies of northern corporations, which profited from keeping the South agricultural. Southern industrialization was hampered by several factors, including discriminatory railroad
rates. The railroads charged low rates for shipping southern raw materials and
unfinished products to northern manufacturing centers but imposed high
rates for transporting southern manufactured goods to other regions.[58]

As part of his attempt to promote New Deal liberalism in the South, President Roosevelt encouraged the drafting of the *Report on Economic Conditions
of the South*. It drew national attention to southern poverty and identified discriminatory freight rates as a major cause.[59] Praising Roosevelt's initiative,
in 1938 Cunningham set up an independent women's pressure group, the
Women's Committee for Economic Policy (WCEP), to seek reform.[60] Since
she was employed full-time, she recruited Lillian Collier, President of the
TFWC's Fourth District (1938–1940), to chair the WCEP and Margaret Reading, granddaughter of the first University of Texas Dean of Women and a
widow who operated a farm in Waller County, to be secretary.[61]

Cunningham considered freight-rate reform a women's issue because of
the effect family poverty had on mothers and children. She expected it to stimulate economic growth, resulting in higher income for parents, thus making
it possible to eradicate child labor.[62] When Lyndon Johnson became a U.S.
Senate candidate in 1941, Cunningham instructed Collier and Jane McCallum
to ask him if he would make freight-rate reform his top priority if elected. Apparently his reply was satisfactory, because Cunningham endorsed Johnson
and the WCEP campaigned for him.[63]

The WCEP advocated two other reforms especially beneficial to women
and families: a fully funded teacher retirement scheme and pensions for the
needy aged. In 1930 over 80 percent of Texas teachers were poorly paid women
without state retirement benefits; as state employees, they were also excluded
from the 1935 federal Social Security Act. Women's organizations, including
the TFWC, had been advocating a state retirement scheme for teachers since
the 1920s.[64] Legislation establishing a Teacher Retirement System financed by
equal contributions from the teacher and the state had passed in 1937, but without an appropriation; pressure from the WCEP helped secure funding in 1941.

The WCEP was also concerned with poverty among elderly women. In
1930 white women lived an average of 3.8 years longer than white men, and
as the differential increased during the following decades, women made up a
rising proportion of the population over 65. Elderly women were especially
likely to be poor in the 1930s because of the lack of federal or state income-
support programs. Even insured men's wives and widows were excluded from
benefits under the Social Security Act.[65] Although the Texas legislature acknowledged the problem in 1935 by passing legislation to provide pensions
for the destitute elderly, the scheme was not implemented because legislators

disagreed on how to finance it. The WCEP opposed using a sales tax to fund the pensions as corporate interests urged and declared victory when its lobbying helped secure the financing by increasing oil and gas taxes in 1941.[66]

ALTHOUGH SHE WAS LESS ACTIVE IN WOMEN'S VOLUNTARY ORGANIZATIONS than in previous decades, in the 1930s Cunningham belonged to the Texas Federation of Women's Clubs, the Texas branch of the American Association of University Women and the Business and Professional Women's Club of Bryan-College Station.[67] A popular speaker, she frequently appeared on the platform at TFWC meetings. In September 1938 the General Federation of Women's Clubs appointed her chair of its national Committee on Urban-Rural Cooperation, with a seat on the Board of Directors.

Her style in working with women's groups is suggested by an incident at the GFWC's headquarters in 1939. After Cunningham moved a resolution in support of a New Deal agricultural policy, Clara Driscoll, Texas's Democratic National Committeewoman, opposed it in a "crashing speech," punctuated with her walking cane. Cunningham then went to the podium and requested that the audience rise for prayer before they voted. According to a witness, the ten-minute prayer Cunningham offered was "the damnedest campaign speech you have ever heard in your life." The vote was nearly unanimous in favor of Cunningham's resolution. After the meeting, Driscoll hissed: "Minnie Fish, don't you ever pray on me again as long as you live!"[68]

Cunningham became part of the movement to transform the Democratic Party into the "women's" party when she accepted an appointment as Senior Specialist in the AAA's Washington, D.C., Information Division in March 1939 and was placed in charge of what she referred to as the AAA's "women's division."[69] Her official duties included planning and implementing educational programs about the farm program among both rural and urban women nationwide; cooperating with women's organizations to disseminate information on AAA programs; and advising Department of Agriculture officials on women's reaction to those programs.[70] But her coworkers realized that she was more important than her title implied.[71] Unofficially, she was to convert women into New Deal supporters. Although her job's political dimension was confidential, the DNC's Women's Division was aware of her work and occasionally invited her to speak at Democratic Party meetings.[72]

The similarities between Cunningham's unofficial duties and what women did for the Democratic Party under Molly Dewson's Reporter Plan suggest that her real function was to extend the Reporter Plan to rural and small-town women. Under Dewson's direction, the Women's Division became the DNC's most politically active and effective special division during the 1930s.[73] Her

Reporter Plan created a grassroots women's movement by recruiting liberal women to teach other women in their communities about New Deal policies. The female reporters were not regular party members but "saleswomen" who promoted New Deal reforms rather than the election of local Demo- crats.[74] Although Cunningham had no formal connection with the DNC's Women's Division, Dorothy McAllister, its director from 1937 to 1940, held her in high regard, apparently because of Cunningham's AAA work.[75] May Thompson Evans, its assistant director, remembered Cunningham as having done "great work" among agricultural women.[76]

Cunningham's appointment (as senior information specialist in the AAA) was one of several initiatives the Roosevelt administration took in 1939 to en- hance its appeal in the approaching election. The midwestern farm vote was a source of special concern.[77] Aware that many farmers perceived a conflict between their economic interests and those of organized labor, CIO leader Sidney Hillman proposed holding conferences that would bring together farmers and workers to reestablish a sense of mutual interest. Secretary of Agriculture Henry Wallace endorsed Hillman's idea, and shortly afterward the AAA appointed Cunningham and assigned her to arrange a series of rural- urban women's conferences.[78]

Cunningham welcomed the CIO's increasing importance in the Roosevelt administration because its opposition to racial- or gender-based employment discrimination was stimulating the growth of working-class left feminism.[79] While AFL unions ignored women workers, the CIO recruited them and ad- vocated gender equality, including equal pay, for them. Encouraged by its poli- cies, Cunningham formed ties with CIO national headquarters while she was in Washington, D.C., and later received CIO support when she ran for gover- nor of Texas.

Cunningham's first AAA project was organizing the April 1939 rural-urban women's conference in Washington. Her desire to establish a link with the working-class women's movement is suggested by the participants. While representatives from the major women's voluntary organizations were in- vited, seven of the twenty-five urban women were union members: four from CIO unions, two from the AFL, and Rose Schneiderman, longtime leader of the Women's Trade Union League. To develop a sense of shared interests be- tween rural and urban women, Cunningham encouraged the participants to identify themselves as consumers rather than as producers.[80] She had Dr. Hazel Stiebeling, the Bureau of Home Economics' senior food economist, report on her nationwide survey that found poverty to be the crucial factor in inade- quate diets, and Cunningham asked the women to consider why there should be poverty and ill health in the midst of abundance.[81] Eleanor Roosevelt sig- naled her support by hosting the participants at the White House following the conference's conclusion.

The Washington conference was the beginning of a nationwide program. By 1943 Cunningham had helped organize twenty-five state and more than a thousand county and community rural-urban conferences, all patterned after the Washington model. They encouraged participatory democracy by using group discussion instead of lectures by experts; stimulated a female consciousness by having the women view themselves as a sisterhood of consumers rather than as members of conflicting class or interest groups; and attributed ill health resulting from poor diets to low income rather than to ignorance.[82]

WHEN PRESIDENT ROOSEVELT ESTABLISHED THE NATIONAL DEFENSE Advisory Commission (NDAC) in May 1940 to coordinate war mobilization planning, he appointed Harriet Elliott, who had worked for the DNC Women's Division in 1935–1936, as the Consumer Division's commissioner. With women's letters pouring into Washington offering to help the defense effort, Elliott asked her assistant, Caroline Ware, to find someone with public relations skills who had contacts with national and local women's organizations. Ware, one of the few white faculty teaching at all-black Howard University and active in the wartime movement to desegregate the capitol, recommended Cunningham.[83]

Early in July, Elliott informed President Roosevelt that she had appointed Cunningham chief of the Consumer Division's Civic Contacts Unit to "work with civic and other groups for the mobilization of human resources."[84] This was a temporary arrangement under which the AAA loaned Cunningham to the NDAC. Although it meant a salary increase, she did not welcome the change: "The Defense Commission has taken me over—and I'm not sure I like that."[85]

Nevertheless, she proceeded to make arrangements for the national conference of civic organizations held in Washington in August. Representatives from eighty-four organizations were selected to provide a mixture of racial, class, and religious groups, reflecting the left-feminist desire to draw working-class and black women into public affairs. Among the groups Cunningham invited were at least five black organizations, including the NAACP and the National Association of Colored Women.

Starting with the conviction that national defense required a healthy population, Cunningham guided the conference discussion into ways that civic organizations could improve the health of low-income groups. In addition to an educational campaign to eliminate vitamin deficiency diseases such as pellagra, she suggested an adult education program to explain what a healthy diet should include, and how to plant vegetable gardens to reduce food costs.[86] But the conference's unstated goals were more important than any specific proposals: women learned that national defense required antipoverty initiatives and that they could contribute to the war effort by helping low-income groups.

Although reluctant to impose a detailed program of action on the participants, Cunningham urged the lay groups to form local defense committees that included all races and classes.[87] The conference accepted this along with several other suggestions that reflected Cunningham's preference for participatory democracy: decentralization, with lay groups rather than the NDAC taking the initiative in forming local defense committees; community discussion groups similar to the AAA rural-urban meetings she had been organizing; and a national educational program that used film, radio, and other media to draw groups that were isolated by poverty, race or recent immigration into the movement.[88] Eleanor Roosevelt ended the conference with an address that Cunningham considered a great success: "She knows what women can do [and] . . . heavens how she works to pump them up to do something."[89]

The ethnically and racially diverse staff Cunningham assembled reflected her concern that the Civic Contacts Unit not limit itself to establishing links with elite white women. It included a black woman, Frances Williams, a member of the NAACP's Board of Directors who had been the national YWCA's advisor on relations with "Negroes," and a male "ethnic," Dr. Frank E. Manuel, a recent Harvard Ph.D. who later became a distinguished Marxist historian. The unit's weekly reports indicate staff members met with black men's and black women's organizations, and with both CIO and AFL trade union leaders as well as farm groups.[90]

Cunningham was also responsible for preparing a special issue of the *Consumers' Guide* on "Food and Nutrition in Relation to National Defense."[91] The issue included a national nutrition program, with a list of suggested action proposals. The response to the special issue was overwhelming: thousands of individuals requested copies. While most who wrote were simply concerned citizens, many were health professionals. The Tennessee Commissioner of Public Health, for example, asked Cunningham for additional copies for the Tennessee State Nutrition Council, while Extension Service nutritionists in several states requested extra copies to use in their teaching.[92] By mid-November, 300,000 copies of the special issue had been distributed, and requests continued to arrive.[93]

Cunningham's tenure at the NDAC ended abruptly in the midst of this frenzied activity. Wayne Darrow, the AAA's Division of Information Director, informed Elliott in December that they needed Cunningham back.[94] Elliott acquiesced, assuring him that even though Cunningham had worked under "great difficulties," she had made a "real contribution" to the Consumer Division.[95]

After rejoining the AAA on January 2, 1941, Cunningham resumed her efforts to convert farm women into New Deal supporters. In addition to organizing rural-urban conferences, she also created a farmer fieldwoman program. Although her official mission was to explain AAA farm policies, unofficially AAA leaders encouraged her in this initiative because they believed New Deal opponents, such as the American Farm Bureau Federation, were turning rural Americans into Republican voters who threatened the New Deal's survival. Since Claude Wickard, the AAA's North Central Division Director, was an enthusiastic advocate, the farmer fieldwomen developed in this region first. By mid-1941 most midwestern states had a state farmer fieldwoman and many had also begun appointing county farmer fieldwomen.[96]

The state farmer fieldwomen were expected to organize AAA auxiliaries for the wives of farmers participating in AAA programs, to organize rural-urban conferences in each county, and to explain AAA programs to women's organizations, such as the Federated Women's Clubs, Parent-Teacher Associations, and home demonstration groups.[97] The latter became a source of controversy when farmer fieldwomen went beyond explaining the AAA's philosophy to making presentations about nutrition and other matters that the Extension Service home demonstration agents considered their jurisdiction.

Although Cunningham went to great lengths to establish harmonious relations with the home demonstration women, they considered the farmer fieldwomen a rival organization.[98] They expressed their resentment in a December 1940 National Home Demonstration Council resolution criticizing the farmer fieldwoman program as an unnecessary duplication of the home demonstration agent's services. The tensions between the two groups were part of a larger clash between the AAA and conservative agricultural organizations, such as the Extension Service. Criticism from Extension Service personnel resulted in a review of the farmer fieldwoman program that imposed restrictions, but allowed it to continue.[99]

REALIZING THAT THE SECOND WORLD WAR WAS INCREASING WOMEN'S opportunities in public affairs if they would only use them, Cunningham attempted to empower women by "poking them up" into becoming active citizens. In a speech to the District of Columbia's Home Economics Association, she called for the "regeneration of our citizenship" through action in support of the war effort. She was especially indignant at war-profiteering by unscrupulous businessmen. Cunningham urged women living near military bases to monitor prices and rents and to organize public pressure against it whenever they found it. She insisted that women's groups had a right and a patriotic duty to defend the public against profiteering. Fully aware that this could pit them against wealthy and socially prominent businessmen, Cunningham challenged them to act: "Will you stand and fight for your country?"[100]

She also reminded white women's organizations that including racial minorities in their activities was essential to developing the national unity necessary for a successful war effort.[101] Welcoming the wartime pressures that threatened to undermine traditional patterns of race relations, she remained friends with Frances Williams even after they ceased working together at the NDAC. When Williams planned a visit to Boston, Cunningham offered an introduction to her close friend, Dorothy Brown. She urged Dorothy to make a special effort to help Williams, because she was a "very fine person" and because race relations was among the problems "vexing" national unity.[102]

The departure of many husbands and farm laborers for the armed forces after 1941 shifted rural gender roles, with women assuming greater responsibility for farm operations. Cunningham encouraged farm women to view themselves as war workers making a contribution as essential as that of the urban women who entered defense plants. She believed that increased responsibilities entitled women to increased rights. There was thus a note of triumph in her 1942 letter informing Eleanor Roosevelt that the AAA had decided to allow farm women to vote in the elections for its community and county committeemen and to be elected to these committees as well.[103]

The First Lady was eager to publicize women's contributions to the war effort, but she depended upon women like Cunningham to provide her with examples. She used Cunningham's information in her wartime radio broadcasts and as a source in preparing her "My Day" column.[104]

Cunningham also met several times with Eleanor in the White House and may have expressed her concern that the men who made government policies often had little awareness of their implications for women.[105] When sugar was rationed, for example, commercial bakeries were allowed 80 percent of their prewar level, but housewives who wanted to make jam were only allotted 50 percent of their prewar consumption.[106] Viewing this as another in a series of slights against women, Cunningham urged Dr. Louise Stanley, Director of the Bureau of Home Economics and Human Nutrition, to make a written protest. Privately, she lamented: "I wish we had a *fierce* bunch of women sitting all the time in Washington who were independent and would raise cane."[107]

She, along with Eleanor Roosevelt and the Women's Division of the DNC, also wanted more women appointed to policy-making positions. President Roosevelt had appointed more women to high office in the 1930s than any of his predecessors, but he had not continued this practice during the war.[108] Cunningham shared the conviction that this resulted in women's interests being neglected. When President Roosevelt considered creating a new group of advisors in 1942, Cunningham and Bertha Friant, a AAA colleague, met with Vice President Henry Wallace "regarding the lack of women in policy-making positions."[109] They urged him to ask the President to include a woman

among the new appointees and suggested three possibilities. But Wallace reported that Roosevelt's response had been: "My God, no."[110]

Cunningham's job required frequent travel—by train and before air conditioning was widely used—to organize rural-urban conferences and to speak
to women's groups. By 1942 she admitted that she was "weary and home-
sick," tired of that "damn Hitler," and intended to go to Texas in November,
come what may.[111] While in Texas, she surveyed public attitudes for the Hogg
Mental Health Foundation and was alarmed at the level of racial animosity.
The increased white resentment against blacks stemmed in part from Roosevelt's 1941 executive order prohibiting racial discrimination in hiring under
defense contracts and creating a Fair Employment Practices Committee to
enforce it. Southern white supremacist groups, such as the misnamed Christian Americans, encouraged racial hatred by spreading reports that the government was attempting to force employers to hire blacks instead of whites.
In June 1943 when white resentment erupted into a race riot in Beaumont,
Cunningham wrote to Eleanor Roosevelt, asking her to have the FBI investi-
gate the "Nazi" group that had instigated the riot.[112]

CUNNINGHAM'S AAA WORK REFLECTED HER VISION OF A WOMEN'S
movement linked with the political Left. She encouraged women to become
politically active but sought to channel that activism in support of New Deal
reforms. She organized discussion groups on public issues, including foreign
policy, to educate women; the meetings she held on "Winning the War on the
Spiritual Front" illustrate her approach. Since churchwomen's groups frequently needed a speaker, Cunningham used a noncontroversial title to secure bookings. But in her presentation she urged women to speak out for the
establishment of a United Nations to preserve peace in the postwar world.[113]
This shrewdly linked women's special interest in peace with one of the Roosevelt administration's controversial foreign policy goals in a nonthreatening
manner.

Through hundreds of grassroots meetings like this during her four years
with the AAA, Cunningham felt that she made great strides in switching farm
women's conversation from "preserving fruit to preserving democracy."[114]
But in training farm women to become active citizens, she was undermining
traditional gender roles as well as increasing support for the New Deal. Conservative farm organizations, such as the Extension Service and the Farm Bureau, objected to both and responded by urging Congress to cut funds for
AAA information work.

The 1942 congressional elections gave Republicans and anti–New Deal
Democrats control of Congress. In 1943 the New Deal came under sustained

congressional attack: its advocates were dismissed and several programs were eliminated.[115] Harry Schooler, who led the AAA fight against the Farm Bureau and as AAA North Central Regional Director was in charge of the region with the most fully developed farmer fieldwoman program, was forced to resign. Wayne Darrow, who had brought Cunningham to Washington to establish the farmer fieldwoman program, also resigned. By July 1943 Cunningham was politically isolated and her job in jeopardy.[116]

The new Congress was eager to assist anti–New Deal farm organizations, such as the American Farm Bureau Federation, in their efforts to weaken New Deal farm programs. Encouraged by the Farm Bureau, Congress included in the 1943 Appropriations Act a clause prohibiting the use of federal funds to pay AAA regional, state, or county information employees. The work they had been doing was turned over to the Extension Service, a Farm Bureau ally.[117] This ended Cunningham's farmer fieldwoman program.

The Appropriations Act led directly to Cunningham's resignation. On July 15, 1943, N. E. Dodd, AAA Chief, announced that the Extension Service would immediately become responsible for the information duties previously performed by AAA state and local employees. While not denying funding for national information officers, such as Cunningham, the Act made it impossible for her to continue her women's programs by making her dependent on an agency—the Extension Service—that opposed them. Rather than continue in the ineffectual role that the Appropriations Act allowed, Cunningham followed the advice she had given an angry friend a year earlier: "For goodness sake don't waste that magnificent rage by spraying it all over the universe. Harness it and make it saw wood."[118]

She therefore resigned from the AAA in a manner designed to inflict maximum political damage on the anti–New Deal forces. In her resignation letter to the Texas congressional delegation, she warned that anti–New Deal groups were undermining the freedoms for which Americans were fighting the war.[119] She accused M. L. Wilson, Extension Service Director, of depriving AAA employees of freedom of speech through the "gag" order, even though this was one of the four freedoms Roosevelt had identified as American war aims. She claimed Wilson's "gag" order also endangered the war food production program, which depended on AAA employees being free to explain the administration's production goals to farmers. Acknowledging that these were serious charges, Cunningham insisted that she could not remain silent while American soldiers were dying on the battlefields in defense of freedom of speech. She was resigning, she concluded, in order to be free to speak for the nation's farm women who wanted the Congressmen to know "this thing is wrong and we will not stand for it."[120]

Shortly after she returned to Texas, Cunningham informed Eleanor Roosevelt that she had resigned from the AAA "in behalf of free speech." She explained that under the "gag" rule a AAA employee could legally attack the government's agricultural war program but could not legally speak out in support of it. Assuring the First Lady that she remained glad that she had "stood up to be counted," Cunningham noted that many people had contacted her since her return to Texas and that she was doing her best to provide leadership in support of the war effort.[121]

Several individuals with ties to the Left recommended Cunningham for other positions. Apparently at Eleanor Roosevelt's request, the DNC staff obtained the approval of prominent black women (including Crystal Bird Fauset, the administration's highest ranking African American woman) to appoint Cunningham to a position in the Fair Employment Practices Committee's Atlanta office.[122] Harold Young, Vice President Wallace's chief aide, and Charles Marsh, the radical newspaper publisher, both urged the CIO to appoint Robert H. Montgomery as its southwest regional political operative with Cunningham as his assistant. They endorsed her because she had the "widest personal following among farmers and within women's organizations of any woman in the southwest."[123] But she chose to remain in Texas and develop a grassroots movement to defend the New Deal against its enemies.

AT WAR WITH THE TEXAS REGULARS,
1944 – 1946

SHORTLY AFTER CUNNINGHAM RETURNED TO TEXAS, SHE ANNOUNCED IN a radio interview that women had special home-front responsibilities: "They must see to it that the ways of democracy are preserved."[1] This was an appeal to women to join with her to prevent a small group of wealthy men known as the Texas Regulars from seizing control of the state Democratic Party and subverting the democratic process. The Regulars had emerged in the 1930s, but wartime developments strengthened the movement. Large corporate interests resented new federal regulations, such as rationing and price controls, so much that they seemed convinced that Texas was fighting three enemies: Germany, Japan, and the federal government.[2] They expressed their discontent by financing anti-Roosevelt political groups. The result in Texas and other southern states was an attempt by nondemocratic methods to prevent President Roosevelt's reelection in 1944.[3]

Cunningham played a major role in organizing the liberal political coalition that resisted the anti-Roosevelt movement. She revitalized the pro-Roosevelt Texas Farmers' Union (TFU) and helped link it with the state's labor movement by establishing the Texas Social and Legislative Conference. She set up the Austin office that served as the liberals' state headquarters, and created an independent women's organization associated with the liberal coalition. Finally, when no other New Deal Democrat would challenge Texas's anti–New Deal governor, she entered the 1944 gubernatorial race to rally Roosevelt's supporters.

WHEN CUNNINGHAM RETURNED TO TEXAS LATE IN 1943, ANTI–NEW DEAL forces were threatening to take over the state. The Texas Farm Bureau Federation, the state's dominant farm organization, was part of this movement and had taken over the pro–New Deal Texas Agricultural Association. One of Cunningham's first steps after returning to Texas was to encourage a revolt against this. She took the floor during a Farm Bureau meeting to contrast the independent status of Texas farm leaders under the TAA with their servile status under the Farm Bureau: "This thing is all wrong, and we farmers will not stand for it."[4]

Since the farm vote was crucial to controlling state politics, Cunningham worked through the TFU to rally farmers behind the New Deal. By the end of 1943 Frank Overturf, the TFU's secretary, was acknowledging the "tremendous impetus" Cunningham and her old friend Caswell Ellis had given the TFU.[5] During the following year Cunningham and Ellis recruited new TFU members in the Austin area and advised Overturf on how to increase statewide membership.[6] Cunningham was appointed to the TFU's policy committee in 1944[7] and later that year was one of the featured speakers at its annual convention, sharing a platform with James Patton, the National Farmers' Union president.[8] Cunningham's efforts had attracted the NFU's attention even before the convention; in June its journal had identified her as a leader of the movement to rebuild the TFU.[9] But Texas farmers could not sustain a successful political movement by themselves. Cunningham knew that anti–New Deal forces had relied upon setting the farmer against the industrial worker "to an enormous degree" to gain political power.[10] To prevent this, she planned a farmer-labor organization that resembled the Political Action Committee the national CIO had established in 1943 to unite workers, farmers, and progressives.

Cunningham's initiative resulted in the formation of the Texas Social and Legislative Conference (TSLC).[11] She urged Overturf to join forces with other New Deal groups.[12] The first step was to bring James Carey, the CIO's national secretary, and James Patton to Dallas for a state farmers meeting.[13] Overturf chaired the meeting, while Cunningham introduced the speakers and made a presentation.[14] The participants agreed that Texas liberal groups needed closer cooperation. Encouraged by Cunningham, the TFU convened the February 1944 Fort Worth meeting that established the TSLC. Although Cunningham was the prime mover and a TFU delegate, she was unable to attend because she was nursing her sister Ella Traylor, who was dying of cancer.[15]

The TSLC played a key role in the development of the Texas Left between 1944 and the mid-1950s. Acting as the Left's political action committee, it drew progressive groups together to promote suitable political candidates and a common legislative agenda. Challenging class and racial barriers to full citizenship, it advocated a true secret ballot; an end to the poll tax; a federal ballot for members of the armed forces;[16]and equal educational and employment opportunities regardless of race, color, or creed. Texas CIO unions provided the largest bloc of delegates at the initial meeting and a majority of the executive committee members. Cunningham's allies, Marion Storm and Margaret Reading, were on the executive committee, and Storm became the TSLC's executive secretary and Research Director in 1948.[17]

Cunningham was also instrumental in setting up the Austin office that served as the unofficial liberal state headquarters for the next two decades.[18] The TSLC financed it under Cunningham's direction in the Littlefield Building downtown, which years earlier had housed the Texas Equal Suffrage Association.[19] Known simply as the 711 Littlefield office, it functioned as an information clearinghouse for Texas liberals. Marion Storm, Cunningham's protégée, became the office manager, and Austin women provided the volunteer labor for the office's mass mail-outs.

NEW DEAL SUPPORTERS NEEDED RALLYING IN 1944 BECAUSE SOUTHERN Democrats were conspiring to prevent President Roosevelt's reelection. They planned to have state Democratic conventions choose uninstructed electors who would deny Roosevelt their electoral college vote, even if he received a majority of a state's popular vote. Their strategy was to throw the election into the House of Representatives, where the southern states were disproportionately strong and could select a more conservative nominee. In Texas the anti-Roosevelt Democrats—called Regulars—were financed by oil and gas interests. Because George Butler, the state Democratic Executive Committee chairman, was one of their leaders, the Regulars were able to use the party organization to pack the precinct meetings with their followers and secure a majority of state convention delegates.[20]

Although all branches of the federal government were involved in reforms that threatened fundamental changes in southern racial and class structures, the Texas Regulars directed their animosity against Roosevelt. In addition to holding him responsible for the growing trade union movement, the Regulars urged the "restoration of the supremacy of the white race," which they claimed the Roosevelt administration had undermined. They especially resented the Supreme Court's 1944 *Smith v. Allwright* decision, which had opened the Texas Democratic primary to black voters. They also denounced Roosevelt for establishing the Fair Employment Practices Committee, which attempted to stop racial discrimination in employment, and for congressional efforts to abolish the poll tax, which reduced black voting.[21]

Roosevelt's supporters were taken by surprise by the Regulars' control of the state convention. When Alvin Wirtz, a Roosevelt leader and former Undersecretary of the Interior, moved that no person should be chosen as a Texas elector unless they agreed to vote in the electoral college for the party's nominee, fistfights and a "near riot" broke out. After his motion was ruled out of order and an appeal defeated, Cunningham, who chaired the Walker County delegation, and the other Roosevelt Democrats held a separate convention. It elected Cunningham one of its four officers[22] and then selected electors and delegates pledged to support the party's presidential nominee.[23]

Although the Regulars used racial issues to attract white voters, Cunningham believed they were motivated by the adverse effect of rationing and price controls on "their own financial holdings," whereas the Roosevelt Democrats supported controls necessary for the war effort.[24] Governor Coke Stevenson joined the oil and gas industry in denouncing wartime price controls and gasoline rationing, but he stayed in the background and allowed his appointee, George Butler, to direct the Regulars' campaign.[25] Stevenson's involvement with the Regulars became apparent, however, when they selected him to head their delegation to the National Democratic Convention.[26]

Convinced that the Regulars were little more than Texas "fascists," Cunningham had already began searching for a pro-Roosevelt candidate to challenge Stevenson.[27] After consulting with her circle of female political activists, she chose J. Frank Dobie, the well-known author and University of Texas Professor of English. Since Dobie was a visiting professor at the University of Cambridge at the time, Cunningham established a "Draft Dobie" organization and convinced John Henry Faulk, Dobie's close friend, to help persuade him to run.[28] After she came to Austin to direct the campaign, "things really picked up," according to Faulk, but despite a flood of telegrams, Dobie refused.[29] When no other Roosevelt supporter came forward, Cunningham decided to run, despite the financial sacrifice: "You can't just lean back and let them run over you."[30] Since she didn't even have the $100 required for the filing fee, she had lumber valued at that amount cut from the pine trees on the land she had inherited.[31]

Cunningham did not expect to win, but she felt morally obligated to run. She explained to Carrie Chapman Catt that she became a candidate because "we were only responsible to God for what we did ourselves and not for what other people did or did not do."[32] She was not, however, simply making a moral gesture; she expected her candidacy to weaken the anti–New Deal forces. If she remained a private citizen, her efforts to publicize Stevenson's role in the Regulars' conspiracy would be ignored; but as a candidate, the press would report her statements. Also, if faced with a serious challenge, Stevenson might stay in Texas and campaign instead of becoming one of the anti-Roosevelt movement's leaders at the Democratic National Convention.[33]

A March 1944 Texas opinion poll indicated nearly two-thirds of those polled supported Roosevelt.[34] If she could convince these voters that Stevenson had "entered into a conspiracy to destroy the American system of party government" in an attempt to prevent Roosevelt's reelection, the governor's bid for another term could be endangered.[35]

Cunningham's candidacy attracted national attention. Impressed by her "flashing wit and biting tongue," liberals at the DNC in Washington hoped she would turn out enough New Deal supporters to defeat several anti–New Deal Texas congressmen seeking reelection.[36] *PM*, the New York City left-liberal journal, claimed that Texas conservatives were taking her very seriously because she was known as a "dynamo of organizing and propaganda ability."[37]

Cunningham described her campaign as a "straight, hot attack on the governor and his anti-war activities."[38] Her platform had one plank: "Full support for the war."[39] She charged Stevenson with obstructing the war effort by opposing gasoline and rubber rationing and suggested that he seemed more concerned with protecting the business community, especially the oil and sulfur industries, against government regulation than with defeating the Axis powers.[40] Although Stevenson received royalty income from oil leases, it was not his personal integrity that she questioned. What she found outrageous was that the governor would serve as the spokesman for "selfish interests which put personal gain before winning the war."[41]

Cunningham also attacked Stevenson for contributing to the climate of racial prejudice. After Roosevelt issued Executive Order 8802 in 1941 banning racial discrimination in hiring under government defense contracts, Stevenson claimed the order should not apply in Texas because it conflicted with state segregation laws. He also denounced the Supreme Court decision allowing blacks to vote in Texas Democratic primary elections as a "monstrous threat to our peace and security."[42] Cunningham thought Stevenson's encouragement of racial enmity not only wrong in itself but dangerously divisive at a time when national unity was needed to wage war successfully.[43]

Although Stevenson generally ignored Cunningham, some of his supporters conducted a race-baiting campaign against her. In one incident, she addressed a religious organization, apparently a YWCA, whose audience included blacks. The racial slurs hurled at her for speaking to a racially mixed audience distressed her friends, but Cunningham was not deterred. "The time is *never* going to come when I will be so little free that I cannot cooperate with a religious organization and serve it as a teacher."[44]

Because politics was still considered a male domain in 1944, press coverage of Cunningham's campaign focused on gender, just as in her 1928 Senate race. Although Miriam Ferguson had served as governor, she had been perceived as her husband's surrogate, and many papers considered the novelty of an independent female candidate the most newsworthy aspect of Cunningham's campaign. When she announced her candidacy, headlines proclaimed: "Woman Opens Her Campaign for Governor."[45] Some headlines implied skepticism about her fitness for a "man's" job: "Mrs. Cunningham Qualified for Office, She Says."[46] Assuming that men could not be expected to vote for a woman, even friendly papers suggested that victory would depend on a heavy female turnout: "Will Women Rise to the Occasion?"[47]

In one respect, electoral conditions in 1944 were unusually favorable for a female candidate. More than 600,000 Texans were in the armed forces, and many were unable to vote because Stevenson had refused to call a special session of the legislature to waive the normal requirements. As a result, women were a majority of eligible voters, and Cunningham made special efforts to stimulate a female consciousness that would bring women to the polls. Her campaign material claimed that because of the stake women had in the war, it was of "paramount importance" that women hold positions of governmental authority. This drew attention to Stevenson's failure to appoint a single woman to a policy-making position.[48]

Cunningham also attempted to attract female voters by stressing her service to women's organizations dating back to the suffrage movement. In addition to her work for the national League of Women Voters and the General Federation of Women's Clubs, she cited her membership on the YWCA's National Board. When she ran for governor, she was a member of the National YWCA's Committee on Agriculture and of the National Federation of Business and Professional Women's Clubs Vocational Guidance Committee. Cunningham had maintained her ties with the Texas Federation of Women's Clubs during the war and was one of the speakers at its 1942 convention.[49] Although the TFWC's constitution prevented it from endorsing candidates, it placed Cunningham's paid political ad in a highly visible position inside its journal's front cover and buried Stevenson's ad in the back.[50]

The women's network Cunningham had developed over the previous quarter century rallied to help her candidacy. Such groups as the Texas League of Women Voters, the Corpus Christi Business and Professional Women, and the Tarrant County Women's Good Government League sponsored her speaking engagements. Jane McCallum, Cunningham's chief lieutenant in the suffrage movement, was in charge of her Austin office, assisted by Mrs. Claude Hill, former Texas LWV president, and Mrs. Sam J. Smith, former Texas Federation of Women's Clubs' president who had managed Cunningham's 1928 Senate campaign.[51] Another former TFWC president, Florence Floore, the Senate campaign's treasurer, was one of the largest campaign contributors.[52]

Cunningham's campaign also drew young women without previous political experience into politics. After hearing one of Cunningham's radio addresses, Kathleen Voigt volunteered her services and became one of Texas's top politi-

cal organizers in the 1950s.[53] Marion Storm, a key postwar assistant, became
her campaign manager.[54] Liz Sutherland (Carpenter), a recent University of
Texas journalism graduate, served as Cunningham's press secretary.[55] Later a
founder of the National Women's Political Caucus, Carpenter acknowledged
that it was Cunningham who helped her develop a "political conscience."[56] As
Liz Carpenter, she became Lady Bird Johnson's White House staff director
and press secretary.

Although the press portrayed her as the "women's candidate," Cunningham was well aware that her chance of winning was minimal if only women
voters supported her. She attempted to appeal to the major components of
Roosevelt's electoral coalition: organized labor, farmers, and the elderly. She
anticipated support from the elderly because of her earlier work to improve
old age pensions through the Women's Committee on Economic Policy and
because Stevenson had cut old age pensions by 10 percent in order to reduce
the state deficit. Pointing out that this was equivalent to imposing a 10 percent
income tax on the elderly, she questioned the fairness of singling out one of
the state's most poverty-stricken groups to bear the burden of achieving fiscal
stability.[57]

Cunningham also drew support from organized labor, farmers, and from
the black community. The national CIO's Political Action Committee, the
Texas Federation of Labor, and the railroad brotherhood all endorsed her.[58]
Herman Wright, one of Texas's two main CIO lawyers in the 1940s, helped finance her three campaign radio broadcasts.[59] The TFU as well as many farmers who had belonged to the Texas Agricultural Association supported her.[60]
The National Farmers' Union published a laudatory article in its journal describing Cunningham as "fluent, fiery and effective."[61] Although black leaders
did not endorse candidates in the election, one of the state's most important
black newspapers identified Cunningham as a "fair-minded woman," which
readers would probably have interpreted as a coded endorsement.[62]

In July, Cunningham informed Eleanor Roosevelt that the "fight" was
going well and that her opportunity for being elected had risen from "practically nothing to at least a good fighting chance."[63] Objectively, however, she
had little chance of winning. She entered the race at the last minute without
a campaign fund or an organization and never secured the funding necessary
for a serious challenge. J. Frank Dobie had refused to enter the race because
he thought $100,000 was the minimum necessary to mount a serious cam-
paign. Cunningham received $1,685 in donations, which she supplemented
with $950 borrowed from her hometown bank.[64] Originally she had not even
planned to campaign, but in response to requests from supporters, she traveled over 1,600 miles by car during a two-and-a-half-week period in which she
stopped briefly at the major eastern and central Texas cities.[65]

Cunningham's campaign climaxed with three radio addresses broadcast
during the week prior to polling day. Each was directed at a different audience:

women, soldiers, and then to all voters. She needed a high turnout by female voters to have any chance of success, and her first radio address was intended to motivate them. She suggested that women whose husbands and sons were risking their lives to preserve democracy had a special responsibility to go to the polls. She also sought to arouse gender consciousness by denouncing the Regulars for removing Clara Driscoll from her position as Texas National Committeewoman: "Not only Clara Driscoll was insulted but every woman in the state of Texas was insulted."[66]

Cunningham had predicted she would get a majority of the women's vote, but women rarely vote as a gender bloc, and 1944 was no exception.[67] After conducting an informal statewide poll of women voters, the *Arlington Citizen's* editor reported that a majority of the women interviewed believed the governor's position was "no job for a woman" and claimed they would not vote for one under any circumstances.[68]

When the ballots were counted, Cunningham finished second behind Stevenson with 48,039 votes, more than twice as many as any of his other challengers. Although she received less than 6 percent of the total vote, contemporaries were amazed that she had done so well in a poorly financed campaign lasting only a few weeks against an incumbent governor.[69]

Several factors probably widened Stevenson's margin of victory. Only 22 percent of those eligible voted, the lowest turnout for a Democratic gubernatorial primary since 1920.[70] This hurt Cunningham more than Stevenson, since a low turnout normally benefits the conservative candidate.[71] The state's election laws probably suppressed the number of votes for Cunningham. The poll tax excluded many low-income persons, whom she considered her most likely supporters. The early voter registration requirement, combined with Cunningham's late announcement of her candidacy, meant that only those who had registered and paid their poll tax, which was several months before they knew Cunningham would be a candidate, were eligible to vote for her.[72] Finally, although Cunningham would probably have benefited more than Stevenson from a high African American turnout, in some areas African Americans risked death if they attempted to vote. In Cunningham's hometown, a black man who voted despite the protests of local whites was beaten by an enraged crowd armed with hatchets, clubs, and ropes. Cunningham, who witnessed the mob violence, saved the man from being lynched by calling the county sheriff.[73]

Although she did not win, Cunningham considered her campaign a success. Instead of leading the Texas delegation at the Democratic National Convention and helping organize an anti-Roosevelt movement, Stevenson stayed home to campaign. Cunningham was elated at having accomplished her primary goal: "We scared him out of going to Chicago."[74] She also believed her campaign worthwhile because it increased the turnout of the "little people," rank-and-file Roosevelt Democrats. Despite the efforts by self-proclaimed pro-Roosevelt leaders, such as Lyndon Johnson, to bargain with the Regulars for power and influence, "the exciting thing has been that the people's movement rose and swept over the 'leaders.'"[75] This contributed to the defeat of two prominent anti-Roosevelt congressmen, Martin Dies and Richard Kleberg. It also helped the pro-Roosevelt forces elect a majority of both the Democratic county chairmen and delegates to the fall state convention.[76]

The struggle with the Regulars forced liberal Democrats to organize on a statewide basis for the first time. Walter G. Hall, one of their leaders, considered it the "beginning of the modern Texas liberal movement."[77] Cunningham's group of female volunteers, working out of the 711 Littlefield office, was at the center of this effort. Paul Holcomb, a liberal Austin editor, reported that "hundreds" of women worked day and night to mobilize Roosevelt supporters statewide. When the Roosevelt Democrats gained control of the party at its September state convention, Holcomb credited the women working under Cunningham's direction for their success.[78] This was a crucial defeat for the Regulars: the convention replaced the anti-Roosevelt electors with a new slate pledged to support the party's nominee and elected a state Democratic Executive Committee composed of loyal Democrats.[79]

Although many individuals contributed to the loyal Democratic majority, Cunningham believed her pre-convention organizing efforts were decisive. While the big city convention delegations were anti-Roosevelt, those from the rural counties gave the Roosevelt forces a majority. Cunningham, who chaired the Walker County delegation, was "thrilled" by the rural response because she had helped establish the Texas Agricultural Mobilization Committee and revitalized the TFU in order to create a New Deal majority among farmers.[80]

With so many men in the armed forces, women played an unusually important role in the 1944 presidential campaign. The DNC's election plan reflected this gender imbalance. Aware that women comprised 60 percent of the potential voters, the DNC recommended that the party "harness the feminine energy of the country." Convinced that winning depended on a high voter turnout, it proposed creating a nonpartisan "Get Out the Vote" organization, which would be especially concerned with stimulating increased female voting. It recommended that Cunningham be appointed to this organization because she was the "best southern woman." Since grassroots women's participation would be crucial to making full use of "unused female energy," it also proposed that Cunningham be asked to review the plan.[81] Although an ostensibly nonpartisan get out the vote organization was established that focused on increasing the women's vote, we have been unable to determine whether Cunningham was involved.[82] She was, however, on the DNC women's division's "key women" list for the 1944 campaign.[83]

President Roosevelt had kept a careful eye on the Texas Regulars' revolt, and both he and Eleanor followed Cunningham's campaign with interest.

During the campaign Eleanor encouraged her and assured her that Franklin was anxious that she do well.[84] Following her defeat, Cunningham directed the Texas women's campaign for Roosevelt during the fall presidential election. She was identified in this capacity when she met with President Truman in the White House in 1945.[85] While it is impossible to determine the extent to which the women's campaign helped Roosevelt carry the state, his Texas opponents considered it important; they tried to discredit it by claiming it was a "militant" women's movement.[86]

CUNNINGHAM RECOGNIZED THAT THE SECOND WORLD WAR HAD CREATED new opportunities for women and that in running for governor she was helping shift gender boundaries. During her campaign she claimed that it was of "paramount importance" that women be given positions of authority in government, and she continued to urge this after her defeat.[87] Following the June 1944 White House Women's Conference, which had been organized to press for the appointment of more women to policy-making positions in the federal government,[88] the American Association of University Women's Texas branch convened a similar conference in Austin.[89]

Chaired by Dallas judge Sarah Hughes, the meeting drew about 200 women to hear Cunningham and others discuss the need for greater female involvement in governing Texas. Apparently disappointed at clubwomen's reluctance to become involved in controversial matters, Cunningham insisted that current events involved real issues, not just "material with which to reply to a club roll call."[90] She warned her audience that if women were to have greater opportunities to participate in state government, they must "take firm stands on controversial questions" and be willing to "attack those who undermine our freedom." Among the barriers to women's future opportunities in government, she identified: "control of government by a corrupt minority," "economic power used for political intimidation," and "racial stresses stirred up for political purposes."[91]

Cunningham was eager to have more women elected to high office and considered Sarah Hughes one of Texas's most electable women. When a Dallas congressional seat became vacant, Cunningham encouraged her to run for it. But when Hughes delayed announcing her candidacy, Cunningham grew impatient and began to have doubts about "the wisdom of my choice" in selecting her.[92] Eventually Hughes did run, winning the first round in the 1946 primary. But she was defeated in the runoff after everyone in the all-male Texas congressional delegation except for Wright Patman endorsed her opponent on the ground they didn't want a woman joining their Washington club.[93]

While middle-class feminists were preoccupied with placing women in positions of authority, left feminists were also concerned with the postwar status of women workers. Female labor leaders feared that the reconversion to a peacetime economy would bring a sharp reduction in women's employment and the permanent removal of protective legislation that had been suspended during the war. Frieda Miller, head of the Women's Bureau, invited Cunningham to a Washington, D.C., conference of national women's leaders interested in defending women workers against these threats.[94] Cunningham attended as a National Farmers' Union representative.

Conference participants were divided on the question of whether women could maintain wartime gains. Those from northern states were most optimistic, emphasizing women's accomplishments, such as establishing the principle of equal pay for female workers. Cunningham, however, warned that the women in war plants were only under contract for the war's duration and that in Texas there were forces pushing for a postwar labor force "altogether without women employees."[95] She joined with trade union women in pressing for policies to prevent discrimination against women when layoffs occurred and for the appointment of informed women to public postwar planning bodies to protect women worker's interests.[96]

The conference participants also expressed concern that the wartime relaxation of protective legislation might be continued in peacetime. In several areas the prewar limit of eight hours per day and forty-eight hours per week for women had been increased to ten and fifty-four. Miller was surprised when Cunningham announced that, as a result of a private agreement between a labor leader and a state senator, it had been extended to ten and seventy in Texas. Although Cunningham questioned the labor leader about the matter afterward, he "didn't see that we [women] had a right to be bitter" about not being consulted.[97]

Cunningham's position on protective legislation reflected her left feminism. By 1945 the issue of whether protective legislation should be resumed had become a source of class conflict between middle-class women's organizations, who opposed it, and working-class women's groups, who were determined to restore it.[98] Despite her close ties with middle-class women's organizations, Cunningham joined with female trade unionists in urging the restoration of protective legislation and minimum wage legislation to address the problem of women's low pay.[99]

THE FIGHT AGAINST THE TEXAS REGULARS DID NOT END WITH Roosevelt's reelection. Unable to gain control of the Democratic Party, the Regulars turned to higher education. After some of Governor W. Lee O'Daniel's wealthy financial backers complained that Texas colleges had radicals on their faculties, he met secretly with several of them in 1940. They agreed at the

Houston "Gag Conference" to seize control of the schools' governing boards in order to get rid of faculty they considered subversive.[100] O'Daniel implemented the plan by appointing Regulars to the University of Texas Board of Regents, and Coke Stevenson continued this policy when he succeeded O'Daniel as governor.[101]

Between 1940 and 1944 these anti–New Deal Regents repeatedly intervened in UT's internal affairs, seeking to suppress dissenting opinions. They attempted to fire three prominent economists, including Dr. Robert Montgomery, Cunningham's close friend and ally; they were saved by tenure, but several untenured faculty were dismissed. By 1944 the Regents had, according to Cunningham, created an atmosphere of "intellectual terrorism" at the University of Texas.[102] The attack on academic freedom culminated with President Homer Rainey's dismissal without explanation in 1944, after he publicly defended the faculty's right to freedom of speech.[103] Later, during the Texas Senate hearing on the matter, a Regent explained that Rainey had been an unsatisfactory President because he was "ultra-liberal on the Nigger question."[104]

Rainey's firing precipitated a crisis that attracted national attention. The American Association of University Professors censured the university administration and kept UT on its blacklist until 1953.[105] Cunningham suggested the Regents who fired Rainey were seeking to establish a "home-grown fascism."[106] She accused them of trying to wreck the university "and use the pieces as building material for private fortunes."[107] After attending the Board of Regents' sessions in which Rainey was terminated, she proposed that the Texas Exes, the UT alumni association, hold regional "fighting" conferences in the state's major cities to defend the university.[108]

Rainey's supporters, led by J. R. Parten, the chairman of the Board of Regents when Rainey was hired, met late in November to plan the defense. Former state Attorney General Robert Lee Bobbitt, a participant in the meeting, worked with Cunningham on a daily basis during the months immediately afterward.[109] He wrote to Sarah Hughes encouraging women to establish an organization to defend the principles that Texas boys were fighting for in the war.[110] Within a few weeks, Cunningham was sending out letters announcing the formation of the Women's Committee for Educational Freedom. The WCEF's initial funding came from UT alumni and an anonymous donor of "unquestionable" integrity, probably Parten.[111]

Cunningham formed this new group because there was no organization open to all women who wished to defend educational freedom. Prospective members were informed that the UT crisis was not an isolated incident but part of the Texas Regulars "conspiracy" to seize control of the Texas Democratic Party.[112] Cunningham realized that politicians did not fear most women's groups because they preferred study to action. But she intended the WCEF to be different; it would be a "fighting committee."[113] She informed a friend that she and her allies were on the eve of launching "our great battle."[114] When Jane McCallum expressed alarm over what the WCEF's opponents were saying about it, Cunningham encouraged her to "buck up and sass the folks who have been trying to scare you."[115]

Convinced that Texas women had enough power "to do anything we desire to do," Cunningham wanted to channel that desire along constructive lines.[116] Since education had traditionally been a women's issue, she believed the attack on higher education could revive the women's movement if it aroused a female consciousness. Partly for this reason, she claimed that Texas women had a special obligation to the "sons and daughters of Texas" to protect their educational opportunities.[117] The WCEF's position, she pointed out, had been endorsed by the four largest and most powerful women's organizations: the Federation of Women's Clubs, the Business and Professional Women's Clubs, the Parent-Teacher Associations, and the AAUW.[118]

The WCEF originally included some of Texas' most influential political women: Marguerite Fairchild, a Regent who voted against firing Rainey; Clara Driscoll, national Democratic Committeewoman from 1928 to 1944; Judge Sarah T. Hughes; and Dr. Minnie Maffett, who had recently completed her term as the President of the National Federation of Business and Professional Women's Clubs. Jane McCallum, a former Texas secretary of state, chaired the committee until poor health forced her to resign,[119] and Cunningham persuaded Lillian Collier to take over. Both women had the financial security and leisure that Cunningham lacked. Cunningham became the WCEF's secretary, establishing a pattern that would be repeated over the next two decades in other groups: Cunningham did the planning and developed the strategy while someone happy to follow her guidance held what was ostensibly the leadership position.

The seventy-five women who attended the WCEF's first meeting in January 1945 adopted three objectives: Rainey's reinstatement, the resignation of the three remaining UT regents who voted to dismiss him, and legislation increasing the Board of Regents to fifteen members, with at least one-third of them women.[120] Reviving a strategy used in the suffrage campaign, Cunningham had recruited a woman from each of the thirty-one senatorial districts, so that after the meeting each state senator could be lobbied by a WCEF member from his district. Not all of the senators were grateful; some hid in phone booths to avoid meeting with their female constituents. Afterward the women reported to Cunningham so she could determine which senators needed additional pressure.[121] She had not planned to lobby the governor, but she agreed when some of her group suggested it. Although the press portrayed them as a band of "militant" women, Stevenson was not persuaded to urge the anti-Rainey board members to resign or to include a woman among his new appointees.[122]

When it became known that Stevenson's new nominees were, with one exception, all Regulars or Republicans, the WCEF demanded a more representative board. The women asked their state senators to reject Stevenson's nominees and reminded them that the September 1944 state Democratic convention had committed the party to opposing restrictions on academic freedom. Cunningham, coauthor of the resolution, insisted that since all the senators had run as Democrats, they were bound by the party's platform.[123] Although the WCEF was unable to prevent the Senate from confirming Stevenson's nominees, the women and their allies generated so much pressure that the Senate acted in secret session, where votes were not recorded.[124]

Asked if she thought the WCEF should abandon the fight, Cunningham quoted the U.S. commander at Bastogne's reply when urged to surrender: "Nuts." Recognizing that the struggle would require political action, she urged WCEF members to prepare for a two-year fight that would culminate in the "great clean up of 1946"—the next elections.[125] To wage this fight more effectively, the WCEF initiated a membership drive. By March 1946 it had grown from the seventy-five original participants to nearly 2,000 women, with members in every county.[126] Many of these were UT alumni or the wives of recently demobilized servicemen.[127]

Cunningham realized that some WCEF members would be pressured to withdraw by their husbands. She therefore did not encourage women to become members "who, because of their husband's business connections, think they must be tactful."[128] Instead, she announced that the committee was seeking those "who are free to stand on their own feet and fight."[129] Recruiting women who fit this description was a challenge. Cunningham gave Marjorie Barksdale, the spouse of a University of Texas-Arlington professor, the names and addresses of women whom she thought would be receptive for a WCEF recruiting trip to North Texas. But Barksdale's reports were disappointing. Some women she approached supported academic freedom, but they refused to join the WCEF because it would endanger their husbands' jobs. Even though Barksdale stressed that the WCEF was an educational rather than a political organization, others declined to join because they didn't want to be involved with politics "in any form." Several of these were the leaders of local women's clubs, whom Cunningham was especially eager to recruit.[130]

Although it began as an attempt to defend academic freedom at the University of Texas, the WCEF was concerned with all educational issues. When the Texas legislature considered endorsing an amendment to the U.S. Constitution setting a 25 percent ceiling on federal income tax, the WCEF argued that there could be no educational freedom without adequate financial support for education and urged legislators to "fight this vicious measure to the last ditch."[131] When state representative Jim Wright (later Speaker of the U.S. House of Representatives) introduced legislation to raise Texas teachers' salaries, among the lowest in the nation, the WCEF endorsed his bill and invited Wright to be the guest speaker at its 1947 annual meeting.[132]

The WCEF also sought to protect educational freedom in the selection of public school textbooks. Under Texas law the State Board of Education selected textbooks used in the public schools. The Texas Regulars' strategy included controlling sources of information in order to turn public opinion against liberalism. Maco Stewart Jr., a multimillionaire Regular, chaired the Board but delegated responsibility for recommending textbooks to his employee, Lewis V. Ulrey, an admirer of Adolph Hitler and a vocal critic of communism, Jews, racial equality, and unions. When Ulrey successfully pressured a publisher into withdrawing a textbook on Russia from Board consideration because it was not sufficiently anticommunist, the author sought support from the WCEF and other groups concerned with educational freedom.[133]

When the Board agreed to the WCEF's request for a hearing on how it selected textbooks, both Cunningham and Lillian Collier testified.[134] Cunningham focused on the illegality of Ulrey's role in deciding what books the Board would consider, while Collier warned that by allowing Ulrey to make such decisions, textbooks could become a means of promoting the "propaganda of a small special interest group."[135] The adverse publicity generated by the hearing may have contributed to Stevenson's decision not to reappoint Stewart when his term expired.

But defending academic freedom at UT remained Cunningham's central concern. Her two-step strategy began with shaping public opinion. The WCEF mailed out 20,000 copies of Bernard DeVoto's *Harper's* article on the University of Texas crisis, 30,000 copies of an *Austin American* editorial on the new Regents' confirmation, and 15,000 booklets composed of *Austin American* articles on the Senate hearing.[136] The second step was to send a questionnaire on academic freedom to 50,000 people. Since 80 percent of the replies were favorable, a leaflet announcing this overwhelming public support was mailed to members of the legislature.[137] Finally, the WCEF prepared a candidate questionnaire before the 1946 elections. Again reviving strategy used thirty years earlier in the suffrage campaign, it mailed copies to WCEF members in each county asking them to seek the cooperation of local women's clubs in presenting the questionnaire to legislative candidates and to arrange for the responses to be publicized locally.[138]

But the key to defeating the Regulars, Cunningham knew, was the 1946 gubernatorial election. The new governor would head the state Democratic Party and appoint the UT Board of Regents. If the new governor owed his election to Cunningham's women's movement, women could expect to receive positions of authority in the party and in the new administration, just as they had in the federal government after Molly Dewson helped secure Roosevelt's election in 1932. Cunningham wanted Congressman Wright Patman to run, but he refused.[139] Homer Rainey was her second choice. After meeting with President Truman in the White House about a possible Rainey candidacy, Cunningham informed him that Truman "genuinely appeared to want us to succeed."[140]

Rainey had never run for public office and was reluctant to become a candidate until he was sure he had a chance of winning. He agreed to enter the race after J. R. Parten, a wealthy independent Texas oil man, promised financial assistance. Parten asked Cunningham to help generate the broad public support that Rainey needed. Under Cunningham's direction, the WCEF organized Rainey for Governor clubs around the state.[141] Cunningham recruited and trained young women, many of them UT graduates, for this. For years afterward Helen Hill and Laura Gowin referred to themselves as "paratroopers" because they dropped into towns unannounced to organize Rainey supporters. Following Cunningham's instructions, they dressed as proper ladies, even wearing white gloves, and met with the town's clergymen to identify local Rainey supporters.[142] The enthusiastic response helped convince Rainey to enter the race, and the clubs later became his grassroots campaign organization.[143]

The possibility that Cunningham's grassroots movement might sweep a reform candidate into office alarmed the Regulars. They took her seriously enough to smear her as a communist, but their crude and inaccurate attempts to portray Cunningham's network of liberal women as communists implicitly complimented her organizational skills. One, for example, warned that the "Cunningham-Collier gang" had succeeded in drawing the various Texas "Red groups" together. "The old she red foxes of the outfit may have known what they were doing, but it is doubtful about the youngsters."[144]

One of the many former UT students who participated in Rainey's campaign called it a "full-blown populist attack on the Texas economic and political establishment."[145] Several of Rainey's themes were central to Cunningham's own thinking: the need for higher teacher salaries, old age pensions, abolition of the poll tax, and, especially, an end to the system under which 70 percent of Texas residents had incomes beneath the federal poverty level, even though the state had over half the nation's oil and gas reserves and a world monopoly on sulfur. Financed by small donations, while the big money went to his opponents, Rainey's campaign resembled a people's crusade. Being underfunded, it depended on voluntary workers. The WCEF provided many of these, and it became the nucleus of Rainey's women's campaign.[146] Officially Cunningham directed the women's campaign, but she also advised the men running the overall campaign (most of whom had no previous experience directing a campaign).[147] She sold most of the timber on her farm to raise money for the campaign, even though this considerably worsened her own precarious financial position.[148] Although Rainey led in the polls up to election day, he finished second in the primary behind Beauford Jester, the establishment's candidate.

Since no candidate received enough votes to win the nomination, a runoff between the top two candidates followed. Parten took direct control of Rainey's campaign during this stage. He considered the WCEF to have been more effective than Rainey's other organizations and urged Rainey's staff to make better use of it to get out the vote. Rainey also began paying more attention to female voters. Assisted by the WCEF, he devoted an entire statewide radio broadcast to the ways in which Texas law and custom relegated Texas women to subordinate roles.[149]

Despite these changes, Rainey was defeated by smear tactics. Although he was an ordained Baptist minister, the opposition claimed that Rainey supported academic freedom in order to encourage the spread of atheism. Even though many trade unionists were unenthusiastic about him, voters were warned that the "Communist-dominated" CIO would take over the state if he won. Perhaps most damaging of all were the planted rumors that he was a "nigger lover," who would allow blacks into the University of Texas.[150] This was an especially effective issue because Heman Sweatt, a black man, had attempted to enroll in the segregated UT Law School a few months earlier; after being rebuffed, he had filed a lawsuit that eventually ended its whites-only policy. Cunningham insisted that Rainey would have won but "for the millions [of dollars] and [the] Ku Klux [Klan] stuff they pulled in July and August."[151]

Given her emotional and financial investment in Rainey's campaign, Cunningham must have been devastated by his defeat. She was also shocked that she had not been able to carry her precinct for him; it was the first time since she had the right to vote that she had lost her own precinct. Rainey's last-minute attempt to reassure white segregationists by supporting racially segregated polling places may have been a factor.[152] In the past Cunningham had relied on the black vote to carry her precinct, but this time "astonishingly enough it was the black vote we lost."[153] Blacks did not vote against Rainey, they simply stayed home.

The enormous effort WCEF members expended on Rainey's behalf may have contributed to the organization's decline after 1946. Its financial problems increased in the months following the election. Because members were not required to pay dues, the WCEF had been financially insecure from the beginning. When debts began to accumulate in 1945, each member was asked to make a five-dollar donation, but only eighty-three did.[154] Expenditures had exceeded expenses so greatly by February 1946 that Cunningham urged members to make any donations that they were planning to make for the year right away.[155] In 1947 she was forced to plead for immediate donations to pay bills.[156] While the WCEF lingered until 1951, financial difficulties apparently were responsible for its reduced level of activity after 1946.[157]

Although she did not gain the governor's seat for herself in 1944 or for Dr. Rainey in 1946, Cunningham played a major role in resisting the efforts by Texas Regulars to seize control of the state Democratic Party and the University of Texas. Outraged at the Regulars' attempt to subvert democracy while servicemen were dying to defend it, Cunningham mobilized women and liberal men against them. She valued democracy so highly, in part, because it implied that women should have an equal opportunity to participate in political life; the Regulars, in contrast, considered politics the preserve of wealthy white males. One of her most significant accomplishments between 1944 and 1946 was to generate a new consciousness that women were entitled to exercise authority in public affairs and that they were morally obligated to fight for this right if it was denied. This sense of female empowerment helps to explain why the WCEF became the most important Texas women's movement since the suffrage campaign.

10

LEFT FEMINISM, 1947–1964

ALTHOUGH THE NATIONAL WOMEN'S MOVEMENT IS OFTEN MISDIAGNOSED as moribund in the 1940s, a promising left-feminist movement was emerging when the war ended. It combined mass support from female trade unionists with articulate spokeswomen, such as Betty Goldstein (Friedan).[1] This movement has been overlooked, in part, because of its differences from post-1968 feminism. Left feminists usually opposed the Equal Rights Amendment (ERA) and, instead of emphasizing the sexual reforms prominent in the later form of feminism, focused on economic issues crucial to working-class women: equal pay, controlling the price of consumer goods, and maintaining women's employment opportunities.

Cunningham had begun writing a column for the *State Observer*, an Austin liberal journal, in September 1944 and used it to promote left feminism. Although an equal pay advocate, she concentrated on issues such as the full employment bill (which became the 1946 Employment Act) and the maintenance of price controls. Left feminists, realizing that high wartime employment levels had expanded women's job opportunities, feared that without the full employment bill women would be driven out of the labor force, as they had been in the 1930s. Cunningham urged her readers to support the bill and lobbied the Texas congressional delegation for it. Fearing that working-class women's budgets would be adversely affected by the elimination of price controls, left feminists also defended the Office of Price Administration (OPA), which became a key battleground between the Left and the Right when the war ended. Claiming that 66 percent of Texas women wanted the OPA to continue, Cunningham publicized the lobbying by women's groups to identify it as a women's issue.[2]

Cunningham also shared the left-feminist opposition to the Equal Rights Amendment. The ERA has become virtually synonymous with feminism since 1970, but when the National Woman's Party proposed the blanket bill (which became the ERA) in 1922, most national women's organizations opposed it. Cunningham presented the LWV's case against the bill at the 1922 National Consumers' League's annual conference.[3] The fundamental objection was that the bill confused identical treatment with equality. Cunningham warned that "blanket legislation would achieve identity of status but would operate to produce inequality of conditions for women. . . ."[4] She shared the conviction of most female reformers that the ERA would invalidate the protective legislation that addressed women's special needs, such as minimum wage laws, mothers' pensions laws, and laws requiring maternity leave before and after childbirth. Implicit in her opposition was an awareness of the ERA's class implications: while middle-class business and professional women would gain protection against job discrimination, working-class women would lose legal safeguards against economic exploitation.

During the Second World War congressional support for the ERA increased, and both major political parties endorsed it. Alarmed by this trend, in September 1944 the Women's Bureau of the Department of Labor organized the National Committee to Defeat the UnEqual Rights Amendment. Cunningham became a member of its Advisory Committee, along with Molly Dewson, former head of the DNC Women's Division, Congresswoman Helen Gahagan Douglas, and Carrie Chapman Catt, former NAWSA president, among others.[5] By 1945, the national LWV and the National Consumers' League were among the forty-three national organizations supporting the committee.[6]

After Texas Senator W. Lee "Pappy" O'Daniel announced that he planned to vote for the ERA, Cunningham publicly opposed what she termed the "Unequal Rights Amendment."[7] Since O'Daniel's positions were usually decided by his wealthy financial backers, Cunningham surmised that they wanted the ERA to pass. As employers, they expected the ERA would eliminate the labor legislation protecting women and, by forcing unprotected women to compete for jobs with returning soldiers, would create a plentiful supply of low-paid labor. As Cunningham had anticipated, when the Senate voted on the ERA in 1946, it was supported by Republicans and southern Democrats who favored fewer government restrictions on employers.

By 1947 Cunningham had attracted a group of female political activists who shared her commitment to enhancing women's political power. Although a few suffrage campaign veterans, such as Jane McCallum and Mary Ellis, helped when they could, because of age or family commitments they played a minor role. Cunningham's postwar women's network thus consisted almost entirely of a new generation, most of whom were young enough to be her daughters, if not her granddaughters. Some, like Lillian Collier and Margaret Reading, had been her close friends since the 1930s. Others, such as Marion Storm and Mary Weinzierl, were drawn into Cunningham's circle by her 1944 gubernatorial race and the struggle to defend the University of Texas. Although she was revered for her role in winning woman suffrage, it was her political expertise and her willingness to sacrifice for others that attracted followers.

Women had campaigned for suffrage in the early twentieth century in part because they believed that as voters they could help reform government. This unfulfilled project remained one of Cunningham's central concerns after 1945. While men often viewed politics as a means of advancing self-interest, she expected women to be altruistic. Women were a majority of the electorate, and Cunningham was convinced that if they were aware of their power to clean up Texas politics, they would do so. But women's participation rate in postwar elections, in part due to the poll tax, remained low—only 25 percent of the potential Texas female voters voted in the 1948 presidential election—and, privately, Cunningham was often frustrated with women's reluctance to become politically active.[8]

Part of the difficulty was that politics was still a male preserve. No independent woman had been elected to high state office since 1920 (Governor Miriam Ferguson was considered a proxy for her husband); none had been appointed to high state office since 1927. In 1944 there were only four women among the Texas Legislature's 181 members. Although national party rules required each state to select a National Committeewoman, the conservative men who controlled the state party usually selected a "safe" woman who could be trusted not to challenge male authority. Hilda Weinert, National Committeewoman from 1944 to 1956, was the spouse of a prominent Texas Regular and shared the Regulars' disdain for Cunningham's group. When the latter invited the director of the DNC Women's Division to speak in Texas, they warned her not to tell Weinert, lest she attempt to prevent the appearance.[9]

As a former suffragist, Cunningham was especially sensitive to gender discrimination, but like other left feminists, she rejected sex-antagonistic rhetoric: "This putting of men against women or women against men leads to nothing constructive."[10] Convinced that forming alliances with men who supported increased opportunities for women was a more effective means of achieving change, she did much of her political work after 1946 in gender-integrated left-liberal groups. Strengthening political liberalism was crucial to improving women's opportunities because liberals, unlike their opponents, genuinely believed in democracy, and "it is only in a democracy that women are regarded as people at all."[11] In Texas's masculine political culture, women were rarely leaders of mixed-sex political groups except for left-liberal organizations, such as the People's Legislative Committee (PLC).

Cunningham and Bob Eckhardt, an Austin labor lawyer and CIO lobbyist, formed the PLC in an attempt to strengthen the Left after conservatives gained control of the state Democratic Party at its September 1946 convention. Alarmed by the Texas CIO's organizing drive begun earlier that year (part of the CIO's Operation Dixie), employers succeeded in getting the convention to adopt an anti-union platform, including a resolution condemning strikes. Shocked by their defeat, seventy-five liberal delegates met immediately after the convention and agreed to establish the PLC. Cunningham and Eckhardt intended it to become the first "people's" political movement since the Populist Party.[12]

The proportion of female leaders on the PLC's interim committee was exceptionally high; in addition to its chair, Cunningham, they included Margaret Carter of Fort Worth, Kathleen Voigt of San Antonio, Marion Storm of Austin, Tosca DaMommio of Dallas, and Mrs. Kirke Steele of Corsicana. The male members included some of the state's leading liberals: J. Edwin Smith, a prominent Houston labor lawyer; D. B. Hardeman, who became Sam Rayburn's principal aide; Dr. John Granbery, the *Emancipator*'s editor; Jim Wright, later Speaker of the U.S. House of Representatives; and Eckhardt, the PLC's secretary-treasurer, who later became a U.S. Congressman.[13] Although the PLC leadership was predominantly Caucasian, the members included blacks and Hispanics.[14]

The PLC's program reflected Cunningham's conviction that class was fundamental to politics: "In politics, property . . . dominates persons; the rich encroach on the poor and keep them poor."[15] She urged the abolition of the poll tax, but did so on class rather than racial grounds. While the poll tax did exclude "Negroes" from the electorate, its wider effect was to reduce voting by low-income people of all races.[16]

During the Second World War, American liberal ideology underwent a profound change as concern with maintaining wartime economic growth led liberals to abandon their prewar critique of big business. But the PLC continued to view big corporations, especially in the oil industry, as a threat to democracy, in part because high ranking corporate employees were prominent in the Texas Regular movement. This perception gained credibility when the Texas Democratic Executive Committee chairman admitted in 1947 that "the oil industry today is in complete control of state politics and state government."[17]

In order to make Texas more democratic, the PLC sought to reduce corporate influence on government. For this purpose, it proposed the registration of lobbyists and the reporting of corporate retainers accepted by state legislators.[18] It also urged abolishing the poll tax and adopting a secret ballot.[19]

Ballots, although ostensibly secret, were numbered corresponding to the number next to the voter's name on the election roll, thus making the person who voted against the establishment's candidate vulnerable to reprisals.

The PLC viewed itself as an advocate for the "little people"—workers, family farmers, and small businessmen—of all races against big corporate interests. While the Texas Regulars were defending white supremacy, the PLC sought government "which will not discriminate against any person because of race, creed, or national origin" and which would guarantee "equality of economic opportunity." In 1946 this implied a radical challenge to the South's class and racial structures.[20]

The PLC began auspiciously. Donations at the initial public meeting totaled $250, while the representatives from the seven largest cities pledged $5,300 toward operating expenses.[21] But by early 1947 so little money had been turned in that Cunningham worried that the PLC was "not the darling of anybody's heart."[22] Marion Storm's admission that "Mrs. Cunningham has been working desperately, raising money" conveys the sense of crisis PLC leaders felt.[23]

Cunningham attributed the PLC's financial difficulties to competition from the ADA (the Union for Democratic Action until January 1947), a national liberal organization that she initially welcomed. After attending the meeting that established a Texas ADA branch, Cunningham encouraged James Loeb, the national director, to return and "nurse the Dallas group into effective growth."[24] But her attitude changed after she became convinced that the ADA's national leaders were attempting to "destroy" the PLC by instructing Jackson Valtair, head of its Texas chapter, to absorb the PLC into the ADA's Texas branch.[25]

Cunningham's concern was well-founded. Valtair did not think Texas could support two liberal groups and rejected Cunningham's offer to cooperate. Cunningham considered the PLC's alliance with the Texas labor movement crucial to its effectiveness and was infuriated when Valtair asked Texas labor leaders to work with the ADA rather than the PLC. She informed Leon Henderson, the ADA national chairman, that she had been "working with Labor when the century was in its teens," whereas Valtair had just emerged.[26] She withdrew her charges against the national ADA leaders after Loeb denied her accusations but dropped Valtair from the PCL.[27]

Despite its initial difficulties, by 1947 the PLC was having an impact on Texas politics. Recruiting middle-class intellectuals like J. Frank Dobie helped it gain enough financial stability to concentrate on political work. The *Dallas Morning News*, the state's most important conservative paper, identified it as Texas's only "dangerous" liberal organization. The PLC gained national attention when the *Nation* singled it out in an article on Texas reform movements.[28] Even her rivals admitted that Cunningham had the state's largest liberal following next to Homer Rainey.[29] Jack Carter, one of Fort Worth's leading liberal Democrats, acknowledged late in 1947: "In all probability . . . if there is any work done next year [to organize liberal Democrats] on a state wide basis a few people like you and Marion [Storm] that have always done the work will end up doing it."[30]

Maintaining the PLC became more difficult after Marion Storm died in a car crash in 1950. Cunningham considered her almost a daughter; Storm was her protégée who would probably have succeeded her when age made it impossible for Cunningham to continue. Without Storm to run the Austin office that served as liberal headquarters, PLC membership declined to such an extent that by December 1953 Cunningham admitted that the time had come to abandon it.[31]

The PLC was affiliated to the Texas Social and Legislative Conference (TSLC), which continued to be an important vehicle for Cunningham's reforming efforts until the mid-1950s. Financed mainly by Texas CIO unions, the TSLC attempted to coordinate the political work of its affiliated groups. It was distinctive in that it brought women and liberals together with blacks, Hispanics, and organized labor. By 1949 the Texas Progressive Voters' League (a black organization) and the American G.I. Forum (Hispanic veterans) had affiliated.[32] In San Antonio, blacks and Hispanics (along with white liberals) provided the TSLC's main base of support by 1952. When the TSLC faced a financial crisis in 1951, Houston black leader Carter Wesley pledged a special donation from his organization (apparently the Progressive Voters' League) to help cover the deficit.[33]

Cunningham was one of the "sparkplugs" who sustained the TSLC during the postwar decade.[34] She was a long-serving Executive Committee member; and for shorter periods, she was, successively, Nominations Committee chair, Policy Committee member, and Resolutions Committee member, but this does not convey the influence she wielded.[35] According to Bob Eckhardt she was the person who really made things happen in the TSLC, and he credited her with his election as the TSLC chair.[36] Marion Storm was the TSLC's Executive Secretary and Research Director until her death, after which Margaret Reading, also a member of Cunningham's inner circle, succeeded her.

Contemporaries remembered Cunningham and Marion Storm "running" the TSLC from Austin's Littlefield Building, which served as Cunningham's unofficial headquarters. The TSLC paid the office rent, and in return the female staff maintained a 6,000-person mailing list, which enabled them to mobilize liberal voters when needed.[37] Cunningham taught her supporters that the key to being a successful activist was to "Stamp the letter first, then address the envelope. That way you'll write it and mail it."[38]

WHEN CUNNINGHAM WAS THE GUEST SPEAKER AT THE 1945 DALLAS Business and Professional Women's Club's annual public relations dinner, she was introduced as a "rugged farmer of Walker County."[39] She cherished this image of herself as one of the "little people" who supported themselves by their own labor. Unable to afford more than a part-time hired man, she did most of her farm work herself, taking pride, for example, in feeding hay to her livestock from the back of her jeep.

Despite owning a large acreage, Cunningham was not financially well off. She didn't have a refrigerator, an outdoor "sanitary disposal" (septic tank), or running water in her house until Mary and Caswell Ellis loaned her $500 in 1947. Because the soil was exhausted from too many years of growing cotton, she had switched to raising cattle, but low farm prices and prolonged drought in the 1950s left her impoverished. Her financial situation was so precarious that she sold sections of her farm to meet living expenses and to finance her political causes; by 1964 only 500 of the original 1187 acres remained.[40]

On an least two occasions following the war, Cunningham attempted to reestablish her ties with the Department of Agriculture. She sought appointment to the joint committee to examine the relationship between the Farm Bureau and the Extension Services that Secretary of Agriculture Clinton Anderson created in 1945. Congressman Wright Patman urged President Truman to appoint her, but even though Truman endorsed that recommendation, she was not chosen.[41]

She came closer to an appointment in 1949. When Secretary of Agriculture Charles Brannan introduced a farm plan that increased financial support for small family farmers, the Farm Bureau attacked it. Cunningham defended the Brannan Plan, claiming that the Farm Bureau had always been the mouthpiece of big corporate farmers who were Republicans or Dixiecrats in politics.[42] The Department of Agriculture then began preparing a series of farm-labor conferences to generate support for the plan and obtained Civil Service Commission authority for a ninety-day appointment for Cunningham.[43] Texas political leaders were informed that Brannan was "going ahead" with her appointment, and she was asked to call him collect on July 6. Apparently she did, but shortly afterward Brannan wrote to the women who had recommended her that they had not been able to reach a mutually satisfactory agreement.[44]

Despite her preoccupation with Texas affairs, Cunningham maintained her Washington, D.C., political connections. She remained a member of the Woman's National Democratic Club and visited her Club friends when she was in Washington.[45] Bertha (Mrs. Julien) Friant, the WNDC's President in 1949–1950, had been a special friend when they worked for the AAA, and they remained close. Helen Fuller, the *New Republic*'s Washington political correspondent (later its political editor), was one of Cunningham's most valued friends. She also kept up her ties with Gladys Tillett, the director of the DNC Women's Division from 1941 to 1947, and visited her in Washington.[46]

Shortly after Harry Truman became President in 1945, Cunningham went to the White House to brief him on Texas politics. She also visited with DNC staff and lobbied the Texas congressional delegation, but securing Truman's support for Texas's loyal Democrats was her main objective.[47] She emerged convinced that Truman would back them in their struggle with the Regulars for control of the Texas Democratic Party. Although she later criticized Truman for requiring federal employees to take a loyalty oath and for proposing to draft striking railway workers, her belief that Texas loyal Democrats could count on his assistance probably contributed to her support for him in the 1948 presidential election.[48]

Cunningham and other left feminists were confronted with a dilemma in that election. They were drawn to Henry Wallace, the new Progressive party's candidate, because he articulated their vision of a society without class and racial barriers. But as a third-party candidate, he had no chance of winning. If they voted for Wallace instead of Truman, they risked helping elect the Republican, Tom Dewey. Cunningham had worked for Wallace's renomination as Vice President in 1944, and when he, as Secretary of Commerce, led the fight for the full employment bill in 1945, she offered to help organize women in support of it. When Wallace spoke in Texas in 1947, he made complimentary remarks about Cunningham, intended to secure her assistance in the approaching struggle with Truman.[49]

But even though she shared Wallace's domestic policy views, Cunningham, along with the CIO and many other left liberals, did not back him.[50] ADA liberals rejected Wallace because he accepted Communist support, but this was not Cunningham's position; she defended him against the red-baiting in Texas. She objected to Wallace's candidacy because it would damage the Left, at both the state and national level. If Texas liberals deserted the Democratic Party to work for Wallace, it would be easier for the corporate interests they had been battling to gain control of the state party. She regarded the "Third Party stuff" as "either escapist wishful thinking or Republican strategy." If the latter, she considered it a shrewd tactic, because the one thing that could guarantee a Republican victory would be a massive shift by liberal Democrats to Wallace.[51]

Privately, Cunningham also cautioned her friends against assuming that Wallace would be a liberal president, despite his attacks on segregation and his advocacy of New Deal policies. Although she admired Wallace for his "conscience and his courage," she cautioned that he had a very illiberal record as Secretary of Agriculture. Wallace had appointed the men responsible for destroying New Deal agricultural programs. His appointees "ignored the progressive movement in the South and gave their support and patronage to the worst political element down here." Also, Wallace's Department of Agriculture treated blacks worse than any other government agency. Since the great majority of African Americans were farmers, Cunningham considered this a "pretty serious" matter.[52]

While Wallace's candidacy threatened to split off the Democratic left wing, the defection of conservative southerners decimated the party's right wing. Angered by Truman's 1948 proposal of federal antilynching and anti–poll tax legislation, they formed the States' Rights Party, committed to maintaining racial segregation, and nominated Strom Thurmond, South Carolina's Governor, for President. In Texas the oilmen backing the Regulars also encouraged the states' rights movement because they wanted to control the offshore oil deposits, but they concealed their financial interest behind anti–civil rights rhetoric that aroused white voters.[53] Many Texas Regulars, including the National Committeeman Wright Morrow, became Dixiecrats (as States' Rights Party members were called). Because of this, loyal Democrats attempted to remove Morrow from his DNC seat. Cunningham asked Truman to intervene against Morrow when the DNC Credentials Committee reviewed his role in the Dixiecrat revolt, but while other Dixiecrats were dropped, Morrow was not.[54] Outraged, Cunningham denounced the DNC as a group of "dumb bunnies" who didn't understand who Morrow represented.[55]

The Dixiecrats' defection enabled loyal Democrats to gain control of the state party at its September 1948 convention. Cunningham's women's group played an important role in electing the loyal Democrats who dominated, and she appeared poised to wield significant influence in the party.[56] Three of her women were subsequently elected to the State Democratic Executive Committee: Lillian Collier, Marion Storm, and Virginia (Mrs. J. Edwin) Smith.[57] Cunningham was working to have Storm elected vice-chair of the executive committee in 1950 and probably would have succeeded under normal circumstances.[58] But midyear Storm died unexpectedly, and the Dixiecrats regained control when Governor Allan Shivers purged the loyal Democrats, including Cunningham's allies, from the executive committee. This was a watershed for Cunningham. Instead of becoming an influential advisor to the party's executive committee, she had to fight, as an outsider, for the right of liberals to even participate in the Texas party.[59] The struggle was embittered by incompatible visions: a Democratic Party open to women, minorities, and workers that sought to eliminate racial discrimination versus an elite-dominated white male supremacist party committed to segregation and female subordination.

The state conventions were a key battleground in Shivers's efforts to drive liberals out of the party. At the 1950 Mineral Wells convention, for example, liberals were subjected to measures designed to discourage them from attending future conventions. The keynote speaker (picked by Shivers) claimed that the liberal delegates, including Cunningham, were Communists; repeated smears like this made liberalism a dirty word, weakening its grassroots support. Denied rooms in local hotels, liberal delegates were forced to stay up to 100 miles from the convention hall. When they attempted to caucus in a nearby park, mounted police with billy clubs threatened to arrest them. Since only half the liberal delegates were assigned convention hall seats, they had to rotate, with half waiting outside in the blazing Texas sun. Liberals were seated in the back of the hall with disabled mikes and were not allowed to make motions or speak from the floor. After the convention many found their cars had been impounded and a substantial fee was required to reclaim them.[60] Cunningham was a leader of the liberals who fought back. Looking back on the struggle a decade later, U.S. Senator Ralph Yarborough singled out Cunningham, Collier, and Frankie Randolph for their role in transforming the party from a closed right-wing club to one that admitted liberals.[61]

Although the States' Rights Party was short-lived, its supporters remained disaffected from the national Democratic Party. Convinced that openly joining the GOP would be political suicide, most worked within their state Democratic Party while backing Republicans in presidential elections. In Texas, Governor Shivers, who controlled the Democratic Party organization, began covert preparations in 1951 to deliver the state to the Republican candidate in the next presidential election. When state party leaders declined to resist his scheme, Cunningham and Lillian Collier asked the national party for assistance. Although the DNC refused to intervene, Sam Rayburn, Speaker of the U.S. House of Representatives, urged the women to form a loyalist group.[62] Working at the grassroots, they began forming loyal Democratic county clubs during the summer of 1951.[63] Cunningham also persuaded the Texas Social and Legislative Conference to help with the precinct level organizing.[64] The campaign to ensure that Texas Democrats would support the national Democratic candidate in 1952 was strengthened when Cunningham's women's group joined with other liberals to form a statewide organization, the Loyal Democrats of Texas, in October 1951.[65]

Shivers was one of three southern Democratic governors who endorsed the Republican candidate, Dwight Eisenhower, in 1952. He also ensured that the state Democratic convention urged Texas Democrats to vote for the Republican presidential and vice presidential candidates, which Cunningham likened to Judas betraying Christ.[66] Since this left Adlai Stevenson, the Democratic candidate, without a state organization, Rayburn appealed to Cunningham's women's group to help organize a Stevenson campaign.[67] Because Democratic women regarded her as their "elder statesman," Cunningham found that "the heat had been put on me" to do something.[68] In October she and Lillian Collier set up a "Texas Women for Stevenson" committee and used the 711 Littlefield office's files to organize women by congressional district.[69] But despite their efforts, Eisenhower carried Texas as well as three other southern states in what had previously been the solidly Democratic south.

With closet Republicans in charge of the state Democratic Party organization, most Democratic politicians kept their heads down. Liberal Democrats considered Cunningham and Frankie Randolph, a wealthy Houston liberal, the party's "saviors," because they led the fight to regain control of the state Democratic Party.[70] Randolph built a racially integrated precinct organization (a rival to the segregated official party structure) that transformed Houston into a loyal Democratic bastion. Cunningham helped create two statewide organizations that gave loyal Democrats an alternative to the Shivercrat-controlled state party: the Texas Democratic Women's State Committee (TDWC) and the Democratic Organizing Committee (DOC), a gender-integrated group that replaced the defunct Loyal Democrats of Texas.[71]

Cunningham established the TDWC in February 1953 to encourage independent women's political activism on the national party's behalf.[72] The TDWC's constitution required members to support national Democratic candidates, but not those of the state party, leaving them free to oppose Shivercrats.[73] Its motto conveyed its self-image as a populist movement seeking to make the Texas Democratic Party democratic: "They have the money, but we have the people."[74] Having created the TDWC, Cunningham could have chaired it, but she chose to be the treasurer.[75] The other officers, Lillian Collier, chair, and Margaret Reading, secretary, were her two closest allies. The vice presidents included some of the state's most important liberal activists: Margaret Carter, Kathleen Voigt, Orissa (Mrs. Bob) Eckhardt, and Louise (Mrs. L. N. D.) Wells of Dallas.[76] The TDWC's funding was so inadequate that Cunningham, Collier, and Margaret Carter did much of the work on a volunteer basis.[77]

The TDWC's immediate objective was to repeal the Election Code's cross-filing clause that Shivercrats were using to encourage Democrats to vote for Republicans. When the Texas House of Representatives considered a bill to do this, Cunningham sent out an "SOS" to 1,500 loyal Democrats urging them to write supporting letters to their representatives immediately.[78] The TDWC-induced flood of telegrams helped defeat an attempt by the Shivercrats to recommit it to committee. A TDWC lobbyist proudly reported: "No one knew our strength, Minnie Fish."[79] Although Shivers's organization called a second vote and pressured the legislators into having the bill sent back to committee, the TDWC and its allies ended cross-filing the following year.[80]

Sharing a common reform agenda with other groups that were part of the Texas Left, in some years the TDWC simply adopted the Texas Social and Legislative Conference's program. In addition to eliminating cross-filing, the

TDWC's other priority was abolishing the poll tax (which in southern states disenfranchised women, especially married women, more than men because the husband often declined to pay his wife's poll tax).[81] Due to Shivers's misuse of the police for his political ends, the TDWC also sought a ban on using armed state police at elections and political conventions.[82]

Although the TDWC program made no reference to school desegregation, in her December 1955 Christmas greeting to the membership—drafted at a time when many Texas communities were deeply divided by the issue of whether to comply with the Supreme Court's recent Brown decision—Cunningham encouraged them to recognize the rights of *all* human beings. Since some members had reservations about desegregation, Cunningham avoided direct mention of race in a coded message that used nonconfrontational language. Noting that the "right to life, liberty and the pursuit of happiness" was still controversial in some southern communities, Cunningham, paraphrasing a Negro spiritual, reminded her readers that "All God's chillun got dignity." Implicit in her text was the message that TDWC members should fight to secure the rights of all "little people," blacks as well as whites.[83]

By the mid-1950s the TDWC's statewide membership included black women, female college professors, lawyers, clergymen's spouses, and the wives of Democratic politicians.[84] The affiliation of the women's divisions of loyal Democratic organizations, such as Frankie Randolph's Harris County Democrats, increased the TDWC's membership so much by May 1955 that its constitution had to be revised.[85] National Democratic leaders considered it a promising state organization, and prominent Democratic women, such as Eleanor Roosevelt and India Edwards, spoke at its meetings.[86] In 1959 Senator Ralph Yarborough identified the TDWC as one of the main reasons liberal Democrats were much stronger than they had been at the beginning of the decade.[87]

The TDWC also sought to construct a women's political culture by preserving the memory of independent women's political action. It honored Cunningham and four other suffrage campaign leaders on the thirty-sixth anniversary of the Primary Suffrage Act. Mary Ellis explained the suffrage campaign's techniques, Cunningham brought campaign photographs, and Jane McCallum described the 1920s Petticoat Lobby that women established to promote their legislative goals. Since Cunningham was seventy-five years old that month, the event also became her birthday party. After considering purchasing a diamond for her, Cunningham's friends honored her with a gift they knew she would value more: a $1,000 TDWC life membership.[88]

Ironically, while Democratic women were building their own state organization, they lost their separate space in the national party. After Steve Mitchell became DNC chair in 1952, he abolished the Women's Division and integrated women into the main DNC structure.[89] Although Cunningham had once been acting head of the Women's Division and had often sought assistance from India Edwards, the most recent director, she apparently did not resent its demise. Her only surviving comment is a wry reference to Mitchell having "integrated India" into the DNC.[90] She may have thought the merger would make it harder for the DNC to ignore women's issues. Also, since she was seeking Mitchell's assistance against the Shivercrats, it would have been impolitic to be critical.[91]

Cunningham first met Mitchell when he came to Texas in 1953, at Rayburn's request, to create a new organization, the Democratic Advisory Council (DAC), which the DNC recognized as the state party. The DAC's stated purpose was to provide a Democratic structure that was loyal to the national party and, by combining liberal and conservative loyal Democrats, that could defeat the Shivers-controlled party. But Rayburn also wanted it to replace the DOC, claiming that the latter was too far to the left to be able to oust Shivers. Some liberals suspected that he opposed the DOC because he didn't control it. Cunningham was among the DOC's Steering Committee members who overcame their doubts and voted for Rayburn's proposal to merge the DOC into the DAC.[92] At first this seemed a wise decision. Members of her women's group obtained important DAC positions: Lillian Collier was on the Steering Committee, Margaret Carter became Director of Women's Activities, and Kathleen Voigt was the secretary. Voigt created the state's most powerful grassroots organization by recruiting blacks and Hispanics, but Rayburn refused to allow the DAC to help the liberal Ralph Yarborough when he ran against Shivers in the 1954 gubernatorial election.[93] In part because of this, Cunningham eventually admitted that the DAC had been a "great mistake."[94]

The 1954 gubernatorial campaign has been portrayed as the closest that Texas has come to a class struggle since the Populist insurgency of the 1890s.[95] Shivers, one of Senator Joseph McCarthy's supporters, used for his own political advantage the nationwide red scare that McCarthy had unleashed. Shivers's attacks on organized labor and his opposition to school desegregation, despite the Supreme Court's Brown decision, drove trade unionists, blacks, and Hispanics into Yarborough's camp, dividing the electorate along class and racial lines.[96] Yarborough, in contrast, spoke for the underprivileged, pledging that he would "put the jam on the lower shelves where the little people can reach it."[97] He also made gender an issue by attacking Shivers's failure to appoint a single woman to a major political position during his five years in office.[98]

Cunningham and Collier directed Yarborough's women's campaign. Their "Democratic Women for Yarborough" committee mailed out weekly bulletins to women and recruited the female volunteers who did much of the campaign's envelope stuffing and telephoning.[99] The committee drew attention to Shivers's involvement in a land scandal by distributing wooden clothespins to women voters with a request that they help hang out the Shivers administration's "dirty linen."[100]

Yarborough's dependence on the women's committee for election work—and on Frankie Randolph for financial assistance—gave them leverage on his platform. The white electorate was so adamantly in favor of racial separation that Yarborough originally endorsed segregated schools. But Cunningham and Frankie Randolph considered desegregation a moral issue and warned him that they would not back him if he maintained his position.[101] Yarborough subsequently refrained from attacking the Brown decision or making the usual pledge to fight to preserve segregation. This alarmed segregationist voters, however, and probably contributed to his defeat.[102]

Cunningham believed the Establishment's control of the press was a crucial factor in preventing liberal candidates from winning elections; only five of the state's one hundred daily newspapers had endorsed Yarborough. She took the initiative in founding the *Texas Observer* as a liberal voice, shortly after Yarborough's defeat. When Paul Holcomb put the *State Observer* up for sale, she decided to mortgage her farm in order to buy it. But because she intended to become the paper's editor, Holcomb refused to sell to her, claiming he didn't want it to become a "petticoat paper."[103] Undaunted, Cunningham and Lillian Collier persuaded Franklin Jones to turn over the *East Texas Democrat* to them, arranged for Frankie Randolph to provide the financing, and merged the two papers into the *Texas Observer*.[104] As the publisher, Randolph is often credited as the *Observer's* founder, but Jones considered Cunningham the prime mover: "Sometimes gently persuading, at other times pointedly needling, but always persistently driving toward her objective, Minnie Fish kept things moving until there emerged the *Texas Observer*."[105]

Expecting to edit the new journal, Cunningham was disappointed when Randolph appointed Ronnie Dugger, the *Daily Texan's* former editor, instead.[106] Having envisioned it as a Democratic Party house organ, Cunningham was also disconcerted when Dugger insisted that the *Observer* be an independent paper.[107] Nevertheless, she sat on both its Editorial Advisory Board and its Board of Trustees, contributed articles, and organized a campaign to attract new subscribers to help the journal survive its financially precarious early years.[108]

THE STRUGGLE FOR CONTROL OF THE TEXAS DEMOCRATIC PARTY intensified in 1956 when Rayburn proposed that Lyndon Johnson—rather than Governor Shivers—head the Texas delegation to the national convention and be the state's favorite son presidential candidate. Johnson's candidacy divided liberals. Although they had helped him gain his Senate seat in 1948,

Johnson's voting record had been illiberal, and he had helped Shivers defeat the liberals in 1952.[109] Some of Cunningham's closest female political friends, including Kathleen Voigt, advocated a temporary tactical alliance with Johnson, making it clear she was proposing a "weekend romance with Lyndon, but didn't want to marry him."[110] But Cunningham and Frankie Randolph opposed any connection. Cunningham felt betrayed by Johnson's shift away from New Deal liberalism after Roosevelt's death and by his refusal to help the loyal Democrats against the Regulars. She considered him a "ruthless maneuverer," concerned only with his own advancement: "He has no principles—none of that stuff I call integrity."[111]

In the midst of the battle between the state's two most powerful politicians, the Texas Democratic Women's State Committee drafted Cunningham to run against Shivers and Johnson as a "favorite daughter" candidate for President and as the Texas delegation's chair at the national convention.[112] The TDWC proposed that precinct conventions elect a delegation composed of "plain, honest men and women, none of whom occupy official position in either State or Federal governments"; if this proposal had been adopted, it would have excluded both Shivers and Johnson.[113]

Cunningham's candidacy provided "at least token leadership" for those reluctant to vote for either Johnson or Shivers. The "incredible impertinence" of challenging the governor and the U.S. Senate Majority Leader meant playing David to their Goliath, but the audacity only made it more appealing. Since Adlai Stevenson's Texas supporters had no leader "and apparently no plans to fight the loss of the Texas Delegation," Cunningham ran as his proxy in the Democratic primary.[114] It was crucial to have a candidate who could entice liberals to the polls, because only Democratic primary voters could participate in the precinct conventions, which selected the delegates to the county conventions, which then picked delegates to the decision-making state convention.[115] Cunningham's campaign was almost entirely a female effort. She announced her candidacy at a meeting of the San Antonio Democratic Women for Good Government club, and the top people in her campaign organization were all women. Mary Weinzierl was her campaign manager, and her campaign committee consisted of thirteen women drawn from ten different senatorial districts.[116]

During her campaign, Cunningham concentrated on attacking Johnson, who pretended to be a moderate when needing liberal support but was no less a defender of big corporate interests than Shivers. She rejected the assumption that liberals would have influence with Johnson if they backed him, "because he's already controlled—by Brown and Root [the Houston construction company that had made substantial donations to Johnson's election campaigns dating back to the 1930s]!"[117] The differences between Cunningham and Johnson were evident in their contrasting economic policies. Johnson had used his Senate position to protect the oil and gas companies that dominated Texas politics. Cunningham opposed them on issues they considered vital: she supported federal ownership of offshore oil deposits and opposed the oil-depletion allowance. Johnson had voted for the anti-union Taft-Hartley Act, but Cunningham opposed similar Texas "right-to-work" legislation, because employers used it to import scab labor to defeat strikes.[118]

Black leaders, such as Garlington J. Sutton of San Antonio, endorsed Cunningham because she was the only candidate who advocated enforcing the Supreme Court's Brown decision.[119] Her position was particularly courageous because she lived in East Texas, where White Citizens' Councils were especially strong. Shivers, in contrast, encouraged resistance to the Brown decision, while Johnson avoided discussing it.[120]

Cunningham drew little support in the precinct conventions, but the DAC's grassroots political organization that Kathleen Voigt, her ally, had built helped Johnson defeat Shivers. At the May state convention, liberal delegates combined with Johnson's to select him as Texas's favorite son presidential candidate. But after loyal Democrats voted to eject the Shivercrats from the State Democratic Executive Committee, Johnson turned against the liberals and had the vote reversed.[121]

Frankie Randolph's selection as national committeewoman was the liberals' sole convention victory and illustrates the difficulty that independent women had in gaining party positions. Politician's wives were usually selected for women's positions, because the male party leaders could control them. But Cunningham and her allies wanted the position to go to a woman who had worked for the party, rather than someone who was her husband's proxy. When Johnson attempted to impose Beryl Ann Bentsen (Congressman Lloyd Bentsen's wife) on the convention, the delegates rebelled and elected Randolph despite Johnson's furious opposition.[122]

Determined to prevent the liberals from gaining control of the party, Johnson helped the Shivercrats defeat them at the September state convention by replacing the two largest liberal delegations with pro-Shivers groups. Anticipating objections, Johnson brought an armed sheriff's posse into the convention to deter resistance.[123] Ignoring the liberal majority, the Johnson-Shivercrat forces then elected a new state Democratic Executive Committee without any liberal members.[124]

Some liberals never forgave Johnson for allying with Texas McCarthyites and using force—to a degree unusual even by Texas standards—to gain control of the party organization. Even Cunningham was shocked that Johnson had armed guards in the convention hall aisles ready to suppress any resistance: "Believe it or not three men with guns stood over *me* when I went to the mike . . . to announce my county vote. They held a button on the mike and if you said anything 'impolite' they cut the connection and left you futilely whispering." Because of his actions, "I have a 'vocation' to be a thorn in Lyndon's side until *he* is *outside*."[125]

Underlying Cunningham's anger was a concern that Johnson had undermined her efforts to establish participatory democracy. She shared Margaret Carter's belief that the real conflict in the 1950s was between those who wanted grassroots democracy and those who discouraged the "masses" from participating in politics.[126] Since the Second World War, Cunningham had been encouraging the "little people" to become politically active by arguing that the Democratic Party stood for democracy. Johnson's actions quashed this vision and made it more difficult to persuade ordinary Democrats to pay their poll tax and participate in party conventions.

Determined "to fight this thing out,"[127] Cunningham and other outraged liberals replaced the DAC with a new organization, the Democrats of Texas (DOT), that was not controlled by Johnson or Rayburn. Chaired by Frankie Randolph, the DOT became the state's most effective postwar liberal Democratic organization. It brought together Cunningham's female activists, loyal Democrats, liberal Mexican American leaders, black leaders, and organized labor.[128] Despite being seventy-four years old, Cunningham was one of the DOT's most respected leaders and was elected to its Executive Board.[129] Although liberal candidates had suffered repeated defeats in the 1950s, with the DOT's assistance Ralph Yarborough was elected to the U.S. Senate in 1957.[130]

DURING THE 1940S AND 1950S, CUNNINGHAM BECAME INCREASINGLY outspoken against segregation. Because it impeded economic modernization and kept the South impoverished, she thought segregation was bad economic policy as well as morally wrong: "The South will never have its place in the sun so long as it pursues the policy of racial discrimination."[131] Since the South's economy depended on black labor, discrimination was illogical; it encouraged blacks to migrate to the North to escape. She also endorsed the black teachers' campaign to have racially based pay scales replaced by an equal pay policy, recognizing that it was both a racial and a gender issue (most black teachers were women).[132]

Although East Texas whites were determined to maintain segregated schools, Cunningham helped undermine support for it in Walker County. After the *Sweatt v. Painter* (1950) ruling that "separate but equal" was not constitutional unless the nonwhite schools were truly equal, Texas officials urged school districts to maintain segregation by upgrading their black schools. Reformers hoped resistance would erode when white property owners realized how high their property taxes would be to preserve separate school systems. Cunningham followed this strategy when she chaired her school district's Tax

Equalization Board in 1951. It raised property taxes substantially in order to improve the local black school. She was elated when property owners flooded the board with protests, including one who lamented: "If it's gonna cost that much to get the black bastards educated, maybe we'd just as well put 'em in with our children!"[133]

Cunningham was outraged when white southerners resisted the Brown decision by closing public schools and sending their children to private academies. "I get so mad about the school situation I'm incoherent," she told the *Texas Observer*, not only because she favored integration but because "the schools belong to all the people," and the affluent whites were turning their backs on the poorer children of both races. Furious, she insisted there "ought to be a fighting women's organization to take up this school thing."[134]

Too old — and too poor — to start a fighting women's organization herself, Cunningham urged younger women to do so during the 1958 ceremony recognizing her contributions to the Democratic Party. Since 1939 the national party had sponsored Democratic Woman's Day annually to honor its most active women. After Katie Louchheim, the DNC's director of women's activities, authorized National Committeewoman Frankie Randolph to select the Texas woman, Randolph picked Cunningham to be honored as "Mrs. Democrat."[135] Cunningham's Austin friends hosted a celebration at which her long-time friend Dr. Robert Montgomery spoke, but she attended the Houston event that Randolph chaired. Houston was in the midst of a heated battle over school desegregation, and Randolph and her allies, including Verna (Mrs. Olon) Rogers, the school board president in the mid-1950s, had been threatened with violence because they wanted Houston to comply with the Brown decision.[136]

Instead of allowing the event to focus on her accomplishments, Cunningham used it to endorse school integration. Privately, she admitted: "I'm taking advantage of this "honoree" nonsense to start a riot on the desegregation business." She claimed that the press "tempered my remarks down so as not to melt the type." She praised Verna Rogers for keeping Houston public schools open, while other southern cities closed theirs to prevent integration. With the previous year's violence in Little Rock, Arkansas, fresh in her mind, Cunningham demanded: "Are we going to sit by and let people like [Governor] Faubus destroy the public school system in America?" She concluded by appealing to the women to ensure that Texas did not undergo a similar tragedy.[137]

IN THE 1960 PRESIDENTIAL ELECTION. CUNNINGHAM ALMOST single-handedly carried her own county for John Kennedy. Despite being seventy-eight years old and in poor health, in the last two months before the election, she worked frantically to rouse support for him.[138] Discovering that there was no organized Kennedy campaign in Walker County, she established a Democratic headquarters in New Waverly. To raise the rent for the building, she persuaded friends to donate used clothing, which she sold to black and Hispanic families when they came to town on Saturday mornings to do their weekly shopping. Cunningham recruited Bill Kilgarlin (later a Texas Supreme Court Justice) and other liberal Democrats to speak while people examined the clothing, thus simultaneously making the rent and informing the voters.[139] Although Walker County had gone Republican in recent presidential elections, Cunningham's efforts helped carry it for Kennedy. Aware that he had barely carried Texas, Kennedy acknowledged her assistance and invited her to his inauguration. Cunningham was so proud that she saved the green coat she wore to his Inaugural and never wore it again.[140]

Since 1946 Cunningham had lived alone in her five-room unpainted pine house with her cat, Alice. Although there were four comfortable rocking chairs, the house lacked modern conveniences, including a telephone. This was partly due to the expense, but Cunningham insisted that reading was a more effective way to get information. She read widely and recommended C. Vann Woodward's class interpretation of the New South, *Origins of the New South, 1877–1913*, as well as other books on American politics. From the grove of trees next to the house, she harvested pecans, which she sold at a roadside stand to raise money for her political causes. She kept a .410 shotgun to defend her large garden against raiding armadillos.[141]

By 1961 Cunningham had been hospitalized several times with heart problems. Nevertheless, she went to the state capitol in August to lobby against the sales tax bill, because regressive taxes take disproportionately more income from low-income groups. In the extreme heat she suffered a heart attack. After spending several weeks in a hospital, she was allowed to return home, even though it had neither a telephone nor air conditioning. When Louisa Pearson Hugg and her husband visited her, they found the house unbearably hot. Although Cunningham admitted being afraid that she might lie down and not be able to get up again, she refused to consider staying with the Huggs until she was stronger. She insisted, among other objections, that the crows would eat the pecans off of her trees if she didn't totter out and fire her old gun in the air to scare them away.[142]

During the last year of her life, Cunningham urged others to continue the work she had begun. Her final words to the Texas Democratic Women's State Committee were "Divest yourself of outside interests and concentrate on your Democratic Party and your women's committee."[143] This was not simply partisan advice. Cunningham's lifelong left-liberal activism reflected her conviction that a liberal Democratic movement provided the most effective organized expression of Christ's social teachings: "Democracy with a little 'd' was what Jesus Christ was standing for on earth."[144]

Cunningham fell and broke her hip in 1964 and never recovered. She died in the hospital of congestive heart failure on December 9, 1964.[145] The *New York Times* and *Washington Post* obituaries noted her national importance as a woman suffrage leader and as a founder of the national League of Women Voters and the Woman's National Democratic Club.[146] The honorary pall bearers at her funeral suggest her importance in Texas politics: U.S. Senator Ralph Yarborough, Congressman Bob Eckhardt, and gubernatorial candidate Don Yarborough. She was buried in the Hardy Cemetery near New Waverly, a Democratic donkey brooch pinned to her dress.[147]

EPILOGUE

ALTHOUGH SHE DIED BEFORE THE LATE 1960S FEMINIST REVIVAL, Cunningham participated in the women's movement's two earlier stages: the "triumphant" period of successful suffrage campaigns and important reform legislation, such as the Sheppard-Towner and Cable Acts, and the period from the mid-1920s to the 1960s, when independent women's political action became more difficult. Reflecting on the movement's loss of energy and focus after the 1920s, Cunningham admitted that it was "maddening to think that we somehow didn't carry on as vigorously as we could have done" and "puzzling to wonder why. . . . Did the League of Women Voters turn us away from fighting to studying? *Something happened. What?*"[1] Although reluctant to criticize women, she concluded that the national LWV's Republican-leaning, upper-middle class leaders had "dehydrated" it, turning it from the "fighting organization" that had been contemplated into a nonpartisan one concerned with studying the issues.[2] But even as she lamented traditional women's organizations' reluctance to continue the struggle after gaining the vote, Cunningham was establishing new women's groups—fighting organizations—that allied with left-liberal forces seeking race, class and gender reform.

This new strategy emerged in the 1930s during the feminizing of the Democratic Party. Cunningham and other women reformers envisioned a left-liberal party that could become a vehicle for empowering women and securing their legislative goals. The attempt to build a progressive Democratic Party—both a national and, after 1943, a state party—was the central thread running through her life from that point on. In a conservative state such as Texas, this meant constructing an electoral coalition linking blacks, Hispanics,

women, male reformers, and organized labor that could sustain liberal politics. She initiated this coalition by helping to form the Texas Social and Legislative Conference and by encouraging other liberals to build on that foundation. That coalition—although not solely Cunningham's creation—was an
important part of her political legacy. It enabled liberals to gain control of the
Texas Democratic Party in 1976 for the first time since 1948 and to elect liberals to state offices in the following years, culminating with Ann Richards's
election as governor in 1990.[3]

During the 1950s, when the race issue overshadowed everything else, Cunningham acquired a reputation for being the "conscience of Texas politics" by
stiffening the backbone of liberal politicians who were tempted to do what
was politically advantageous rather than what was morally right.[4] Because
she saw politics in moral terms, she could be impatient with fence-sitters and
was known to have a "tart tongue for wishy-washy males."[5] Some politicians
resisted her advice for fear of becoming unelectable. But Texas's two most
successful liberal politicians of the late 1950s—Ralph Yarborough and Bob
Eckhardt—valued it. Cunningham was the "brains" behind the women's
campaigns that helped elect Yarborough to the U.S. Senate, and he acknowledged her importance.[6] Eckhardt, who gained national attention as a liberal
member of the U.S. House of Representatives after serving several terms in
the Texas legislature, also sought Cunningham's advice. He would drive out
to her New Waverly home and listen carefully while she laid out strategy.
Because her political judgments were shrewd and he needed her women's
group's assistance, Eckhardt usually followed her advice.[7]

Cunningham was a legendary figure in Texas by the 1950s, but women
who encountered her remember a very genuine, unpretentious, down-to-
earth person more concerned with promoting other women than her own
ego.[8] "If you want a stepping stone," she advised a very young Liz Carpenter,
"you have to be one."[9] Although she could be a southern lady when necessary,
contemporaries considered her to be a very "tough minded" woman who told
people exactly what she thought and did not shrink from conflict.[10] Her frank
speaking was "awe inspiring" for younger women accustomed to the deferential language expected from ladies.[11]

Cunningham's involvement in groups seeking racial and class reforms
after 1945 may have obscured the extent to which she remained committed to
women's interests, but those who knew her had no uncertainty. Texas Supreme
Court Justice Oscar Mauzy claimed that Cunningham taught a generation of
young Texans (including himself) that women and minorities were entitled to
equal treatment in public life.[12] She was especially concerned with encouraging young women to become politically active. Dell Sackett (Goeres), state
CIO office secretary and a TDWC member, recalled: "Minnie Fish always had
her hand on my back pushing me into politics."[13] One of Cunningham's most

successful protégées, Billie Carr, became known as the "godmother" of Texas liberal Democrats while serving as Texas's Democratic National Committee-woman and a DNC member from 1972 to 2000.[14] Kathleen Voigt perceived Cunningham as a bridge between the suffragists and the new generation of female activists (including herself) emerging in the 1950s.[15] Others who watched her mentoring women suggest that because of Cunningham, the revival of women's political activism in Texas began in the Fifties rather than in the Sixties.[16]

In 1992 the Texas Historical Commission erected a marker on Highway 75, north of New Waverly, near where Cunningham's home had been. At the dedication ceremony, Liz Carpenter remembered Cunningham as a "dynamo" who devoted her life to saving democracy from its enemies. She concluded that in a civilized society, a few idea-driven people can make a difference: Cunningham was one of them.[17]

Notes

INTRODUCTION

1. *Texas Monthly*, December 1999: 139.
2. On the "generation of 1880," see Susan Ware, *Beyond Suffrage: Women and the New Deal* (Cambridge: Harvard University Press, 1981).
3. Our use of the term "left feminism" is derived from Ellen Carol DuBois, *Woman Suffrage and Women's Rights* (New York: New York University Press, 1998), 243.
4. Leila Rupp and Verta Taylor, *Survival in the Doldrums: The American Women's Movement, 1945 to the 1960s* (New York: Oxford University Press, 1987).
5. Ruth Rosen, *The World Split Open: How the Modern Women's Movement Changed America* (New York: Penguin, 2000), 34.
6. Chandler Davidson to Harold Smith, 24 February 1998, reporting on his interviews with Texas liberals active prior to 1960.
7. MFC to Eleanor Roosevelt, 12 July 1944, box 1717, folder 100, ER Papers, FDR Library.
8. Anne Firor Scott, "Epilogue," in *Votes for Women: The Struggle for Woman Suffrage Revisited*, ed. Jean H. Baker (New York: Oxford University Press, 2002), 191.
9. MFC to Dorothy Brown, 29 April 1921, box 8, folder 243, Dorothy Kirchwey Brown Papers, SL.
10. MFC to J. Frank Dobie, 4 April 1944, box 2P363, Alexander Caswell Ellis Papers, CAH-UT.
11. MFC to Jane McCallum, 27 July [1944], box G, McCallum Family Papers, part I, AHC-APL.
12. Jo Freeman, *A Room at a Time: How Women Entered Party Politics* (Lanham, Md.: Rowman & Littlefield, 2000), 5, 242 n. 11.
13. Ibid., x.

CHAPTER 1

1. Minnie Fisher Cunningham, "Crossing Over," TS, box 1, folder 5, Minnie Fisher Cunningham Papers, UH. Cunningham wrote this unpublished memoir sometime during the 1930s; quotations are from the foreword.
2. "Walker County," *The New Handbook of Texas*, ed. Ron Tyler et al., 6 vols. (Austin: Texas State Historical Association, 1996), 6: 799–801; D'Anne McAdams Crews, comp., *Huntsville and Walker County, Texas: A Bicentennial History* (Huntsville: Sam Houston State University Press, 1976), 482; MFC, "Crossing Over," 2–4.
3. Walker County Genealogical Society and Walker County Historical Commission, *Walker County, Texas: A History* (Dallas: Curtis Media Corp., 1986), 359–360; Eighth Census of the United States, 1860, Texas, Schedule 1, Population, p. 86; "Walker County," *New Handbook of Texas*.
4. Seventh Census of the United States, 1850, Alabama, Schedule 2, Slave Inhabitants, shows William P. Fisher holding 127 slaves in Lowndes County and John C. Abercrombie holding 56 in Macon County.
5. Eighth Census of the United States, 1860, Texas, Schedule 2, Slave Inhabitants, 34–38. John Abercrombie owned 56 slaves, Lorenzo Fisher held 52, and John Fletcher Fisher owned 43. William and Horatio Fisher's standing in Walker County is derived from *United States Historical Census Data Browser*, http://fisher.lib.virginia.edu/census/. Only one planter in Walker County owned more than 100 slaves.
6. Value of real estate and personal estate are recorded in the 1860 population census as follows: William P. Fisher, $11,130/$81,725; H. W. Fisher, $15,000/$51,750; L. C. Fisher, $17,150/$51,120; John F. Fisher, $24,500/$29,020; John C. Abercrombie, $41,659/54,395. Wealthholding ranks are determined according to the tables in Randolph B. Campbell and Richard G. Lowe, *Wealth and Power in Antebellum Texas* (College Station: Texas A&M University Press, 1977), 138, 140, 142.
7. Tommy Yett, ed., *Members of the Legislature of the State of Texas from 1846 to 1939* (Austin: n.p., 1939), 29; MFC, "Crossing Over," 26–44 (quotation at 37). Horatio Fisher's Company, the Abercrombie Light Guards, became Co. G, Seventh Texas Cavalry, CSA.
8. Ninth Census of the United States, 1870, Texas, Schedule 1, Population, 45; MFC, "Crossing Over," 36, 64–65.
9. "Waverly," *The New Handbook of Texas*, 6: 853; Charles P. Zlatkovich, *Texas Railroads: A Record of Construction and Abandonment* (Austin: University of Texas Bureau of Business Research, 1981), 27.
10. "New Waverly," *New Handbook of Texas*, 4: 1006; MFC, "Crossing Over," 76–77. Provisioning railroad construction crews put extra money in the pockets of many southern farm families; see Edward Ayers, *The Promise of the New South: Life After Reconstruction* (New York: Oxford University Press, 1992), 9.
11. On the postwar economy, see Gavin Wright, *Old South, New South: Revolutions in the Southern Economy Since the Civil War* (New York: Basic Books, 1986), and Howard N. Rabinowitz, *The First New South, 1865–1920* (Arlington Heights, Ill.: Harlan Davidson, 1992). Ayers, *Promise of the New South*, 18–20, documents the spread of villages.
12. MFC, "Crossing Over," 93–94.
13. Ibid., 77–78, 84–85.

14. Ibid., 36; MFC to Reuben Brigham, 4 March 1940, Records of the Federal Extension Service, U.S. Dept. of Agriculture, box 643, RG33, NA; MFC, handwritten biographical sketch, box 4J459, Lillian Collier Papers, CAH-UT.

15. Amy Thompson McCandless, *The Past in the Present: Women's Higher Education in the Twentieth-Century South* (Tuscaloosa: University of Alabama Press, 1999), 20; Charles William Dabney, *Universal Education in the South*, 2 vols. (Chapel Hill: University of North Carolina Press, 1936), 1: 412–428; 2: 385, 408.

16. MFC, "Crossing Over," 93.

17. Ibid., 96–97, 100–103.

18. Ibid., 17–19, 103.

19. MFC, handwritten biographical sketch, Collier Papers.

20. MFC, "Crossing Over," 88–89. The horse was sold years later to drovers collecting mounts for Theodore Roosevelt's Rough Riders; see MFC to Bess Furman, 25 February 1953, box 24, Furman Papers, LC.

21. MFC, "Crossing Over," 100, 36; Rev. G. M. Coe, sermon preached at MFC's funeral, printed in "Memorial Tribute to Mrs. Minnie Fisher Cunningham, a Great American, March 19, 1882–December 9, 1964," copy in Cunningham file, General Federation of Women's Clubs Archives, Washington, D. C.

22. MFC, "By Countryside and Town," *State Observer*, 7 May 1945, compares World War II servicemen to Foxe's martyrs. "I Believe" is reprinted in "Memorial Tribute to Mrs. Minnie Fisher Cunningham." On Methodist women, see Mary Frederickson, "Shaping a New Society: Methodist Women and Industrial Reform in the South, 1880–1940," in *Women in New Worlds: Historical Perspectives on the Wesleyan Tradition*, ed. Hilah F. Thomas and Rosemary Skinner Keller (Nashville: Abingdon Press, 1981).

23. MFC, "Crossing Over," 69, 86–87, 99.

24. Gaines M. Foster, *Ghosts of the Confederacy: Defeat, the Lost Cause, and the Emergence of the New South, 1865–1913* (New York: Oxford University Press, 1987); Grace Elizabeth Hale, *Making Whiteness: The Culture of Segregation in the South, 1890–1940* (New York: Pantheon, 1998), chap. 2; MFC, "Crossing Over," 48.

25. MFC, "Crossing Over," 27–28; W. Fitzhugh Brundage, "White Women and the Politics of Historical Memory in the New South, 1880–1920," in *Jumpin' Jim Crow: Southern Politics from the Civil War to Civil Rights*, ed. Jane Dailey, Glenda Elizabeth Gilmore, and Bryant Simon (Chapel Hill: University of North Carolina Press, 2000), 117.

26. "Walker County," *New Handbook of Texas*.

27. MFC, "Crossing Over," 69. She wrote as fact, probably from misunderstanding accounts of black officeholding heard as a child, that George Wood, her father's slave, had represented Walker County in the legislature and that Horatio was the first white man elected justice of the peace for their precinct after Reconstruction. No George Wood is listed in J. Mason Brewer, *Negro Legislators of Texas* (Austin: Jenkins Publishing, 1970), 126, or in Merline Pitre, *Through Many Dangers, Toils, and Snares: The Black Leadership of Texas, 1868–1900* (Austin: Eakin Press, 1983), 206. Horatio Fisher's immediate predecessor as justice of the peace, William Whitley (elected 1874), is designated as white on the 1871 voters' roster for Walker County. See box 2-12/561, Records of the Secretary of State, Election Returns, TSL.

28. *Members of the Legislature of the State of Texas from 1836 to 1939*, 97. We have reconstructed the rest of his political career from the Walker County files in boxes 2-12/585, 589, 595, 599, 606, 618, 624, 635, 640, 652, 661, 672, 681, 690, 697, and 706, Records of the Secretary of State, Election Returns, TSL.

29. *Houston Post-Dispatch*, 27 July 1928, copy in Beulah Grimmet Papers, TWU; F.F.F. Moss, untitled TS, box 18, McCallum Family Papers, part I, AHC-APL; Liz Carpenter, speech at dedication of MFC historical marker, New Waverly, Texas, 25 March 1992, copy in authors' possession.

30. MFC, "Crossing Over," 81.

31. C. Vann Woodward, *Origins of the New South, 1877–1913* (Baton Rouge: Louisiana State University Press, 1951), 185–186; MFC, "Crossing Over," 103.

32. "Crossing Over," 103–104. Since prices were marked up by 10 percent or more, Sallie got less value for her produce; see Robert S. Maxwell and Robert D. Baker, *Sawdust Empire: The Texas Lumber Industry, 1830–1940* (College Station: Texas A&M University Press, 1983), chap. 9, which describes company stores.

33. The literature on Populism is vast. See especially Robert McMath, *Populist Vanguard: A History of the Farmer's Alliance* (Chapel Hill: University of North Carolina Press, 1975), and McMath, *American Populism: A Social History, 1877–1898* (New York: Hill and Wang, 1993); Bruce Palmer, *"Man over Money": The Southern Populist Critique of American Capitalism* (Chapel Hill: University of North Carolina Press, 1980); and Lawrence Goodwyn, *Democratic Promise: The Populist Movement in America* (New York: Oxford University Press, 1976), which emphasizes Texas. Quotation is from Ayers, *Promise of the New South*, 218.

34. See especially Gregg Cantrell and D. Scott Barton, "Texas Populists and the Failure of Biracial Politics," *Journal of Southern History*, 55 (November 1989): 659–692; and Lawrence Goodwyn, "Populist Dreams and Negro Rights: East Texas as a Case Study," *American Historical Review* 76 (December 1971): 1435–1456.

35. Alwyn Barr, *Texas Politics: Reconstruction to Reform, 1876–1906* (Austin: University of Texas Press, 1971), 117–139; Donna A. Barnes, *Farmers in Rebellion: The Rise and Fall of the Southern Farmers' Alliance and People's Party in Texas* (Austin: University of Texas Press, 1984), 138–139; Robert C. Cotner, *James Stephen Hogg: A Biography* (Austin: University of Texas Press, 1959).

36. Walter L. Buenger, *The Path to a Modern South: Northeast Texas Between Reconstruction and the Great Depression* (Austin: University of Texas Press, 2001), 15.

37. Roscoe Martin, *The People's Party in Texas: A Study in Third-Party Politics* (Austin: University of Texas Press, 1933), 73, Map 1, 177, 236 n. 19; *Houston Post-Dispatch*, 27 July 1928 (quotation). Across the South generally, Populists tended to do less well in black majority counties because white Democrats felt greater pressure to maintain political unity and saw to it that Populists were "counted out" at the ballot box. See Ayers, *Promise of the New South*, 278–282. There is no study of Walker County to explain the Democrats' looser grip on power.

38. Marjorie Spruill Wheeler, *New Women of the New South: The Leaders of the Woman Suffrage Movement in the Southern States* (New York: Oxford University Press, 1993), 115–125.

39. Rebecca Edwards, *Angels in the Machinery: Gender in American Party Politics from the Civil War to the Progressive Era* (New York: Oxford University Press, 1997), 122–135; Glenda E. Gilmore, *Gender and Jim Crow: Women and the Politics of White Supremacy in North Carolina, 1896–1920* (Chapel Hill: University of North Carolina Press, 1996), 91–118. The term "white male supremacy" is Stephen Kantrowitz's; see his *Ben Tillman and the Reconstruction of White Supremacy* (Chapel Hill: University of North Carolina Press, 2000).

40. J. Morgan Kousser, *The Shaping of Southern Politics: Suffrage Restriction and the Establishment of the One-Party South, 1880–1910* (New Haven: Yale University Press, 1974), 39–41, 63–71, 196–208. As Michael Perman shows in *Struggle for Mastery:*

Disfranchisement in the South, 1888–1908 (Chapel Hill: University of North Carolina Press, 2001), no generalization can accurately encompass the diversity of state disfranchisement movements. In Texas, the poll tax was part of the "reform" agenda initiated by Hogg Democrats to bring the former Populists back into the party.

41. Gilmore, *Gender and Jim Crow*, 118.

42. Ronnie Dugger, "Spanning the Old to the New South: Minnie Fisher Cunningham and her Heroine Mother," *Texas Observer*, 21 November 1958; *Austin Statesman*, 24 May 1946; *Houston Post*, 14 July 1994; obituary of Marion Fisher, *Galveston Tribune*, 31 August 1950.

43. For a full account of Marion Sims's medical career, see Seale Harris, *Woman's Surgeon: The Life Story of J. Marion Sims* (New York: Macmillan, 1950), and Deborah Kuhn McGregor, *From Midwives to Medicine: The Birth of American Gynecology* (New Brunswick, N.J.: Rutgers University Press, 1998).

44. *Austin Statesman*, 24 May 1946; Barbara Miller Solomon, *In the Company of Educated Women: A History of Women and Higher Education in America* (New Haven: Yale University Press, 1985), 131–133; Penina Migdal Glazer and Miriam Slater, *Unequal Colleagues: The Entrance of Women into the Professions, 1890–1940* (New Brunswick, N. J.: Rutgers University Press, 1987), 80–83, 1–2 (quotation).

45. *The University of Texas Medical Branch at Galveston: A Seventy-Five Year History by the Faculty and Staff* (Austin: University of Texas Press, 1967), 14–27, 68–69; Henry M. Burlage and Margot E. Beutler, *Pharmacy's Foundation in Texas: A History of the College of Pharmacy, 1893–1976* (Austin: Pharmaceutical Foundation of the College of Pharmacy of the University of Texas, 1978), 41–46, 61, 75.

46. Burlage and Beutler, *Pharmacy's Foundation in Texas*, 42–43, 48 (Cline quotation), 65.

47. Ibid., 70–71. There are numerous accounts of the Galveston hurricane; most recently, see Patricia B. Bixel and Elizabeth H. Turner, *Galveston and the 1900 Storm: Catastrophe and Catalyst* (Austin: University of Texas Press, 2000).

48. Elizabeth Brown Pryor, *Clara Barton, Professional Angel* (Philadelphia: University of Pennsylvania Press, 1987), 328–330; Dugger, "Spanning the Old to the New South" (quotation); MFC to Clara Barton, 13, 19 October 1900, reel 78, Clara Barton Papers, microfilm, LC. We are greatly indebted to Ann Barton at Blagg-Huey Library, Texas Woman's University, for locating the latter letter for us.

49. She was one of the first women pharmacy graduates but not *the* first, as has been widely and erroneously claimed in biographical sketches and most recently by Elizabeth Silverthorne and Geneva Fulgham in *Women Pioneers in Texas Medicine* (College Station: Texas A&M University Press, 1997). The list of pharmacy graduates appears in *The University of Texas Medical Branch at Galveston: A Seventy-Five Year History*, appendix R, 352, and in Burlage and Beutler, *Pharmacy's Foundation in Texas*, appendix J, 553. Four women graduated in the class of 1897 and one in 1900. After Minnie, there were no more until 1905. She was apparently unaware of the 1897 graduates and thought she was the second woman degreed; see Dugger, "Spanning the Old to the New South."

50. Burlage and Beutler, *Pharmacy's Foundation in Texas*, 44–45, 60–61. In 1925 the Ph.G. program was expanded to three years, an intermediate step toward the current Bachelor of Science in Pharmacy degree. The Ph.G. degree was discontinued in 1937.

51. Burlage and Beutler, *Pharmacy's Foundation in Texas*, 45, 61; Dugger, "Spanning the Old to the New South"; Minnie S. Fisher and Dr. E. L. Angier, "To Whom it

May Concern," 26 November 1901, Cunningham binder, Walker County Historical Commission, Huntsville, Texas.

52. Twelfth Census of the United States, 1900, Texas, Schedule 1, p. 5. (Cunningham is listed as Boyd J. Cunningham, which may be either an error or an experiment; he disliked his unusual given name, and in later years his name appeared several times in the Galveston city directories as Benjamin J. Cunningham. In official documents and newspaper accounts he is always identified by his initials alone.) On school teaching, see T. B. Fuller, Superintendent of Schools, White County, Illinois, reference for Beverly J. Cunningham, 2 September 1893, box 2.325/F37, Minnie Fisher Cunningham Papers, CAH-UT.

53. His obituary in the *Galveston Daily News*, 21 March 1928, notes Cunningham's affiliation as a Mason. State records indicate that he was initiated in 1901 and was passed and raised the following year. James D. Ward, Grand Secretary, Masonic Grand Lodge Library and Museum of Texas, to Judith McArthur, 10 December 1998.

54. Dugger, "Spanning the Old to the New South" (quotation); marriage certificate of B. J. Cunningham and Minnie Fisher, Cunningham binder, Walker County Historical Commission; telephone interview with R. M. Traylor III, Conroe, Texas, 28 February 2001.

Chapter 2

1. *Austin American*, 24 May 1946; Walker County Election Returns, 1904, Records of the Secretary of State, TSL.

2. *Directory of the City of Houston, 1905–1906* (Houston: Morrison and Fourmy, 1905), 132, 383, 394; Jim Hudson, *Dickinson: Taller than the Pines* (Burnet, Tex.: Nortex Press, 1979), 55–57, 75, 82; "Synopsis of the Life of Minnie Fisher Cunningham of Fisher Farms," Cunningham biographical file, CAH-UT.

3. *Directory of the City of Galveston, 1906–1907* (Galveston: Morrison and Fourmy, 1906), 113; *Directory of the City of Galveston, 1909–1910*, 121 (in early entries his name is given as Benjamin J. Cunningham); obituary of Beverly Jean Cunningham, *Galveston Daily News*, 21 March 1928; Hugh Williamson, ed., *The Story of Insurance in Texas* (Dallas: John Moranz Associates, 1954), 46.

4. David McComb, *Galveston: A History* (Austin: University of Texas Press, 1986), 134–143; Elizabeth Hayes Turner, *Women, Culture, and Community: Religion and Reform in Galveston, 1880–1920* (New York: Oxford University Press, 1997), 195–197; Bradley Robert Rice, *Progressive Cities: The Commission Government Movement in America* (Austin: University of Texas Press, 1977), 1–18.

5. Turner, *Women, Culture, and Community*, 11–12, 198–215.

6. "Synopsis of the Life of Minnie Fisher Cunningham of Fisher Farms"; *Kansas City Star*, 30 January 1941; MFC to Dorothy Brown, [on reverse of form letter dated 20 November 1920], box 8, folder 243, Dorothy Kirchwey Brown Papers, SL. The children were apparently still with her when she began suffrage work. See Perle Penfield to MFC, 11 August 1914, and MFC to Penfield, n.d., box 11a, folder 4, McCallum Family Papers, part II, AHC-APL. Penfield's letter concludes: "Please remember me to the children," and mentions having given them a swimming lesson; Cunningham, during a vacation in New Waverly, writes that "Josie and Jimsey send love. They are having a glorious time."

7. On the Home for Homeless Children, see Turner, *Women, Culture, and Community*, 139–143. Turner did not find Cunningham listed on the board of lady managers for either of Galveston's two orphanages, so the nature of her involve-

ment is unknown. We were unable to locate the Cunninghams in the 1910 manuscript census for Galveston, which presumably would have listed any children in the household.

8. I. H. Kempner, *Recalled Recollections* (Dallas: Eagan Co., 1961), 39–41, 52; K. C. Ilfet, " A Little History About Ourselves," *First Texas State Dope Sheet*, 10, 25 August 1913, copies in Rosenberg Library, Galveston; Williamson, *Story of Insurance in Texas*, 137. B. J. joined the Texas Bar Association in 1912, when it met in Galveston; see Texas Bar Association, *Proceedings of the Thirty-First Annual Session* (Austin: A. C. Baldwin, 1912), 288.

9. The literature on female voluntary associations is vast. For an overview, see Anne Firor Scott, *Natural Allies: Women's Associations in American History* (Urbana: University of Illinois Press, 1991).

10. "Synopsis of the Life of Minnie Fisher Cunningham of Fisher Farms"; Turner, *Women, Culture, and Community*, 156. There are no membership records for the Ladies' Musical Club beyond 1905, and the city directory lists only one other music circle, the Girls' Musical Club. We are greatly indebted to Elizabeth Turner for searching for Cunningham's name in her database of membership in Galveston women's organizations.

11. Turner, *Women, Culture, and Community*, 158–160, 282.

12. Programs, 1912–1913, 1913–1914, Wednesday Club Records, Rosenberg Library; Nancy Cott, *The Grounding of Modern Feminism* (New Haven: Yale University Press, 1987), 41, 46–47.

13. Turner, *Women, Culture, and Community*, 215–216.

14. "Mrs. Cunningham to Represent National League at Meeting Here," *Macon (Ga.) Telegraph*, 16 January 1923, clipping in Cunningham file, National League of Women Voters headquarters, Washington, D.C.; Turner, *Women, Culture, and Community*, 216–223.

15. *Galveston Daily News*, 4 February 1914; Turner, *Woman, Culture, and Community*, 218, 282.

16. Unidentified newspaper article signed by Cunningham, n.d., Galveston Equal Suffrage Association Records, Rosenberg Library.

17. Marjorie Spruill Wheeler, *New Women of the New South: The Leaders of the Woman Suffrage Movement in the Southern States* (New York: Oxford University Press, 1993), 115–120; Elna C. Green, *Southern Strategies: Southern Women and the Woman Suffrage Question* (Chapel Hill: University of North Carolina Press, 1997), 8–15.

18. A. Elizabeth Taylor, "The Woman Suffrage Movement in Texas," in *Citizens at Last: The Woman Suffrage Movement in Texas*, ed. Ruthe Winegarten and Judith N. McArthur (Austin: Ellen C. Temple, 1987), 16–25.

19. Turner, *Women, Culture, and Community*, 270–274, 356 n. 24.

20. Ronnie Dugger, "Spanning the Old to the New South," *Texas Observer*, 21 November 1958. Obviously, Cunningham was misquoted; she would never have referred to herself as a "suffragette," the label for the British militants. The press and the public, however, rarely grasped the difference between a suffragist and a suffragette.

21. "Mrs. Cunningham to Represent National League at Meeting Here."

22. Judith N. McArthur, *Creating the New Woman: The Rise of Southern Women's Progressive Culture in Texas, 1893–1918* (Urbana: University of Illinois Press, 1998), chap. 5; Cott, *Grounding of Modern Feminism*, 29–30.

23. Victoria Bissell Brown, "Jane Addams, Progressivism, and Woman Suffrage: An

Introduction to 'Why Women Should Vote,'" in *One Woman, One Vote: Rediscovering the Woman Suffrage Movement,* ed. Marjorie Spruill Wheeler (Troutedale, Ore.: NewSage Press, 1995), 179–202; Ellen Key, *Love and Marriage* (New York: G. P. Putnam's Sons, 1911), chap. 7.

24. "Leading Texas Women Work for Ballot," *Houston Chronicle,* 5 July 1914, clipping, box 1, folder 11, GESA Records; Letter to editor, *Houston Post,* 27 December 1916, TS, box 14b, folder 8, McCallum Papers, part II; MFC to J. P. Buchanan, 17 January 1917, box 14, folder 203, Cunningham Papers, HMRC (quotation). See also draft of an unpublished article on democracy for *Holland's Magazine,* [1919], box 13, folder 189, ibid.

25. MFC, "Woman Suffrage," 6 November 1912, Program, 1912–1913, Wednesday Club Records. On maternalist feminism, see Karen Offen, *European Feminism: A Political History* (Palo Alto: Stanford University Press, 2000), 236–239.

26. Unidentified newspaper article signed by Cunningham, n.d., GESA Records.

27. *Galveston Daily News,* 10 March 1912; MFC to Annette Finnigan, 8 May 1914, box 10a, folder 2, McCallum Papers, part II.

28. "Equal Suffrage Play Draws Big Attendance," unidentified clipping, n.d., box 1, folder 5, GESA Records; Sheila Stowell, *A Stage of Their Own: Feminist Playwrights of the Suffrage Era* (Ann Arbor: University of Michigan Press, 1992), 70 n; Larry J. Wygant, "'A Municipal Broom': The Woman Suffrage Campaign in Galveston, Texas," *Houston Review* (1984): 121–123 (quotation).

29. Taylor, "Woman Suffrage Movement in Texas," 26–27; *Galveston Tribune,* 14 June 1913, copy, box 1, folder 11, GESA Records.

30. Elizabeth Hayes Turner, "'White-Gloved Ladies and 'New Women' in the Texas Women Suffrage Movement," in *Southern Women: Histories and Identities,* ed. Virginia Bernhard et al (Columbia: University of Missouri Press, 1992), 152, 154; Turner, *Women, Culture, and Community,* 262, 270, 285.

31. McArthur, *Creating the New Woman,* 117; Annette Finnigan, "Texas Woman Suffrage Association," *Proceedings of the Forty-Sixth Convention of the National American Woman Suffrage Association, November 12–17, 1914* (New York: NAWSA, n.d.), 179–180. On the Women's Political Union, see Ellen Carol DuBois, *Harriot Stanton Blatch and the Winning of Woman Suffrage* (New Haven: Yale University Press, 1997).

32. *Galveston Daily News,* 16 February 1912; MFC to Annette Finnigan, 15 July 1914 (first quotation), 8 May 1914 (second quotation), 2 June 1914 (third quotation), box 10a, folder 4, McCallum Papers, part II.

33. *Galveston Daily News,* 27 April, 3 May 1914.

34. MFC to Finnigan, 2 June 1914; Finnigan to MFC, 22, 29 June 1914; MFC to Finnigan, 24 June 1914 (quotation); all in box 10a, folder 4, McCallum Papers.

35. *Galveston Daily News,* 5 June 1914.

36. MFC to Finnigan, 8 May 1914.

37. MFC to Perle Penfield, 6, 10 July 1914, box 10a, folder 4, McCallum Papers.

38. MFC to Penfield, 10 July (first quotation), 6 July (second quotation) July 1914; Penfield to MFC, 8 July 1914; all in ibid. Finnigan to MFC, 13 July 1914, box 11a, folder 4, ibid.

39. McComb, *Galveston,* 180; Dugger, "Spanning the Old to the New South"; MFC to Penfield, [July 1914], box 10a, folder 4, McCallum Papers; Perle Penfield, "Report of Work, Summer of 1914," box 10a, folder 8, ibid.

40. MFC to Finnigan, 2 June 1914 (first quotation); Finnigan to MFC, 17 June 1914;

Ida B. Deats to MFC, 14 June 1914; MFC to Penfield, [June 1914] (second quotation); all in box 10a, folder 4, McCallum Papers.

41. McArthur, *Creating the New Woman*, 107–108; Finnigan to Marin Fenwick, 23 September 1914, box 11a, folder 1b, McCallum Papers; MFC to Finnigan, 8 November 1914, box 11a, folder 4, ibid.

42. Turner, *Women, Culture, and Community*, 282; MFC to Finnigan, n.d., box 11a, folder 4, McCallum Papers; Finnigan to Mary G. Hay, 22 February 1915, box 11b, folder 6, ibid. The TFWC endorsed suffrage at the following year's convention.

43. McArthur, *Creating the New Woman*, 95; Finnigan to Eva Goldsmith, 7 July 1914, box 11a, folder 1a; and Finnigan to MFC, 7 July 1914, box 10a, folder 4; both in McCallum Papers.

44. Goldsmith to Finnigan, 20 July 1914, box 11, folder 1, ibid.; *Labor Dispatch*, 12 March 1915 (first quotation); Turner, *Women, Culture, and Community*, 275 (second quotation).

45. See for example MFC to Goldsmith, 7 July 1916, box 14, folder 7, McCallum Papers.

46. MFC to Mrs. Fain, n.d.; MFC to Finnigan, [February 1915]; both in box 11a, folder 4, ibid.; *Labor Dispatch*, 30 April 1915 (quotation).

47. *Labor Dispatch*, 12 February 1915.

48. *Labor Dispatch*, 2 April 1915.

49. *Labor Dispatch*, 19 February, 19 March, 9 April 1915 (quotation).

50. Finnigan to Mrs. H. A. Deats, 9 December 1914, box 10a, folder 4, McCallum Papers.

51. MFC to Finnigan, 9 December 1914, box 11a, folder 4, ibid.

52. Mrs. H. A. Deats to Finnigan, 14 December 1914, box 10a, folder 4, ibid.; MFC to Finnigan, 20 December 1914, box 11a, folder 4, ibid.

53. Finnigan to Marin Fenwick, 8 December 1914, box 11a, folder 1b, ibid.; DuBois, *Harriot Stanton Blatch*, 165 (quotation).

54. Finnigan to Anna E. Walker, 14 December 1914, box 11b, folder 9; Finnigan to Dear Club President, 31 December 1914, box 11a, folder 5; Finnigan to MFC, 5 January 1915, box 11a, folder 4; all in McCallum Papers.

55. MFC to Finnigan, [January 1914], box 11a, folder 4, McCallum Papers; Helen Todd to Finnigan, 10 February 1915, box 11b, folder 5, ibid.

56. "Suffragettes Would Bring Speaker Here," n.d. *Fort Worth Star* clipping, box 11a, folder 5, McCallum Papers; MFC to Finnigan, [January 1915], box 11a, folder 4, ibid.

57. Finnigan to MFC, 21 January 1915, ibid.; *HWS*, 6: 632; Dugger, "Spanning the Old to the New South" (quotation).

58. *Houston Daily Post*, 11 April 1915.

59. Finnigan to MFC, 13, 20 February 1915, box 11a, folder 4, McCallum Papers; *Labor Dispatch*, 5 February 1915; Turner, *Women, Culture, and Community*, 281.

60. Finnigan to MFC, 20 February 1915, box 11a, folder 4, McCallum Papers.

61. MFC to Finnigan, n.d., box 11a, folder 4, McCallum Papers; Finnigan to Elizabeth H. Potter, 7 March 1915, box 11b, folder 7, ibid.

62. *Galveston Daily News*, 26 March 1915.

63. MFC to Finnigan, 3 April 1915, and [1915], box 11a, folder 4, McCallum Papers.

64. Finnigan to MFC, 13 (quotation), 20 February 1915; MFC to Finnigan, n.d.; both in box 11a, folder 4, McCallum Papers.

65. Finnigan to MFC, 8 April 1915, ibid.; Elizabeth Fain to MFC, 19 April 1915, ibid.;

Galveston Daily News, 13, 14 May 1915; Taylor, "Woman Suffrage Movement in Texas."

66. Minutes of the Texas Woman Suffrage Association Fifth Annual Convention, Galveston, 12–14 May 1915, box 10a, folder 4, McCallum Papers.

67. Mrs. J. S. Sweeney to Finnigan, 26 March 1915; Finnigan to Sweeney, 5 June 1915; both in box 11a, folder 7, ibid.

CHAPTER 3

1. Elizabeth H. Potter to Jane McCallum, 20 May 1918, Jane Y. and Arthur N. McCallum Family Papers, box 3K84, CAH-UT.

2. Marjorie Spruill Wheeler, *New Women of the New South: The Leaders of the Woman Suffrage Movement in the Southern States* (New York: Oxford University Press, 1993), 38–50.

3. Texas Woman Suffrage Association—Report of Treasurer, 1 January 1916, box 12b, folder 6, McCallum Family Papers, part II, AHC-APL; MFC to W. H. Glynn, 1 January 1916, box 13a, folder 1, ibid. Catt is quoted in Robert Booth Fowler, *Carrie Catt: Feminist Politician* (Boston: Northeastern University Press, 1986), 118.

4. MFC to A. Louise Dietrich, 3 January 1916, box 12a, folder 1, McCallum Papers, part II; MFC to Miss A. A. Stuart, 19 April 1916, ibid.

5. MFC to Benigna Kalb, 13 July 1915, box 12a, folder 2, McCallum Papers, part II; MFC to Mrs. W. K. Knowd, 20 March 1916, box 14b, folder 8, ibid.

6. MFC to Annie Polk, 7 October 1915, box 12a, folder 3, ibid.

7. MFC to Louise Dietrich, 3 January 1916 (quotations); MFC to Kate Hunter, 10 September 1915, box 12b, folder 5, ibid.

8. MFC to Carrie Chapman Catt, 31 December 1915, box 13b, folder 5, ibid.

9. MFC to Kate Hunter, [January 1916], box 12b, folder 5, McCallum Papers, part II; MFC to Dear Executive Board Member, 1916, box 12, folder 168, Cunningham Papers, HMRC; MFC to Miss A. A. Stuart, 19 April 1916, box 15b, folder 6, McCallum Papers, part II; MFC to Anna B. Cade, 12 July 1916, box 14a, folder 3, ibid.

10. Questionnaire for State Presidents, 7 July 1916, reel 59, NAWSA Papers, LC; TESA Annual Report, 1916, box 3, folder 4, McCallum Papers, part I; Report of the President of the Texas Equal Suffrage Association, box 4, folder 2, ibid.; MFC to Dear Suffragist, 28 October 1916, box 13a, folder 3, ibid., part II; MFC to A. C. Ford, 9 November 1916, box 14b, folder 6, ibid.

11. For a full examination of the Southern States Woman Suffrage Conference, see Wheeler, *New Women of the New South*, 135–159.

12. *Galveston Daily News*, 15 May 1915.

13. MFC to Kate Hunter, [1916], box 12b, folder 5, McCallum Papers, part II; MFC to Mrs. J. M. Young, 8 January 1916, box 15b, folder 9, ibid.

14. MFC to Mrs. J. M. Young, 6 July 1916, box 15b, folder 9, ibid. The NWP reported 71 Texas members at the end of 1915 and 182 a year later; see *National Woman's Party Papers* (Bethesda, Md.: University Publications of America, 1977–1981), part II, series 1, reel 87.

15. For a discussion the politics of prohibition, see Lewis L. Gould, *Progressives and Prohibitionists: Texas Democrats in the Wilson Era* (Austin: University of Texas Press, 1974), chap. 2; On the Rio Grande Valley, see Evan Anders, *Boss Rule in South Texas: The Progressive Era* (Austin: University of Texas Press, 1982).

16. MFC to Dear Suffragist, 3 May 1916, box 13a, folder 3, McCallum Papers, part II; A. Elizabeth Taylor, "The Woman Suffrage Movement in Texas," in *Citizens at Last: The Woman Suffrage Movement in Texas*, ed. Ruthe Winegarten and Judith N. McArthur (Austin: Ellen C. Temple, 1987), 28; Jane Y. McCallum, "Texas," *HWS*, 6: 632–633; John C. Granbery to Mrs. James [*sic*] Y. McCallum, 23 November 1921, box 1, folder 9, McCallum Papers, part I; Gould, *Progressives and Prohibitionists*, 170–174.

17. Mary Gray Peck, *Carrie Chapman Catt: A Biography* (New York: H. W. Wilson, 1944), 248–249; Virginia Jeans Laas, *Bridging Two Eras: The Autobiography of Emily Newell Blair, 1877–1951* (Columbia: University of Missouri Press, 1999), 169–170; McCallum, "Texas," 633. Quotation is from Liz Carpenter, speech at dedication of Cunningham marker, Walker County, Texas, copy in authors' possession.

18. Carrie Chapman Catt and Nettie Rogers Shuler, *Woman Suffrage and Politics: The Inner Story of the Suffrage Movement* (1926; reprint, Seattle: University of Washington Press, 1969), 255–256; Peck, *Carrie Chapman Catt*, 250–252; *Dallas Times Herald*, 16 June 1916.

19. Sara Hunter Graham, *Woman Suffrage and the New Democracy* (New Haven: Yale University Press, 1996), 85; MFC to Lutie Stearns, 7 July 1916, box 16, folder 3, McCallum Papers, part II; MFC to Anna E. Walker, 6 July 1916, box 16, folder 1a, ibid.

20. MFC to Tex Armstrong, 7 August 1916, box 14a, folder 1, ibid.; MFC to Lavinia Engle, [August 1916], box 16, folder 2, ibid.

21. MFC to Carrie Chapman Catt, 11 August 1916, box 13b, folder 5, ibid.; MFC to Engle, [August 1916].

22. MFC to Mr. Cheeseborough, 22 August 1916, box 14a, folder 3, McCallum Papers, part II; MFC to Catt, 11 August 1916 (quotation).

23. MFC to Catt, 11 August 1916.

24. Maud Wood Park, *Front Door Lobby*, ed. Edna Lamprey Stantial (Boston: Beacon Press, 1960), 15–17; Fowler, *Carrie Catt*, 143–145.

25. MFC to Catt, 9 April 1917, box 3, folder 1, McCallum Papers, part I; Catt, "Report of Campaign and Survey Committee: A National Survey," 1916, reel 59, NAWSA Papers, LC; Wheeler, *New Women of the New South*, 159–162; Graham, *Woman Suffrage and the New Democracy*, 85–89.

26. MFC to Kate Gordon, 16 February 1917, box 14, folder 209, Cunningham Papers.

27. MFC to Helen Moore, n.d., box 17, folder 4, McCallum Papers, part II. For details of Ferguson's "war" with the University of Texas, see Gould, *Progressives and Prohibitionists*, chap. 7.

28. Helen Knox to Anna Pennybacker, 5 August 1917, Mrs. Percy V. Pennybacker Papers (recataloging in progress), CAH-UT; Mary Gearing to George Brackenridge, 10 December 1917, box 4P162, University of Texas Memorabilia, CAH-UT; MFC to Eleanor Brackenridge, 2 September 1917, box 4, folder 37, Cunningham Papers.

29. MFC to Dear Suffragist, 21 July 1917, box 34, McCallum Papers, part II; MFC, TESA Annual Report, 1917, box 3, folder 4, ibid., part I.

30. Cunningham to Carrie Chapman Catt, 31 July 1917, box 1, folder 8, Cunningham Papers; Dudley K. Woodward to Jane McCallum, 29 January 1920, box 1, folder 9, McCallum Papers, part I; Mary Gearing to George Brackenridge, 10

December 1917, and to Dr. H. Y. Benedict, 2 June 1923, box 4P162, University of Texas Memorabilia; [Women's Committee on Good Government], "An Appeal to the Friends of the University by the Women of Texas," ibid.

31. MFC to Helen Moore, n.d. (quotation); Mary Gearing to George Brackenridge, 14 August 1917, box 4P162, University of Texas Memorabilia; Headquarters Committee of the Woman's Campaign for Good Government, "Campaign Material," ibid.

32. EHL (Edith Hinkle League), memorandum, 3 August [1917], box 4P162, University of Texas Memorabilia; "Accusing the Governor, Speaker Fuller Charges That—", ibid.; MFC to Carrie Chapman Catt, 28 August 1917, box 1, folder 8, Cunningham Papers; MFC to George Peddy, 20 August 1917, box 34, McCallum Papers, part II. This box contains letters from MFC to numerous individuals and groups regarding the campaign to impeach Ferguson.

33. MFC to Catt, 28 August 1917 (first quotation), and 26 September 1917 (second quotation), ibid.

34. MFC to Dear Suffragist, 7 April 1917, box 12, folder 169, Cunningham Papers; *Houston Post*, 20 May 1917. On the Liberty Loan, see box 20, folders 294–299, Cunningham Papers.

35. Mark Thomas Connally, *The Response to Prostitution in the Progressive Era* (Chapel Hill: University of North Carolina Press, 1980); Anna Howard Shaw to Raymond Fosdick, 28 May 1917, box 1, RG 165, Records of the War Department, General and Special Staffs, Correspondence with Civilians and Civilian Agencies, NA. On Secretary Baker's "Fit to Fight" campaign, see Allan M. Brandt, *No Magic Bullet: A Social History of Venereal Disease in the United States Since 1880* (New York: Oxford University Press, 1985), chap. 2.

36. Suffrage Convention Bulletin, 17 May 1917, Jessie Daniel Ames Papers, Dallas Historical Society; MFC to Carrie Chapman Catt, 20 June 1917, box 1, folder 8, Cunningham Papers (quotation); MFC to Nannie Webb Curtis, 31 May 1917, box 17, folder 254, ibid.; "Vice Conditions are Horrible in San Antonio," *Home and State*, 15 June 1917.

37. *Dallas Evening Dispatch*, 2 June 1917 (quotation); [Edith Hinkle League] to Mrs. George F. L. Bishop, 26 June 1917, box 17, folder 254, Cunningham Papers; MFC to Newton Baker, 29 May 1917, box 17, folder 260, ibid.; *San Antonio Express*, 6 June 1917; MFC to Newton Baker, 7 June 1917, box 1, RG 165, NA.

38. MFC to Raymond Fosdick, 10 July 1917, box 17, folder 260, Cunningham Papers; "Camp Mothers Replace Vivandieres," *Woman Citizen*, 7 July 1917, 106; Edith Hinkle League to Mrs. E. F. Clay, 2 July 1917, box 17, folder 250, Cunningham Papers.

39. *Galveston Tribune*, 4 July 1917; MFC to Dr. Milton J. Bliem, 19 June 1917, box 17, folder 252, Cunningham Papers; MFC to Nannie Webb Curtis, 6 July 1917, and to Mrs. Gussie Scott Cheney, 31 August 1917, box 17, folder 254, ibid.; MFC, "Report of Work Planned for the Texas Women's Anti-Vice Committee and a Partial Summary of the Field for Work as Seen at the Close of the First Month's Activities," box 18, folder 267, ibid.

40. MFC to Raymond Fosdick, 12 June 1917, box 8, RG 165, NA; MFC to Fosdick, 15, 25 August, 23 October (quotation) 1917, box 17, folder 260, Cunningham Papers; Bascom Johnson to MFC, 2 November 1917, and MFC to Johnson, 3 January 1918, ibid.; MFC to Mary Ellis, 22 January 1959, box 2P363, Alexander Caswell Ellis Papers, CAH-UT. For a full account of the CTCA, see Nancy K. Bristow, *Making Men Moral: Social Engineering During the Great War* (New York:

New York University Press, 1996). Raymond Fosdick gives a first-hand account in *Chronicle of a Generation: An Autobiography* (New York: Harper, 1958), 136–157.

41. MFC to Raymond Fosdick, 19 June 1917, box 8, RG 165, NA; Fosdick to MFC, 23 June 1917, ibid.; Fosdick to MFC, 13 July 1917, box 1, ibid.; Maud Miner to MFC, 17 July, 7 August, 8 September 1917, box 17, folder 257, Cunningham Papers.

42. MFC to My Dear Co-Worker, 15 July 1917, box 18, folder 267, Cunningham Papers; MFC to Mrs. Edward Kneeland, 17 July 1917, and to Sara Toon Lane, 18 August 1917, box 17, folder 250, ibid.; MFC to Maud Miner, 2 September 1917; MFC to Anna Pennybacker, 31 August 1917, Pennybacker Papers; Dora H. Fleming to Pennybacker, 22 September 1917, ibid.

43. MFC to Mrs. E. A. Watters, 27 October, 1917, box 17, folder 266, Cunningham Papers.

44. Elmer Scott to MFC, 9 November 1917, box 17, folder 264, Cunningham Papers; William P. Hobby to MFC, 20 June 1918, box 23, folder 346, ibid.; Minutes of the First Meeting of the Executive Committee of the Texas State Military Welfare Commission, Austin, 20 June 1918, ibid.

45. MFC to Lavinia Engle, 6 April 1917, box 16, folder 2a, McCallum Papers, part II; *San Antonio Express*, 18 May 1917; *Houston Post*, 20 May 1917.

46. MFC to Mrs. A. L. Guerard, 26 September 1917, box 4, folder 48, Cunningham Papers; MFC to Dear Executive Board Member, 6 January 1917, box 12, folder 169, ibid.; Jessie Daniel Ames to TESA Executive Board, 18 January 1918, box 4, folder 42, ibid.; Minutes of the Executive Board, TESA, 23 January 1918, box 4, folder 3, McCallum Papers, part I.

47. MFC to Jane McCallum, 5 January 1918, box 3K84, folder 17, Jane Y. and Arthur N. McCallum Family Papers, CAH-UT.

48. MFC to Helen Moore, 7 December 1917, box 12, folder 269, Cunningham Papers; Moore to Dear Executive Board Member, 12 December 1917, box 11, folder 9, McCallum Papers, part I; MFC to Jane McCallum, 5 January 1918 (quotation).

49. MFC to Lavinia Engle, 6 April 1917, box 16, folder 2a, McCallum Papers, part II; MFC to Dear Executive Board Member, 1 January 1917 [*sic*], box 12, folder 169, Cunningham Papers; MFC to Dear Executive Board Member, 29 January 1918, box 12, folder 170, ibid.; MFC to McCallum, 5 January 1918.

50. Minutes of the Meeting of the Executive Board of the Texas Equal Suffrage Association . . . 23 January 1918, box 4, folder 3, McCallum Papers, part I; Jessie Daniel Ames, memorandum, n.d., box 18, ibid.

51. MFC to McCallum, 5 January 1918; MFC to Dear Suffragist, 19 February 1918, box 4, folder 5, McCallum Papers, part I.

52. MFC to Tom Finty, 28 January 1918, box 4, folder 3, ibid.; MFC to Carrie Chapman Catt, 25 January 1918, box 1, folder 9, Cunningham Papers; Gould, *Progressives and Prohibitionists*, 228–233.

53. Carrie Chapman Catt to MFC, 21 January 1918, box 17, folder 260, Cunningham Papers; Catt, *War Messages to the American People, No. 2: The Home Defense* (New York: National American Woman Suffrage Association, n.d.); *Dallas Morning News*, 15 January 1918; MFC to James Emerson Smith, 28 January 1918, box 4, folder 1, McCallum Papers, part I; Edith Hinkle League to Jane McCallum, 1 May 1918 (handwritten note on reverse), box 15, folder 3, ibid.

54. MFC to C. B. Metcalfe, 28 January 1918; Metcalfe to MFC, 10 February 1918, and

MFC to Metcalfe, 13 February 1918; all in box 14, folder 213, Cunningham Papers.

55. For details of the suffrage bargain, see Judith N. McArthur, "Minnie Fisher Cunningham's Back Door Lobby in Texas: Political Maneuvering in a One-Party State," in *One Woman, One Vote: Rediscovering the Woman Suffrage Movement*, ed. Marjorie Spruill Wheeler (Troutdale, Ore.: NewSage Press, 1995), 315–324.

56. *Austin American*, 31 May 1918; *San Antonio Express*, 31 May 1918 (quotation); MFC to Dear _____, 13 June 1918, box 12, folder 170, Cunningham Papers.

57. Mrs. E. Sampson to Mrs. [Maud Wood] Park, June 1918; Carrie Chapman Catt to Edith Hinkle League, 17 July 1918; MFC to Sampson, 31 August 1918; all in box 3, folder 4, McCallum Papers, part I.

58. Suzanne Lebsock, "Woman Suffrage and White Supremacy: A Virginia Case Study," in *Visible Women: New Essays on American Activism*, ed. Nancy A. Hewitt and Suzanne Lebsock (Urbana: University of Illinois Press, 1993), shows how dishonestly and deftly the antis manipulated the race issue. See also Glenda E. Gilmore, *Gender and Jim Crow: Women and the Politics of White Supremacy in North Carolina, 1896–1920* (Chapel Hill: University of North Carolina Press, 1996), and Elna C. Green, *Southern Strategies: Southern Women and the Woman Suffrage Question* (Chapel Hill: University of North Carolina Press, 1997).

59. MFC to the *[Galveston Daily] News*, 20 November 1916, box 14b, folder 8, McCallum Papers, part II.

60. MFC to Harry Dale, 2 May 1916, RG 233, Records of the House of Representatives, Center for Legislative Archives, NA; MFC to My Dear Sir, [1917], box 12, folder 169, Cunningham Papers.

61. *Houston Post*, 11 April 1915; *Houston Chronicle*, 30 December 1917. The latter is attributed to Cunningham in Willie D. Worley Bowles, "History of the Woman Suffrage Movement in Texas" (master's thesis, University of Texas at Austin, 1939).

62. MFC to T. N. Jones, 13 July 1918, box 3, folder 4, McCallum Papers, part I, AHC-APL (first quotation); MFC to Jane McCallum, n.d., box 3K84, folder 17, Jane Y. and Arthur N. McCallum Family Papers, CAH-UT (second quotation).

63. MFC to _____, 29 May 1918, and MFC to Walter J. Crawford, 17 July 1918, box 14, folder 229, Cunningham Papers; Minutes, Hobby Campaign Committee, Galveston, 30 March 1918, box 14, folder 231, ibid.; Minutes, Women's Hobby Committee, 15 June 1918, ibid.

64. Helen Moore to Annie Webb Blanton, 4 April 1918, box 17, folder 5, McCallum Papers, part II; *Austin American*, 1 June 1918; Debbie Mauldin Cottrell, *Pioneer Woman Educator: The Progressive Spirit of Annie Webb Blanton* (College Station: Texas A&M University Press, 1993), 49–55.

65. MFC to Annie Webb Blanton, 10 June 1918, and Blanton to MFC, 12 June 1918, box 15, folder 225, Cunningham Papers.

66. *Austin American*, 20 August 1917; MFC, "Ellis—Suffrage," TS, box 2P362, Ellis Papers.

67. Alexander Caswell Ellis to MFC, 20 June (quotations), 2, 7, 8, 10 July 1918; all in box 15, folder 226, Cunningham Papers. For a full account of the Blanton campaign, see Cottrell, *Pioneer Woman Educator*, 55–61.

68. Charles Metcalfe to MFC, 16 July 1918, MFC to Metcalfe, 16 July 1918, and Metcalfe to MFC, 14 August 1918; all in box 14, folder 213, Cunningham Papers.

69. [A. C. Ellis], "Shall the Fathers and Mothers of Texas or the Brewers and German-American Alliance O.K. Our State Superintendent of Public Instruc-

tion?" box 15, folder 226, Cunningham Papers; MFC to D. O. Bell, 17 July 1918, and MFC to Dear Suffragist, 22 July 1918, both in ibid. Cunningham's main objection to Doughty seems to have been that he had worked amicably with Ferguson and refused the Texas Women's Anti-Vice Committee an opportunity to address a statewide meeting of county school superintendents in Austin. See MFC to Marion Fisher, 1 August 1917, box 17, folder 255, Cunningham Papers.

70. MFC to Lavinia Engle, 16 July 1918, and Engle to MFC, n.d., box 10, folder 139, Cunningham Papers; McArthur, "Minnie Fisher Cunningham's Back Door Lobby in Texas" (Ferguson quotation).

71. MFC to A. Caswell Ellis, 30 July 1918, box 2P363, Ellis Papers. For a full account of the election, see McArthur, "Minnie Fisher Cunningham's Back Door Lobby in Texas."

72. [Jane McCallum], note, n.d., uncataloged box, McCallum Papers, part I; *Dallas Morning News*, 5 September 1918 (Cunningham quotation).

73. "Spanning the Old to the New South," *Texas Observer*, 21 November 1958.

74. Mrs. R. H. Ward to MFC, [1916], box 4, folder 7, McCallum Papers, part I; Charles B. Metcalfe to MFC, 16 August 1918, box 14, folder 213, Cunningham Papers.

75. MFC to Jane McCallum, partial letter, [ca. 1940], box 4, folder 5, McCallum Papers, part I.

76. *Houston Post*, 20 August 1940; MFC to McCallum, 5 April [1940?], box 7, folder 3, McCallum Papers, part I.

CHAPTER 4

1. *HWS*, 6: 692; MFC to Dear Executive Board Member, 2 September 1916, box 12, folder 168, Cunningham Papers, HMRC; Report of the President of the TESA, [1916–1917], box 4, folder 2, McCallum Family Papers, part I, AHC-APL.

2. Maud Wood Park, *Front Door Lobby*, ed. Edna Lamprey Stantial (Boston: Beacon Press, 1960), 28–29.

3. Sara Hunter Graham, *Woman Suffrage and the New Democracy* (New Haven: Yale University Press, 1996), xv-xvi, 83–90; Carrie Chapman Catt to Anna Pennybacker, 7 July 1919, box 2M125, Mrs. Percy V. Pennybacker Papers, CAH-UT.

4. *HWS*, 5: 516; Graham, *Woman Suffrage and the New Democracy*, 97; MFC to Morris Sheppard, 4 December 1917, box 14, folder 215, Cunningham Papers; MFC to Mary Gearing, 8 December 1917, box 20, folder 301, ibid.

5. [Edith Hinkle League] to Mary Gearing, 22 December 1917, box 20, folder 301, Cunningham Papers; League to Dear Suffragist, 20 December 1917, box 12, folder 169, ibid.; [MFC] to Rena Maverick Green, 16 January 1918, box 4, folder 47, ibid.; MFC to John E. Baker, 4 January 1918, box 4, folder 3, McCallum Papers; Park, *Front Door Lobby*, 133; *Houston Chronicle*, 10 January 1918; Elizabeth Herndon Potter to MFC, 16 January 1918, box 5, folder 60, Cunningham Papers (quotation).

6. Potter to MFC, 16 January 1918 (quotation); Alexander Caswell Ellis to Maud Wood Park, 31 January 1918, and Park to Ellis, 13 May 1918, box 2P362, Ellis Papers, CAH-UT; MFC to Dear Suffragist, 6 January 1918, box 14, folder 205, Cunningham Papers; MFC to Ellis, 3 February 1918, box 2P362, Ellis Papers.

7. Maud Wood Park, "Congressional Work for the Nineteenth Amendment, Supplementary Notes," February 1943, Edna Stantial Papers, *Women's Studies Manuscript Collections from the Schlesinger Library, Radcliffe College* (Bethesda, Md.: University Publications of America), microfilm, series 1, part E, reel 26.

8. Park, *Front Door Lobby*, 20–21, 38–40.
9. "Members of the National Board of the Congressional Committee and Others on Duty in Washington from December 1, 1917, to July 20, 1918," box 9, Maud Wood Park Papers, LC; Park to MFC, 20 May 1918, box 1, folder 3, Cunningham Papers; Park, *Front Door Lobby*, 181, 187.
10. Catt to Maud Wood Park, [August 1918], 4 September 1918, reel 5, Catt Papers, LC; Catt to Park, 21 August 1921, reel 15, NAWSA Papers, LC; Maud Wood Park to Mary Garrett Hay, 6 September 1918, Mary Garrett Hay Papers, *Women's Studies Manuscript Collections from the Schlesinger Library, Radcliffe College*, series 1, part B, reel 1.
11. "The Senate Will Vote," *Woman Citizen*, 21 September 1918, 326–327.
12. *New York Times*, 17 September 1918, 13; *Washington Post*, 17 September 1918, 2; Doris Stevens, *Jailed for Freedom: American Women Win the Vote*, ed. Carol O'Hare (Troutdale, Ore.: NewSage Press, 1995), 146–148.
13. "Report of the Chairman of the Congressional Committee, December 1st, 1917, to March 20th, 1919," box 9, Park Papers, LC; Catt to Maud Wood Park, 18 November 1918, reel 15, NAWSA Papers, LC; MFC to Park, 1 November 1918, box 1, folder 3, Cunningham Papers; Edith Hinkle League to Jessie Daniel Ames, 25 November 1918, box 13, folder 191, ibid.
14. Anna Pennybacker to Mrs. Frank Shuler, 24 November 1919, Pennybacker Papers. This letter, in which Pennybacker writes that she has just learned from a friend of MFC's separation but doesn't "know why this unfortunate step has been taken," is the only reference of which we are aware.
15. Park to MFC, 11 November 1918, box 1, folder 3, Cunningham Papers; Park, *Front Door Lobby*, 30–32.
16. MFC to A. Caswell Ellis, 14 December 1918, box 2P362, Ellis Papers.
17. MFC to Catt, 8 January 1919, Maud Wood Park Papers, *Women's Studies Manuscript Collections from the Schlesinger Library, Radcliffe College*, reel 42; Catt to My Dear President, 11 January 1919, reel 17, NAWSA Papers, LC.
18. Joseph E. Ransdell to Catt, 11 January 1919, Park Papers, reel 42; *HWS*, 6: 117, 407–408; MFC, Expense Account, Florida Trip, 9-20 January [1919], box 11, folder 160, Cunningham Papers; Eleanor Flexner, *Century of Struggle: The Woman's Rights Movement in the United States* (New York: Atheneum, 1974), 313.
19. Catt to My Dear President, 11 January 1919, reel 17, NAWSA Papers, LC; MFC to Jane McCallum, 5 April [1940?], box 7, folder 3, McCallum Papers, part I; Fragment of letter, [1919], box 3, folder 1, ibid. Quotation handwritten later by McCallum.
20. R. M. Dudley to MFC, 31 July 1918, box 14, folder 206 Cunningham Papers; W. L. Dean to MFC, 13 November 1918, box 12, folder 179, ibid.; MFC to Catt, 22 December 1918, uncataloged box, McCallum Papers, part I.
21. MFC to R. M. Dudley, 2 August 1918, box 14, folder 207, Cunningham Papers; MFC to W. L. Dean, 21 November 1918 (quotations), box 12, folder 179, ibid.
22. Vernice Reppert to MFC, 19 December 1918, and 1 January 1919, box 14, folder 205, Cunningham Papers; MFC to Catt, 22 December 1918; Catt to MFC, 23 January 1919, box 9, folder 1, McCallum Papers, part I.
23. Logic favored Crane's interpretation. The only "demand" in the platform was for a prohibition amendment, which the 1916 convention had passed, but Governor Ferguson had refused to submit; the language reflected indignation at his thwarting of the party's will. All of the other planks were "recommended." See *Dallas Morning News*, 4 September 1918.

24. M. M. Crane to Vernice Reppert, 8 January 1919, box 14, folder 205, Cunningham Papers; MFC to Reppert, 23 December 1918, box 4, folder 1, McCallum Papers, part I; MFC to Jane McCallum, 23 December 1918, ibid.

25. W. L. Dean to MFC, 22 November 1918; MFC to Dean, 25 November 1918; Dean to MFC, 1 January 1919, all in box 12, folder 179, Cunningham Papers; MFC to R. E. Thomason, 28 December 1918, box 14, folder 218, ibid.; MFC to Jane McCallum, 30 December [1918] (quotation), box 9, folder 2, McCallum Papers, part I; Catt to Jessie Daniel Ames, 3 January 1919, box 3, folder 1, ibid.

26. MFC to Jane McCallum, 11 December 1918, box 4, folder 1, McCallum Papers, part I; MFC to McCallum, n.d. (quotations), box 9, folder 2, ibid.

27. MFC to Catt, 4, 29 January 1919, box 1, folder 9, Cunningham Papers; Jessie Daniel Ames to MFC, 21, 28 December 1918, box I/18, folder 4, McCallum Papers, part I.

28. Catt to MFC, 27 December 1918, box 1, folder 7, ibid., and 3 January 1919, box 1, folder 9, ibid.

29. *Austin Statesman*, 16 January 1919; MFC to A. Caswell Ellis, n.d., box 2P363, Ellis Papers; Ewing Thomason to MFC, 21 January 1919, box 3, folder 5, McCallum Papers, part I.

30. Vernice Reppert to MFC, 13 December 1918, box 3, folder 2, McCallum Papers, part I; MFC to Jane McCallum, 20 January 1919, box 4, folder 5, ibid.

31. Catt to MFC, 23 January 1919.

32. *Austin Statesman*, 5 February 1919; *Dallas Morning News*, 2 February 1919.

33. The NAWSA had not at first realized that the Texas bill contained an alien disfranchisement clause; Catt and Shuler sent a copy of the South Dakota bill, urging the TESA to have its own bill amended accordingly. Catt to Cunningham, 23 January 1919; Nettie Rogers Shuler to Cunningham, 23 January 1919, box 9, folder 1, McCallum Papers, part I; Jane McCallum to Catt, telegram, 29 January 1919, box 13, folder 6, ibid.

34. Fowler, *Carrie Catt*, 82–86; MFC to Catt, 25 March 1918, box 1, folder 9, Cunningham Papers.

35. MFC to Tom Finty, 25 March 1919, box 11, folder 5, McCallum Papers, part I; MFC to C. S. Fowler, 27 February 1919, box 10, folder 9, ibid. Although Cunningham refers to the legislature having "tacked on" the alien clause, the same provision was in the bill that W. L. Dean prepared for the TESA. See *Dallas Morning News*, 18 January 1919.

36. "State Suffrage Leader Announces Campaign to Secure Amendment," *Houston Chronicle*, clipping, n.d., box 13, folder 183, Cunningham Papers; MFC to Dear County Chairmen, 26 February 1919, MFC to Mrs. Rosser Thomas, 31 March 1919, MFC to Baptist ministers, 8 May 1919, and MFC to Council of National Defense chairs, 19 May 1919; all in box 3, folder 1, McCallum Papers, part I.

37. Nettie Rogers Shuler to MFC, 29 January 1919, box 9, folder 1, McCallum Papers, part I; "Plan of Campaign for Michigan," box 12, folder 1, ibid.; "Outline of Campaign for Carrying the Suffrage Amendment at the Special Election on May 24, 1919," box 3, folder 2, ibid.; MFC to Senatorial District Chairwomen, 27 February 1919, ibid.

38. Catt to MFC, 23 January 1919; MFC to Dear Suffragist, 14 March 1919, box 3, folder 1, McCallum Papers, part I.

39. MFC to Dear Suffragist, 21 March 1919, 15 April 1919, ibid.; Nettie Rogers Shuler to MFC, 11 March 1919, box 13, folder 9, McCallum Papers, part I;

"Program of the M. Eleanor Brackenridge Training School for Volunteer Workers in the Suffrage Campaign," box 13, folder 7, ibid.

40. Nettie Rogers Shuler to MFC, 24 February, 16 May 1919, box 13, folder 4, McCallum Papers, part I; Catt to MFC, 26 December 1918, box 9, folder 1, ibid.

41. MFC to R. M. Dudley, 25 March 1919, box 10, folder 9, ibid.; Jessie Daniel Ames to Miss Benckenstein, 10 April 1919, and Emma Winner Rogers to MFC, 8 April 1919, box 19, folder 1, ibid.; "Rough Estimate of a Budget for the Suffrage Campaign Worked Out on a Basis of Four Months," box 10, folder 8, ibid.; "Report of the Finance Committee, Submission Campaign Fund, March 1st–June 12th, 1919," box 20, folder 1, ibid.

42. Jessie Daniel Ames to Eleanor Brackenridge, 7 June 1919, box 19, folder 2, McCallum Papers, part II; MFC to Newspaper Editors, 10 April 1919, box 10, folder 21, ibid., part I; MFC, Car Cards letter, n.d., box 10, folder 4, ibid.; MFC to Dear Suffragist, 5 May 1919, box 3, folder 1, ibid.; Jane Y. McCallum, "Activities of Women in Texas Politics," in *Texas Democracy: A Centennial History of Politics and Personalities of the Democratic Party, 1836–1936*, 2 vols., ed. Frank Carter Adams (Austin: Democratic Historical Association, 1937), 1: 484.

43. *Ferguson Forum*, 20 February, 17 April, 15, 22 May, 1919; *Woman Citizen*, 17, 24 May 1919; Elna Green, *Southern Strategies: Southern Women and the Woman Suffrage Question* (Chapel Hill: University of North Carolina Press, 1997), 116. Copies of antisuffragist literature can be found in box 9, folder 4, McCallum Papers, part I.

44. MFC to Catt, 5 May [1919], box 3, folder 2, McCallum Papers, part I.

45. MFC to Eleanor Brackenridge, 4 June 1919, box 11, folder 8, McCallum Papers, part I; MFC to Catt, 5 June 1919 (quotation); MFC to Florence Cotnam, 6 June 1919, box 3, folder 29, Cunningham Papers.

46. MFC to Dear Suffragist, 17 May 1919, box 3, folder 1, McCallum Papers, part I.

47. MFC to R. E. Thomason, 28 May [1919], box 10, folder 9, McCallum Papers, part I; Vernice Reppert to MFC, 28 May 1919, box 11, folder 3, ibid.; MFC to Jane McCallum, fragment, [ca. 1940], box 4, folder 5, ibid.

48. MFC to Dear Suffragist, 5 June 1919, box 3, folder 1, McCallum Papers, part I; MFC to Senator R. P. Dorough, 5 June 1919, box 10, folder 9, ibid. On the antisuffragists, see James Ferguson to James B. Wells, 9 June 1919, Wells to R. L. Henry, 9 June 1919, and Wells to D. F. Strickland, 26 June 1919; all in box 2H496, James B. Wells Papers, CAH-UT.

49. A suit against the secretary of state's office would have required the TESA to bring forward witnesses to prove that the irregular ballots actually cost them the number of votes by which the amendment was defeated. If the suffragists lost, they would have had to pay the court costs, which, because the state was entitled to direct the investigation, might have run as high as $50,000–$75,000; TESA would have been required to give bond for it upon initiating the lawsuit. MFC to Catt, 5 June [1919], uncataloged box, McCallum Papers, part I, and 14 June 1919, box 3, folder 2, ibid.

50. Anne F. and Andrew M. Scott, *One Half the People: The Fight for Woman Suffrage* (Philadelphia: Lippincott, 1975), 162; Wheeler, *New Women of the New South*, 33.

51. MFC, circular letter, 21 June 1919, box 4, folder 5, McCallum Papers, part I. James Bernard Seymour, Jr., "'War Within a War': The Effects of the Great War on Social Progressivism in Texas" (Ph.D. diss., Texas A&M University, 1997), 236–238, argues that the alien vote "played a limited role" in defeating the amendment; Susan E. Marshall in *Splintered Sisterhood: Gender and Class in the*

Campaign Against Woman Suffrage (Madison: University of Wisconsin Press, 1997), 159, finds that "counties that were poorer, more nonwhite, slower growing, and German recorded larger antisuffrage margins."

52. MFC to J. C. McNealus, 21 June 1919, and to Hon. J. H. Woods, 19 June 1919, box 12, folder 178, Cunningham Papers; MFC to Mrs. T. A. Coleman, 6 June 1919, box 12, folder 178, ibid.; MFC to Catt, 5 June [1919].

53. MFC to Morris Sheppard, 16 June 1919, box 14, folder 215, Cunningham Papers; MFC to Catt, 2 July 1919, box 3, folder 9, McCallum Papers, part I; Catt to MFC, 23 June 1919, box 1, folder 9, Cunningham Papers.

54. McCallum, "Activities of Women in Texas Politics," 485–487; *Woman Citizen*, 19 July 1919; Graham, *Woman Suffrage and the New Democracy*, 135–136; [MFC], "Ellis—Suffrage," TS, box 2P362, Ellis Papers.

55. MFC to Catt, 2 July 1919; MFC to Jane McCallum, fragment, [ca. 1940], box 4, folder 5, McCallum Papers, part I.

56. MFC to Catt, 1, 9 July 1919, box 1, folder 9, Cunningham Papers; Minutes, New York Section of the Board of Officers, 14 July 1919, reel 61, NAWSA Papers; Catt to Katherine Ludington, 5 August 1919, reel 32, ibid.; Graham, *Woman Suffrage and the New Democracy*, 130–131.

57. MFC to Catt, 15 July 1919, box 1, folder 9, Cunningham Papers; Albert B. Fall to MFC, 4 August 1919, reel 6, NAWSA Papers; Ronnie Dugger, "Spanning the Old to the New South," *Texas Observer*, 21 November 1958; MFC to Jane McCallum, 22 July 1919, box 3K84, folder 17, Jane Y. and Arthur N. McCallum Family Papers, CAH-UT.

58. "Autobiography of Jessie Jack Hooper," TS, 25–26, Jessie Jack Hooper Papers, WSHS.

59. Ibid., 27–28; Carrie Chapman Catt and Nettie Rogers Shuler, *Woman Suffrage and Politics: The Inner Story of the Suffrage Movement* (1923; reprint, Seattle: University of Washington Press, 1969), 352–353; Agenda, Board Meeting, 5 September 1919, reel 61, NAWSA Papers.

60. Nettie R. Shuler to Anna Pennybacker, 29 October 1919, Pennybacker Papers; Elizabeth Skinner to MFC, 7 December 1919, Cunningham Collection, Walker County Historical Commission, Huntsville, Tex.; Shuler to MFC, 20 November 1919, ibid. (Copies also available in the Beulah Grimmet Papers, TWU).

61. Anna Pennybacker to Catt, 10 November 1919, Pennybacker Papers; Nettie R. Shuler to MFC, 15 December 1919, Cunningham Collection, Walker County Historical Commission; MFC to Jane McCallum, [1919], and 18 December 1919, box I/18, McCallum Papers, part I.

62. *HWS*, 6: 334, 337; Anna Pennybacker to MFC, 19 December 1919; Blanche Rogers to MFC, [December 1919], and Lulu Daniel Hardy to MFC, 20 December 1919 (quotation), all in Cunningham Collection, Walker County Historical Commission; A. Elizabeth Taylor, "The Woman Suffrage Movement in Mississippi," *Journal of Mississippi History* 30 (February 1968): 25–31.

63. Catt to MFC, 12 December 1919, Cunningham Collection, Walker County Historical Commission; J. Stanley Lemons, *The Woman Citizen: Social Feminism in the 1920s* (Urbana: University of Illinois Press, 1973), 49–52; Louise M. Young, *In the Public Interest: The League of Women Voters, 1920–1970* (Westport, Conn.: Greenwood, 1989), 33–46. The eight standing committees were American Citizenship, Women in Industry, Child Welfare, Social Hygiene, Improvements in Election Laws and Methods, Study of Food Problems, Unification of Laws Concerning Women, and Research.

64. *Dallas Morning News*, 25, 26 May, 24 June 1920; Kristi Andersen, *After Suffrage: Women in Partisan and Electoral Politics before the New Deal* (Chicago: University of Chicago Press, 1996), 83, 87–88. Women made a smaller showing at the Republican Convention, where they were 3 percent of the delegates and 13 percent of the alternates. The Texas delegation also included three women district delegates; see *Woman Citizen* 4 (12 June 1920): 61.
65. *Dallas Morning News*, 24 June 1920; *Woman Citizen* 4 (15 May 1920): 254; Emily Newell Blair, "Women at the Conventions," *New York Times Current History* 13 (20 October 1920): 27–28; *Dallas Morning News*, 3 July 1920.
66. Norman D. Brown, *Hood, Bonnet, and Little Brown Jug: Texas Politics, 1921–1928* (College Station: Texas A&M University Press, 1984), 170.

CHAPTER 5

1. Barbara Stuhler, *For the Public Record: A Documentary History of the League of Women Voters* (Westport, Conn.: Greenwood, 2000), 40, 78; Carrie Chapman Catt, "The League of Women Voters," *Woman Citizen* 3 (12 April 1919): 957; Catt, "Political Parties and Women Voters," *Papers of the League of Women Voters*, part II, series A, reel 1 (Frederick, Md.: University Publications of America, 1986), microfilm (hereafter cited as LWV Papers).
2. Nancy Cott, *The Grounding of Modern Feminism* (New Haven: Yale University Press, 1987), 106–109; Anna L. Harvey, *Votes Without Leverage: Women in American Electoral Politics, 1920–1970* (Cambridge: Cambridge University Press, 1998), 189–192, 201–203.
3. Hortense Ward to MFC, 1 April 1918, and MFC to Ward, 5 April 1918, box 13, folder 192, Cunningham Papers, HMRC; MFC to Anna Pennybacker, 4 July 1918, box 13, folder 190, ibid.
4. Elizabeth Herndon Potter to MFC, 18 January 1918, box 5, folder 60, Cunningham Papers; Potter to A. Caswell Ellis, 16 January 1918, box 2P362, Ellis Papers, CAH-UT; MFC to Morris Sheppard, 28 January 1918, box 14, folder 215, Cunningham Papers; MFC to Catt, 28 January 1918, box 1, folder 3, ibid. Knowing that whoever was chosen would be in thrall to state party leaders, Cunningham refused to let her name go forward.
5. MFC to Dorothy Kirchwey Brown, [1922], box 8 folder 243, Dorothy Kirchwey Brown Papers, SL. On the integration of women into party structures, see Jo Freeman, *A Room at a Time: How Women Entered Party Politics* (New York: Rowman and Littlefield, 2000), 109–112.
6. "Minnie Fisher Cunningham on Voter Education," in Stuhler, *For the Public Record*, 96–97. On "reformed democracy," see Robert Booth Fowler, *Carrie Catt, Feminist Politician* (Boston: Northeastern University Press, 1986), chap. 6.
7. Minutes of the Annual Convention of the Texas Equal Suffrage Association and the Texas League of Women Voters, 9 October 1919, Texas League of Women Voters Papers, Southwest Collection, Texas Tech University; *San Antonio Express*, 9, 10, 11 October 1919.
8. Jessie Daniel Ames to Mrs. Hiram Knox, 23 July 1919, box 19, folder 4, McCallum Family Papers, part I, AHC-APL.
9. Mrs. George C. Boller to Bill Edwards, 1919, box 1, folder 5, Galveston Equal Suffrage Association Papers, Addendum, Rosenberg Library, Galveston; *El Paso Herald*, 14 October 1920; Emma Louise Moyer Jackson, "Petticoat Politics: Political Activism Among Texas Women in the 1920s" (Ph.D. diss., University of Texas at Austin, 1980), 23.

10. "Proceedings of the Victory Convention of the National American Woman Suffrage Association and First National Congress of the League of Women Voters," 1920, LWV Papers, part II, series A, reel 1; Minutes of the Executive Committee, 17–20 February 1920, LWV Papers, part I, reel 1.

11. Lewis L. Gould, *Progressives and Prohibitionists: Texas Democrats in the Wilson Era* (Austin: University of Texas Press, 1973), 257–265; *Dallas Morning News*, 29 February, 7 March 1920; Jacquelyn Dowd Hall, *Revolt Against Chivalry: Jessie Daniel Ames and the Women's Campaign Against Lynching* (New York: Columbia University Press, 1974), 47 (Bailey quotation).

12. Jessie Daniel Ames, "Texas League of Women Voters," TS, Jessie Daniel Ames Papers, TSL; Texas Equal Suffrage Association Minute Book, 1919–1921, 15–16, Blagg-Huey Library, TWU.

13. MFC to Anna Pennybacker, 13 May 1920, box 22, folder 320, Cunningham Papers, HMRC; Janet G. Humphrey, ed., *A Texas Suffragist: Diaries and Writings of Jane Y. McCallum* (Austin: Ellen C. Temple, 1988), 142–143.

14. Gould, *Progressives and Prohibitionists*, 271–272; MFC to Ruth Potts Spence, 13 May 1920, box 22, folder 320, Cunningham Papers. Neff clipping, box 21, folder 318, ibid.

15. MFC to R. E. Thomason, 14 May 1920; MFC to A. M. Frazier, 28 May, 10, 12, 17 June, and 12 July 1920; Frazier to MFC, 17 June 1920; MFC to Mrs. T. A. Coleman, 28 April 1920 (quotation); Jessie Daniel Ames to Dear Co-Worker, 18 May 1920; all in box 22, folder 322, Cunningham Papers.

16. "An Answer to Neff's Article as Issued by Mrs. E. P. Turner from Mrs. Minnie Fisher Cunningham Personally," *Dallas Morning News*, 18 July 1920; A. M. Frazier to MFC, 16 July 1920, box 22, folder 322, Cunningham Papers.

17. Jessie Daniel Ames to Maud Wood Park, 28 July, 14 August 1920, LWV Subject Files, series I, box 49, LC; Jessie Daniel Ames, "Report of a Year's Work . . . October 14, 1919–October 14, 1920," Texas League of Women Voters Papers; Ames, "Texas League of Women Voters."

18. Texas Equal Suffrage Association Minute Book, 1919–1921, pp. 19–21; "Proceedings of the Second National Convention," 1921, LWV Papers, part II, series A, reel 1, frame 0677 (Cunningham quotation). On the effort to unseat Wadsworth, see Elisabeth Israels Perry, "Defying the Party Whip: Mary Garrett Hay and the Republican Party, 1917–1920," in *We Have Come to Stay: American Women and Political Parties, 1880–1960*, ed. Melanie Gustafson, Kristie Miller, and Elisabeth Israels Perry (Albuquerque: University of New Mexico Press, 1999).

19. "Proceedings of the Third Annual Convention," 1922, LWV Papers, part II, series A, reel 3, 36–37; Harvey, *Votes Without Leverage*, 135–139.

20. Press release, 22, 30 April (MFC quote), reel 55, NAWSA Papers, LC; Rose Young to Dear Friend, 21 April 1920, ibid.; MFC to Anna Pennybacker, 13 May 1920, box 22, folder 320, Cunningham Papers.

21. MFC to Jane McCallum, [1920], box 18, McCallum Papers, part I; Interview with Richard M. Traylor IV, 4 April 1998, New Waverly, Texas, and with R. M. Traylor III, 5 April 1998, Conroe, Texas; Beulah Grimmet to Judith McArthur and Harold Smith, 1 July 2001.

22. At some point Carrie Chapman Catt apparently invited her to take the secretaryship of the Leslie Woman Suffrage Commission, but Cunningham never served and there is no documentation except a small, undated press notice. "Galveston Woman Will Handle Suffrage Fund," unidentified clipping, box 1, folder 11A, Records of the Galveston Equal Suffrage Association. The Leslie

Commission changed secretaries in 1920, but the new appointee was Nora Newell, who served from July 15, 1920 to October 1, 1922. Rose Young, *The Record of the Leslie Woman Suffrage Commission, Inc., 1917–1929* (New York: The Commission, 1929), 63.

23. J. Stanley Lemons, *The Woman Citizen: Social Feminism in the 1920s* (Urbana: University of Illinois Press, 1973), 55–57; Cott, *Grounding of Modern Feminism*, 97–98.

24. Robyn Muncy, *Creating a Female Dominion in American Reform, 1890–1935* (New York: Oxford University Press, 1991), 93–105; Molly Ladd-Taylor, *Mother-Work: Women, Child Welfare, and the State, 1890–1930* (Urbana: University of Illinois Press, 1994), 167–176.

25. Florence Kelley to Mrs. Edward P. Costigan, 18 March 1921, container B12, reel 24, National Consumers' League Papers, LC; MFC to Kelley, 2 April 1921, LWV Papers, part III, series A, reel 1, box I-24. A short biography of Cunningham identifying her as legislative secretary appears in "Proceedings of the Second National Convention," LWV Papers, part II, series A, reel 1.

26. MFC to Jane McCallum, [7 March 1921], box 22, McCallum Papers, part II.

27. Program of Pre-Convention Conferences, Second National Convention, part II, series A, reel 1, LWV Papers; Eleanor Roosevelt to Franklin Roosevelt, 11 April 1921, box 15, folder 8, Roosevelt Family Papers Donated by the Children, FDR Library; Eleanor Roosevelt, "Why I Am a Member of the League of Women Voters," LWV Papers, part II, series A, reel 18.

28. Maud Wood Park to Dear Board Member, 14 May 1921, Maud Wood Park Papers, *Women's Studies Manuscript Collections from the Schlesinger Library, Radcliffe College*, series 1, part D (Bethesda, Md.: University Publications of America), microfilm, reel 44; *El Paso Herald*, 14, 20, 21 October 1920.

29. MFC to Dorothy Kirchwey Brown, 29 April, 7 May 1921, box 8, folder 243, Brown Papers.

30. MFC, Sheppard-Towner Press Release, 6 July 1922, and MFC to Dorothy Kirchwey Brown, 19, 21, 22 July 1921; all in box 8, folder 243, Brown Papers; MFC, "The Women's Joint Congressional Committee is Supporting the Sheppard-Towner Bill," LWV Papers, part III, series A, reel 3, box II-7; *Woman Citizen*, 13 August 1921.

31. MFC to Dear State Chairmen, 2 August 1921, and to Dorothy K. Brown, [summer 1921], box 8, folder 243, Dorothy Kirchwey Brown Papers; MFC to Pattie Ruffner Jacobs, 29 August 1921, LWV Papers, part III, series A, reel 2, box I-21; MFC to Mrs. Julian B. Salley, 2 September 1921, box 4, folder 67, Eulalie Chafee Salley Papers, SCL.

32. Muncy, *Creating a Female Dominion*, 105–106; *Woman Citizen*, 3 December 1921, 6; Lemons, *The Woman Citizen*, 157–160.

33. Carrie Chapman Catt, "Who's Scared?" *Woman Citizen*, 28 January 1922; Maud Wood Park to the *Woman Citizen*, 11 March 1922; MFC to Dorothy Kirchwey Brown, 19 February 1922, box 8, folder 243, Brown Papers.

34. MFC to Dorothy Kirchwey Brown, 19 February 1922, and [April? 1923] (quotation), box 8, folder 243, Brown Papers; MFC to Pattie Ruffner Jacobs, 17 July, 10 October 1922, LWV Papers, part III, series A, reel 2, box I-21; Muncy, *Creating a Female Dominion*, 107.

35. MFC, "Report of the Executive Secretary," in "Proceedings of the Third Annual Convention," LWV Papers, part II, series A, reel 2, and "Proceedings of the Fourth Annual Convention," ibid., reel 4 (quotation).

36. Minutes of the Executive Committee, June 1922, September 1922, ibid., part I,

reel 1; MFC to Marie Edwards and Belle Sherwin, 9 March 1922, ibid., part III, series A, reel 2, box I-26.

37. Marguerite Wells to Maud Wood Park, 14 April 1944, box 9, Park Papers, LC; Park to MFC, 15 July 1922, LWV Papers, part III, series A, reel 1, box I-13; Elizabeth Hauser to Gertrude S. Martin, 13 March 1922, ibid., box I-17; MFC to Amy G. Maher, 26 September 1922, ibid., reel 3, box I-62; Minutes of the Executive Committee, July 1921, ibid., part I, reel 1; MFC to Florence Kelley, 20 July 1922, ibid., part III, series A, reel 2, box I-25; MFC to Maud Wood Park, 26 July 1922, ibid., box I-30.

38. MFC, "Report of the Executive Secretary," in "Proceedings of the Fourth Annual Convention"; Maud Wood Park, "Supplementary Notes, National LWV, Third Year, April 30, 1922 to April 15, 1923," Park Papers, *Women's Studies Manuscript Collections from the Schlesinger Library, Radcliffe College*, reel 43; *Louisville Courier*, 21 January 1923, Cunningham file, LWV headquarters; MFC to Dorothy K. Brown, 8 January [1922], 23 January 1923, 14 February 1923, box 8, folder 243, Brown Papers.

39. Lemons, *The Woman Citizen*, 65–67; Nancy F. Cott, "Marriage and Women's Citizenship in the United States, 1830–1934," *American Historical Review* 103 (December 1998): 1440–1474.

40. Candice Lewis Bredbenner, *A Nationality of Her Own: Women, Marriage, and the Law of Citizenship* (Berkeley: University of California Press, 1998), 86–93; LWV, "Woman's Work is Never Done," TS, Edna Stantial Papers, *Women's Studies Manuscript Collections from the Schlesinger Library, Radcliffe College*, reel 26; MFC, Report on the Cable Act, "Proceedings of the Fourth National Convention," LWV Papers, part II, series A, reel 5. The remainder of the discussion of the bill is drawn from this account.

41. For a full discussion of the remaining difficulties, see Bredbenner, *A Nationality of Her Own*, chap. 3.

42. Press Release, 15 April 1922, LWV Papers, part II, series A, reel 2; MFC to Carrie Chapman Catt, 1, 27 March 1922, ibid., part III, series A, reel 3, box II-3; MFC to Jane McCallum, [1922], box 9, folder 2, McCallum Papers, part I.

43. Maud Wood Park, "Second Year (April 17, 1921 to April 30, 1922), Supplementary Notes," 2, Park Papers, *Women's Studies Manuscript Collections from the Schlesinger Library, Radcliffe College*, reel 43; MFC to Jane McCallum, [1925], box 18, McCallum Papers, part I. Extensive correspondence between Cunningham and Engle documenting preparations for the Pan-American Conference is preserved in box 16, LWV Papers, series II, LC.

44. Park, "Second Year . . . Supplementary Notes," 5–6.

45. "Call to the Third Annual Convention and the Pan-American Conference of Women," LWV Papers, part II, series A, reel 2; "Pan-American Conference of Women," box 15, LWV Papers, series II, LC; *Woman Citizen* 6 (6 May 1922): 12; Freda Kirchwey, "The Pan-American Conference of Women," *The Nation*, 10 May 1922.

46. Evelyn Brooks Higginbotham, "In Politics to Stay: Black Women Leaders and Party Politics in the 1920s," in *Women, Politics, and Change*, ed. Louise A. Tilly and Patricia Guerin (New York: Russell Sage Foundation, 1990), 212–215; Paula Giddings, *When and Where I Enter: The Impact of Black Women on Race and Sex in America* (New York: William Morrow, 1984), 166. Hunton had earlier asked to address the National Woman's Party February convention and been refused.

47. Minutes of the Board of Directors, April 1921, LWV Papers, part I, reel 1; Adele

Clark to Maud Wood Park, 21 May 1921, ibid., part III, series A, reel 3, box I-50; Eulalie C. Salley to Mrs. Basil Manley, 20 April 1921, Salley Papers.

48. MFC to Dorothy Kirchwey Brown, 29 April 1921, box 8, folder 243, Brown Papers.

49. Helen M. Rocca to Mary Jagoe, 11 May 1926, box II: 80, LWV Subject Files, series II, LC (quoting MFC); MFC to Brown, 29 April 1921.

50. Pattie Ruffner Jacobs to MFC, 8 December 1921 (quotation), LWV Papers, part III, series A, reel 12, box I-21; Julia Lathrop to Maud Wood Park, 15 April 1922, and MFC, 16 April 1922, ibid., reel 12, box I-50.

51. Mary Swenson Miller, "Lobbyist for the People: The League of Women Voters in Alabama, 1920–1975" (master's thesis, Auburn University, 1978), 33; Maud Wood Park to Julia Lathrop, 8 June 1922, and Lathrop to MFC, 14 July 1922 [filed], LWV Papers, part III, series A, reel 3, box I-50; Minutes of the Executive Committee, September 1922, November 1922, ibid., part I, reel 1; MFC to Julia Lathrop, 3 October 1922, and MFC, "Report on Activity for the Organization of the Special Committee on Negro Problems," ibid., part III, series A, reel 3, box I-50; Minutes of the Executive Committee, February 1923, ibid., part I, reel 1.

52. Minutes of the Executive Committee, April 1923, LWV Papers, part I, reel 1; National Notes, 25 (June 1923): 6–7, Records of the National Association of Colored Women's Clubs (Bethesda, Md.: University Publications of America, 1993), part I, reel 23; Blanche Rogers to MFC, 6 April 1923, LWV Papers, part III, series A, reel 3, box I-50.

53. "Miss Lathrop's Report," 14 April 1923; MFC to Blanche Rogers, 5 May 1923; Minutes of the Executive Committee, April 1923; Blanche Rogers to MFC, 13 June, 28 September 1923; all in ibid.

54. MFC to Dorothy Kirchwey Brown, [1922], box 8, folder 243, Brown Papers.

55. MFC to Dorothy Kirchwey Brown, 19 February 1922 and [1923?], box 8, folder 243, Brown Papers; MFC to Brown, 18 January 1954, box 9, folder 224, Brown Papers (third accession); MFC to Maud Wood Park, 24 February 1922, LWV Papers, part III, series A, reel 2, box I-30.

56. MFC to Dorothy Kirchwey Brown, 4 July 1923, [summer 1923], and 8 September 1923, box 8, folder 244, Brown Papers; Marion Banister to Brown, 20 September 1923, box 3, folder 71, ibid.

57. Helen H. Gardener to Catt, 3 October 1923, reel 8, NAWSA Papers, LC; Woman Citizen, 20 October 1923.

58. "Notable Women Visit Galveston"; "Mrs. Cunningham Arrives by Boat"; "Former Secretary of League of Women Voters and Children's Bureau Official"; all in Cunningham file, LWV headquarters.

59. MFC to David Rockwell, 11 December 1923, and Rockwell to MFC, 10 January 1924, box 17, Thomas B. Love Papers, Dallas Historical Society.

60. Nora Huston to MFC, 10 April 1924; Huston to Marion Delaney, 12 April 1924; Elizabeth J. Hauser to Huston, 16 April 1924; all in box 86, Adele Clark Papers, VCU; "Proceedings of the Fifth Annual Convention," LWV Papers, part II, series A, reel 5; MFC to Dorothy Kirchwey Brown, [1924], box 8, folder 244, Brown Papers.

61. Minutes of the General Council, 30 April 1924, and Minutes of the Board of Directors, 2 May 1924, LWV Papers, part I, reel 1.

62. MFC to Adele Clark, 27 October 1922, box 81, Clark Papers; "The Light Turned on a Race Riot," Literary Digest 75 (28 October 1922): 11–12.

63. MFC to Blanche Rogers, 9 May 1924, LWV Papers, part III, series A, reel 8, box II-67; MFC to Irene Goins, 9, 31 May 1924, and Goins to MFC, 19 May 1924, ibid.

64. MFC, "Introductory Statement in Regard to the Special Committee on Negro Problems"; "Report of the Special Committee on Negro Problems"; "Notes on Activity of Committee on Negro Problems, April 1924–April 1925"; all in LWV Papers, part III, series A, reel 8, box II-67.

65. Minutes of the Executive Committee, July 1924, LWV Papers, part II, series A, reel 2.

CHAPTER 6

1. "Proceedings of the Fifth Annual Convention," *Papers of the League of Women Voters*, part II, series A, reel 6 (Frederick, Md.: University Publications of America, 1986), microfilm (hereafter cited as LWV Papers).

2. MFC to Jane McCallum, 8 June 1924, box 18, McCallum Family Papers, part I, AHC-APL.

3. MFC to Jane McCallum, [1924], ibid.; MFC to Dorothy K. Brown, [1924], box 8, folder 244, Dorothy Kirchwey Brown Papers, SL.

4. Kristi Andersen, *After Suffrage: Women in Partisan and Electoral Politics before the New Deal* (Chicago: University of Chicago Press, 1996), 80–86; Anna L. Harvey, *Votes Without Leverage: Women in American Electoral Politics, 1920–1970* (Cambridge: Cambridge University Press, 1998), 99–102, 112–119; Jo Freeman, *A Room at a Time: How Women Entered Party Politics* (Lanham, Md.: Rowman and Littlefield, 2000), chap. 5.

5. "Proceedings of the Fourth Annual Convention," LWV Papers, part II, series A, reel 4; Helen Moore to Marguerite Owen, 5 April 1924, LWV Subject Files, series II, box 28, LC.

6. Unidentified St. Petersburg, Fla., newspaper clipping, n.d,. Cunningham file, LWV headquarters, Washington, D.C.

7. Report of the Department of Organization, April 1924–April 1925, and Outline of Regional Secretaries' Duties, LWV Papers, part III, series A, reel 7, box II-58; Report of the Department of Organization, 11 November 1924, ibid., part I, reel 2; MFC to Ruth McIntosh, 21 July 1924, ibid., part III, series 1, reel 8, box II-65.

8. Mark Lawrence Kornbluh, *Why America Stopped Voting: The Decline of Participatory Democracy and the Emergence of Modern American Politics* (New York: New York University Press, 2000); Michael Schudson, *The Good Citizen: A History of American Civic Life* (Cambridge: Harvard University Press, 1998), chap. 4.

9. Minutes of the General Council, Buffalo, 30 April 1924, LWV Papers, part I, reel 1; MFC to Jane McCallum, 8 June 1924, box 18, McCallum Papers, part I (first quotation); MFC to McCallum, n.d., box 22, ibid., part II (second quotation).

10. Report of Advisory Committee on the Get Out the Vote Campaign to the Buffalo Convention, 1924, LWV Papers, part III, series A, reel 5, box II-46; *Get Out the Vote: Why, When, How*, ibid., reel 4, box II-13; "Seven Steep Steps" broadside, Maud Wood Park Papers, *Women's Studies Manuscript Collections from the Schlesinger Library, Radcliffe College* (Bethesda, Md.: University Publications of America) microfilm, series I, reel 43; *Woman Citizen*, 28 June 1924, 21.

11. MFC to Jane McCallum, 8 June 1924.

12. Pattie Ruffner Jacobs to MFC, 25 May [1924], LWV Papers, part III, series A, reel 6, box II-52; MFC to Belle Sherwin, 29 May 1924, ibid., reel 5, box II-42; "Planks Presented by the National League of Women Voters to the Platform Committees of the National Political Parties, June 1924," ibid.

13. MFC to Belle Sherwin, 24, 29 May, 5 June 1924, LWV Papers, part III, series A,

reel 5, box II-42; MFC to Eleanor Roosevelt, 23 May 1924, ibid.; MFC to Dorothy Kirchwey Brown, n.d., box 8, folder 233, Brown Papers.

14. Minutes of the Board of Directors, 30 April, 2 May 1924, LWV Papers, part I, reel 1; MFC to Pattie Ruffner Jacobs, 20 May, 17 June 1924, and Jacobs to MFC, 2 June 1924, LWV Papers, part III, series A, reel 6, box II-52.

15. MFC to Belle Sherwin, 5 June 1924; Eleanor Roosevelt to MFC, 13 May, 5, 10 June 1924, and MFC to Roosevelt, 14 May 1924, LWV Papers, part III, series A, reel 5, box II-42; Virginia Jeans Laas, ed., *Bridging Two Eras: The Autobiography of Emily Newell Blair, 1877–1951* (Columbia: University of Missouri Press, 1999), 294; *New York Times*, 31 March 1924, 2; Blanche Weisen Cook, *Eleanor Roosevelt*, vol. 1, 1884–1933 (New York: Penguin, 1992), 349–350.

16. "Report of a Meeting of the Committee to Assist the Democratic National Committee on Platform Planks of Special Interest to Women," ER Papers, General Correspondence, 1928–1932, box 9, FDR Library.

17. Andersen, *After Suffrage*, 83; "The Democrats in the Garden," *Woman Citizen*, 12 July 1924, 7–9, 24–25; Cook, *Eleanor Roosevelt*, 350.

18. MFC, "Report of Presentation of the Planks to the Democratic Convention at New York, June 1924," LWV Papers, part I, reel 2.

19. "Report of a Meeting of the Committee to Assist the Democratic National Committee on Platform Planks of Special Interest to Women." On Texas, see Norman D. Brown, *Hood, Bonnet, and Little Brown Jug: Texas Politics, 1921–1928* (College Station: Texas A&M University Press, 1984), 183–207.

20. MFC to Dorothy Kirchwey Brown, [July 1924], box 8, folder 244, Brown Papers.

21. MFC to Jane McCallum, 8 June 1924, box 18, McCallum Papers, part I.

22. MFC, "Report on the Campaign to Get-Out-the-Vote," 7 July 1924, LWV Papers, part I, series A, reel 2; MFC to Adelia Pritchard, 14 July 1924, LWV Papers, part III, series A, reel 5, box II-46; "A Tour in the Middle West," *Woman Citizen*, 6 September 1924, 18–19; [MFC], "Report on the Campaign to Get-Out-the-Vote Presented to the Executive Committee, September 15th, 16th, and 17th," and Minutes of the Executive Committee, 17 September 1924, LWV Papers, part I, series A, reel 2; *The A B C of Voting*, ibid., part III, series A, reel 4, box II-13; MFC to Belle Sherwin, 4 September 1924, ibid., reel 8, box II-65; Anne Williams to MFC, 25 September 1924, ibid., reel 5, box II-42.

23. "Report of the Department of Organization . . . November 11, 1924," LWV Papers, part I, reel 2; Hazel Hart to MFC, 8 October 1924; "Status of the Get-Out-the-Vote Campaign as of October 15, 1924; Anne Williams to MFC, 16 October 1924; all in ibid., part III, series A, reel 5, box II-42.

24. MFC to Anne Williams, 13 November 1924; Williams to MFC, 20 November 1924; "Get Out the Vote Campaign 1924, Summarized by Ann Webster," all in ibid.; Helen King Cheeseman, "Report of the Get-Out-the-Vote Campaign," "Proceedings of the Sixth Annual Convention," LWV Papers, part II, series A, reel 6. Washington statistician Simon Michelet calculated turnout somewhat higher, at 52.5 percent; see Harvey, *Votes Without Leverage*, 142.

25. Helen King Cheeseman to MFC, 20, 26, 30, July 1924, LWV Papers, part III, series A, reel 5, box II-44; Conference of Regional Directors, 11–12 November 1924, ibid., part 1, reel 2.

26. On independent or female-defined partisanship, see Andersen, *After Suffrage*, 43–44, 100, and Melanie Gustafson, Kristie Miller, and Elisabeth Israels Perry, eds., *We Have Come to Stay: American Women and the Political Parties, 1880–1960* (Albuquerque: University of New Mexico Press, 1999), xiii. Catt is quoted in "On the

Inside," *Woman Citizen*, 6 March 1920, 948, and Hay in "Proceedings of the Third Annual Convention, 1922," LWV Papers, part II, series A, reel 3, p. 46.

27. MFC to Dorothy Brown, [1922], box 3, folder 243, Brown Papers.

28. Brown, *Hood, Bonnet, and Little Brown Jug*, chap. 6.

29. Emma Louise Moyer Jackson, "Petticoat Politics: Political Activism Among Texas Women in the 1920s" (Ph.D. diss., University of Texas at Austin, 1980), 282–283; MFC to Belle Sherwin, 2 September 1924, LWV Papers, part III, series A, reel 8, box II-65. For a gender analysis of Miriam Ferguson's campaign, see Shelley Sallee, "'The Woman of It': Governor Miriam Ferguson's 1924 Election," *Southwestern Historical Quarterly* 98 (July 1996): 1–16, and Nancy Beck Young, "'Me for Ma': Miriam Ferguson and Texas Politics in the 1920s and 1930s," in *We Have Come to Stay*, ed. Gustafson, Miller, and Perry.

30. Brown, *Hood, Bonnet, and Little Brown Jug*, 247–250; MFC to Dorothy K. Brown, 28 November 1924, box 8, folder 244, Brown Papers; *San Antonio Express*, 26 October 1924.

31. Jane Y. McCallum, "Activities of Women in Texas Politics," in *Texas Democracy: A Centennial History of Politics and Personalities of the Texas Democratic Party, 1836–1936*, ed. Frank Adams (Austin: Democratic Historical Association, 1937), vol. 1: 492.

32. Minutes of the Board of Directors, November 1924, and Report of the Department of Organization, 11 November 1924, both in LWV Papers, part 1, reel 2; Report of the Department of Organization, April 1924–April 1925, LWV Papers, part III, series, 1, reel 7, box II-58; Hazel Hart to MFC, 9 December 1924, ibid., reel 5, box II-42.

33. MFC to M.L.G., 11 November 1924, ibid.; Helen Moore to Belle Sherwin, 13 November 1924, Miss [Hazel] Hart to Miss [Belle] Sherwin and Miss [Gladys] Harrison, 8 December 1924; all in LWV Subject Files, II-28, LC.

34. Virginia Scharff, *Taking the Wheel: Women and the Coming of the Motor Age* (New York: Free Press, 1991), 117; MFC to Dorothy K. Brown, 18 October 1924, box 8, folder 244, Brown Papers.

35. MFC to Mrs. T. A. Coleman, 8 November 1918, box 19, folder 288, Cunningham Papers, HMRC; [MFC] to Julia Jaffray, 19 June 1920, box 2G445, Elizabeth Ring Papers, CAH-UT; Paul M. Lucko, "The Next 'Big Job': Women Prison Reformers in Texas, 1918–1930," in *Women and Texas History: Selected Essays*, ed. Fane Downs and Nancy Baker Jones (Austin: Texas State Historical Association Press, 1993), 74–76.

36. Jackson, "Petticoat Politics," 99–101; MFC to National Committee on Prisons and Prison Labor, 11 June 1920, and Jessie Daniel Ames to Elizabeth Ring, 7 October 1920, box 2G445, Ring Papers; MFC to Dorothy K. Brown, 8 September 1923, [October 1923], box 8, folder 244, Brown Papers.

37. Minutes of the Executive and Survey Committees, Texas Committee on Prisons and Prison Labor, 25 October 1924, box 2G445, Ring Papers; Program, Sixth Annual Convention, Texas League of Women Voters, 13–15 October 1925, TLWV Papers, microfilm, TWU; MFC to Jane McCallum, November 1924, box 18, McCallum Papers, part I.

38. Lucko, "The Next 'Big Job,'" 79–86; Jane McCallum, "Prison Reform Achievement of Petticoat Lobby," *Austin American-Statesman*, 13 October 1946; MFC to Jane McCallum, November 1924.

39. MFC to Jane McCallum, 18 June 1925, box 22, McCallum Papers, part II.

40. Helen H. Gardener to MFC, 7 July 1925, Helen Hamilton Gardener Papers,

Women's Studies Manuscript Collections from the Schlesinger Library, Radcliffe College, series 1, part A, reel 5.

41. MFC to "My dearest Chief" [Maud Wood Park], 4 July [1925]; MFC to "My dearest Lady" [Helen Gardener], 21 July 1925; MFC to "My dear Chief," 21 July 1925 (quotations); all in reel 6, NAWSA Papers, LC.

42. Maud Wood Park to Calvin Coolidge, 29 July 1925; Park to Charles Curtis, 12 August 1925; Curtis to Park, 14 August 1925; reel 6, NAWSA Papers.

43. MFC to "My Dear Chief" [Park], 4 August 1925, ibid.

44. MFC to Dorothy Brown, 31 August 1925, box 8, folder 244, Brown Papers; Charles Curtis to Maud Wood Park, 14 August 1925; and Rena B. Smith to Park, 7, 14 August 1925, and 15, 17, 18 September 1925, reel 6, NAWSA Papers; *Washington Post*, 18 August 1925.

45. Rena B. Smith to Maud Wood Park, 14 August 1925; "A Woman Civil Service Commissioner," *Equal Rights*, 8 August 1925, 205; "Government Workers' Council Urges Appointment of Experienced Woman," ibid., 22 August 1925, 223; MFC to Park, 28 September 1925, reel 6, NAWSA Papers.

46. Jane Norman Smith to Calvin Coolidge, 18 September 1925; Caroline Spencer to Alice Paul, 18 September 1925; Jessie Dell to Paul, 21 September 1925; all in *National Woman's Party Papers* (Sanford, N.C.: Microfilming Corporation of America, 1979), series 1, reel 30.

47. MFC to Dorothy Kirchwey Brown, 31 August 1925, box 8, folder 244, Brown Papers; "Miss Dell Appointed," *Equal Rights*, 26 September 1925, 259; MFC to Jane McCallum, 29 August 1925, box 9, folder 2, McCallum Papers, part I.

48. Nancy F. Cott, *The Grounding of Modern Feminism* (New Haven: Yale University Press, 1987), 102–105; Melanie Susan Gustafson, *Women and the Republican Party, 1854–1924* (Urbana: University of Illinois Press, 2001), 134; Andersen, *After Suffrage*, 5–6; Harvey, *Votes Without Leverage*, 6–9, 181–208.

49. Andersen, *After Suffrage*, 85–87; Laas, *Bridging Two Eras*, 220–221, 305.

50. Diary, 1922, box 7, folder 51, Emily Newell Blair Papers, Western Reserve Historical Society, Cleveland, Ohio.

51. Elizabeth Carpenter, "Democratic Club Celebrates—and Recalls," *Washington Post*, 16 May 1952; "The Story of the Woman's National Democratic Club," *Democratic Digest* 12 (April 1935): 19; Club Letters and Minutes, 1922–1926, Woman's National Democratic Club Archives, Washington, D.C. (hereafter cited as WNDC Archives); "History of the Woman's National Democratic Club, 1922–1961," TS, 12, ibid.; Jewell Fenzi and Allida Black, *Democratic Women: An Oral History of the Woman's National Democratic Club* (Washington, D.C.: WNDC Education Fund, [2000]), 6–7.

52. "The History of the Woman's National Democratic Club," *The Bulletin*, vol. 3, no. 6 (June 1928): 6; Emily Newell Blair, "Advance of Democratic Women," *Democratic Digest* 17 (April 1940): 38; Laas, *Bridging Two Eras*, 246–247.

53. MFC to Helen Gardener, 21 July 1925, and MFC to Maud Wood Park, 28 September 1925, reel 6, NAWSA Papers; Minutes of the Special Meeting of the Board of Governors, 24 October 1925, Club Letters and Minutes Book, 1922–1926, WNDC Archives; Mrs. Charles S. Hamlin, "The Woman's National Democratic Club," *Democratic Bulletin* 8 (March 1933): 12.

54. Jesse H. Jones to Emily Newell Blair, 2 December 1925, box 183, Jesse Jones Papers, LC; MFC to Mrs. A. A. Jones, 16 September 1926, box 2, folder 16, Blair Papers; Laas, *Bridging Two Eras*, 311.

55. Minutes of a Special Meeting of the Board of Governors, 5 December 1925, Club Letters and Minutes Book, 1922–1926, WNDC Archives; MFC to Dorothy K. Brown, 25 December 1925, box 8, folder 244, Brown Papers.

56. MFC to Mrs. J. Borden Harriman, 17 September 1926, box 2, folder 16, Blair Papers; Laas, *Bridging Two Eras*, 311; MFC to Dorothy K. Brown, 2 December 1925, box 8, folder 244, Brown Papers.

57. Minutes of the Meeting of the Board of Governors, 19 December 1925, 6 January 1926, 10 March 1926, Club Letters and Minutes Book, 1922–1926, WNDC Archives.

58. "Introducing *The Bulletin*," *The Bulletin*, vol. 1, no. 1 (February 1926): 3; Minutes of the Board of Governors, 14 April 1926, WNDC Archives; MFC to Dorothy Kirchwey Brown, n.d., box 8, folder 244, Brown Papers; Dorothy Girton, "Chronology of the Publication Now the *Democratic Digest*," box 2, India Edwards Papers, Harry S Truman Library.

59. MFC to Mrs. [A. A.] Jones, 27 March 1926, Executive and House Committee Reports, 1924 [*sic*]; MFC, Report of the Editorial Committee, 12 May 1926, Board of Governors Minute Book, WNDC Archives; MFC to "Dear Club President," 22 April 1926, box 8, folder 246, Brown Papers.

60. MFC to Jane McCallum, [9 May 1926], box 22, McCallum Papers, part II.

61. *Woman Citizen*, 26 August 1926, 35; Corinne Frazier, "Class in Political Organization Inaugurated by Woman's National Democratic Club," *The Bulletin*, vol. 1, no. 5 (June 1926): 4; "A Summer Training School of Political Organization," *The Bulletin*, vol. 3, no. 6 (June 1928): 12; MFC, "Report on the School of Political Organization," Board of Governors Meetings Minute Book, 1926–1927, WNDC Archives; MFC, "A Democratic School of Politics at Washington, D. C.," *Women's Democratic News*, vol. 2, no. 4 (August 1926): 11; MFC to Emily Newell Blair, 28 August 1926, box 2, folder 16, Blair Papers.

62. "Reminiscences of Florence Jaffrey Harriman," *Columbia University Oral History Project*, microfiche, 35; Freeman, *A Room at a Time*, 87.

63. MFC, "Red Herrings," *Woman Citizen*, October 1926, 25. Sallie Hert's article for the Republicans, "National Housekeeping," was published on the facing page.

64. "The Address of Mrs. Minnie Fisher Cunningham of the Woman's National Democratic Club, Saturday night, October 2nd at Station W.R.C. of the Radio Corporation of America in Washington City," box 17, McCallum Papers, part I; "Democrats on the Air," *The Bulletin*, vol. 1, no. 8 (October 1926): 2; *Washington Post*, 3 October 1926; MFC to Jane McCallum, 10 October [1926], box 22, McCallum Papers, part II, and [1926], box 18, ibid., part I.

65. Plan of Work, Budget for 1927, House and Executive Committee Meetings Minute Book, 5 April 1926; MFC to Mrs. H. P. Hamlin, 9, 13, 17, September 1926, WNDC Archives.

66. C. L. Shaver to MFC, 24 August 1926, box 2, folder 15, Blair Papers; MFC to Mrs. A. A. Jones, 16 September 1926, and MFC to Emily Newell Blair, 12 May 1927, ibid.; MFC to Mrs. H. P. Hamlin, [September 1926], Hamlin to MFC, 15 September 1926, WNDC Archives.

67. 13 October 1926, Board of Governors Minute Book, 1926–1927; Board of Governors to Clem Shaver, n.d., House and Executive Committee Meetings Minute Book, 1926; 6 December 1926, ibid., all in WNDC Archives.

68. Fenzi and Black, *Democratic Women*, 12; Edith Wilson to MFC, 15 February 1927, box 42, Edith Bolling Wilson Papers, LC; 2 June 1926, Board of Governors

Minute Book; 13, 20 December 1926, House and Executive Committee Meetings Minute Book, WNDC Archives; MFC to Emily Newell Blair, 7 January 1927, box 2, folder 16, Blair Papers.

69. 13 April, 11, 20 May 1927, Board of Governors Minute Book, 1926–1927, WNDC Archives; MFC to Clem Shaver, 15 April 1927, box 2, folder 16, Blair Papers.

70. Carpenter, "Democratic Club Celebrates"; Fenzi and Black, *Democratic Women*, 17, 20; MFC to Emily Newell Blair, 16 April [1927], 12 May 1927, Blair Papers.

71. 20 May 1927, Board of Governors' Minute Book, 1926–1927; 9 May 1927, Executive Committee Meetings Minute Book, 1927–1929; MFC, "Report of Ways and Means Committee, 25 April 1927," Executive Committee Meetings Minute Book, 1926–1927, WNDC Archives; MFC to Blair, 12 May 1927.

72. Frances [Mrs. Cordell] Hull and MFC to Edith Wilson, 4 November 1927, Wilson Papers; MFC to Edith Wilson, 15 October, 17 December 1927, ibid.; "An Appreciation," *The Bulletin*, vol. 3, no. 6 (June 1928): 9; Hamlin, "The Woman's National Democratic Club," 13; Caroline [Reilley?] to MFC, 7 May 1928, box 18, McCallum Papers, part I.

73. Minutes of the Executive Committee, 9 November 1927; "Report of Minnie Fisher Cunningham," Minutes of the Board of Directors, 9 November 1927, WNDC Archives.

74. Board of Governors Minutes, 21 December 1927; Mrs. Rose Yates Forrester to Clem Shaver, 4 January 1928; Report of the Executive Committee to the Board of Governors, 8 February 1928, WNDC Archives.

75. *The Bulletin*, vol. 2, no. 11 (December 1927): 6, and vol. 3 no. 1 (January 1928): 5; Minutes of the Executive Committee, 19 December 1927, WNDC Archives; *Washington Evening Star*, 9 February 1928.

CHAPTER 7

1. Cott, *The Grounding of Modern Feminism*, 321, n. 38; *Woman Citizen*, 18 November 1922. Andersen, *After Suffrage*, 114–121, has since shown that women were making respectable, if less visible progress in winning local and state office.

2. *Baltimore American*, 10 November 1922 (clipping in Cunningham file, LWV headquarters, Washington, D.C.).

3. MFC to Maud Wood Park, 26 July 1922, LWV Papers, part III, series A, reel 2.

4. MFC to Jane McCallum, 25 December 1926, box 18, McCallum Papers, part I.

5. *Dallas Morning News*, 20 July 1927; *Houston Post-Dispatch*, 24 July 1927. Four woman sat in the House of Representatives in 1927. Three of them held seats formerly filled by their husbands—two were widows and a third replaced a spouse serving time in federal prison. The fourth, Mary Norton of New Jersey, had been handpicked by the mayor of Jersey City and backed by the Democratic machine. See Freeman, *A Room at A Time*, 231–232, on the importance of male sponsorship.

6. Humphrey, *A Texas Suffragist*, 142; MFC to Dorothy Brown, [1922], and 1 September 1922, box 8, folder 243, Dorothy Kirchwey Brown Papers, SL.

7. *Washington Post*, 22 July 1927; Jackson, "Petticoat Politics," 572; *The Bulletin*, vol. 2, no. 8 (September 1927): 5; *San Antonio Light*, 20 September 1927; Minnie Fisher Cunningham, "Too Gallant a Walk," *Woman's Journal* 14 (January 1929): 13.

8. Outline of the Senate Campaign in MFC's hand, box 17, folder 3, McCallum Papers, part I; MFC to My Dear Co-Worker, 12 January 1928, box 8, folder 245, Brown Papers.

9. Emily Newell Blair, "Men in Politics as a Woman Sees Them," *Harper's Magazine*, May 1926: 703–709; Mrs. Franklin D. Roosevelt, "Women Must Learn to Play the Game as Men Do," *Redbook*, April 1928: 78–79, 141–142.

10. Blair, "Men in Politics as a Woman Sees Them"; Andersen, *After Suffrage*, 140 (cartoon).

11. [MFC], "Basis of Selection of Planks in Platform," box 18, McCallum Papers, part I.

12. MFC to Dorothy K. Brown, n.d., box 8, folder 245, Brown Papers; *Texas Voters News*, vol. 3, no. 2 (February 1928); Fannie C. Potter, ed., *History of the Texas Federation of Women's Clubs, 1918–1938*, vol. 2 (Dallas: n.p., 1941), 73–79, 158.

13. MFC to Jane McCallum, 4 April 1927, box 18, McCallum Papers, part I; MFC Campaign Fund Receipts, 20 December 1927, box 8, folder 245, Brown Papers.

14. A. Caswell Ellis to MFC, 29 August 1927, box 2P363, Alexander Caswell Ellis Papers, CAH-UT.

15. MFC to Ellis, 30 July 1918, ibid.

16. A. Caswell Ellis to MFC, 28 June 1928, box 2P363, Ellis Papers; MFC to the Ellises, March 1928, ibid.

17. On the ascendancy of "advertised" political style in the early decades of the twentieth century, see Michael E. McGerr, *The Decline of Popular Politics: The American North, 1865–1928* (New York: Oxford University Press, 1986).

18. A. Caswell Ellis, "To the Democrats of Texas," TS; MFC to Ellis, [December 1927], box 2P363, Ellis Papers. Copies of Cunningham's campaign brochure can be found in box 8, folder 245, Brown Papers, and in box 113, Adele Clark Papers, VCU.

19. Ellis to MFC, 28 June 1928.

20. *Dallas Morning News*, 9 March 1928; *Fort Worth Star-Telegram*, 3 March 1928; *Huntsville Item*, 8 March 1928 (quotations).

21. *Huntsville Item*, 8 March 1928; *Austin Statesman*, 7 March 1928; MFC to A. Caswell Ellis, 13 March [1928], box 2P363, Ellis Papers; MFC to Dorothy Kirchwey Brown, [March 1928], box 8, folder 245, Brown Papers.

22. *The Dope Sheet: Journal of the First Texas Prudential Insurance Company*, 15 August 1925: 2–3, copy in Rosenberg Library, Galveston; Obituary of B. J. Cunningham, *Galveston Daily News*, 22 March 1928; Death Certificate, Beverly J. Cunningham, Bureau of Vital Statistics, Texas Department of Health, Austin; Will of Beverly Jean Cunningham, No. 7991, Probate Records, Galveston County Courthouse.

23. MFC to Dorothy Kirchwey Brown, [April 1928], box 8, folder 245, Brown Papers.

24. Dugger, "Spanning the Old to the New South," *Texas Observer*, 21 November 1958.

25. *Dallas Morning News*, 9 March 1928. On the Democratic candidates in 1928, see Douglas B. Craig, *After Wilson: The Struggle for the Democratic Party, 1920–1934* (Chapel Hill: University of North Carolina Press, 1992), 92–130. Walsh quotation appears in press release, box 18, McCallum Papers, part I.

26. Glenda Eileen Morrison, "Women's Participation in the 1928 Presidential Campaign" (Ph.D. diss., University of Kansas, 1978), 25, 52–53, 60.

27. *Austin American*, 22, 24, 25, June 1928; Jackson, "Petticoat Politics," 557–561; *Houston Post-Dispatch*, 17, 20 June 1928.

28. Brown, *Hood, Bonnet, and Little Brown Jug*, 382–402; *Fort Worth Star-Telegram*, 21 June 1928; *Houston Post-Dispatch*, 4 July 1928. On the divided Democrats and the

1928 convention, see David Burner, *The Politics of Provincialism: The Democratic Party in Transition, 1918–1932* (New York: Knopf, 1970); Allan J. Lichtman, *Prejudice and the Old Politics: The Presidential Election of 1928* (Chapel Hill: University of North Carolina Press, 1979), and Craig, *After Wilson*.

29. Freeman, *A Room at a Time*, 140, 188–189; *Houston Post-Dispatch*, 7 July 1928; *Dallas Morning News*, 8 July 1928.

30. MFC to Dear Co-Workers, 14 July 1928, box 113, Clark Papers; *Austin American*, 7, 19 July 1928; *Fort Worth Star-Telegram*, 15 July 1928.

31. *Houston Post-Dispatch*, 4 July 1928; *Austin Statesman*, 10 July 1928; *Austin American*, 12 July 1928; *Dallas Morning News*, 17, 18 July 1928.

32. Decca Lamar West, historian of the Texas Federation of Women's Clubs, wrote an open letter to Cunningham's campaign manager declaring that Cunningham's former apostasy rendered her unworthy of Democratic office and gave the letter to Connally's people for release to the Dallas papers. Decca Lamar West to Mrs. Sam J. Smith, [1928], box 86, Tom Connally Papers, LC.

33. *Fort Worth Star-Telegram*, 13 July 1928.

34. *Austin American*, 28 June 1928. She also spent time helping the League of Women Voters' delegation secure convention seats and find housing in Houston. See Gladys Harrison to MFC, 25 February 1928; Belle Sherwin to MFC, 3 March 1928; MFC to Sherwin, 17 March 1928; all in League of Women Voters Subject Files, box II-84, LC.

35. Elinor Morgenthau to Brown, 21 May 1928, and Eleanor Roosevelt to Brown, 16 May 1928, box 8, folder 245, Brown Papers. The candidates' expense reports have not survived, but a newspaper account indicates that Cunningham never approached the $10,000 limit imposed by the state election laws. As of July 19, she reported expenditures of $5,349 and contributions of just $3,808. By contrast, Alvin Owsley had spent nearly $8,000, and Tom Connally reported some $5,000 for July alone. See *Austin Statesman*, 2, 19, July 1928; *Austin American*, 19 July 1928.

36. MFC to Dorothy Brown, n.d., box 8, folder 245, Brown Papers.

37. [Adele Clark] to Nell Doom, n.d.; Doom to MFC, n.d.; Doom to Dear——, n.d.; Ruby Neale Long to Clark, 19, 21 July 1928; all in box 113, Clark Papers.

38. *Dallas Morning News*, 25 July 1928 (Cunningham quotation); Suggestions from Mrs. True Worthy White on Publicity, and *Bulletin of the University Methodist Church*, vol. 1, no. 24 (15 June 1928); both in box 113, Clark Papers.

39. *Christian Science Monitor*, 14 July 1928; MFC, "Too Gallant a Walk," 13; MFC to "Dearest Dorothy," n.d., box 8, folder 245, Brown Papers.

40. *Houston Chronicle*, 24 July 1928; MFC to M. M. Crane, 14 June 1928, box 3N106, Martin McNulty Crane Papers, CAH-UT.

41. *Fort Worth Star-Telegram*, 12 July 1928; *Houston Chronicle*, 4 March 1928; MFC press release, Wichita Falls, 11 July 1928, box 18, McCallum Papers, part I; MFC campaign poster, Jessie Daniel Ames Papers, TSL; *Dallas Morning News*, 14 (Owsley quote), 17, 19, 20, 21 July 1928; *Houston Post-Dispatch*, 21, 27 July 1928.

42. Tom Connally, *My Name is Tom Connally* (New York: Thomas Y. Crowell, 1954), 120–124.

43. Ibid., 124; MFC to M. M. Crane, 14 June 1928.

44. Press release, Beaumont, n.d., box 113, Clark Papers; Crane to MFC, 16 June 1928; Nell Doom et al. to Crane, 5 July 1928; and Crane to Doom, 9 July 1928; all in box 3N106 Crane Papers. Fanny F. F. Moss to MFC, n.d., box 18, McCallum Papers, part I.

45. Blair, "Men in Politics as a Woman Sees Them": 708–709; *Dallas Morning News*, 21 July 1928.

46. *Dallas Morning News*, 19, 21 July 1928.

47. Ruby Neale Long to Adele Clark, [1928], box 113, Clark Papers; MFC, "Too Gallant a Walk," 46.

48. *Dallas Morning News*, 20, 21, 22, 26, 28 July 1928; *Houston Post-Dispatch*, 24, 25 July 1928; *Fort Worth Star-Telegram*, 25 July 1928.

49. "To the Woman Voters of Texas," box 113, Clark Papers, and *Dallas Morning News*, 21 July 1928.

50. Mabel C. Willard to Adele Clark, 12 July 1928; Ruby Neale Long to Clark, 17, 19 July 1928; Long to Anna B. Cade, 17 July 1928; Dorothy Brown to Clark, 18 July 1928; all in box 113, Clark Papers. Clark to Brown, 22 July 1928, box 8, folder 246, Brown Papers; *Houston Post-Dispatch*, 25 July 1928.

51. MFC to Dorothy Kirchwey Brown, n.d., box 8, folder 245, Brown Papers; *Fort Worth Star-Telegram*, 22 July 1928; Brown, *Hood, Bonnet, and Little Brown Jug*, 406–407; Alexander Heard and Donald Strong, *Southern Primaries and Elections, 1920–1949* (Freeport, N.Y.: Books for Libraries Press, 1950), 167–170.

52. MFC, "Too Gallant a Walk," 47; MFC to Larry [LaRue Brown], 7 August [1928], box 8, folder 245, Brown Papers; MFC to Jane McCallum, n.d., box 18, McCallum Papers, part I.

53. MFC to Dorothy Kirchwey Brown, 1 August [1928] (first quotation), and [August 1928] (second quotation), box 8, folder 245, Brown Papers; MFC to Adele Clark, 2 August [1928], box 113, Clark Papers; Fanny F. F. Moss to Cunningham, n.d.; Ella [?] to MFC, 16 August [1928], box 2.325/F37, Cunningham Papers, CAH-UT.

54. Untitled reminiscence of Kate Hunter, TS, box 3, folder 6, McCallum Papers, part I.

55. MFC to Larry [Brown], 7 August [1928]; MFC to Jane McCallum, 13 March 1929, box 18, McCallum Papers, part I; MFC, "Too Gallant a Walk," 12, 46–47. Texas did not elect its first woman U.S. Senator, Kay Bailey Hutchison, until 1993.

56. Adele Clark to Dorothy Kirchwey Brown, 22 July 1928, box 8, folder 246, Brown Papers; Long to Adele Clark, [1928] box 113, Clark Papers.

57. Connally, *My Name is Tom Connally*, 122.

58. Kristie Miller, *Ruth Hanna McCormick: A Life in Politics* (Albuquerque: University of New Mexico Press, 1992), 158, 160, 187; MFC, "Too Gallant a Walk," 46, 47.

59. Emily Blair to MFC, 26 July 1928, box 113, Clark Papers; MFC to A. C. Ellis, 15 November [1928], and n.d., box 2P363, Ellis Papers; MFC, "By Countryside and Town," *Texas Observer*, 12 February 1957; MFC to Dorothy Kirchwey Brown, 1 March 1929, box 8, folder 245, Brown Papers.

60. MFC to Belle Sherwin, 13 August 1928, box II: 135, LVW Subject Files, series II, LC; MFC to Maud Wood Park, 16 August [1928], box 5, Park Papers, LC.

61. [Liz Carpenter], biographical sketch of MFC, box 2.325/F37, Cunningham Papers, CAH-UT.

62. Roosevelt, "Women Must Learn to Play the Game," 141; Morrison, "Women's Participation in the 1928 Presidential Campaign," 106.

63. MFC to Jane McCallum, 13 March 1929.

CHAPTER 8

1. Ellen Carol DuBois, *Harriet Stanton Blatch and the Winning of Woman Suffrage* (New Haven: Yale University Press, 1997), 277.

2. Mason, who met Cunningham in the LWV in the 1920s, became the CIO's southern public relations representative in 1937. Cunningham's name appears on one of Mason's CIO mailing lists, and Cunningham invited Mason to the NDAC's national meeting in 1940. Reel 65 (Texas), series 5, Lucy Mason Papers, *Operation Dixie: The C.I.O. Organizing Committee Papers, 1946–1953* (Sanford, N.C.: Microfilming Corporation of America, 1980), microfilm. Virginia Durr met Cunningham in the 1930s in Washington, D. C., and thought very highly of her. Virginia Durr, interview by Harold Smith, 28 April 1996, and Jean Begeman Bergmark, interview by Harold Smith, 26 August 2001.

3. Robyn Muncy, *Creating a Female Dominion in American Reform, 1890–1935* (New York: Oxford University Press, 1991), xi.

4. Sidney M. Milkis, *The President and the Parties: The Transformation of the American Party System since the New Deal* (New York: Oxford University Press, 1993), 62–66.

5. Susan Ware, *Beyond Suffrage: Women in the New Deal* (Cambridge: Harvard University Press, 1981), 1; Susan Ware, *Partner and I: Molly Dewson, Feminism, and New Deal Politics* (New Haven: Yale University Press, 1987), 210–211; Blanche Wiesen Cook, *Eleanor Roosevelt: Vol. 2, 1933–1938* (New York: Viking, 1999), 368; Jo Freeman, *A Room at a Time: How Women Entered Party Politics* (Lanham, Md.: Rowman and Littlefield, 2000), 89–91, 195–196.

6. [DNC staff], "Gallup Vote Total: 1944 Predictions and Deductions," 10 April 1944, box 31, folder "Texas C-F 1933–45," Democratic National Committee Papers, FDR Official File, OF 300, FDR Library.

7. MFC to Dorothy [Brown], [late 1928], box 8, folder 245, Brown Papers, SL.

8. Mary Dewson to Louis Howe, 22 November 1934, reel 6, Mary (Molly) Dewson Papers, *The Papers of Eleanor Roosevelt, 1933–1945* (Frederick, Md., University Publications of America, 1986), microfilm. Dewson eventually decided not to appoint anyone to the Council.

9. Anna L. Harvey, *Votes Without Leverage: Women in American Electoral Politics, 1920–1970* (New York: Cambridge University Press, 1998), 144–146.

10. MFC to Dorothy Brown, 28 June [1930], box 8, folder 245, Brown Papers.

11. MFC to Belle Sherwin, national LWV President, 14 February 1929, box II:135, folder "C" miscellaneous, LWV Subject files, series II, LWV Papers, LC.

12. "Suffrage Luncheon," TS, 26 March 1930, 26, box 2, folder 7 "Speeches and Notes," Cunningham Papers, UH.

13. Gearing chaired the University of Texas Home Economics Department throughout the interwar period.

14. MFC to Dorothy Brown, [1930], box 8, folder 245, Brown Papers.

15. *Texas Parent Teacher*, 9 (December 1930): 12.

16. Bess Heflin, Lucy Rathbone, and W. E. Gettys to Dr. Theophilus Painter, [University of Texas] President, 25 March 1949. Records of the Office of the President, University of Texas Archives, CAH-UT.

17. The tablet disappeared in the early 1950s, but the LWV has photos of it.

18. "Suffrage Luncheon," 27.

19. Emma Louise Moyer Jackson, "Petticoat Politics: Political Activism Among Texas Women in the 1920s" (Ph.D. diss., University of Texas, 1980), 440.

20. MFC to Dorothy Brown, [1940?], box 7, folder 162, Brown Papers; box 205, Texas LWV Miscellaneous file, series III, LWV Subject Files, LWV Papers, LC; *Houston Chronicle*, 11 November 1929.

21. U.S. Department of Agriculture personnel memorandum, 9 July 1930, MFC federal personnel file. Cunningham rented most of her land to Polish tenant farm-

ers during the 1930s. Although the acreage was substantial, most of it was worn out from being planted in cotton too often and it generated little income.

22. Apparently Cunningham and the woman who headed the home demonstration unit were the only high ranking females in the Texas Extension Service in the 1930s. In 1933 Texas A&M College was sued unsuccessfully by parents seeking to force it to enroll female students. Henry C. Dethloff, *A Centennial History of Texas A&M University, 1876–1976* (College Station: Texas A&M University Press, 1975), 413.

23. MFC to Dorothy Brown, 7 May [1931?], box 8, folder 245, Brown Papers.

24. MFC to Margaret Carter, 14 September [1945], box 15, folder 9, Margaret Carter Papers, Collection 239, UT-A.

25. Texas Agricultural Extension Service, *Annual Report 1935*, 52.

26. MFC to Clara Bailey, Assistant, Office of Information, Cooperative Extension Service, Washington, D. C., 25 June 1937, box 449, folder A-C TX, RG 33, Federal Extension Service Papers, NA-CP.

27. "Mrs. Cunningham Runs For Governor of Texas," *National Union Farmer*, 15 June 1944, 3.

28. In 1934 the FERA authorized the purchase of cotton for the production of two million mattresses; by August, forty states had mattress-making projects under way. Nancy E. Rose, *Put to Work: Relief Programs in the Great Depression* (New York: Monthly Review Press, 1994), 67–68.

29. Sidney Baldwin, *Poverty and Politics: The Rise and Decline of the Farm Security Administration* (Chapel Hill: University of North Carolina Press, 1968), 62–64; *The Rural Community Work Center*, black and white film, 1934. RG 33, item 494, Federal Extension Service Papers, NA-CP; Eleanor Roosevelt to Rex Tugwell, 20 June 1935, box 291, series 70, ER Papers, FDR Library.

30. ER to MFC, 6 November 1934, box 2679, series 190, ER Papers, FDR Library.

31. MFC to Kate Adele [Hill], 12 August 1942, box 7, folder 169, Brown Papers; MFC to Sam Rayburn, 10 October 1943, box 1, folder 1, Cunningham Papers, UH.

32. Texas Agricultural Extension Service, *Annual Report 1938*, 171; Minutes of the Board of Directors, Texas Agricultural Association, 24 January 1938. Minutes of the Board of Directors, October 1937–October 1960, microfilm, Texas Farm Bureau Papers, Texas Collection, Baylor University.

33. MFC to Kate Adele [Hill], 12 August 1942; *The Spade*, October 23, 1943.

34. MFC to Dorothy Brown, 1 March 1929, box 8, folder 245, Brown Papers.

35. MFC to Dorothy Brown, [30 August 1931?], box 8, folder 245, Brown Papers.

36. MFC to Jane [McCallum], [1932], box G, folio 141, McCallum Papers, part I, AHC-APL.

37. MFC to Dorothy Brown, "Election Night" [November 1932], box 6, folder 127, Brown Papers.

38. MFC to Mrs. [Edith] Helm (E. R.'s secretary), 30 December 1934, box 1333, series 100, 1935, ER Papers, FDR Library.

39. Lionel V. Patenaude, *Texans, Politics and the New Deal* (New York: Garland, 1983), 88–93.

40. ER to Colonel Lawrence Westbrook, 21 December 1934, box 1324, series 100, 1934, ER Papers, FDR Library.

41. John Kenneth Galbraith, *A Life in Our Times: Memoirs* (Boston: Houghton Mifflin, 1981), 24.

42. Don E. Carleton, *A Breed So Rare: The Life of J. R. Parten, Liberal Texas Oil Man, 1896–1992* (Austin: Texas State Historical Association, 1998), 152.

43. Otto B. Mullinax to Harold L. Smith, 2 October 1998; Bernard Rapoport, as told to Don Carleton, *Being Rapoport: Capitalist with a Conscience* (Austin: University of Texas Press, 2002), 33, 37–38.

44. Creekmore Fath, interview by Judith N. McArthur and Harold L. Smith, 12 January 1996.

45. "Official Minutes of the Women's Division of the Democratic Party of the State of Texas," 24 November 1936, box 48a, McCallum Papers.

46. MFC to Jane [McCallum], September [1940], box 9, folder 2, McCallum Papers.

47. *State Observer*, 28 March 1949, 3.

48. Richard K. Scher, ed., *Politics in the New South*, 2d ed. (Armonk, N.Y.: M. E. Sharpe, 1997), 45.

49. Texas Agricultural Extension Service, *Annual Report 1941*, 15.

50. Daphne A. Roe, *A Plague of Corn: The Social History of Pellagra* (Ithaca: Cornell University Press, 1973), 131.

51. Texas Agricultural Extension Service, *Annual Report 1938*, 166.

52. Wilson chaired the Nutrition Policy and Planning Committee, which was formed in September 1940 to advise Harriet Elliott, the National Defense Advisory Commission's Commissioner for Consumer Protection, concerning nutrition and national defense. On Cunningham, see M. L. Wilson to Harriet Elliott, 12 November 1940, box 713, folder "Advisory Commission to the Council for National Defense," General Correspondence of the Extension Service June 1907–June 1943, RG 33, Federal Extension Service Records, NA-CP.

53. M. L. Wilson to Harriet Elliott, 12 November 1940, box 1, National Defense Advisory Commission Records, Office of Price Administration Papers, RG 188; "Proceedings of the National Nutrition Conference for Defense, May 26–28, 1941," 237.

54. Texas Agricultural Extension Service, *Annual Report 1941*, 16.

55. "Back the Gruber Dig," *Kansas City Star*, 30 January 1941, 1; Harvey Levenstein, *Paradox of Plenty: A Social History of Eating in Modern America* (New York: Oxford University Press, 1993), 55.

56. Lillian Collier circular letter to voters, [1944], box 1, folder 7, Cunningham Papers, UH; *Women at Work For Universal Peace*, Texas Federation of Women's Clubs Yearbook, 1942–1945 (TFWC: 1945), 33; Francis Foyt (Lillian Collier's daughter), interview by Patricia Cunningham, 28 April 1984, in her "Too Gallant a Walk: Minnie Fisher Cunningham and Her Race for Governor of Texas in 1944" (master's thesis, University of Texas, 1985), 61.

57. "Minnie Fisher Cunningham Speaks on Taxes at McLennan Council," *Farmers' Banner*, 1 July 1938, 3; MFC, "Tips on the Tariff," [1938?], box 1, folder 13, Kate Adele Hill Papers, Texas A&M University.

58. MFC to Jane [McCallum], 25 September [1937], box G, folio 116, McCallum Papers, part I; Ronnie Dugger, *The Politician: The Life and Times of Lyndon Johnson* (New York: W. W. Norton, 1982), 311; Creekmore Fath interview by Patricia Cunningham, 8 November 1983, in "Too Gallant a Walk," 54.

59. David L. Carlton and Peter A. Coclanis, eds., *Confronting Southern Poverty in the Great Depression: The Report on Economic Conditions of the South with Related Documents* (New York: St. Martin's, 1996), 77. The report became the "bible" for southern New Dealers and led to the formation of reform groups, such as the Southern Conference for Human Welfare. Patricia Sullivan, *Days of Hope: Race and Democracy in the New Deal Era* (Chapel Hill: University of North Carolina Press, 1996), 67.

60. MFC to Jane [McCallum], [3 December 1939], box G, folio 142, McCallum Papers, part I.

61. Although Collier chaired the committee, she acknowledged that Cunningham was the "brains" behind the various groups in which they were involved. Lillian Collier, interview by author, 6 February 1968, in Glenn K. Polan, "Minnie Fisher Cunningham" (master's thesis, Sam Houston State College, 1968), 18. WCEP members in 1940 included Jane McCallum, former Texas Secretary of State, and two former TFWC presidents: Mrs. Sam J. Smith and Mrs. Florence Floore. Lillian Collier to Emily Perkins, 4 June 1940, folder "Perkins. Correspondence with 4th District 1938–40," Texas Federation of Women's Club Papers, uncataloged, Collection 32, TWU.

62. MFC to Jane [McCallum], 13 October [1940], box 18, folio 17, McCallum Papers, part I.

63. MFC to Jane [McCallum], 23 April [1941], box G, folio 151, McCallum Papers, part I; Lillian Collier circular letter to County Superintendents, 19 May 1941, box 4J468, Lillian Collier Papers, uncataloged, CAH-UT; Mrs. Max Brooks, Chair, Austin Women's Division, LBJ for Senator, to MFC, 9 May 1941, box 21, folder "Key Women in Texas 1941," LBJ House of Representatives Papers, LBJ-A.

64. Ralph Steen, *Twentieth Century Texas: An Economic and Social History* (Austin: Steck, 1942), 247.

65. Wives and widows obtained coverage under the 1939 Social Security Amendments Act. Alice Kessler-Harris, *In Pursuit of Equity: Women, Men, and the Quest for Economic Citizenship in 20th Century America* (New York: Oxford University Press, 2001), 131–141.

66. Lillian Collier to Mrs. Charles [Gladys] Tillett, 28 April 1941, box 260, "Texas," Correspondence 1937–1944, DNC-Women's Division Papers, FDR Library; Raymond Brooks, "Petticoat Lobby Rejoices Over New Resource Tax," *Austin Statesman*, May 1941, box 4J459, Collier Papers, CAH-UT.

67. *Texian Who's Who: A Biographical Dictionary* (Dallas: The Texian Co., 1937), 112.

68. Creekmore Fath, cited in Carlos Vidal Greth, "Ahead of Her Time," *Austin American-Statesman*, October 7, 1990.

69. Although the AAA did not have a distinct unit called the "women's division," Cunningham used this term because it conveyed a sense of her responsibility for outreach to the nation's women.

70. John T. Whalen, AAA Chief Personnel Officer, to Secretary of Agriculture, 2 March 1939, MFC federal personnel file.

71. Wayne Rasmussen (one of Cunningham's coworkers in the Department of Agriculture, 1939–1940, and later the Department's historian), interview by Harold L. Smith, 2 June 1996.

72. Lorena Hickok, Executive Secretary, Women's Division, DNC, to Carl Hamilton, Assistant Secretary of Agriculture, 27 February 1942, box 697, 1942, Personnel 19-20, Records of the Secretary of Agriculture, General Correspondence, 1906–1975, RG 16, NA-CP.

73. Milkis, *The President and the Parties*, 64–65.

74. Ware, *Beyond Suffrage*, 80; Freeman, *A Room at a Time*, 91–92. There were 30,000 women reporters by 1940. Ware, *Partner and I*, 198–199.

75. Creekmore Fath, interview by Harold Smith, 12 January 1996.

76. May Thompson Evans, interview by Thomas F. Soaper, 30 January 1978, p. 39, ER Oral History Project. FDR Library.

77. The Department of Agriculture had been concerned about farm women's opposition to the AAA since the mid-1930s, and this increased as the 1940 election
approached. Katherine Jellison, *Entitled to Power: Farm Women and Technology,
1913–1963* (Chapel Hill: University of North Carolina Press, 1993), 74, 83–86.

78. Steven Fraser, *Labor Will Rule: Sidney Hillman and the Rise of American Labor* (New
York: The Free Press, 1991), 436. Eleanor Roosevelt was also pressuring the De-
partment of Agriculture to appoint more women to responsible positions. Edith
Helm (ER's secretary) to Henry Wallace, 11 November 1936, box 2446, 1936, file
"Women," Records of the Secretary of Agriculture, General Correspondence,
1906–1975, RG 16, NA-CP.

79. Ruth Milkman, *Gender at Work: The Dynamics of Job Segregation during World War
II* (Urbana: University of Illinois Press, 1987), 1, 36; Nancy F. Gabin, *Feminism in
the Labor Movement: Women and the United Auto workers, 1935–1975* (Ithaca: Cornell University Press, 1990), 231.

80. U.S. Department of Agriculture, *Digest of the Rural-Urban Women's Conversations,
1940*, 23.

81. *Ibid.*, 6–8.

82. *State Observer*, 12 November 1945, 3.

83. Harriet Elliott to ER, 10 September 1940, reel 8, *The Papers of Eleanor Roosevelt,
1933–1945*, microfilm; Ernestine L. Friedmann to Hilda Smith, 3 July 1940, box
17, folder 291, Hilda W. Smith Papers, SL.

84. Harriet Elliott to FDR, 11 July 1940, box 27, National Defense Advisory Commission 1940–1941, Caroline Ware Papers, FDR Library.

85. MFC to Dorothy Brown, 28 June [1940], box 7, folder 162, Brown Papers.

86. "Official Report of the Proceedings [of] . . . Group 5. The Consumer Advi-
sor's Office and Organized Civic Groups," 1 August 1940: 37, box 15, NDAC-
Consumer Division Records, Office of Price Administration Papers, RG 188,
NA-CP (hereafter cited as OPA Papers).

87. "Official Report of the Proceedings [of the] . . . Consumer Advisors Conference
of National Lay Organizations," 1 August 1940: 47, box 15, NDAC-Consumer
Division Records, OPA Papers, RG 188, NA-CP.

88. List of conclusions of Group 5 from the Consumer Advisors Conference, box
15, folder 203.011, Consumer Division-NDAC Records, OPA Papers, RG 188,
NA-CP.

89. MFC to Jane [McCallum], September [1940], box 9, folder 2, McCallum Papers,
part I.

90. Weekly Operations Program Report, 25 September and 23 October 1940, box 3,
folder 012.02, War Production Board Policy Documentation File, RG 179, NA-CP.

91. "Food and Nutrition in Relation to National Defense," *Consumers' Guide*, 6 (September 1940): 1–16.

92. MFC to Mr. W. C. Williams, Commissioner of Public Health, Tennessee, 30 October 1940, box 2, folder 200.02, NDAC Records, OPA Papers, RG 188, NA-CP.

93. "NDAC Weekly Report," No. 17, 13 November 1940, p. 653, box 4, folder
012.02–012.1, War Production Board Policy Documentation Files, RG 179,
NA-CP.

94. Wayne Darrow to Harriet Elliott, 9 December 1940, MFC federal personnel file.

95. Harriet Elliott to Wayne Darrow, 12 December 1940, MFC federal personnel
file.

96. "The Farmer Fieldwomen of the AAA North Central Division," September
1941, pp. 2–3, box 750, 1942, file "Women," Records of the Secretary of Agri-

culture, General Correspondence, 1906–1975, RG 16, NA-CP. Perhaps because of the political nature of Cunningham's work, it was kept very quiet, and the Department of Agriculture appears to have no institutional memory of the Farmer Fieldwoman program.

97. Ibid., 5–6.
98. MFC to Grace Frysinger, Extension Service, 6 December 1939, box 642, folder "Agricultural Adjustment Administration," Conn - D. C. 1939–1940, RG 33, General Correspondence 1907–1943, Federal Extension Service Records, NA-CP.
99. "The Farmer Fieldwomen of the AAA North Central Division;" MFC to Reuben Brigham, 30 September 1941, and Reuben Brigham to MFC, 14 October 1941, box 792, folder "Agricultural Adjustment Administration," Federal Bureau - D.C. 1941–1942, RG 33, Federal Extension Service Records, NA-CP.
100. MFC, "The Place of Home Economists in the Defense Program," *Journal of Home Economics*, 33 (March 1941): 152–155.
101. MFC, "The Feminine Touch," *Today and Tomorrow*, 1 (April 1941): 13.
102. MFC to Dorothy Brown, 8 January 1942, box 7, folder 169, Brown Papers. Williams was sufficiently impressed with Cunningham that after the latter resigned her AAA position, Williams endorsed her for a new appointment. Neal Townley, DNC, to Malvina Thompson (ER's secretary), 20 December 1943, box 891, folder 70, ER Papers.
103. MFC to ER, 9 September 1942, box 1242, series 95, 1942, ER Papers, FDR Library.
104. MFC to ER, 27 March 1942, box 1120, series 90, 1942, ER Papers; ER to MFC, 16 September 1942, box 1242, series 95, 1942, ER Papers, FDR Library. See ER, "My Day" column, 14 September 1942.
105. Eleanor's appointments diary indicates Cunningham met with her in the White House on at least three occasions during the twelve months from March 1942 to March 1943.
106. Amy Bentley, *Eating for Victory: Food Rationing and the Politics of Domesticity* (Urbana: University of Illinois Press, 1998), 107.
107. MFC to Dorothy Brown, 12 August [1942], box 7, folder 169, Brown Papers.
108. Ware, *Beyond Suffrage*, 127.
109. Bertha Friant to Henry Wallace, 31 August 1942, box 26, General Correspondence, Papers as Vice-President 1941–1945, Henry Wallace Papers, FDR Library. Friant was a Democratic Party activist who worked in the Department of Agriculture.
110. Henry Wallace diary, 2 September 1942, in *The Price of Vision: The Diary of Henry A. Wallace 1942–1946*, ed. John Morton Blum (New York: Houghton Mifflin, 1973), 114.
111. MFC to Dorothy [Brown], Sunday [1942?], box 7, folder 169, Brown Papers.
112. MFC to Dr. Robert Sutherland, Director, The Hogg Foundation, 10 December 1942, box 2605, series 170, ER Papers, FDR Library; MFC to Eleanor Roosevelt, 27 June 1943 and E. Roosevelt's Administrative Officer to MFC, 2 July 1943, box 862, folder 70, 1943, ER Papers.
113. MFC to Jane [McCallum], 10 January, 22 June 1943, box G, part I, McCallum Papers.
114. [Liz Carpenter], "Memorandum on Mrs. Cunningham," n.d., box 2.325/F37, folder 92–291, Cunningham Collection (unprocessed), CAH-UT.
115. Alan Brinkley, *The End of Reform: New Deal Liberalism in Recession and War* (New York: Random House, 1995), 140–145.

246 NOTES TO PAGES 164–167

116. William Block, *The Separation of the Farm Bureau and the Extension Service* (Urbana: University of Illinois Press, 1960), 41; Charles M. Hardin, *The Politics of Agriculture* (New York: Free Press, 1952), 138.

117. Block, *The Separation of the Farm Bureau and the Extension Service*, 40.

118. MFC to Kate Adele [Hill], 12 August 1942, box 7, folder 169, Brown Papers.

119. It was published in the National Farmers Union journal. See "Women's Leader Quits Triple-A to Lead Fight Against 'Gag' Rule," *National Farmer Banner*, 15 August 1943.

120. MFC to Texas Congressmen, 5 August 1943, box 98, Cunningham, Minnie F., 1943, Central Correspondence Files, AAA Papers, RG 145, NA-CP.

121. MFC to ER, 29 September 1943, box 862, series 70, ER Papers, FDR Library.

122. Wayne Darrow to MFC, 10 January [1944], box 2P363, A. C. Ellis Papers, CAH-UT; Neal Townley, DNC Interoffice memorandum to Malvina Thompson (ER's secretary), 20 December 1943, box 98, Cunningham, Minnie F., Central Correspondence Files, AAA Papers, RG 145, NA-CP; Merl E. Reed, *Seedtime for the Modern Civil Rights Movement: The President's Committee for Fair Employment Practice, 1941–1946* (Baton Rouge: Louisiana State University Press, 1991), 223. Fauset had been the DNC's head of "Colored Women's Activities" since 1936.

123. Unsigned memorandum by Charles Marsh, "TEXAS (Dallas): Consultant Professor Robert H. Montgomery," 18 November 1943; Harold Young to Sidney Hillman, 26 November 1943. Both documents are in the Henry Wallace Papers, University of Iowa.

CHAPTER 9

1. "Editor's Notes," *Texas Federation News*, 21 (November 1943): 3.

2. MFC to Robert L. Sutherland, 10 December 1942, box 2605, series 170, ER Papers, FDR Library.

3. George N. Green, *The Establishment in Texas Politics: The Primitive Years, 1938–1957* (Westport, Conn.: Greenwood, 1979), 16–20.

4. "Hard Riding With A Burr Under the Saddle!" *The Spade*, 23 October 1943.

5. Frank Overturf to Alexander C. Ellis, 13 December 1943, box 2P 364, Ellis Papers, CAH-UT.

6. A. C. Ellis to James Patton, 26 April 1944, box 2P 364, Ellis Papers; Frank Overturf to MFC, 19 May 1944, box 2P 364, Ellis Papers.

7. Frank Overturf to J. Frank Dobie, 16 November 1944, folder "Farmers Educational and Cooperative Union," J. Frank Dobie Papers, HRC-UT.

8. Program of the "Texas Farmers Union—Annual Convention," 9 August 1944, box 2P 364, Ellis Papers.

9. *National Union Farmer*, 15 June 1944, 3.

10. "Official Report of the Proceedings . . . [of the] Conference on Post-War Adjustment of Women Workers," 4–5 December 1944, p. 47, box 176, Records Relating to Women Workers in World War II, 1940–1945, Women's Bureau Papers, RG 86, NA-CP.

11. Bob Eckhardt claimed Cunningham "designed and set up" the TSLC. Bob Eckhardt, interview by Harold Smith, 12 January 1996; TSLC Executive Committee minutes, 9 December 1951, p. 4, and *What Is the Texas Social and Legislative Conference?*, 5 pp. booklet, n.d., box 1, folder 6, Texas Social and Legislative Conference Records, Collection AR 120, UT-A.

12. Frank Overturf to Alexander Caswell Ellis, 14 September 1943, box 2P 364, folder "Farmers Union," Ellis Papers.

13. MFC to John Granbery, 10 March [1944], box 2P 417, folder "March 1944," John Granbery Papers, CAH-UT.

14. Program of "State Farmers Meeting," 20 November 1943, box 2P 364, Ellis Papers.

15. MFC to John Granbery, 10 March [1944]. Granbery Papers.

16. The Roosevelt administration pressed for a federal ballot to ensure that state laws would not deprive servicemen and servicewomen of the right to vote in the 1944 elections, but southern political leaders opposed this because it would enable black soldiers to vote. Robert A. Garson, *The Democratic Party and the Politics of Sectionalism, 1941–1948* (Baton Rouge: Louisiana State University Press, 1974), 45.

17. TSLC press release, 23 February 1944, box 10, folder 2, Texas AFL-CIO Papers, series 26, Collection AR 110, UT-A. Reading was the Texas Agricultural Mobilization Committee's representative, while Storm, the granddaughter of a U.S. Congressman, represented the Associated Texans. TSLC, *A Peoples' Legislative Platform for Texas*, 1946, box 20, folder 1, Margaret Carter Papers, Collection 239, UT-A.

18. Margaret Carter, interview by Chandler Davidson, 25 October 1975, p. 27, Southern Historical Collection, A-309–1, UNC.

19. Frank Overturf, Texas Farmers' Union, to MFC, 16 March 1944, box 2P 364, Ellis Papers.

20. Nathan Robertson, "How Big Business Plotted Texas Anti-Roosevelt Revolt," *PM*, 2 June 1944, 3.

21. Green reproduces the Texas Regulars' platform in *The Establishment in Texas Politics*, 50.

22. "Pro-Roosevelt and Antis in Full Cleavage," *Austin American*, 24 May 1944, 6.

23. Seth McKay, *Texas Politics, 1906–1944* (Lubbock: Texas Tech Press, 1952), 434.

24. "Texans Plot Third Party Against FDR," *PM*, 25 May 1944, 4.

25. Green, *The Establishment in Texas Politics*, 56.

26. Lorraine Barnes, "Mrs. Cunningham Says Coke Tied Up With Move to 'Steal Election' Regardless of Vote," *Austin American*, 15 June 1944, 1–2.

27. MFC to Harold Young, 5 April 1944, box 16, folder "Cun-Cur," Henry Wallace Papers, FDR Library.

28. John Henry Faulk, interview by Patricia Cunningham, 1983, quoted in her "Too Gallant a Walk: Minnie Fisher Cunningham and Her Race for Governor of Texas in 1944" (master's thesis: University of Texas, 1985), 67.

29. John Henry Faulk to J. Frank Dobie, 27 March 1944, folder "Faulk, John Henry," J. Frank Dobie Papers, HRC-UT.

30. Patricia Cunningham, "Too Gallant A Walk," 68.

31. Margaret Carter, interview by Patricia Cunningham, 12 August 1984, quoted in Patricia Cunningham, "Too Gallant A Walk," 86.

32. MFC to Carrie Chapman Catt, 24 August 1944, Carrie Chapman Catt Papers, LC.

33. MFC, interview by Lorraine Barnes, quoted in her "She's a Favorite Joan of Arc," *Austin Statesman*, 22 October 1947, 6.

34. Green, *The Establishment in Texas Politics*, 46.

35. William E. Keyes, "Eight Man, One Woman Race For Governor Is Launched With Flag-Day Addresses," *Austin American*, 15 June 1944, 6.

36. Gardner Jackson, "'Minnie Fish' Perils Connally Machine," *PM*, 23 May 1944.

37. Ibid.

38. MFC to Carrie Chapman Catt, 24 August 1944, Catt Papers, LC.

39. *Austin American*, 15 June 1944, 1.

40. MFC, press release, 15 June 1944, box 1, folder 7, Cunningham Papers, UH.

41. "Mrs. Cunningham Qualified for Office, She Says," *Galveston Daily News*, 19 July 1944.

42. Dallek, *Lone Star Rising*, 316.

43. "Mrs. Cunningham Raps Stevenson in First Address," *Dallas Morning News*, 15 June 1944, 2.

44. MFC to Jane McCallum, 27 July [1944], box G, folder "Miscellaneous Correspondence 128–153," McCallum Papers, Part I, AHC-APL.

45. "Woman Opens Her Campaign for Governor," *Houston Chronicle*, 15 June 1944.

46. "Mrs. Cunningham Qualified for Office, She Says," *Galveston Daily News*, 19 July 1944.

47. "Will Women Rise to the Occasion?" *State Observer*, 19 June 1944.

48. MFC, circular letter to female voters, 1944, box G, folder "Miscellaneous Correspondence 101–127," McCallum Papers, Part I; *Austin American*, 15 June 1944.

49. *Federation News*, 20 (November 1942).

50. *Federation News*, 22 (July 1944).

51. "Mrs. Cunningham to Keynote Race Wednesday," *Austin American*, 11 June 1944.

52. Cunningham campaign financial report, 12 July 1944. Record of Campaign Expenditures, Secretary of State, TSL.

53. Kathleen Voigt, interview by Harold L. Smith, 16 October 1996.

54. Cunningham campaign financial report, 27 June 1944. Records of Campaign Expenditures, Secretary of State, TSL.

55. MFC to Jane [McCallum], [1944], box G, folder "Miscell. Corresp. 128–153," folio 149. McCallum Papers, Part I.

56. Barbara Karkabi, "Minnie Fish 'Looked Like A Wren, But She Was Really An Eagle,'" *Houston Chronicle*, 2 March 1986.

57. Barnes, "Mrs. Cunningham Says Coke Tied Up With Move to 'Steal Election' Regardless of Vote," 2.

58. Eleanor Roosevelt to MFC, 23 July 1944, box 1717, Series 100, 1944, ER Papers, FDR Library. Although Cunningham was never the subject of an FBI investigation, FBI agents monitoring the CIO reported that it was supporting her candidacy. J. Kevin O'Brien, Chief, FBI Freedom of Information–Privacy Acts Section, to Judith N. McArthur, 22 July 1998; FBI agent's report from San Antonio, Texas, 14 July 1944, File No. 100–5942, FBI Records.

59. MFC to Mary [Ellis], [1944], box 2P 363, Ellis Papers.

60. Gardner Jackson, "'Minnie Fish' Perils Connally Machine."

61. *National Union Farmer*, 15 June 1944, 3.

62. "Discussion of the Primary Ballot," *The Informer*, 22 July 1944, 1.

63. MFC to ER, 12 July 1944, box 1717, Series 100, 1944, ER Papers, FDR Library.

64. MFC campaign final financial report, 1 August 1944. Records of Campaign Expenditures, Secretary of State, TSL.

65. Ronnie Dugger, "Spanning the Old to the New South," *Texas Observer*, 21 November 1958, 2; Carlos Vidal Greth, "Ahead of Her Time," *Austin American Statesman*, 7 October 1990, 4.

66. "A Message to the Women of Texas," radio broadcast script, 19 July 1944, box 1, folder 7, Cunningham Papers, UH. The Texas Regulars replaced Driscoll with Hilda (Mrs. H. H.) Weinert, the spouse of a banker and oilman who was a prominent Regular.

67. *Dallas Morning News*, 19 July 1944, 1.
68. "You Want to Defeat Stevenson? Woman Candidate Can Not Do It," *Arlington Citizen*, 15 July 1944.
69. John Henry Faulk, interview by Patricia Cunningham, "Too Gallant A Walk," 118.
70. Chandler Davidson, *Race and Class in Texas Politics* (Princeton: Princeton University Press, 1990), 24, 55.
71. The low turnout was partially due to people losing their eligibility to vote as a result of being in the armed forces or moving away from home to work in a war factory. Liberal Democrats believed the vast majority who were disenfranchised were Roosevelt Democrats.
72. Davidson, *Race and Class in Texas Politics*, 51.
73. "Voter Beaten, Jailed," *The Informer*, 29 July 1944, 1. There were 551 lynchings recorded in East Texas between 1882 and 1943. Chandler Davidson, *Biracial Politics: Conflict and Coalition in the Metropolitan South* (Baton Rouge: Louisiana State University Press, 1972), 15.
74. *Dallas Morning News*, 19 July 1944, 1.
75. MFC to ER, 12 July 1944, box 1717, Series 100, 1944, ER Papers, FDR Library. Cunningham believed Johnson had betrayed the pro-Roosevelt Democrats by negotiating with the Regulars. MFC to Homer Rainey, 14 July 1945, file 1381, Rainey Papers, WHMC.
76. MFC to Carrie Chapman Catt, 24 August 1944, Catt Papers; "Fights Cause Rump Sessions in Both Camps," *Houston Post*, 30 July 1944, 1, 10.
77. Walter Hall, interview by Ronnie Dugger, cited in Dugger, *The Politician: The Life and Times of Lyndon Johnson* (New York: W. W. Norton, 1982), 262.
78. Paul Holcomb, "How Texas Became a No-Party State," *State Observer*, 19 October 1953, 3. Anti-Roosevelt spokesmen also acknowledged the important role Cunningham's women's group played in mobilizing Roosevelt's supporters. *Houston Post*, 20 January 1945, 4.
79. Davidson, *Race and Class in Texas*, 159–160.
80. Unsigned memorandum by [MFC], "T.A.M.C. No. 16," 23 October 1944, reel 9, Cunningham Papers, HMRC; Margaret Reading, "Texas Farmers in the Fight," *The Emancipator*, 7 (November 1944): 11.
81. [DNC], "Gallup Vote Total 1944: Predictions and Deductions," 10 April 1944, box 31, folder "Texas C-F 1933–45," Democratic National Committee Papers, FDR Official File OF 300, FDR Library.
82. "Franchise Education Group Led by Kaiser Starts Drive for Big Registration and Vote," *New York Times*, 1 October 1944, 40.
83. "Key Women–1944 Campaign," folder 78, box 2, General Subject Files, subseries 1.1, Democratic National Committee Materials, series 1, Gladys Avery Tillett Papers #4385, Southern Historical Collection, UNC.
84. ER to MFC, 23 July 1944, box 1717, Series 100, 1944, ER Papers, FDR Library.
85. Memorandum by [Matthew J. Connelly, Secretary to the President], 10 November 1945. Official File 3369, 1945, Harry S. Truman Papers, Truman Library.
86. "University in Politics?" *Houston Post*, 20 January 1945, 4.
87. "Mrs. Cunningham Qualified for Office, She Says."
88. "Conference at the White House," *Independent Woman*, July 1944, 225; Susan Hartmann, *The Home Front and Beyond* (Boston: Twayne, 1982), 149.
89. "Texas Holds Its Own White House Conference," *Independent Woman*, November 1944, 358.

90. Untitled text of MFC speech, [7 September 1944], box 2, folder "Speeches and Notes," Cunningham Papers, UH.

91. "Dr. Rainey Reviews History of Women in Government Service at White House Meeting," *Austin American*, 8 September 1944.

92. MFC to Jane McCallum, 11 September [1945], box G, untitled folder, folio 95, McCallum Papers, Part I.

93. James W. Riddlesperger, "Sarah T. Hughes: Biography of A Federal Judge" (master's thesis, North Texas State University, 1980), 29.

94. Frieda Miller to MFC, 26 October 1944, box 175, Records Relating to Women Workers in World War II, 1940–45, Women's Bureau Records, RG 86, NA-CP.

95. "Official Report of the Proceedings . . . [of the] Conference on Post-War Adjustment of Women Workers," 4–5 December 1944, p. 45, box 176, Records Relating to Women Workers in World War II, 1940–1945, Women's Bureau Records, RG 86, NA-CP.

96. *State Observer*, 11 December 1944, 3. On the conference, see Kathleen A. Laughlin, *Women's Work and Public Policy: A History of the Women's Bureau, U.S. Department of Labor, 1945–1970* (Boston: Northeastern University Press, 2000), 29.

97. "Conference on Post-War Adjustment of Women Workers," 99.

98. Susan M. Hartmann, "Women's Organizations During World War II: The Interaction of Class, Race, and Feminism," in *Woman's Being, Woman's Place: Female Identity and Vocation in American History*, ed. Mary Kelley (Boston: G. K. Hall, 1979), 319.

99. "Conference on Post-War Adjustment of Women Workers," 125.

100. Don E. Carleton, *A Breed So Rare: The Life of J. R. Parten, Liberal Texas Oil Man, 1896–1992* (Austin: Texas State Historical Association, 1998), 242.

101. Green, *The Establishment in Texas Politics*, 83–84.

102. MFC to FDR, 21 November 1944, file 3535, President's Personal File, FDR Papers, FDR Library.

103. Green, *The Establishment in Texas Politics*, 86–87.

104. D. F. Strickland, testimony in "An Educational Crisis: A Summary of Testimony Before A [Texas] Senate Committee Investigating the University of Texas Controversy," 15–28 November 1944, 2.

105. Alice Carol Cox, "The Rainey Affair: A History of the Academic Freedom Controversy at the University of Texas, 1938–1946" (Ph.D. diss., University of Denver, 1970), 133; Green, *The Establishment in Texas Politics*, 89.

106. MFC to FDR, 21 November 1944, file 3535, President's Personal File, FDR Papers, FDR Library.

107. *State Observer*, 23 October 1944, 3.

108. *State Observer*, 30 October 1944, 3; MFC to Homer Rainey, 13 October 1944, file 632, Rainey Papers.

109. MFC to ER, 26 January 1945, box 2954, folder 190, Miscellaneous, 1945, ER Papers, FDR Library.

110. Robert Lee Bobbitt to Sarah T. Hughes, 13 December 1944, file 673, Rainey Papers.

111. MFC to Margaret Carter, 31 March 1945, box 21, folder 4, M. Carter Papers, Collection 239; Carleton, *A Breed So Rare*, 314, 320.

112. "Mrs. Cunningham Pledges Hard Fight," *Daily Texan*, 21 January 1945; MFC circular letter to WCEF members, 9 January 1945, box 15, folder 9, Margaret Carter Papers, Collection 239.

113. MFC to John Granbery, [January 1945], box 2P 420, folder 2, Granbery Papers.

114. Ibid.

115. MFC to Jane McCallum, 9 March [1945], box G, untitled folder, folio 97, McCallum Papers, Part I.
116. "UT Interested Women March on Capitol," *Austin American*, 19 January 1945, 19.
117. Ibid.
118. *State Observer*, 29 January 1945.
119. Women's Committee for Educational Freedom minutes, 25 April 1945, box 2, folder 10, Cunningham Papers, UH.
120. "UT Interested Women," *Austin American*, 19 January 1945, 1.
121. Ibid., 1, 19.
122. "Militant Women Seek Rainey's Reinstatement," *San Antonio Light*, 18 January 1945; "Stevenson Pooh-Poohs Blacklisting," *Austin American*, 19 January 1945, 1.
123. "Women Stress Free Education Platform," *Austin Statesman*, 19 January 1945, 8.
124. Carleton, *A Breed So Rare*, 322.
125. Jane McCallum and MFC to WCEF members, 6 February 1945, box 2, folder 10, Cunningham Papers, UH.
126. *State Observer*, 21 January 1946, 1; Lillian Collier and MFC to "Ladies and Gentlemen," 10 January 1946, file 1417, Homer Rainey papers; MFC to Mrs. Frank Dobie, 31 March 1946, folder "Cunningham, Minnie Fisher," J. Frank Dobie Papers, HRC-UT.
127. MFC to Mrs. Frank Dobie, 31 March 1946.
128. "Mrs. Cunningham Pledges 'Hard' Fight," *Daily Texan*, 21 January 1945.
129. Ibid.
130. Marjorie Barksdale to MFC, 27 February, 11 March 1946, box 21, folder 4, Margaret Carter Papers, Collection 239.
131. "Resolutions Passed by Women's Committee for Educational Freedom" at the 25 April 1945 meeting, box 15, folder 9, Carter Papers, Collection 239.
132. Collier and MFC to WCEF members, 7 February 1947, box 15, folder 9, Carter Papers, Collection 239. Higher pay for teachers was a women's issue in two respects: women comprised the vast majority of teachers while mothers could anticipate better education for their children.
133. Green, *The Establishment*, 59, 63–64.
134. MFC to Homer Rainey, 1 December [1945], file 1390, Rainey Papers.
135. Women's Committee for Educational Freedom press release, 10 December 1945, box 2, folder 7, McCallum Papers.
136. "The Women's Committee for Educational Freedom," 6 pp. pamphlet, n.d., box 2, folder 7, McCallum Papers.
137. Ibid.
138. Collier and MFC to WCEF members, 29 May 1946, box 21, folder 4, Carter Papers, Collection 239.
139. MFC to Wright Patman, 13 July 1945, box 82 C, Wright Patman Papers, LBJ Library.
140. MFC to Homer Rainey, 22 November 1945, file 1245, Rainey Papers.
141. MFC to Mrs. E. C. [Marjorie] Barksdale, 27 February, 28 February 1946, box 21, folder 4, Carter Papers, Collection 239.
142. Forest Hill (Helen Hill's spouse), interview by Harold L. Smith, 9 March 2000.
143. Carleton, *A Breed So Rare*, 350, 359.
144. Memorandum by Lewis Valentine Ulrey, "The Red's Attack the Educational Setup in Texas," 1 July 1946, file 1364, Rainey Papers. We are grateful to Nancy Beck Young for drawing our attention to this and other references in the Rainey Papers.

145. Bernard Rapoport as told to Don Carleton, *Being Rapoport: Capitalist with a Conscience* (Austin: University of Texas Press, 2002), 65.
146. Carleton, *A Breed So Rare*, 359.
147. Ronnie Dugger, "Spanning the Old to the New South," 2; Bernard Rapoport, interview by Harold Smith, 15 March 2000.
148. Ronnie Dugger, "White Dresses, Yellow Parasols," *Texas Observer*, 2 May 1956, 3.
149. Carleton, *A Breed So Rare*, 367.
150. Green, *The Establishment*, 95–96.
151. MFC to Dorothy Brown, 1 January 1947, box 8, folder 185, Dorothy K. Brown Papers, SL.
152. Patricia Sullivan, *Days of Hope: Race and Democracy in the New Deal Era* (Chapel Hill: University of North Carolina Press, 1996), 217.
153. MFC to John Granbery, 27 August 1946, box 2P 426, folder 2, Granbery Papers.
154. WCEF minutes, 10 October 1945, box 15, folder 9, Carter Papers, Collection 239.
155. Collier and MFC to WCEF members, 23 February 1946, box 21, folder 4, Carter Papers, Collection 239.
156. Collier and MFC to WCEF members, 18 January 1947, box 15, folder 9, Carter Papers, Collection 239.
157. Lillian Collier and Margaret Reading to WCEF members, 17 March [1951], box 1, folder 4, TSLC Papers, Collection 120. Since the WCEF's records apparently have not survived, it has not been possible to determine how much longer it continued.

CHAPTER 10

1. Daniel Horowitz, *Betty Friedan and the Making of the Feminine Mystique: The American Left, the Cold War, and Modern Feminism* (Amherst: University of Massachusetts Press, 1998), 125; Nancy F. Gabin, *Feminism in the Labor Movement: Women and the United Auto Workers, 1935–1975* (Ithaca: Cornell University Press, 1990), 140–41, 231; Sharon Hartman Strom, *Political Woman: Florence Lascomb and the Legacy of Radical Reform* (Philadelphia: Temple University Press, 2001), 189.
2. *State Observer*, 26 November, 10 December 1945, 3; *State Observer*, 22 April, 20 May 1946, 3; MFC to Dr [Homer] Rainey, 22 November 1945, file 1245, Rainey Papers, WHMC.
3. Mary [Molly] Dewson to MFC, 25 October 1922, box I-25, Part III, reel 2, LWV Papers.
4. Untitled memorandum by MFC on Blanket Amendment, [1924], box II-53, Part III, reel 6, LWV Papers.
5. Dorothy McAllister to Maude Wood Park, 15 March 1947, reel 15, NAWSA Papers.
6. Cynthia Harrison, *On Account of Sex: The Politics of Women's Issues, 1945–1968* (Berkeley: University of California Press, 1988), 20; Kathleen A. Laughlin, *Work and Public Policy: A History of the Women's Bureau, U.S. Department of Labor, 1945–1970* (Boston: Northeastern University Press, 2000), 37.
7. *State Observer*, 22 January 1945, 3.
8. *State Observer*, 6 October 1947; "Women in Politics: New Factor?" *Texas Observer*, 5 September 1956, 3; Beulah Grimmet, interview by Harold L. Smith, 31 December 1999.
9. Elizabeth Carpenter, "Women Voters Could Take Over," *Houston Post*, 7 April 1952; Margaret Carter to Chase Going Woodhouse, DNC Women's Division's Director, 11 October 1947, box 21, folder 3, Margaret Carter Papers, Collection 239, UT-A.

10. *State Observer*, 6 October 1947, 3.
11. MFC to Wright Patman, 29 August 1946, box 83A, file "Democratic Executive Committee-State 1946," Wright Patman Papers, LBJ Library.
12. "Still Fighting," *Texas Week*, 7 December 1946, 9.
13. People's Legislative Committee minutes, 7 December 1946, box 2, folder 6, Cunningham Papers, UH.
14. [John Granbery], "Light Overcoming Darkness," *Emancipator*, 9 (March 1947): 3.
15. *State Observer*, 26 February 1945, 3.
16. *State Observer*, 26 September 1949, 1.
17. Alan Brinkley, *The End of Reform: New Deal Liberalism in Recession and War* (New York: Random House, 1995), 4–8; "Bob Calvert and Class Legislation," *Texas Spectator*, 2 (10 March 1947): 7; Untitled PLC pamphlet, [1946], box 13, folder 7, Carter Papers, Collection 239.
18. "A People's Legislative Program," [1946], attached to MFC to Dorothy Brown, 1 January 1947, box 8, folder 185, Dorothy Brown Papers, SL.
19. People's Legislative Committee, "Bulletin No. III," 17 February 1947, box 2P 428, folder 1, Granbery Papers, CAH-UT.
20. People's Legislative Committee, "A People's Legislative Program," [1946], box 39, McCallum Papers.
21. MFC circular letter to PLC members, 17 December 1946, box 2P 427, Granbery Papers.
22. MFC to Margaret Carter, 19 April 1947, box 21, folder 4, Carter Papers, Collection 239.
23. Marion Storm, PLC, to John Granbery, 28 April 1947, box 2P 429, Granbery Papers.
24. MFC to Dr. James Loeb, Jr., April 1946, series 3, chapter file 1943–1965, reel 78, ADA Papers, microfilm, WSHS.
25. MFC to Margaret Carter, 15 February 1947, box 21, folder 4, Carter Papers, Collection 239; James Loeb to MFC, 8 March 1947, series 3, chapter file 1943–65, reel 78, ADA Papers, microfilm.
26. MFC to Leon Henderson, 5 March 1947, box 46, folder 1, Dallas chapter, series 3, ADA Papers.
27. MFC to James Loeb, 10 March 1947, series 3, chapter file 1943–1965, reel 78, ADA Papers, microfilm.
28. MFC to Margaret Carter, 19 April 1947, box 21, folder 4, Carter Papers, Collection 239; A. G. Mezerik, "Under the Sign of the Flying Red Horse," *The Nation*, 3 May 1947, 512; *Proceedings of the Fifteenth Annual Convention of the Texas State Industrial Union Council*, 63, cited in Murray E. Polakoff, "The Development of the Texas C.I.O. Council" (Ph.D. diss., Columbia University, 1955), 433.
29. Jackson Valtair to N. Panek, 1 November 1946, ADA Papers.
30. Jack Carter to MFC, 28 November 1947, box 2, folder 8, Cunningham Papers, UH.
31. MFC to Walter G. Hall, 7 July 1950, box 46, Walter G. Hall Papers, Rice University; MFC to Jack Carter, 28 December 1953, box 3, folder 11, Carter Papers, Collection 265.
32. Polakoff, "The Texas C.I.O. Council," 425.
33. TSLC Executive Committee minutes, 17 August 1952, p. 4 and 9 December 1951, p. 4, TSLC Papers, UT-A.
34. Stuart Long, interview by Chandler Davidson, June 1976, pp. 16–17, box 1, Texas Oral History Program, Rice University.
35. MFC to Walter and Virginia Hall, 26 December 1951, box 46, folder VI, Walter

G. Hall Papers, Rice University; TSLC Executive Committee minutes, 1950 and 1951, box 1, folder 7, TSLC Papers, collection 120, UT-A; Programs of TSLC annual conventions, box 10, folder 2, Texas AFL-CIO Papers, series 26, Collection 110, UT-A.

36. Robert Eckhardt, interview by Judith McArthur and Harold L. Smith, 12 January 1996.

37. Mark Adams, "Texas Needs a Forum on Public Affairs." Speech presented at the TDWC's eighth annual meeting, 25 May 1961, box 4J476, Collier Papers; TSLC, *A Report 1951*, 1951, p. 6, Parten Papers, uncataloged, CAH-UT.

38. Liz Carpenter, "Remarks at Dedication of Marker for Minnie Fisher Cunningham," 25 March 1992, 1.

39. *State Observer*, 12 February 1945, 3.

40. MFC to Mary [Ellis], 26 June [1947], box 2P363, Alexander Caswell Ellis Papers, CAH-UT; MFC to Jane [McCallum], 9 March [1945], box G, McCallum Papers, Part I, AHC-APL; MFC to Kathleen [Voigt], 25 June [1953], box 5, folder 8, Democratic Advisory Council Papers, UT-A; Barbara Karkabi, "Minnie Fish 'Looked Like A Wren,' But She Was Really An Eagle," *Houston Chronicle*, 2 March 1986; R. M. Traylor III, interview by Harold L. Smith, 5 April 1998.

41. Lillian Collier to Wright Patman, 1 February 1946, Collier Papers, uncataloged, CAH-UT; Wright Patman to President Truman, 17 December 1945; Matthew Connelly, Secretary to President Truman, to Wright Patman, 21 December 1945; both in File 3369, White House Central Files: Official Files, 1945–1953, Truman Presidential Papers, Truman Library. Clinton Anderson to Wright Patman, 7 January 1946, Collier Papers.

42. *State Observer*, 18 April 1949, 1; *State Observer*, 22 August 1949, 1.

43. PGH to Mr. Herrill, 20 July 1949, MFC federal Personnel File; Donald Dawson, Administrative Assistant to President Truman, to William H. Kittrell, 17 June 1949, File 3369, Truman Papers.

44. Charles Brannan to Mrs. Grace Martin, 20 July 1949, RG 16, Secretary of Agriculture Papers, General Correspondence 1906–1975, NA-CP.

45. It was apparently through her Club membership that Cunningham was invited to the 29 May 1946 White House tea with Bess Truman. Guide to the "Records of the White House Social Office, 1945–1953," p. 9, Truman Library.

46. MFC to Margaret Carter, 11 July [1945], 14 September [1945], box 15, folder 9, Carter Papers, Collection 239.

47. MFC to Homer Rainey, 22 November 1945, box 41, Rainey Papers.

48. *State Observer*, 14 October 1946, 15 September 1947.

49. MFC to Harold Young, 12 May 1944, box 16, Henry Wallace Papers, FDR Library; MFC to Henry Wallace, 2 March [1945], reel 32, Henry Wallace Papers, University of Iowa, microfilm; "Full Text of Wallace's Speech," *Texas Spectator*, 2 (26 May 1947): 10.

50. James C. Foster, *The Union Politic: The CIO Political Action Committee* (Columbia: University of Missouri Press, 1975), 91.

51. *State Observer*, 5 January 1948, 29 March 1948, p. 3; MFC to Jack Carter, 17 November 1947, box 1, folder 2, Cunningham Papers, UH.

52. MFC to Jack Carter, 17 November 1947, ibid.

53. George N. Green, *The Establishment in Texas Politics: The Primitive Years, 1938–1957* (Westport, Conn.: Greenwood, 1979), 108–109.

54. MFC to President Truman, 23 August 1949, file 3369, White House Central Files: Official Files, 1945–1953, Truman Papers; Kari Frederickson, *The Dixiecrat*

Revolt and the End of the Solid South, 1932–1968 (Chapel Hill: University of North Carolina Press, 2001), 197.

55. *State Observer*, 29 August 1949, 2.
56. Paul Holcomb, "How Texas Became a No-Party State," *State Observer*, 19 October 1953, 3.
57. Lillian Collier to India Edwards, 26 June 1950, box 2, General Correspondence, India Edwards Papers, Truman Library.
58. MFC to Walter G. Hall, 7 July 1950, box 46, Walter G. Hall Papers, Rice University.
59. Green, *The Establishment*, 141.
60. Billie Carr, "Memories of Conventions Past," *Texas Observer*, 1 October 1976, 5.
61. Pat Mathis, interview by Harold L. Smith, 9 April 2000.
62. Don E. Carleton, *A Breed So Rare: The Life of J. R. Parten, Liberal Texas Oil Man, 1896–1992* (Austin: Texas State Historical Association, 1998), 409.
63. Lillian Collier to Major Parten, 23 July 1951, Parten Papers.
64. TSLC Executive Committee minutes, August 1951, box 12, folder IIa, Hall Papers.
65. Carleton, *A Breed So Rare*, 411.
66. *State Observer*, 13 October 1952, 3.
67. Carleton, *A Breed So Rare*, 420.
68. MFC to W. G. Hall, 7 October 1952, box 46, folder 6, Hall Papers.
69. Lillian [Collier] to W. G. Hall, 13 October 1952, box 46, folder 6, Hall Papers.
70. Franklin Jones, Sr. to Louisa Hugg, 13 July 1984, in *The Itch of Opinion: The Public and Private Letters of Franklin Jones, Sr., Vol. 3, 1881–1884 Firestarter Files*, ed. Ann Adams (Oak Harbor, Washington: Packrat Press, 1985), 265; Oscar Mauzy, interview by Harold L. Smith, 7 March 2000.
71. Mauzy, interview by Harold L. Smith, 7 March 2000.
72. Margaret Carter to Helen Fuller, February 1953, box 10, folder 4, Carter Papers, Collection 239.
73. TDWC, "Constitution and By-Laws," n.d., box 9, folder 224, Brown Papers.
74. MFC to Dr. W. H. Bryant, 31 August 1955, box 2, folder 8, Cunningham Papers, UH.
75. MFC to Mrs. A. W. Brisbin, 22 October 1955, box 2, folder 8, Cunningham Papers, UH.
76. Lillian Collier to Major Parten, 6 March 1953. Parten Papers.
77. MFC to Mrs. A. W. Brisbin, box 2, folder 8, Cunningham Papers, UH.
78. MFC circular letter, "SOS Democrats," n.d., attached to Lillian Collier to Major Parten, 6 March 1953, Parten Papers.
79. Kathleen [Voigt] to MFC, [1953], box 4J482, Collier Papers.
80. Margaret Carter to Stephen A. Mitchell, DNC Chairman, 17 February 1953. box 12, folder 11, Carter Papers, Collection 239.
81. Sarah Wilkerson-Freeman, "The Second Battle for Woman Suffrage: Alabama White Women, the Poll Tax, and V. O. Key's Master Narrative of Southern Politics," *Journal of Southern History*, 68 (May 2002): 333–374.
82. Lillian Collier, circular letter to TDWC members, 10 December 1954, Parten Papers.
83. MFC, "I Believe," included with Lillian Collier circular letter to TDWC members, 10 December 1955, series 26, collection 110, Texas AFL-CIO Papers.
84. Lillian Collier, circular letter to TDWC members, 23 November 1955, box 40, General Political Files, State File: Texas, Stephen A. Mitchell Papers, Truman Library. The TDWC encouraged the formation of city and county Democratic

women's organizations, such as the Travis County Democratic Women's Committee. Sally Hunter Graham, *A Voice for the People: A History of the Travis County Democratic Women's Committee* (Austin: TCDWC, 1985), 2.

85. Lillian Collier, circular letter to TDWC members, 19 May 1955, box 8, miscellaneous political correspondence, 1954–1956: C, Mitchell Papers.

86. Lillian Collier, circular letter to all TDWC members, 10 January 1956, 28 January 1956, box 49a, McCallum Papers, Part II.

87. Ralph Yarborough to Ed Idar, 11 June 1959, box 4J489, Collier Papers.

88. Circular letter from Lillian Collier to "loyal Democrats," 6 April 1954, Parten Papers; Lucille Cooper to Jack Carter, 4 February 1954, box 3, folder 11, Carter Papers, Collection 265.

89. Sean J. Savage, *Truman And The Democratic Party* (Lexington: University Press of Kentucky, 1997), 84–85.

90. MFC to Margaret Carter, 10 July 1953, box 3, folder 11, Carter Papers, Collection 265.

91. Lillian Collier, circular letter to TDWC members, 10 December 1954, Parten Papers.

92. Charles W. Stephenson, "The Democrats of Texas and Texas Liberalism, 1944–1960: A Study in Political Frustration" (master's thesis, Southwest Texas State College, 1967), 32.

93. Julie L. Pycior, *LBJ and Mexican Americans* (Austin: University of Texas Press, 1997), 97; Ronnie Dugger, "DOC, DAC and DOT," *Texas Observer*, 4 April 1958, 8.

94. MFC to [Gerald] Mann, 22 October 1955, box 2, folder 8, Cunningham Papers, UH; Carleton, *A Breed So Rare*, 444.

95. Lawrence Goodwyn, "Dugger's Observer" *Texas Observer*, 27 December 1974, 5.

96. Pycior, *LBJ and Mexican Americans*, 93.

97. William Wayne Justice, "Yarborough's Legacy," *Texas Observer*, 23 February 1996, 8.

98. *Austin American*, 3 August 1954, 9.

99. MFC to Dell [Sackett], 27 July [1954]; Dell [Sackett] to Lillian [Collier] and MFC, 3 August 1954; Dell [Sackett] to MFC, 7 August 1954. box 4Za46, Ralph Yarborough Papers, CAH-UT.

100. Claire Banister, "Yarborough 'Pin Voter' Clubs Form," *Austin American*, 3 August 1954, 1.

101. *Texas Observer*, 20 December 1954, 3; Billie Carr, interview by Harold L. Smith, 11 September 2000; Lawrence Goodwyn, interview by Harold L. Smith, 18 November 2001; Creekmore Fath, interview by Patrick Cox, quoted in Cox, *Ralph Yarborough: The People's Senator* (Austin: University of Texas Press, 2001), 113.

102. Green, *The Establishment*, 156; Cox, *Yarborough*, 113.

103. Franklin Jones, Sr., "Minnie Fish: A Reminiscence," *Texas Observer*, 22 January 1965, 12.

104. Franklin Jones, Sr., "The Birth of the Observer," *Texas Observer*, 11 March 1977, 28.

105. Jones, "Minnie Fish: A Reminiscence," 12.

106. Mary Marrs Weinzierl, interview by Ann Fears Crawford, 6 February 1985, quoted in Crawford, "Mrs. Democrat: Minnie Fisher Cunningham Runs For Governor," unpublished paper, February 1985, 17.

107. Franklin Jones, Sr. to Ann Adams, 19 February 1983, in *The Itch of Opinion*, ed. Adams, 151.

108. Franklin Jones to Ronnie Dugger, 19 November 1984, ibid., 293–294; "New Pa-

pers' Trustees Meet for First Time," *Texas Observer*, 13 December 1954; Ronnie Dugger, interview by Molly [Randolph] Luhrs, 13 May 1970, p. 6, box 7, Frankie Randolph Papers, Rice University.

109. Green, *The Establishment*, 145.
110. Kathleen Voigt, interview by the author, 26 July 1976, quoted in Green, *The Establishment*, 172.
111. Dugger, "Spanning the Old to the New South," 2.
112. *Houston Chronicle*, 16 April 1956, 14B.
113. See resolution attached to MFC to Barry Bingham, 16 April 1956, box 574, Adlai Stevenson Papers, Princeton University.
114. MFC to Bingham, 16 April 1956.
115. Chandler Davidson, *Race and Class in Texas Politics* (Princeton: Princeton University Press, 1990), 155, 158.
116. "Who Will Go With 'Minnie Fish' to Chicago And A Real Victory?" election leaflet, Cunningham file, Sam Houston State University Library; Untitled memorandum by Laura Perea, 30 April 1956, 2, box 1, folder 6, Cunningham Papers, UH.
117. Ronnie Dugger, "White Dresses, Yellow Parasols," *Texas Observer*, 2 May 1956, 3.
118. "Why We Are Against Lyndon Johnson as Favorite Son and Leader of the Delegation," Cunningham file, Sam Houston State University library; "Why We Are For Minnie Fisher Cunningham as Favorite Daughter and Leader of the Delegation," Cunningham file, Sam Houston State University library.
119. "Why We Are For Minnie Fisher Cunningham as Favorite Daughter and Leader of the Delegation." Sutton was elected to the Texas legislature in 1972 and became the chairman of the Legislative Black Caucus.
120. Robyn Duff Ladino, *Desegregating Texas Schools: Eisenhower, Shivers, and the Crisis at Mansfield High* (Austin: University of Texas Press, 1996), 38.
121. Green, *The Establishment*, 174.
122. Margaret Carter, interview by Chandler Davidson, 25 October 1975, p. 58, A-309-1, Southern Historical Collection, UNC.
123. Robert Dallek, *Lone Star Rising: Lyndon Johnson and His Times 1908–1960* (New York: Oxford University Press, 1991), 505.
124. Green, *The Establishment*, 178; Davidson, *Race and Class*, 164.
125. MFC to Dorothy Brown, 12 April 1957, box 9, folder 224, Brown Papers.
126. Margaret Carter, interview by Chandler Davidson, April 1976, p. 29, Texas Oral History Program, Rice University.
127. MFC to Dorothy Brown, 23 June 1957, box 9, folder 240, Brown Papers.
128. Pycior, *LBJ and Mexican Americans*, 100.
129. DOT Executive Board minutes, 18 May 1957, box 8, folder 5, series 26, Texas AFL-CIO Papers, collection 110; Dave Richards, interview by Harold L. Smith, 9 June 2002.
130. MFC to Dorothy Brown, 12 April 1957, box 9, folder 224, Brown Papers.
131. *State Observer*, 11 November 1946, 3.
132. Merline Pitre, *In Struggle Against Jim Crow: Lulu B. White and the NAACP, 1900–1957* (College Station: Texas A&M University Press, 1999), 57.
133. MFC to Virginia [Smith], 6 August 1951, box 46, folder VI, Hall Papers, Rice University; Margaret Carter, interview by the author, 12 August 1984, quoted in Cunningham, "Too Gallant A Walk," 126.
134. Dugger, "Spanning the Old to the New South," 2.
135. *Austin American-Statesman*, 19 October 1958.

136. "Minnie Fish Honored," *Texas Observer*, 24 October 1958, 4; William Henry Kellar, *Make Haste Slowly: Moderates, Conservatives, and School Desegregation in Houston* (College Station: Texas A&M University Press, 1999), 56, 61.

137. MFC to Dorothy Brown, 24 October 1958, box 9, folder 240, Brown Papers; Walter Mansell, "Faubus Clan Hit By 'Minnie Fish,'" *Houston Chronicle*, 19 October 1958, p. B8.

138. MFC to Dorothy Brown, 27 December 1960, box 9, folder 240, Brown Papers.

139. Louisa Hugg note on MFC, n.d. Hugg Papers, TWU.

140. John F. Kennedy to MFC, 19 January 1961, quoted in Glenn K. Polan, "Minnie Fisher Cunningham" (master's thesis, Sam Houston State College, 1968), 3; Beulah Grimmet, interview by Harold L. Smith, 31 December 1999.

141. Dugger, "Spanning the Old to the New South," 1, 3.

142. Louisa Pearson Hugg to Franklin Jones, Sr., n.d., and MFC to Louisa Hugg, 12 September 1961, Hugg Papers.

143. Franklin Jones, "Minnie Fish: A Reminiscence," 12.

144. Dugger, "Spanning the Old to the New South," 2.

145. Death certificate, Minnie Fisher Cunningham; "'Mrs. Democrat' Cunningham Dies," *Houston Post*, 10 December 1964.

146. *New York Times*, 12 December 1964, 31; *Washington Post*, 12 December 1964, C3.

147. Mrs. R. H. Bush, "Tribute to Minnie Fisher Cunningham," in "Memorial Tribute to Mrs. Minnie Fisher Cunningham: A Great American," Texas Democratic Women's State Committee, [1965].

EPILOGUE

1. MFC to Jane McCallum, September [1940], box 9, folder 2, McCallum Family Papers, part I, AHC-APL.

2. Ronnie Dugger, "Spanning the Old to the New South," *Texas Observer*, 21 November 1958, 2.

3. Chandler Davidson, *Race and Class in Texas Politics* (Princeton: Princeton University Press, 1990), 195; Dave Richards, *Once Upon a Time in Texas: A Liberal in the Lone Star State* (Austin: University of Texas Press, 2002), 243, 246.

4. Mark Adams, "Texas Needs a Forum on Public Affairs." Speech presented at the TDWC's eighth annual meeting, 25 May 1961, box 4J476, Collier Papers.

5. Dugger, "Spanning the Old to the New South," 2.

6. Pat Mathis (Ralph Yarborough's legislative aide 1959–1962), interview by Harold Smith, 9 April 2000; Dell Sackett [Goeres] interview by Harold Smith, 6 September 2000; Chandler Davidson, recalling his interview with Ralph Yarborough, to Harold Smith, 22 February 1998.

7. Nadine Eckhardt, interview by Harold Smith, 10 April 2000; Orissa Eckhardt Arend to Harold Smith, 9 June 2002.

8. Jean Dugger Sherrill, interview by Harold Smith, 20 June 2002.

9. Liz Carpenter to Judith McArthur, 15 January 2001.

10. Pat Mathis interview.

11. Billie Carr interview by Harold Smith, 11 September 2000.

12. Oscar Mauzy interview by Harold Smith, 7 March 2000.

13. Dell Sackett [Goeres] interview by Harold Smith, 8 September 2000.

14. Billie Carr interview; Davidson, *Race and Class*, 180–181.

15. Kathleen Voigt, interview by Harold Smith, October 16, 1996.

16. Nadine Eckhardt interview.

17. Liz Carpenter, "Remarks at Dedication of Marker for Minnie Fisher Cunningham," 25 March 1992.

INDEX